Computation and Complexity in Economic Behavior and Organization

This book presents a model of computing and a measure of computational complexity that are intended to facilitate the analysis of computations performed by people, machines, or a mixed system of people and machines. The model is designed to apply directly to models of economic theory, which typically involve continuous variables and smooth functions, without requiring an analysis of approximations. The model permits an analysis of the feasibility and complexity of the calculations required of economic agents in order for them to arrive at their decisions. The treatment contains applications of the model to game theory and economics, including a comparison of the complexities of different solution concepts in certain bargaining games, to the trade-off between communication and computation in an example of an Edgeworth Box economy, and to problems of economic organization.

Kenneth R. Mount is Emeritus Professor of Mathematics at Northwestern University, where he has spent 40 years on the faculty. Professor Mount received the E. Leroy Hall Award for excellence in teaching at Northwestern, and he also served as a visiting professor and researcher in France and Argentina. Professor Mount's articles and coauthored articles have appeared in leading refereed publications such as the *Journal of Mathematical Economics*, *Advances in Mathematics*, *Proceedings of the American Mathematical Society*, *Econometrica*, *Journal of Complexity*, and *Economic Theory*. His professional research has been supported by the National Science Foundation, NATO, and UNESCO.

Stanley Reiter is Morrison Professor of Economics and Mathematics in the Weinberg College of Arts and Sciences and Morrison Professor of Managerial Economics and Decisions Sciences in the Kellogg School of Management, Northwestern University, where he directs the Center for Mathematical Studies in Economics and Management Science. He previously served as Krannert Professor of Economics and Mathematics at Purdue University. A Fellow of the American Academy for the Advancement of Science, the American Academy of Arts and Sciences, the Guggenheim Foundation, and the Econometric Society, Professor Reiter is the editor of *Studies in Mathematical Economics* (1987), coeditor of *Information, Incentives, and Economic Mechanisms* (1987), and associate editor of the journals *Economic Design* and *Complex Systems*.

Additional Praise for *Computation and Complexity in Economic Behavior and Organization*

"This book summarizes the research done over the past two decades by these two pioneers in the theory of bounded rationality in organizations. Anyone who is trying to model economic agents in an organization, and especially anyone who is concerned with the processing of information by organization, will find this an important reference. The models in this book, where agents are information processors within a network, are significantly richer than the conventional model of a single boundedly rational agent as a finite automaton. This approach offers a fresh perspective and tools for modeling computational complexity in an organization, tools that will be very valuable in capturing within a model the limited computational capabilities of both individuals and organizations. The treatment is both insightful and rigorous, making the book particularly suitable to advanced graduate students and researchers."

– In-Koo Cho, *University of Illinois*

"This book opens a challenging new path in the theory of organization. An organization's task is to compute a function of certain external variables. A well-designed organization does so quickly. It breaks the task into subtasks, each requiring a unit of time to complete, with the result becoming an input for a higher subtask. Some of the subtasks can be performed simultaneously. The challenge is to arrange the subtasks in a network so as to minimize the total elapsed time until the full task is finished. This is a novel and fruitful way to look at efficient organizations and to compare the difficulty of the tasks they undertake. Some general results are obtained and they are illustrated in a rich assortment of examples, including resource-allocating organizations and games. Contemporary work in the economic theory of organization has many motives and many approaches. Those who seek to move it in new directions ought to make a serious study of this book."

– Thomas Marschak, *University of California, Berkeley*

"Mount and Reiter overcome the idiosyncratic, problem specific nature of previous models of computation and complexity by developing an approach based around the most common building blocks of economic models: real numbers and smooth functions. On the technical side this powerful innovation opens the way for the use of classical analysis and algebra in analyzing complexity of decision-making. At the same time the use of real numbers and smooth functions makes Mount and Reiter's approach immediately applicable to standard models in game theory and organizational economics. The detailed examples in the text allow the applied theorist to see this new approach at work in familiar problems without having to master all the theoretical underpinning of this powerful new theory."

– Kieron Meagher, *University of New South Wales, Australia*

Computation and Complexity in Economic Behavior and Organization

KENNETH R. MOUNT
Northwestern University

STANLEY REITER
Northwestern University

CAMBRIDGE
UNIVERSITY PRESS

CAMBRIDGE UNIVERSITY PRESS
Cambridge, New York, Melbourne, Madrid, Cape Town, Singapore, São Paulo

Cambridge University Press
The Edinburgh Building, Cambridge CB2 8RU, UK

Published in the United States of America by Cambridge University Press, New York

www.cambridge.org
Information on this title: www.cambridge.org/9780521800563

First published 2002
This digitally printed version 2007

A catalogue record for this publication is available from the British Library

Library of Congress Cataloguing in Publication data

Mount, Kenneth R.

Computation and complexity in economic behavior and organization / Kenneth R. Mount, Stanley Reiter.

p. cm.

Includes bibliographical references and index.

ISBN 0-521-80056-0

1. Economics, Mathematical. 2. Organizational behavior. 3. Computational complexity. I. Reiter, Stanley. II. Title.

HB135 .M744 2002
330'.01'51 – dc21 2001035644

ISBN 978-0-521-80056-3 hardback
ISBN 978-0-521-03789-1 paperback

To Bertha, Cynthia, John, Lisa and Greg.

K.R.M.

To Nina, Carla, Frank, Carrol and Miles.

S.R.

Contents

Acknowledgments

We are indebted to Tom Marschak for extensive comments on an earlier version of this book, a debt that cannot adequately be recognized in the references. We are also grateful to Tim Van Zandt and to Leo Hurwicz for their interest and for helpful discussions. We thank Fran Walker for her help in preparing the manuscript, including some graphics, and for her cheerful patience in dealing with many changes in its evolution. Thanks also to Sondra Fargo for a very helpful editorial contribution.

Portions of Section 6.1 and Appendix B appeared in Mount, K. R. and S. Reiter, "A lower bound on computational complexity given by revelation mechanisms," *Economic Theory*, 7, 237–266. Copyright Springer-Verlag 1996.

Example 1 in Section 7.1 appeared in Reiter, S. "Coordination of Economic Activity: An Example," *Review of Economic Design*, 2001. Copyright Springer-Verlag 2001.

Research reported in this book was supported by National Science Foundation Grants IST-8314504, IST-8509678, and IRI-9020270/01.

1 Introduction

1.1. THE MODELING OF COMPUTING AND ECONOMIC AGENTS

This book presents a model of computing, called the modular network model, and a measure of complexity, intended to apply to computations performed by a mixed system of people and machines. Applications of the model to problems in game theory and economics are also presented.

The model has two primitives: a set, usually denoted $\mathcal{F}$ of elementary functions or elementary operations, and a set of directed graphs. The modeler can choose the set of elementary operations to fit the problem at hand. It is assumed that an elementary operation is carried out in one unit of time. Every computation is described as a superposition of elementary operations. Choice of the set of elementary operations permits limitations on computing capabilities to be expressed formally. It also gives the modeler control over the level of reduction of analysis. The topology of the directed graph can also be restricted by the modeler, though in this book we do not do so; instead we assume that any directed graph is available.

These features facilitate the application of the model to human agents and to economic models. Parallel and distributed computing and the dispersion of information among agents are naturally expressed in this model. In each application the modeler can choose the set of elementary functions to suit the problem. The class of elementary operations may include functions of real variables, as well as functions whose domains are discrete sets, as, for instance, functions defined on strings from a finite alphabet. When the alphabet is finite and the elementary functions are Boolean, the model is equivalent to the finite-state automaton model.

Computing with real numbers offers some important advantages in the context of scientific computing (see Blum et al., 1998). It is also relevant to applications in economic theory. Economic models typically use real variables and functions of them. A model of computing in which the elementary operations are functions of real variables allows that model to be directly applied to standard economic models, without requiring an analysis of approximations in each application. In cases in which the analysis in the economic model is itself numerical, then, as is the case with numerical analysis generally, computation is necessarily finite and typically is carried out by persons who use a finite-state machine. This raises a question about the relationship between the analysis of complexity in our model when real variables are involved and the complexity of the corresponding computation performed by a finite-state automaton that uses a finite alphabet. Instead of analyzing this question case by case, we show (in Chapter 6, Theorem 6.2.1) that the measure of complexity of a function obtained from the continuum model (real variables and smooth functions) is a limit of a sequence of measures of complexity obtained from finite networks, equivalent to sequential machines, computing approximations to the smooth function in question. The limit theorem presented in Chapter 6 shows that when regularity assumptions are satisfied, our model of computation, and the measure of complexity obtained in it, is an idealization of finite computing in the same sense in which measurement with real numbers is an idealization of measurement with rational numbers.

Real computing opens connections to classical mathematics. When computing is done over a finite alphabet, the technical machinery of analysis available is combinatorial mathematics, which is difficult and, in the setting of standard economic models, awkward. In contrast, when the alphabet is the real numbers, or real vectors, the apparatus of classical analysis is available. In this book the class of elementary operations is often taken to be the class of functions of at most r variables, each a d-dimensional real vector, whose value is also a vector in a d-dimensional Euclidean space. In terms of machines, the parameter d can be thought of as the *size* of a register, and the parameter r as the number of registers. When a human being is doing the computing, the parameter d may refer to the number of modalities of perception via the senses. Smoothness conditions are sometimes imposed. A person typically receives visual, auditory, and other sensory inputs simultaneously. In our model, the number of these is d. Further, a person can perceive more than one input at a time, but not very many. In our model the number of these is r. According to a classic paper (Miller, 1956) for a human being the number r is approximately seven. A modular network whose elementary functions satisfy the restrictions imposed by r and d is called an (r, d) network. Much of the analysis in this book concentrates on analysis of (r, d) networks.

How can an (r, d) network represent computations performed by a system consisting of human beings and machines? When the class of elementary functions consists of functions between Euclidean spaces (or between smooth manifolds), it is not obvious that the (r, d)–network model can represent computations performed by human beings, or by a combination of people and machines. However, we can extend the model so that more abstract computations can be reduced to computations with real quantities. For this purpose

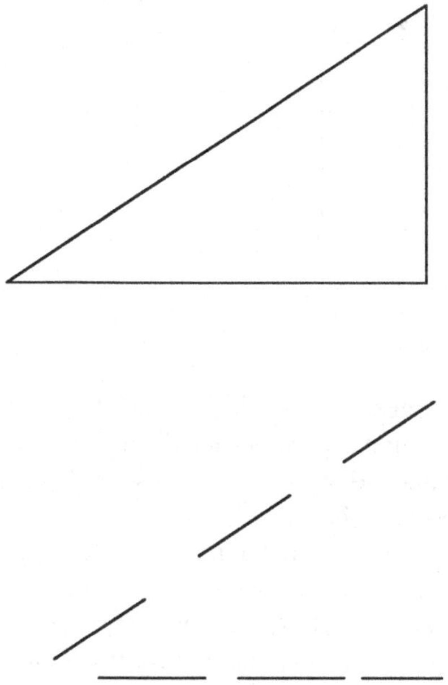

Figure 1.1.1.

we introduce the idea of an *encoded version of a function*, and its computation. The formal definition appears in the first section of Chapter 4. Here we make do with an informal description sufficient to understand the example that follows.

Human beings are good at detecting patterns in low dimensions. For instance, people have little trouble recognizing the pattern shown in Figure 1.1.1 as a triangle.

We continue to recognize a triangle even if the corners, and perhaps other pieces of the perimeter, are missing, or if the sides are slightly curved. Recognizing a pattern can be thought of as computing a function that expresses the relation between a subset of the plane, and the act of saying that it is a particular pattern, in our example a triangle. Thus, recognizing a pattern is represented as evaluating a function, ρ, whose value at the subset shown in Figure 1.1.1 is the word *triangle*. The domain of ρ is the set of subsets of the plane, not a Euclidean space, and the range of ρ is the set of English words, or some suitable subset of it, also not a Euclidean space. In the case of pattern recognition by a human being, it is natural to consider ρ to be an elementary function. When it is possible to encode the more abstract domain and range of the function in terms of elements of Euclidean spaces, then, as Figure 1.1.2 shows, evaluating ρ becomes equivalent to evaluating a function, h, whose domain and range are Euclidean spaces. Although h may be complex if evaluated by a machine,

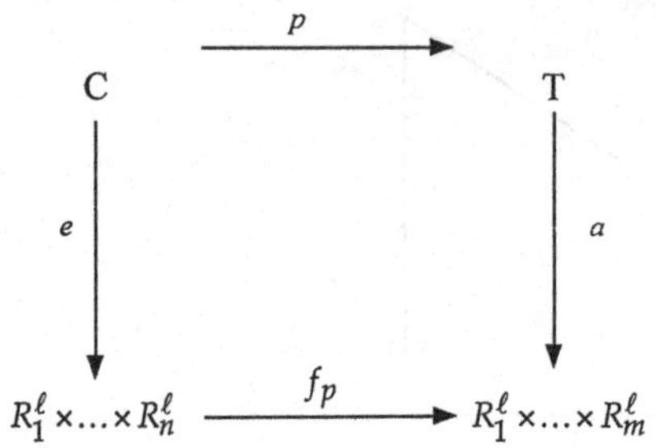

Figure 1.1.2.

when ρ is elementary for a human agent, and the (fixed) encoding and decoding functions are elementary, the function h becomes an elementary function in a modular network model that applies to the system consisting of human agent and machine. Figure 1.1.2 shows the scheme.

More broadly, the standard models of computer science are not convenient for expressing the characteristics of human beings, in particular, economic agents, as information processors. A machine can easily do some things that people find difficult. Other things are easy and natural for people and difficult for machines. Machines have no special difficulty in handling high-dimensional data, whereas human beings do. Human beings are good at recognizing patterns in low-dimensional data, whereas that task can be quite difficult for a machine. Reading handwriting is relatively easy for literate human beings, and quite complex for machines. The widespread and heavy use of computers to generate two-dimensional visual representations of high-dimensional or complex data so that a human being can study them graphically, rather than look at a printout of the underlying function in the form of numerical data, testifies to the special ability of humans to see patterns in low dimensions; it also testifies to the limitations of humans to comprehend the same information presented in another form. The standard models of computing represent these tasks independently of who is to perform them, and the complexity of a task is the same whether the computation is done by a human or a machine. A model in which reading handwriting can be a simple task if done by a human being and a complex one if done by a digital computer would come closer to capturing computation done by persons equipped with machines.

Computers are sometimes used directly by human beings, who determine and control their inputs, and receive and use their outputs. (Some computational devices are internal to other machinery, such as the computers used to control automobile engines and the like. In these cases the interaction with humans is more remote.) In some cases when a human being is an active participant in the course of a computation, with the result that the whole computation depends on both the actions of the machine and of the person, it is nevertheless possible to focus entirely on the analysis of the computation performed by the machine.

But when, as in some economic models, the object of the analysis includes the person, it is not appropriate to separate the person from the machine. When these situations are important, there is need for a model of computation that facilitates analysis of computational problems to be solved by a combination of human and machine resources. The modular network model allows operations that can be carried out by a person to be included in the set of elementary functions. When an encoded version of such an elementary function exists, it can be included in the set of elementary functions of an (r, d) network. Then the analysis of the entire computational task of human and machine can be modeled and analyzed seamlessly. (Analysis of some examples of computations performed by a combination of humans and machines are presented in the first section of Chapter 4. Also see Mount and Reiter, 1998.) Of course, the entire computation might also be represented in one of the classical models of computing, a Turing machine, or a finite-state automaton. Some work along this line is in the literature. The finite-state automaton model and the Turing machine model have been used in game theory (Neyman, 1985), where computational issues also arise. In game theory, as in economic theory generally, it is assumed that players are fully rational and have unlimited computational abilities and resources. These assumptions provide a basis for deep analysis of situations in which the interests of agents may run together, and also conflict to some extent. As in economic theory, there are attempts to weaken the assumptions of full rationality and unlimited computational capabilities. The finite-state automaton model has been used to analyze the complexity of strategies, and the Turing machine model has been used to study the complexity of games. The questions addressed are, for a given game: "How difficult is it for a player to carry out a given strategy in that game?" and: "How difficult is it to solve the game?"[1] Regarding the first question, Aumann (1981) suggested using finite-state automata to measure the complexity of strategies. The measure is the number of states of the smallest automaton that can execute the strategy. (see Gilboa and Zemel, 1989). This is called *strategic complexity*. Infinitely repeated games have been studied in this way (Rubenstein, 1979, 1986; Abreu and Rubenstein, 1988; and Cho, 1995). There is substantial literature in which finite-state automata or Turing machines are used to restrict strategic complexity (Kalai and Stanford, 1988; Kalai, 1996). With respect to the second question, the standard model of computational complexity in computer science, namely the classification of computations based on the asymptotic theory of complexity classes, has been used to analyze the complexity of solving games. (Also see Ben-Porath, 1989; Kalai et al., 1993; Papadimitriou, 1992.) Ben-Porath (1986) showed that there is an advantage to a player in a repeated two-person zero-sum game with patient players from having a larger automaton. The

[1] Kalai (1996) surveys the literature relevant to these questions and provides a bibliography listing the basic papers.

advantage can be considerable, but the automaton must have an exponentially larger number of states. We address these questions in Chapter 5 in the context of the modular network model of computing.

The idea that human cognition is modeled well by Turing machines, or finite-state versions of them, is widely asserted, but it remains controversial.[2]

There is another issue that deserves a brief comment here. An economic agent experiences his environment directly. How that agent represents his environment in his own mind is usually not observable by others. The economic analyst considering the agent's behavior in his environment "constructs" her own model of the situation in which she can deduce the optimal action of the agent. We apply the (r, d)-network model to the analyst's model in order to analyze the computational complexity of the decisions of the agent. Because the analyst's choice of how to model the agent's situation may have arbitrary elements in it, the measure of complexity might reflect those arbitrary elements, and consequently might be misleading. It is therefore important that the model of computation and the complexity measure it defines do not depend on a particular parameterization of the problem. We want the measure of complexity to be invariant with respect to transformations of the problem that preserve its essential elements. Specifically, we want the measure of complexity to be the same under coordinate changes in the spaces of the variables that define the computation. The methods of analysis in Chapter 3 are coordinate free; in Chapter 4, where the model is applied to analyzing the trade-off between communication and computation in finding the equilibrium of a decentralized message process, we show explicitly that the result is invariant under appropriate coordinate transformations of the underlying spaces.[3] There is a second reason why invariance of the measure of complexity under coordinate transformations is important. Changing coordinate systems can implicitly perform computations without our taking explicit notice of them. For instance, to solve a system of linear equations without doing any work, just assume that the coordinate system is one that makes the matrix of the system diagonal. There are also other ways of "smuggling" computation, but these are ruled out in our analyses by regularity conditions.

[2] Put briefly, the assertion is that the human brain (mind) is a Turing machine. Among others, Roger Penrose does not subscribe to this assertion. His book (Penrose, 1994) is an excellent guide to the issues and to the literature. It is not necessary for our purpose here to take a position on this question. Even if it were the case that the brain is a Turing machine, it would not necessarily be useful in applications to economic agents or economic organizations to model them as executing algorithms in which the elementary steps are evaluations of Boolean functions over a finite alphabet.

[3] This is done in steps, beginning with linear coordinate transformations, and ending with general nonlinear coordinate transformations. We show the invariance under linear coordinate transformations explicitly. The proof for nonlinear transformations is tedious and does not lead to any new insight. We therefore refer the reader to Mount and Reiter (1990), where it is presented in full.

1.2. COMPLEXITY, MATHEMATICS, AND HUMAN CAPACITIES

There is a direct connection between the (r, d)–network model and certain classical problems in mathematics. For instance, when we restrict attention to analytic functions, computation of a function F by an $\mathcal{F}$ network, where $\mathcal{F}$ is taken to be the class of analytic functions of two variables, is related to Hilbert's 13th problem. That problem asks whether an analytic function of several variables can be expressed as a superposition of analytic functions of two variables. This is the same as asking whether an analytic function of several variables can be computed by a (2, 1) network whose modules are analytic functions. There is literature stemming from Hilbert's 13th problem that includes contributions by Kolmogorov and others, such as Kolmogorov (1961a, 1961b) and Arnol'd (1963); also see Lorentz (1966). Kolmogorov first showed that each continuous function of n real variables could be written as a superposition of functions of three variables. Arnol'd showed that only functions of two variables are required. Kolmogorov refined this result and showed that each continuous function of n variables could be written as a superposition of continuous functions of one variable and the binary function of addition. In general, the functions required for superposition, besides addition, are not differentiable. The situation is more complicated when the functions in the superposition are required to be smooth. It is known that there are s times differentiable functions of n variables that cannot be written as a finite superposition of s times differentiable functions of fewer variables (see Lorentz, 1966 or Vitushkin, 1961). In this book we work mostly with elementary functions that are twice continuously differentiable, d-vector–valued functions of r variables, each a d-dimensional real vector. Sometimes real analytic functions are used as elementary functions, as in the paper by Mount and Reiter (1998). That paper presents some of the ideas of our model in a less technical setting, and it also presents some applications of the model to human computing, specifically to Chernoff faces in pattern-recognition problems (Chernoff, 1973).

In our model, *computability* and *complexity* are *relative* concepts. The complexity of a given computation can be different depending on the class $\mathcal{F}$ of elementary functions (and, if relevant, the class of graphs permitted). Consider a polynomial of degree ten in one variable, and consider the function that associates the array of its roots with the vector of its coefficients. A person who knows the coefficients and must compute the roots can be in one of at least three situations. She may not have a computer available, or she may have a computer but not have a program for the task, or she may have a computer equipped with a program for computing the roots of polynomials from the coefficients, for example, the program Gauss, or Mathematica. A person without access to a computer, or one using a personal computer that lacks a program for that purpose, would find this a time-consuming task – a complex task. However, that same person using a computer equipped with Gauss or Mathematica could accomplish the task with a few keystrokes. In that case it would be sensible in many situations to regard the function that associates the roots to the coefficients as an elementary operation, and not pursue the analysis to more detailed levels of the program doing the work. To require that every computation be reduced to a fixed given level of elementary operations, such as Boolean functions over a finite alphabet, results in a model that is awkward to apply to computations done in the context of economic problems by economic agents or by economic theorists, whether they do or do not have access to computing machines.

The idea that complexity is a relative concept is in keeping with practice in mathematics. There the notion of solution to a problem is also relative. For example, what does it mean to solve a differential equation? Among other possibilities, it can mean to find an integral, perhaps expressed in some abstract form, or it can mean to find the solution trajectories numerically. The complexities of these two tasks can be quite different. In mathematics a problem can be considered as solved in cases that are quite different. For instance, a problem might be considered solved if it is shown to be equivalent to another problem for which a solution is known, or to one that is known to have a solution, or to one for which there is an algorithm.

1.2.1. Complexity and Computability

In the $\mathcal{F}$-network model, the complexity of a function F relative to the class $\mathcal{F}$ ($\mathcal{F}$ complexity) is the minimum over all $\mathcal{F}$ networks $\mathcal{N}$ of the number of sequential steps in the longest path in the network $\mathcal{N}$. We also refer to this as the *time* it takes $\mathcal{N}$ to compute F. When we take account of the resources used to evaluate elementary functions, the time can vary depending on the assignment of elementary operations to agents (see Chapter 7). If the $\mathcal{F}$ complexity of F is infinite, then F is not $\mathcal{F}$ computable; that is, it is not computable by networks with modules in the class $\mathcal{F}$. We will sometimes refer to the complexity of F, omitting reference to the class $\mathcal{F}$ when it is clear which class is being used.

Note that the complexity of a function depends only on the class of elementary functions, and not on a particular algorithm that might be used to compute it. In some cases, in which the functions being computed are smooth and the set of elementary functions is appropriately specified, we are able to give lower bounds, sometimes exact, on the complexity of a function F in terms of properties of F alone, that is, independently of the algorithms used. This means that the complexities of, say, different polynomial or rational functions (functions in the standard complexity class P) can be compared without having to count the steps of the algorithms being used to compute them. In the case of smooth functions between Euclidean spaces (or, more generally, smooth manifolds) the lower bound on computational complexity is determined by the number of variables that the function *actually* depends on (as distinct from the number of its nominal arguments). The calculation of the lower bound does not require specification in detail of the computations performed by any algorithm that computes the function. This analysis is presented in Chapter 6.

One of our aims in proposing the modular network model is to provide a formal structure in which to study the process of figuring out what actions are best, or at least desired, for agents in given situations, when that process is subject to constraints that in one way or another impose costs. Thus, our approach can be located within the rational-choice paradigm. It is a model of rational choice when there are costs of figuring out what to choose. Radner has called this approach one of costly rational choice (Radner, 1997, 2000). This is rational choice in a model that includes constraints on information processing (see Rubinstein, 1998, p. 22; Gilboa and Samet, 1989).

The idea that elementary operations can be chosen at the discretion of the analyst may appear objectionable. Wouldn't it be sounder to identify the fundamental capabilities of human beings and to base the set of elementary operations on them? If the level of resolution they determine is too fine, then higher-level compositions of them could be formed in a way analogous to the way computer instructions in a high-level language are ultimately related to machine language instructions. A difficulty with this idea is that if we mean by the inherent capabilities of human beings those that are genetically determined, then those capabilities are likely the same today as they were fifty thousand years ago. However, we know that there are information-processing tasks that are elementary for people in contemporary societies but were impossible for people who lived only a few hundred years ago. It seems appropriate that the difficulty of an information-processing task should depend on the currently operative capabilities, recognizing that those capabilities change from time to time.

1.3. COMPUTING AND ECONOMIC ORGANIZATION

Historically, the main analysis of economic organization and of the coordination of economic activity has been General Equilibrium Theory. Adam Smith's insight into the workings of a market economy was that persons – economic agents – motivated by self-interest and guided by market prices are led to take actions that produce socially efficient outcomes. *Socially efficient* has come to mean *Pareto optimal*. In the 1950s this insight was given a rigorous but somewhat incomplete formal treatment, known as the classical theorems of welfare economics. The First Welfare Theorem asserts that in a certain class of economic environments, a competitive equilibrium corresponds to or determines an efficient social state. This result makes Smith's insight rigorous, but it is incomplete in several ways. First, *market economy* means perfectly competitive markets, in which all economic actors are price-takers who do not consider the effects of their actions on the actions of others. In economies with finitely many agents, price-taking behavior is not in general consistent with fully rational self-interest. Second, the proposition that prices established in competitive markets suffice to guide economic action to socially efficient outcomes is not true in all economic environments, partly because equilibrium competitive prices do not exist in some environments, and partly because in some environments where they do exist they do not necessarily correspond to socially efficient outcomes. For instance, the existence of significant indivisibilities in commodities can allow nonefficient competitive equilibria. Furthermore, in environments with externalities, competitive market prices are generally not adequate to guide economic agents to socially efficient actions.

Even in environments in which the First Welfare Theorem is valid, it does not adequately support the claim that competitive prices guide economic agents to take socially efficient actions. The theorem tells us that if the economic agents are taking competitive equilibrium actions, then the outcome will be efficient. It says nothing about how the market process will find a competitive equilibrium even when it is unique. (Competitive equilibria are not in general unique, even in the most classical environments.) Thus, there must be some process that arrives at and selects a particular equilibrium, even when the equilibrium prices are different, and even more so when different equilibria are associated with the same prices.

One of the important properties claimed for the market organization is that it economizes on the information that agents need to know, and on the need to transfer information among agents. It is therefore essential that the process of finding an equilibrium from a possible multiplicity of them does not compromise this claim. In the case of a single market, the idea of adjusting the price to reduce the difference between supply and demand was known to the English classical economists, and in the case of multiple markets, Walras' *tatonnements* extended the idea to simultaneous adjustments of all prices. Pareto (1927, pp. 233–34) compared the market mechanism to a machine for computing equilibria. The economic environment was viewed in a way that modern computing theory would call *distributed*. Memory or observation of the environment is local; each individual economic agent observes only that part of the environment that pertains to him, such as his own preferences, or production possibilities. All other information must be communicated among the agents. The computation was conceived as an iterative process of price adjustment beginning in some state of the economy and eventually converging to a competitive equilibrium price. In environments in which the equilibrium corresponding to a given price is unique, and in which the First Welfare Theorem is valid, we are assured that finding a competitive equilibrium is equivalent to finding an efficient profile of actions and hence an efficient economic allocation.

This approach was formalized by Samuelson (1947, pp. 269–75) in terms of systems of differential equations. It was subsequently shown that the class of environments for which systems of differential equations such as the ones proposed by Samuelson converge even locally is quite restricted (see Scarf, 1960; Arrow and Hurwicz, 1958; and Arrow et al., 1959). More elaborate adjustment systems based on Newton's method can converge, but they require communication of much more information among the agents (see Smale, 1976a, 1976b, and Saari and Simon, 1978). In computational terms they have much higher communication complexity – so much higher as to call into question their feasibility.

Arrow and Hurwicz (1960) adopted a computational approach to calculating efficient allocations for economies with a well-defined goal function, such as one in which a single utility function is to be maximized. The problem then becomes a well-defined maximization. They used linear and nonlinear programming techniques to extend the class of environments for which pricelike adjustment processes could achieve efficient outcomes. Their idea of computation is the same kind of iteration as used in classical models of price adjustment. Hurwicz (1960) broadened the concept of a *decentralized economic mechanism*, with the aim of finding mechanisms that would have the informational and incentival advantages claimed for the market, but that would also generate efficient or desired outcomes in a class of environments where the market is not guaranteed to do so. Hurwicz's mechanisms are iterative message-exchange processes analogous to Walrasian tatonnement, but with messages that are not necessarily prices. This development gave rise to the field of *mechanism design*. Research in mechanism design has split into two somewhat separate lines: mechanisms that focus on incentive compatibility (game forms) but ignore informational efficiency, and decentralized mechanisms that focus on informational efficiency but ignore incentives. There are a few papers that study the informational requirements of implementing goal functions (sometimes called *social choice functions*) by game forms. Different game theoretic solution concepts are used, such as dominant strategy, Nash, or Bayesian equilibria (see Reichelstein, 1984 or Reichelstein and Reiter, 1988). A game form whose equilibria match the given goal function is said to *implement* that goal function; a decentralized mechanism whose outcomes match the goal function while ignoring incentives is said to *realize* that goal function. Results, such as lower bounds on the informational requirements of realizing a goal function, apply directly to informational requirements of implementing that goal function. This is a direct consequence of the fact that an equilibrium strategy profile of a game form is also the message correspondence of a decentralized mechanism, with the same outcome function, that realizes that goal function.

The issue of stability that exists for the market mechanism also arises with respect to the class of decentralized message-exchange processes. As with the market, the process of converging from some initial message complex to an equilibrium or final message is a kind of computation. It was shown by Reiter (1979) in an example, by Mount and Reiter (1983) in a more general setting, by Hurwicz (1986, p. 326), and in greater generality by Jordan (1987). Jordan (see p. 200) showed that the information required to realize Pareto optimal allocations by locally stable decentralized mechanisms cannot be less than the requirements for local stability of the competitive mechanism, which are known to be large. The combination of incomplete environmental coverage and the unexpectedly high informational requirements of markets and of tatonnementlike message-exchange processes suggests that we reexamine the problem of coordinating and organizing economic activity in a different framework than one built on General Equilibrium Theory.

Recall that in the General Equilibrium Model, economic activity consists of the actions of individual agents constrained by feasibility conditions and coordinated by market equilibrium prices. In particular, production is carried out by abstract agents called *producers*, each an individual decision maker. Even the most casual observation of the existing economy reveals that a good deal of economic activity is carried on in formal organizations comprising many individuals, and that their activities are coordinated by mechanisms that are not markets and do not resemble markets. The formal organizations we observe include firms; not-for-profit entities, such as hospitals; universities; organizations whose members are organizations, such as trade associations and sports leagues; and so on. It is tempting to have one or another of these in mind and to base a model on that. However, existing formal organizations tend to be quite complex things. For instance, a firm is a legally defined entity that has rights, privileges, and obligations that can differ from the legal rights and obligations of natural persons, and from those of other firms. A firm has an identity that distinguishes it from other firms. Which firm should we study? In contemporary economic theory the prevalent conception of a firm is essentially legal. A firm is seen as a collection of assets with an owner, an agent who has the legal right to control the use of the assets, and the right to the residual income from them. A firm that has more than one person in it generally has mechanisms for coordinating and controlling its internal activities. A firm is generally also a participant in mechanisms external to it that coordinate its actions with those of other economic entities. A given firm can change its internal coordination mechanisms without changing its identity as a firm. The mechanisms that coordinate the firm's actions with those of other economic agents can change without changing the identities of any of the agents effected.

Rather than theorize about firms, or other complex organizations, we focus on coordination mechanisms, whether they operate within firms or across firms. We use an extension of the $\mathcal{F}$-network model to define coordination mechanisms, to analyze their structure and performance, and to compare them. We use the $\mathcal{F}$-network model of computation to study choice between alternative mechanisms for coordinating economic activity. The $\mathcal{F}$-network model is extended to one of distributed computation in which resources are required to perform the elementary operations. This model provides a basis for choosing efficient coordination mechanisms and for addressing questions of organizational structure. The program sketched in the following paragraphs is presented formally, with examples, in Chapter 7.

Suppose a class of possible environments is given, where an environment is specified by a vector of real parameters. Suppose that a goal function defined on the class of environments is also given, associating with each environment an *outcome* or *action* that is desired for that environment. Suppose further that there are restrictions on the combinations of parameters an agent can observe. Those restrictions constrain the initial distribution of information about the environment among agents. Given a class $\mathcal{F}$ of elementary functions, we suppose there is a nonempty set of algorithms each represented by an $\mathcal{F}$ network that can compute the goal function. Note that, when the network is one that computes the optimal action in minimal time, a goal function determines (up to an equivalence relation on the modules called simple equivalence) the modules of $\mathcal{F}$ networks that compute it (see Chapter 6). In any case, the possibilities of parallel computation implicit in the goal function show up in the $\mathcal{F}$ networks it determines. Next we add to the $\mathcal{F}$ network model the requirement that each module of the network be evaluated by an agent, human or machine, subject to the condition that the evaluation takes one computational step, and that no agent can evaluate more than one module at a time.This is called the *parallel constraint.*

It is also assumed that the input nodes of the network are assigned to agents subject to the conditions governing the observability of input variables. An *assigned network* is one in which every module of the network is assigned to an agent. An assigned network represents an execution of the algorithm that the unassigned $\mathcal{F}$ network specifies. The assigned network specifies a computation carried out by the agents to whom modules are assigned in the pattern determined by that assignment. An assigned network determines several quantities of interest. These include the length of time required to compute the value of the goal function (*delay*); the number of transmissions of the value of a variable from one agent to another agent (a *crosslink*); the number of such transmissions from an agent to herself, that is, a retrieval from that agent's memory (a *selflink*); and the number of agents involved in the computation. These quantities depend on the environment, and hence bounds on them depend on the class of environments for which the goal function is defined. These quantities are determinants of the cost of carrying out the computation. Generally we do not have a fully specified cost function, but even in the absence of a cost function, one can examine the efficient frontier in the space of the four cost determinants.

We call an efficient, assigned $\mathcal{F}$ network a *coordination mechanism.* It specifies a multiperson organization for computing the decisions or actions required in each environment in the domain of the goal function. Different coordination mechanisms can be compared by comparing the performances and structures of the assigned $\mathcal{F}$ networks that define them. In Chapter 7 we consider coordination mechanisms in the context of production. Two types of mechanisms are considered, depending on the kind of communication channels used. One type of mechanism uses *market channels*; the other uses *direct channels*. The goal function, which defines the coordination problem, also determines the class of $\mathcal{F}$ networks that can compute the goal function, and therefore also determines the class of assigned networks to be considered. The performance of assigned networks in this class that use market channels can be compared with that of networks that use direct channels. An example (Example 1) is studied in which the First Welfare Theorem holds and competitive equilibrium exists. In this example, satisfactory coordination means achieving "just-in-time" production. There are two subcases. In one, the market mechanism cannot coordinate production, whereas a direct mechanism can. In the other, both mechanisms achieve satisfactory coordination, but the direct mechanism is less costly. A second example (Example 2) with several parts shows the sensitive dependence of efficient coordination mechanisms on the particular specifications of the coordination problem. Examples 1 and 2 appear in Section 7.2 before the formal model, which is presented in Section 7.3. They are intended to motivate the formal model. They implicitly conform to the structure of that formal model, but because they are simple, they can be understood without first working through the formal model. In a variant of Example 2, we see that the relationship between the structure of a network that uses direct channels and the parameters that define an environment determines where there are natural breaks between coordinating units, suggesting boundaries between organizational units. We take up the question whether to combine organizational units into a larger structure. This requires elaborating the cost model to include comparing the effect of converting an external channel into an internal one as a result of combining initially separated units into one larger one. A third example (Example 3) illustrates a case in which the structure of the assigned network is independent of the number of parameters. This example also suggests how the number of parameters may limit the scale of the organization.

The desire to understand multiperson organizations and mechanisms motivates a growing literature in which information processing is modeled explicitly in the context of multiagent economic behavior and decision making. Van Zandt's survey and review of a large part of this literature provides an excellent orientation (Van Zandt, 1998). The $\mathcal{F}$-network model is, in certain respects, more general than the models discussed there. In particular, the models of Radner (1993), Radner and Van Zandt (1992), and Van Zandt (1998) are, insofar as elementary operations are concerned, specializations of the $\mathcal{F}$-network model in which the class $\mathcal{F}$ consists of associative operations, such as addition, and finding the maximum of two numbers. Radner (1993) and Radner and Van Zandt (1992) study the routine computations of a bureaucracy, in which successive waves of inputs are processed by a fixed network. They study the cost of computing, including delay. One question addressed is about the nature of returns to scale in information processing, a question suggested by classical arguments about determinants of the size of the firm. They find decreasing returns to scale.

Van Zandt (1998), using associative elementary functions, considers the effects of computational delay on decision-making when the organization is operating in a sequence of environments generated by a (known) stochastic process. His computational model is one of real-time parallel processing with associative elementary operations. In his model it is possible to make decisions more quickly by allowing managers "closer" to the observed environment to make certain decisions by using only their own information. These decisions are generally not optimal, because they ignore other relevant information, but to use all the information would entail more delay and therefore make the decision less timely. Van Zandt derives optimal decision rules for this problem and relates these to the structure of organization.

In Chapter 4 we consider a pure-exchange economy with two agents and two goods in which the agents have quadratic utility functions. In this class of environments, the Walrasian trade is given by the function

$$F(x, z, x', z') = (z - z')/(x - x'),$$

where (x, z) are the parameters of the first agent and (x', z') are the parameters of the second agent (see Hurwicz et al., 1980). It is known that the smallest message space that can realize this goal function is one whose dimension is two. We examine the complexity of the computation involved in this example. We show that there is a trade-off between communication requirements and computational complexity. We derive the efficient frontier in the space whose coordinates are message space size m and complexity τ – the minimum time (number of steps) needed to compute F – and show that this frontier is invariant under independent transformations of coordinates in the parameter spaces of the two agents, whether linear or nonlinear.

1.4. CHAPTER SUMMARIES

Chapter 2, $\mathcal{F}$ Networks, presents the $\mathcal{F}$-network model and discusses the relation of that model to finite automata and modular networks. If a function can be computed in finite time, then the computation can be analyzed by using a network with a graph that is a directed tree. It is shown that conditional branching is not ruled out by this restriction (see Section 2.1.2). For the exposition to be made self-contained, the graph theory used in the formal model is included in the chapter. The language of Chapter 2 is used in the subsequent chapters.

Chapter 3 presents the Leontief Theorem and the generalization of it used to analyze $\mathcal{F}$ networks. Most of the sections that follow use the analytic techniques developed in this chapter. The mathematical tools used can be found in a standard undergraduate multidimensional differential calculus course. The article by Simon (1986) covers all the required concepts.

The first section of Chapter 4 extends the $\mathcal{F}$-network model to make it applicable to computations carried out by human agents; the second section of Chapter 4 contains an introduction to decentralized mechanisms, message spaces, and realizing goal functions. This section lays the groundwork for the next section, which presents a two-agent two-commodity Edgeworth Box economy and derives its set of Pareto optimal trades. This determines a goal function. In the fourth section we analyze the communication and complexity requirements of decentralized mechanisms that realize this goal function. The trade-off between message space dimension and computational complexity is explicitly determined.

In Chapter 5 we study two related issues that arise in connection with games. In Section 5.1 we consider two-person bargaining games, and we compare the complexity of two solutions namely; the Nash solution and the Kalai–Smorodinsky solution. Two bargaining games are studied, one with a quadratic boundary, and the other with a cubic boundary. We show that in these games the Kalai–Smorodinsky solution is simpler than the Nash solution. Indeed, it appears that the Nash solution is probably not computable in games with a cubic boundary, in spite of the fact that the class of elementary functions used is large. The techniques introduced in Chapter 3 play a heavy role in this analysis.

In Section 5.2 we take up a related question. Does a player who has a superior set of elementary functions to compute with have an advantage in games? We consider two games. The first is a two-player concave–convex zero-sum game played under a time constraint; the second is a class of two-player noncooperative games we call "Ready or Not" games. As might be expected, because our measure of complexity is time, time is involved in these games.

Chapter 6 presents a lower bound on the computational complexity of vector-valued and twice-differentiable functions defined on product spaces. Functions in this class arise as goal functions to be realized by decentralized mechanisms. The lower bound on complexity is determined by the number of variables the goal function actually depends on. The analysis uses the generalized Leontief Theorem. It also uses the concept of a universal object from category theory. However, no knowledge of category theory is required to understand this chapter. The proof of the generalized Leontief Theorem provides a constructive method for expressing a goal function in terms of subsets of variables. When the underlying parameter space is a product space, the construction produces a partition of the set of variables into subsets such that the partition respects the given structure of the parameter space as a product, and enables us to write the goal function as a superposition of functions, each of which is defined on one of the subsets in the partition. The theorem and its proof are presented in the Appendix to Chapter 6.

In the second section of Chapter 6 we compare the measure of complexity of a C^2 function F computed by networks that use C^2 elementary functions of two real variables, with the time needed to compute a discrete approximation to F by a finite network. Considering approximations of increasing accuracy, and passing to the limit, we show that the time needed to compute a C^2 function

F by networks using elementary functions that are C^2 real-valued functions of two real variables is a limit of times taken by finite networks that compute finite approximations to F. In the limiting process studied here, the *structure* of the approximating networks remains fixed, whereas the size of the alphabet is allowed to vary. This may be interpreted to say that the same algorithm is used to compute each of the finite approximating functions and the limiting function, whereas increasingly many symbols are used to encode the finer approximations as we pass to the limit, much as the number of positions in a sequence of progressively finer rational approximations to a real number increases. We interpret these results to mean that the $\mathcal{F}$-network model of computing is an idealization of finite computing in the same sense in which measurement with real numbers is an idealization of rational measurement.

Chapter 7 addresses the organization of economic activity. The focus of analysis is on coordination problems, and their implications for organizational structures. The ideas are presented first in examples. Among other things, the examples reveal how apparently small differences in coordination problems can make large differences in the organizational structures that are designed to solve those problems. The examples are followed by a formal model that embodies a computational approach to economic organizations. The formal model uses an extension of the (r, d)–network model of computing presented in Chapters 2 and 3. The analysis of the examples implicitly uses the formal model, but, because the examples are so simple, they can be followed without knowing the formal model. The advantage of reading the examples before the formal model is, we hope, that it will make the formal model more intuitive, and more convincing.

2 $\mathcal{F}$ Networks

2.1. GRAPHS AND TREES

In this chapter we introduce the definitions and geometry of $\mathcal{F}$ networks. $\mathcal{F}$ networks are the devices that are used to represent algorithms and to compute functions. They are constructed as compositions of functions chosen from a class $\mathcal{F}$ of primitive functions. The terms *composition* and *superposition* are used interchangeably. The rules of composition or interconnection are represented by a directed graph, that is, a digraph, that shows the order in which the elementary operations are carried out. The general outline of this chapter is similar to discussions of finite automata – a standard topic in machine theory. The definitions in this section differ little from those of usual developments of the theory of finite automata, with the exception that we allow the primitive functions to be chosen from classes of functions that include functions defined on topological spaces. Thus elements of $\mathcal{F}$ will generally not be binary functions, or even functions that have a finite number of values. The main focus of this chapter is on the graph that represents the computation. Assuming that each primitive function of $\mathcal{F}$ computes its value with a delay of one unit of time, our goal is to determine the minimum delay required to compute a given function. For an arbitrary function the analysis of $\mathcal{F}$ networks that compute the function can be difficult. That analysis is greatly simplified by showing that if a function can be computed in a time t by a network represented by a digraph, that network can be replaced with a new network whose digraph is a simple tree with a single root, a fan-in (Definition 2.1.10), that computes the same function in the same time t. This may require extending the class of functions $\mathcal{F}$ to include a small class of constants and projections. A fan-in is a particularly simple tree. If the graph of the $\mathcal{F}$ network is a fan-in, then the function it computes is presented as a finite superposition of functions in $\mathcal{F}$. The maximum number of compositions in a chain of compositions occurring in a superposition is the length of the superposition. Length is an indicator of the time required for a superposition to compute a given function. Bounds on the lengths of superpositions are explored in Chapter 6. For a given function and algorithm for computing it, the expression of that algorithm as a fan-in is determined mainly by the original digraph and the time t. The principal graph theoretic advantage of working with a fan-in is that the time t required to compute the value of a function is also the length of the longest path from a leaf, a vertex where a variable is introduced, to its root, the vertex where the value of the computation is read. Representing a function as a finite superposition of functions of $\mathcal{F}$, makes available classical analytic techniques of function theory. These techniques can be used to analyze the depth of the superposition and hence the minimum length of the fan-in required to compute the function.

In this chapter we present the formal definitions required from graph theory along with the formal definition of what it means for an $\mathcal{F}$ network to compute a function in time t. We relate this to graph theory and machine theory. We include several examples of functions computed by algorithms represented by $\mathcal{F}$ networks. We describe the process of reducing the computation of an $\mathcal{F}$ network that computes a function in time t to an $\mathcal{F}$ network that is represented by a fan-in of length t. Theorem 2.1.4 is the formal statement that this reduction can be made. The proof of the theorem is in Appendix A.

The definitions and results given in this section are, with some slight modifications, materials that can be found in Arbib (1960), Berge (1973), or Knuth (1973b). Some variants from these texts are taken from MacLane (1971).

Definition 2.1.1. A directed graph (or digraph) $G = [V, A]$ is a set V with elements that are called *vertices*, *points*, or *nodes*, a set A called the set of *arcs of* G, and a function $a \mapsto [\iota(a), \tau(a)] = \overrightarrow{\iota(a)\tau(a)}$, from A to $V \times V$. The vertex $\iota(a)$ is called the *initial vertex* of the arc a and $\tau(a)$ is called the *terminal vertex* of the arc a. Each directed graph also has a set of *empty arcs*, one such empty arc for each element of V. The empty arc for the vertex v is denoted by $\epsilon(v)$. An empty arc at vertex v has the vertex v as both its initial and its terminal vertex. An empty arc is not an arc.[1]

An arc that has the initial vertex equal to the terminal the vertex is a *loop*. Note that a loop is an arc; thus an empty arc is not a loop.

Figure 2.1.1 represents a simple directed graph. The elements of the set V of vertices are represented by the small circles labeled v_1, v_2, v_3, and v_4.

[1] The proof of Theorem 2.1.4 requires the construction of maps between digraphs. A map between digraphs carries vertices to vertices and should carry arcs to arcs. However, it is useful to be able to construct a concept of map that eliminates some arcs. In order to be able to discuss such "maps" it is convenient to be able to carry an arc to an "empty arc" and avoid cumbersome special-case statements when arcs are to be eliminated. We would also like to be able to replace a digraph with a (loopless) tree. Thus, if each vertex of a graph is to have an empty arc, to avoid loops we require the rather peculiar statement that an empty arc should not be listed as an arc (see MacLane, 1971, p. 48).

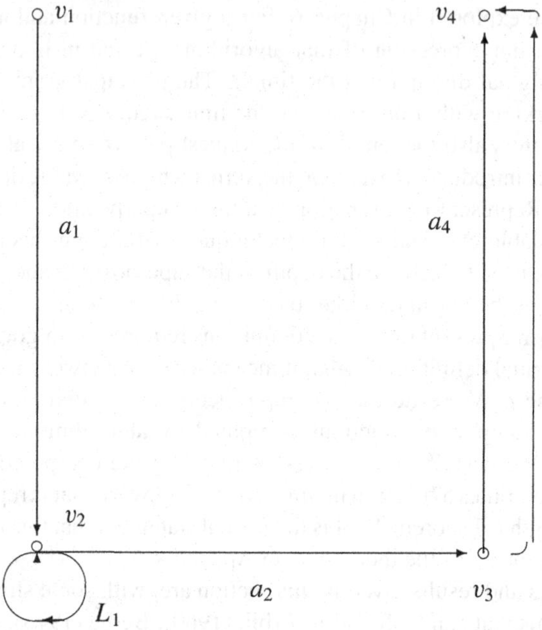

Figure 2.1.1.

The arcs are represented by curves drawn between the vertices. An arrow on an arc indicates the order of initial vertex to terminal vertex. Thus A has five elements: a_1, a_2, a_3, a_4, and L_1. The arc a_1 has as initial vertex the vertex v_1 and as terminal vertex the vertex v_2. The arc L_1 is a loop with v_2 as both initial and terminal vertices. The function $a \mapsto \overrightarrow{\iota(a)\tau(a)}$ assigns an initial vertex and a terminal vertex to the arc a. On arc a_1, $a_1 \mapsto \overrightarrow{v_1 v_2}$, indicating that the initial vertex of a_1 is v_1 and the terminal vertex of a_1 is v_2. The terminology *digraph* does not appear in Berge (1973) or Arbib (1960).

In some cases we wish to ignore the order, initial vertex to terminal vertex, that is assigned to the arcs of a digraph. In such a case we assign to an arc a represented by the ordered string $\overrightarrow{\iota(a)\tau(a)}$ the *nonordered set* $\{\iota(a), \tau(a)\} = \overline{\iota(a)\tau(a)}$ and call the arc an *edge* between the vertices $\iota(a)$ and $\tau(a)$. When the order assigned to the arcs of a directed graph G is ignored, then the resulting graph is a *nondirected graph.* If we replace the arcs of a digraph with edges, the result is the *associated nondirected graph.* Figure 2.1.1 can also represent a nondirected graph. All we need do is ignore the arrow heads on the arcs. For example, in Figure 2.1.1 the arc a_1, where $a_1 \mapsto \overrightarrow{v_1, v_2}$, can also be viewed as an edge between v_1 and v_2 where $a_1 \mapsto \{v_1, v_2\} = \overline{v_1 v_2}$.

If G is a digraph and v is a vertex of G, then the *out-degree of* v is the number of arcs that have v as the initial vertex. The *in-degree of* v is the number of arcs that have v as the terminal vertex. Empty arcs have no effect on in-degree or out-degree.

In Figure 2.1.1 the in-degree of v_2 is 2 because a_1 and L_1 both have as a terminal vertex the vertex v_2. The vertex v_3 has out-degree 2 and in-degree 1, whereas v_4 has out-degree 0 and in-degree 2.

If G is a (nondirected) graph, then a *chain C of length q* (where q is a positive integer) in G is a sequence of edges $L = (a_1, \ldots, a_q)$ such that the edge $a_r, 2 \leq r \leq q - 1$, of the sequence has *one* of the vertices, $\iota(a_r)$ or $\tau(a_r)$, in the set $\{\iota[a_{(r-1)}]\tau[a_{(r-1)}]\}$ and the other vertex, $\iota(a_r)$ or $\tau(a_r)$, is in the set $\{\iota(a_{r+1}), \tau(a_{r+1})\}$. For a chain L of length q in a graph G, the edge a_1 is between a vertex u and a vertex that is also a vertex of a_2. Similarly, the arc a_q is between a vertex v and a vertex w. One of the vertices, say w, is also a vertex of a_{q-1}. The other vertex, v, is the endpoint of the chain. The vertices u and v are the *endpoints of the chain C*. The chain C *joins* the vertices u and v. From Berge (1973), a chain is *elementary* if the vertices of the arcs in the chain are all distinct. A chain in a digraph is a sequence of vertices and arcs that form a chain in the associated nondirected graph.

In Figure 2.1.1 the sequence of edges $\Gamma = (a_1, a_2, a_3, a_4)$ is a chain of length 4 with the vertices v_1 and v_3 as endpoints. The loop L_1 is also a chain that has endpoints v_2 and v_2.

A *cycle in G* is a chain that has endpoints that coincide and is such that no edge appears twice in the sequence. An empty arc, that is, the edge associated with an empty arc, is not a cycle. The chain $\Delta = (a_4, a_3)$ in Figure 2.1.1 is a cycle. However, the chain $(\{L_1, L_1\})$ is not a cycle because the arc L_1 occurs twice in the chain.

A *path P of length q* in a digraph G is a sequence of q arcs and empty arcs $a_1, \ldots, a_r$ in which the initial vertex of a_j is the terminal vertex of a_{j-1} such that the total number of arcs (not including empty arcs) is q.[2] The path P is denoted by $\langle a_1, \ldots, a_q \rangle$. In Figure 2.1.1 the sequence $\langle a_1, L_1 \rangle$ is a path of length 2 whereas the sequence $\langle a_4, a_3 \rangle$ is not a path because the initial vertex of a_3 is not the terminal vertex of a_4. If, for each i, $a_i \mapsto \overrightarrow{u_i v_i}$, then vertex v_q is the *terminal vertex of the path*, and the vertex u_1 is the *initial vertex of the path*.

A path can encounter the same vertex many times, and it can use the same arc many times.

In the graph of Figure 2.1.1 the sequence of arcs that starts at the vertex v_1 proceeds along arc $a_1 \mapsto \overrightarrow{v_1 v_2}$ to the vertex v_2, traverses the empty arc[3] $\epsilon(v_2)$, follows the loop L_1, and ends by following the arc $a_2 \mapsto \overrightarrow{v_2 v_3}$ to the vertex v_3 is the path $\langle a_1, \epsilon(v_2), L_1, a_2 \rangle$.

A digraph G is *connected*, that is, connected as a nondirected graph, if for each pair of vertices u and v there is a chain in G that joins u and v. A digraph is without cycles if the associated nondirected graph is without cycles.

[2] An empty arc has length zero.

[3] Empty arcs are not shown. Arcs are denoted by lines or curves. As noted in footnote 2, empty arcs have initial and terminal vertices, but are not arcs. They are introduced as identity elements in compositions of arcs.

Definition 2.1.2. (From Berge, 1973). A *tree* is a digraph that is connected and has no cycles.

Between each two vertices of a tree there is at most one edge. Berge (1973, Theorem 1, Chap. 3) shows that between each two vertices of a tree, there is a unique (elementary) chain.

A vertex R in a digraph is a *terminal vertex* if there is no arc in the graph with R as the initial vertex. A vertex I in a digraph is an *input vertex* if no arc in the graph has I as the terminal vertex.

Input vertices of a digraph are places where variables are introduced into a superposition and a terminal vertex is where the function's value is read.

A tree diagram is an easy way to represent a superposition. This is an old technique; indeed, Cayley (1857) used trees to represent compositions. The function $\sin(x^2)$ is the superposition of the function $\sin(x)$ and the function x^2. When a function is written as a superposition of functions chosen from some collection $\mathcal{F}$, one can count the number of superpositions used between a variable and the value computed by the composition. That number usually depends on the variable chosen, but the maximum over all the variables is an indicator of the complexity of the function relative to the class $\mathcal{F}$. For example, if the elementary functions that are used for superpositions are $A(x, y) = (x + y)$, $B(x, y) = xy$, $E(x, y) = x^2 + y^2$, $C(x, y) = x - y$, and $D(x, y) = x/y$, then $A(x, y)$ is simpler than $A[x, B(x, y)]$. The function $A[B(x, y), E(z, w)]$ is less complicated than $f(x, y, z, w) = C\{D[A(x, y), B(z, w)], E(x, y)\}$. A representation of a superposition by a tree is constructed by assigning to the composition a digraph with component functions assigned to the vertices of the graph and with the arcs indicating the substitutions of variables to be made. The discussion of an example, which follows Figure 2.1.2, makes the construction clear. Figure 2.1.2. represents an example of a function of several variables computed as a superposition. The function is

$$f(x, y, z, w) = C\{D[A(x, y), B(z, w)], E(x, y)\}.$$

The diagram that represents the composition the tree of Figure 2.1.2, where the vertices have functions A, B, C, D, and E assigned and the arcs of the diagram indicate the order of the composition. Because the graph in Figure 2.1.2 has, at most, one arc connecting a pair of vertices, we can uniquely identify an arc by signifying its initial and terminal vertices.

The variable x is entered at the vertices labeled x_1 and x_2, and the variable y enters the computation at the vertices labeled y_1 and y_2. The variables z and w enter at the input vertices labeled z and w, respectively. One reads the value computed at vertex C. The same variable x is placed at the vertices labeled x_1 and x_2, but these distinct vertices require different labels. We use subscripts to represent the distinctions.

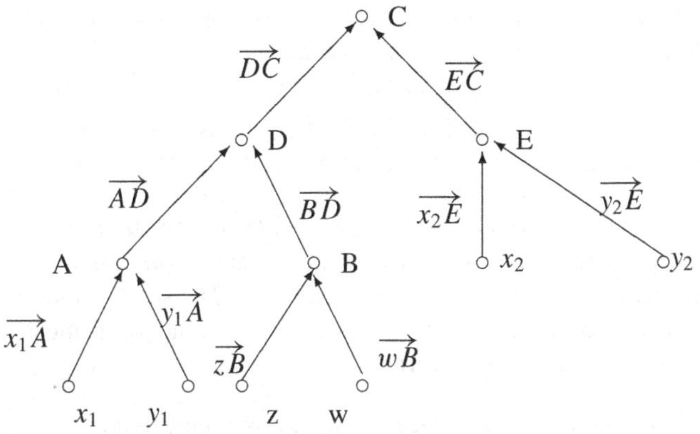

Figure 2.1.2.

The graph in Figure 2.1.2 represents the computation of $f(x, y, z, w)$; however the graph does not make clear the relation between the arcs of the diagram and the variables that appear in the functions A, B, C, D, and E. This is a minor labeling issue, but it must be dealt with. As an example of the problem, the function $D(x, y)\ x/y$ is certainly different from the function $D'(x, y) = D(y, x) = y/x$. An arc from a vertex that represents a function to a vertex that represents a second function indicates that the value of the function at the initial vertex of the arc is to be substituted for one of the variables of the function at the terminal vertex, but the arc does not indicate into which variable the substitution is to be made. In Figure 2.1.2, if D is a vertex that is to represent the function x/y, should one evaluate at D the function $A(x, y)/B(z, w)$ or the function $B(z, w)/A(x, y)$? The notation $C\{D[A(x, y), B(z, w)], E(x, y)\}$ makes the choices clear.

A way to avoid the labeling ambiguity in the tree representation is to introduce an order among the arcs that end at a particular vertex, and specify orderings for the variables of the functions of $\mathcal{F}$. We also need to avoid ambiguity when computations are represented by directed graphs that are not necessarily trees. Arbib (1960) and Knuth (1973b, p. 305) have a method to avoid the problem. We follow their procedure. The method begins with Definition 2.1.3. Before we give that definition, we require a bit more notation.

Notation. *Suppose U is a nonempty set and that Λ denotes a collection of empty sequences (or empty strings). Denote by U^* the set of finite sequences of elements chosen from the set $U \cup \Lambda$. The set U^* has the concatenation of sequences (or strings) as a composition operation. Two elements of U^* are equal if it is possible to derive one from the other by adding or eliminating empty sequences or strings. Thus, if w is an empty sequence, then the sequence* *of arcs* $\langle a_1, w\rangle$ *is the same as the sequence* a_1. *We abuse the notation by denoting the collection of equivalence classes also by* U^*.

Composition in the collection of equivalence classes U^* is again concatenation. Empty strings act as identity elements in the set U^*.

Definition 2.1.3. An *ordered directed graph* (from Arbib, 1960, p. 32) or *ordered digraph* consists of a digraph $G = [V, A]$ and an *order function* Γ defined on the vertices V of G with values in the set $\overline{A}^*$. The set $\overline{A}$ is the union of the set of arcs A with the set of empty arcs of G. The function Γ must satisfy the following conditions for each vertex v of G:

(i) each arc of the sequence $\Gamma(v)$ is an arc with terminal vertex v or is the empty arc $\epsilon(v)$,
(ii) each nonempty arc with terminal vertex v occurs exactly once in the sequence $\Gamma(v)$.

The function Γ counts the arcs that terminate at v. Arc 1 is first in the sequence $\Gamma(v)$, arc 2 is the second in the sequence, and so on. The vertex v is a place holder for a function of variables $x_1, \ldots, x_n$. The function $\Gamma(v)$ indicates the order of assignment of arcs to variables. For example, if the in-degree of a vertex v is three, then three arcs a, b, and c terminate at the vertex v. Setting $\Gamma(v) = bca$ indicates that arc b is to be connected to the variable x_1 of the function assigned to v.

To make an ordered graph of the tree in Figure 2.1.2, we labeled each vertex with the name of the function assigned to that vertex. Thus the function $C(x_1, x_2)$ is assigned to the vertex C. Because

$$f(x, y, z, w) = C\{D[A(x, y), B(z, w)], E(x, y)\},$$

the order function Γ for the tree must represent that composition. Set $\Gamma(C) = \overrightarrow{DC}\,\overrightarrow{EC}$. Arc $\overrightarrow{DC}$ is the first arc and $\overrightarrow{EC}$ is the second arc that ends at C. Vertex D is assigned the function D. Therefore, $\Gamma(D) = \overrightarrow{AD}\,\overrightarrow{BD}$. Thus D is a function of two variables x_1, x_2, and the value from function A is to be substituted for the first variable x_1 of D. Constructing Γ is clearly an easy process, so we do not continue except to note that one assigns to both the vertices x_1 and x_2 the variable x whereas y is assigned to both y_1 and y_2. Arbib uses a cleaner specification of the arcs in an ordered digraph by introducing a function from a vertex to the set of finite sequences of vertices of the graph. We prefer to consider the arcs as primitives and to phrase definitions, as much as possible, in terms of the arcs.

Knuth uses the following definition to discuss trees that are ordered graphs.

An *ordered tree* (from Knuth, 1973b, p. 305) is a digraph T that is a tree such that:

(i) there is a terminal vertex R called the *root*;
(ii) the remaining vertices of T (excluding the root) are partitioned into a sequence of $m \geq 0$ disjoint subsets $T_1, \ldots, T_m$, and each of these sets together with the arcs connecting the vertices of the set is an ordered tree;
(iii) for each $1 \leq i \leq m$, there is a single arc that connects the root of T_i with R and that arc has the root of T_i as the initial vertex and R as the terminal vertex.

The trees $T_1, \ldots, T_m$ are called the *subtrees* of the root R. The notation $R(T_1, \ldots, T_m)$ denotes the sequence of subtrees of the root R.

The concept of an ordered tree is the same as the concept of an ordered digraph without cycles that has one terminal vertex.[4] We use whichever version of ordered tree that is convenient. For most of the discussion of superposition, Knuth's definition is the easiest to use. However, when discussing a digraph that is not a tree, we fall back to Definition 2.1.3.

In a tree, an input vertex is called a *leaf*. A vertex of an ordered tree that is not a leaf or the root is a *node* **or** *branch vertex* (see Knuth, 1973b).

2.1.1. The Network Model

The representation of a superposition of functions by a tree is the goal of this chapter. At first sight a model of computing that considers only computations that can be expressed by trees appears to be severely restrictive. We show in Section 2.1.2. that this is a misleading impression. We construct a model that is based on classical neural network models of computing. Our model is a variant of the concept of automata or the McCulloch and Pitts (1943) concept of neural networks. Automata are not in general representable by trees; they require diagrams that are directed graphs. The next few paragraphs formalize the model of computing we have in mind.

Definition 2.1.4. If Y is a nonempty set and if r is a positive integer, denote by $\mathcal{F}(r)$ the set of all functions from the product of r copies of Y to Y. Assume that $\mathcal{F}$ is a class of functions chosen from the union over r of the $\mathcal{F}(r)$. An $\mathcal{F}$ **module** is a function in the class $\mathcal{F}$. It is assumed that an $\mathcal{F}$ module computes a value in one (finite) unit of time. If at time t $(y_1, \ldots, y_s)$ is input into the function f, then the function outputs the value $f(y_1, \ldots, y_s)$ one unit of time later. If Y is an open set in R^d, a d-fold product of copies of the real numbers r, then we will call a module in $\mathcal{F}(r)$ an (r, d) module.

[4] The sequence of subtrees replaces the sequence of arcs associated with a vertex. If the sequence of subtrees of a root R is $R(T_1, \ldots, T_n)$, then the root R_i of T_i must be connected to R by the arc $\overrightarrow{R_i R}$. An order function for the tree T would have value $\overrightarrow{R_1 R}, \ldots, \overrightarrow{R_n R}$ at the root R.

Notation. *If $f(y_1, \ldots, y_r)$ is an $\mathcal{F}$ module, then $[j, f]$ denotes the jth variable y_j of f.*

Next we use Definition 2.1.4 to define $\mathcal{F}$ networks.

Definition 2.1.5. Suppose Y is a nonempty set and suppose $\mathcal{F}$ is a class of functions, each with domain $Y \times \cdots \times Y$ (an a-fold product $1 \leq a \leq r$) and each function with range Y. An $\mathcal{F}$ **network** is a finite set of $\mathcal{F}$ modules and a function C, *the connection rule*, defined on a subset of the collection of variables of the $\mathcal{F}$ modules of the network with values in the set of modules of the $\mathcal{F}$ network. If a variable $[j, f]$ is not in the domain of the function C, then that variable is an *input line of the network.* Modules in a designated subset of modules of the network are *output lines of the network.*

An $\mathcal{F}$ network $\mathcal{N}$ is represented by an ordered directed graph N in the following way. Each vertex of the graph has a module assignment. That is, each vertex v of the graph represents a module of the network $\mathcal{N}$.

Notation. *If vertex v of the graph is assigned the function f, then we denote f by $\mathcal{N}_v$ or f if there is no danger of confusion.*

If the connection rule assigns a module g to a variable $[j, f]$, then there is an arc $a_{[j,f]}$ in the graph from the vertex that represents g to the vertex that represents f. If $[j, f]$ is not in the domain of the function C, then we introduce a vertex $L_{[j,f]}$ that is an input vertex of the ordered directed graph and we connect that input vertex $L_{[j,f]}$ to the vertex representing f by an arc. Thus in the graph N, each input vertex represents an input line to the network $\mathcal{N}$. The order function Γ of the ordered directed graph assigns to each input vertex of the directed ordered graph the empty arc at that vertex. If f is a module of s variables represented by the vertex f such that the vertex is not an input vertex of the graph, then the function Γ assigns the sequence $a_{[1,f]} \cdots a_{[s,f]}$ to that vertex. We complete the ordered directed graph by adding the empty arc at each vertex.

We illustrate these concepts by constructing an example of a computation carried out by an $\mathcal{F}$ network $\mathcal{N}$. Assume that the set $\mathcal{F}$ consists of three functions, each a function of either two or three variables. The variables and function have values in $\Re^+$, the set of positive real numbers. The functions are assumed to be defined on products of $\Re^+$. We assume that $\Re^+ \times \Re^+$ has coordinates y_1, y_2 and that $\Re^+ \times \Re^+ \times \Re^+$ has coordinates x_1, x_2, and x_3. The functions in $\mathcal{F}$ are $F_1 = x_1x_2x_3$, $F_2 = 1 + y_1 + y_2$, and $F_3 = y_1/y_2$. There are three modules F_1, F_2, and F_3 in the network $\mathcal{N}$. The variables of the function F_1 are $[1, F_1]$, which we identify with x_1; $[2, F_1]$, which we

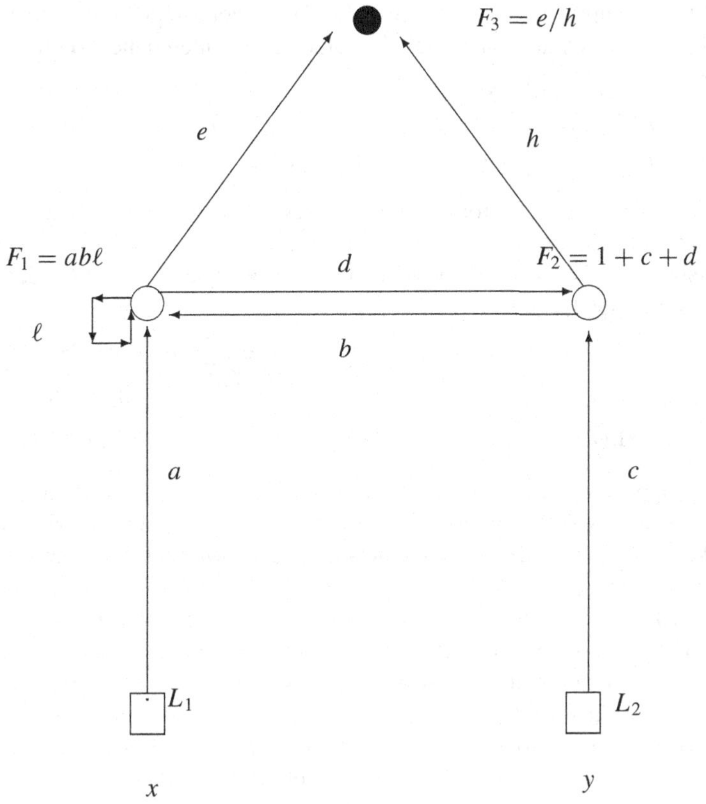

Figure 2.1.3.

identify with x_2; and $[3, F_1]$, which we identify with x_3. The functions F_2 and F_3 are each functions with variables $[1, F_j]$ identified with y_1 and variables $[2, F_j]$ identified with y_2. The input lines to the network are $[1, F_1]$ and $[1, F_2]$. The diagram in Figure 2.1.3 depicts an ordered directed graph that represents the network $\mathcal{N}$. The three vertices labeled F_1, F_2, and F_3 represent the three modules of the network. The black disk labeled F_3 is the output line of the network. Two (open-square) vertices labeled L_1 and L_2 are added to represent the two input lines $[1, F_1]$ and $[1, F_2]$ to the network. The arcs of the graph are

$$a = \overrightarrow{L_1F_1}, \quad c = \overrightarrow{L_2F_2}, \quad \ell = \overrightarrow{F_1F_1},$$
$$e = \overrightarrow{F_1F_3}, \quad b = \overrightarrow{F_2F_1}, \quad d = \overrightarrow{F_1F_2}, \quad h = \overrightarrow{F_2F_3}.$$

In Figure 2.1.3 the first variable $[1, F_1] = x_1$ of F_1 is an input line to the network and receives the variable x. The second variable x_2 of F_1 receives values computed by the function F_2. The second input line of the network is $[1, F_2] = y_1$, and it receives the value y. The interconnection function C is defined as follows:

$$C([1, F_1]) = L_1, \quad C([2, F_1]) = F_2, \quad C([3, F_1]) = F_1, \quad C([1, F_2]) = L_2,$$
$$C([2, F_2]) = F_1, \quad C([1, F_3]) = F_1, \quad C([2, F_3]) = F_2.$$

The order function for the network prescribes the relations between the arcs of the diagram that represent the computation and the variables of the functions assigned to the vertices. For the network $\mathcal{N}$ of Figure 2.1.3, the order function Γ is described as follows.

$$\Gamma(F_1) = ab\ell, \quad \Gamma(F_2) = cd, \quad \Gamma(F_3) = eh,$$
$$\Gamma(L_1) = \epsilon(L_1) \qquad \text{(the empty arc at } L_1\text{)},$$
$$\Gamma(L_2) = \epsilon(L_2) \qquad \text{(the empty arc at } L_2\text{)}.$$

Suppose at a time t each of the functions in the network $\mathcal{N}$ has a specific value; that is, each function is in a *state* described by the value of the function. We assume that each arc of the network carries without delay the value of the function that is at the initial vertex of the arc to the variable to which the arc is joined. At time t the *state of the network* σ_t describes the state of each of the functions in the network. At the end of one unit of time, each function in the network has computed a value that depends on the values given to that function's variables. Each module of the network changes to a new state and thus the whole network changes to a new state σ_{t+1}. If the network $\mathcal{N}$ starts a time $t = 0$ in a state σ_0 (i.e., a value is assigned to each of the modules F_j), which we call the *initial state*, and the inputs at the leaves $L_1 = x$ and L_2 constantly have the values x and y, respectively, then at each time $t > 0$ the output line of the network has a value that is the state of that output line at time t. The state of that output line at time t is the value computed by the network in time t with the input constantly x on the input line $[1, F_1]$ and constantly y on the input line $[1, F_2]$. The computation of a function of a network can be viewed as a flow of changes of state of the network. In the case of the network $\mathcal{N}$, we will make that flow precise. In order to understand the flow of information through the network, we note that the flow can be described by two functions. The first function is the *next-state function* δ that has the possible states of the network as domain and range. The value of the function δ at the state σ is the state of the network one unit of time after the network is in state σ. The second function is the *next-output function* λ whose domain is the collection of possible states of $\mathcal{N}$. At state σ the value $\lambda(\sigma)$ is the state of the output lines of the network one unit of time after the state of the network is σ.

Suppose that the network $\mathcal{N}$ of the diagram in Figure 2.1.3 has the initial state σ_0, in which modules F_1, F_2, and F_3 each have value 1. We describe the next state function λ and the next output function δ when F_1, F_2, and F_3 are

Table 2.1.1. Flow of Information in Figure 2.1.3

	Column		Module		
State	L_1	L_2	F_1	F_2	F_3
σ_0	1	1	1	1	1
σ_1	x	y	1	3	1
σ_2	x	y	$3x$	$2+y$	$\frac{1}{3}$
σ_3	x	y	$3x^2(2+y)$	$(1+y+3x)$	$\frac{3x}{2+y}$
σ_4	x	y	$3x^3(1+3x+y)(2+y)$	$1+6x^2+(1+3x^2)y$	$\frac{3x^2(2+y)}{(1+3x+y)}$

in states f_1, f_2, and f_3, respectively; the input to the network at the variable $[1, F_1]$ is x; and the input to the variable $[1, F_2]$ is y. Therefore,

$$\delta[(f_1, f_2, f_3), (x, y)] = [F_1(x, f_2, f_1), F_2(f_1, y), F_3(f_1, f_2)],$$
$$\lambda[(f_1, f_2, f_3), (x, y)] = F_3(f_1, f_2).$$

We show the flow of computation explicitly in Table 2.1.1. In that table the rows are labeled by the states and the columns are labeled by the modules. We adjoin two columns, L_1 and L_2, which show the values introduced as the inputs of the network that are held constantly at x on L_1 and constantly at y on L_2. Reading down the rows of Table 2.1.1, we see the states and their changes during the steps of the computation.

In the initial state σ_0 the input lines each have the values x on a and y on b. At the end of time $t = 1$ the network is in state σ_1, in which F_1 is in state x, module F_2 is in state $2 + y$, and F_3 is in state 1. At time $t = 5$, when the network is in state σ_5, the module F_1 is in state $3x^4(1 + 3x + y)(2 + y)[1 + y + 3x^2(2 + y)]$, the module F_2 is in state $1 + y + 3x^3(1 + 3x + y)(2 + y)$, and the terminal module F_3 is in state

$$\frac{3x^3(1 + 3x + y)(2 + y)}{[1 + 6x^2 + (1 + 3x^2)y]}.$$

As we remarked in the first paragraph of this chapter, the concept of a $\mathcal{F}$ network is little different from the concept of a modular network found in the literature of computer science, with one exception. Modules of $\mathcal{F}$ network are not required to have finite sets as domain and range. If an $\mathcal{F}$ network consists of modules with finite sets as domain and range, then the network function is a *state-output machine* in which the *present-output function* reads the states of the output lines of the network (cf. Arbib, 1960). A more detailed discussion of the relations between $\mathcal{F}$ networks and automata can be found in Appendix A. In the case in which $\mathcal{M}$ is a finite automaton, there is a modular network $\mathcal{N}$, which is interpreted as a finite automaton that simulates the automaton $\mathcal{M}$.

For a proof, see Arbib (1960, p. 69). Thus what one can compute with finite automata, one can also compute with a modular network.

Now we define what it means for an $\mathcal{F}$ network with r input lines and s output lines to compute a function $F : Y \times \cdots \times Y \to Y \times \cdots \times Y$, where the first product is r-fold and the second is s-fold.

Definition 2.1.6. Suppose that $X = Y \times \cdots \times Y$ is an r-fold product of copies of a nonempty set Y and suppose that $Z = Y \times \cdots \times Y$ is an s-fold product of copies of the set Y. Assume that $\mathcal{F}$ is a class of functions from products of copies of Y to Y. An $\mathcal{F}$ network $\mathcal{N}$ with r input lines $(L_1, \ldots, L_r)$ and s output lines $(O_1, \ldots, O_s)$ can compute the function $F = [F_1(x), \ldots, F_s(x)] : X \to Z$ in time t if the following condition is satisfied.

There is a state σ for the network such that for each element $(x_1, \ldots, x_r) \in X$, if the $\mathcal{F}$ network begins in state σ, and each input line L_i, $1 \leq i \leq r$ is held constant at the value x_i, then for each $1 \leq j \leq s$, at the end of t units of time the state of the output line O_j is $F_j(x_1, \ldots, x_r)$.

Next we say what we mean by the time complexity of a function F of n variables relative to a class of functions $\mathcal{F}$.

Definition 2.1.7. If F is a function of N variables $x_1, \ldots, x_N$ and if $\mathcal{F}$ is a class of functions, then we say that F *has (time) complexity t relative to* $\mathcal{F}$ if there is an $\mathcal{F}$ network that computes F in time t when $x_1, \ldots, x_N$ and constants are inputs to the network, but no $\mathcal{F}$ network with only $x_1, \ldots, x_N$ and constants as inputs can compute F in time less than t.

Many computations are most naturally presented in terms of $\mathcal{F}$ networks with ordered directed graphs that are not trees. Trees are, however, easier to work with and arise naturally when one considers superpositions of functions. If an $\mathcal{F}$ network computes a function in a known time, or, more importantly, if we wish to decide whether a network can compute a function in at most a given time, then we reduce the analysis to considerations of computations represented by directed ordered trees. We show this by carrying out a *delooping* process, or *cycle-removing* process.

Computations carried out by $\mathcal{F}$ networks represented by ordered trees have some very special properties. In particular, such computations are, after an appropriate length of time, stable. The network represented by Figure 2.1.3 computes many different functions depending on the length of time the computation is allowed to run. Ordered trees, in contrast, do not show that kind of instability. To be more precise, we introduce two new concepts.

Definition 2.1.8. (From Knuth, 1973b). The root of an ordered tree is said to be *of level 0 in T.* If T is an ordered tree with root R and subtrees $R(T_1, \ldots, T_m)$, then the *level in T of each vertex in* T_i is one larger than the level of that vertex in T_{i-1}.

The leaves of an ordered tree are at the highest level in the tree. A characteristic of an ordered tree is the length of the longest path. That length is the height of the ordered tree.

Definition 2.1.9. If T is an ordered tree, then the length of the longest path in T is the *height of T.*

We can now say something about the stability of computations carried out by a network represented by an ordered tree. Suppose an $\mathcal{F}$ network is represented by an ordered tree of height t, and that inputs to the network are held constant for the duration of the computation. For times t' greater than or equal to t, the function computed by the network depends only on the input to the network and is independent of the time t'. Once the leaves of a tree have fixed inputs, then during the first unit of time the state of each module directly connected by arcs to the leaves changes, to the value of the function represented by the module. For each unit of time thereafter, the modules in the level next to the top will stay in the same state as long as the inputs remain constant. That is, after the first computation, the states of the top level of modules are stable. After the second unit of time, the modules that are that are two levels from the top will have inputs that are stable; the modules on the tth level from the top become stable after t units of time. There is a formal inductive proof of this fact included in Appendix A. The formal statement is given in the next lemma.

Lemma 2.1.1. *Suppose that Y is a nonempty set and suppose that $\mathcal{N}$ is an $\mathcal{F}$ network represented by an ordered tree T. Suppose that the tree T has height t, the tree has s leaves, and the inputs to the network are from the product $P = Y \times \cdots \times Y$ (an s-fold product). For each element x in P and each time $t' \geq 1$, denote by $f_{t'}(x)$ the value computed by $\mathcal{N}$ in time t'. For each $t' \geq t$, and each x in P, $f_{t'}(x) = f_t(x)$.*

If an $\mathcal{F}$ network is represented by an ordered tree, and if the network computes a function in a time at least as long as the height of the tree, the notation introduced for ordered trees writes the function computed as a superposition of the functions that name the vertices of the tree. Once a computation is represented by an ordered tree, we can identify the function computed, at least for computing times greater than or equal to the height of the tree, with a superposition of the modules of the tree.

Among computations represented by ordered trees, it is easiest to analyze those represented by ordered trees in which every branch vertex is the terminal vertex of exactly r arcs. We can say something about the minimum height such a tree must have if it represents the computation of a function of N variables.

Notation. *If r is a real number, then we denote the smallest integer equal to or larger than r by* $\lceil \mathbf{r} \rceil$ *and denote by* $\lfloor \mathbf{r} \rfloor$ *the largest integer equal to or less than r.*

A simple lower bound is implied by the following lemma. The finite-automaton version of this can be found in Arbib (1960).

Lemma 2.1.2. *Suppose* $r \geq 2$ *is an integer and suppose that T is an ordered tree with N leaves such that each vertex that is not a leaf has in-degree at most r. There is a path in T of length* $\geq \lceil \log_r N \rceil$.

The formal proof is given in Appendix A, but roughly the lemma results from noticing the following. If there are N leaves in a tree, then one minimizes the lengths of paths from leaf to root by maximizing the number of leaves attached to vertices one arc away. When the number of arcs that can terminate in a vertex is r, then one needs $\lceil N/r \rceil$ vertices one arc away from the leaves of the tree. Now consider the vertices one arc away from the leaves as a new set of leaves, and minimize the number of vertices required to divide up the $\lceil N/r \rceil$ vertices and connect them by arcs to a next level of vertices. The number of times one must do this to attain a single root is $\lceil \log_r N \rceil$. A computation bound follows immediately when one assumes that the function to be computed depends on each of the variables. If this is the case, because variables must be placed at the leaves of the representing tree, the tree must have height at least $\lceil \log_r N \rceil$, and thus the computation requires at least time $\lceil \log_r N \rceil$.

Trees with a uniform in-degree for branch vertices are particularly easy to work with. For a fixed r and fixed height N, there is essentially only one such uniform tree. Furthermore, each tree of height N with the in-degree of each vertex at most r can be modeled as a subtree of such a uniform tree. We need to be careful about what "essentially only one" means, and we need a representation of that unique uniform tree. There is a convenient notation that represents the vertices of a uniform tree as lattice points of $\Re^2$, where $\Re$ denotes the real numbers.

Definition 2.1.10. Suppose that T is an ordered tree such that every vertex has in-degree at most r (briefly, an *r tree*). The ordered r tree T is said to be a *complete ordered tree* (cf. Knuth, 1973b, p. 401) if each vertex is either a leaf or is the root of exactly r ordered r-trees. A complete ordered r tree will also be called an *r fan-in*.

If r is an integer greater than 1 and if $M = r^N$, then there is a complete r tree of height N that has M leaves. This complete r tree is denoted by $S[r, N]$ and has an order function denoted by $\Gamma[r, N]$. The following convenient representation of this tree is often of use in Chapter 3. The representation consists of the lattice points (i, j) in the plane, i and j integers, that satisfy the conditions $0 \leq j \leq N$ and $0 \leq i < r^j$. The lattice points (i, j) are at level j in the tree.

For fixed j, write $i = a_{j-1}r^{j-1} + a_{j-2}r^{j-2} + \cdots + a_0$ where $0 \le a_t < r$ for each $0 \le t \le j-1$. The point $(kr^{j-1} + t, j)$ is an initial vertex of an arc with the point

$$a_{j-1}r^{j-2} + a_{j-2}r^{j-3} + \cdots + a_1 = (i - a_0)/r$$

as its terminal vertex.

Each of the points $(i, 1)$ is the initial vertex of an arc that terminates at the root $(0, 0)$. The kth tree associated with the point (i, j) is the tree that has the point $(ri + k, j + 1)$ as the root. That is, the trees are ordered left to right. Thus the order function $\Gamma[r, N]$ assigns the sequence $\overrightarrow{(ri, j+1)(i, j)} \cdots \overrightarrow{(ri + r - 1, j+1)(i, j)}$ to the vertex (i, j). Along the line $y = N$, there are r^N points, and each point along the line $y = N$ is connected to a point on the line $y = N - 1$. Figure 2.1.4 shows an example of this complete ordered tree when $r = 2$ and $N = 3$.

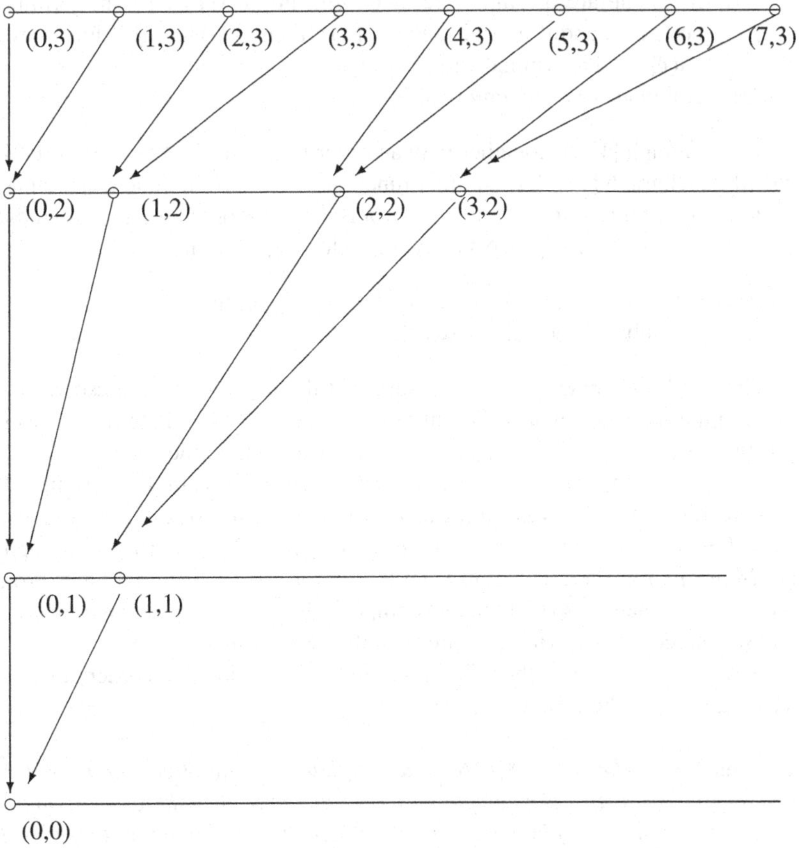

Figure 2.1.4.

The claim that there is essentially only one complete ordered r tree requires the concept of mapping between trees. In order to reduce a computation represented by an ordered directed graph to a computation represented by an ordered tree, we construct maps between directed ordered graphs. The terminology needed for that process is given in the following definition.

Definition 2.1.11. If G is a digraph, then a *map* ϕ from G to G' is a pair of functions a_ϕ, v_ϕ such that:

(a) v_ϕ is a function from the vertices of G to the vertices of G',
(b) a_ϕ is a function from the arcs and empty arcs of G to the set that consists of the union of the set of arcs and empty arcs of G'.

The functions a_ϕ and v_ϕ satisfy the following conditions:

(i) if e is an arc or empty arc of G with initial vertex v_1 and terminal vertex v_2, and if $a_\phi(e)$ is an arc of G', then $v_\phi(e)$ has an initial vertex $v_\phi(v_1)$ and a terminal vertex $v_\phi(v_2)$;
(ii) empty arcs map to empty arcs.

If G is a digraph $[V, A]$ together with an order function, $\Gamma : V \to A^*$, if G' is an ordered digraph $[V', A']$ and order function $\Gamma' : V' \to A'^*$, and if ϕ is a map of digraphs from G to G', then the map ϕ is a map of ordered directed graphs if the functions a_ϕ and v_ϕ also satisfy the following condition:

(iii) if v is a vertex of G and if $\Gamma(v) = a_1, \ldots, a_t$, then $a_\phi(a_1), \ldots, a_\phi(a_t)$ is a subsequence of $\Gamma'[v_\phi(v)]$.

The conditions placed on arcs ensure that the map on paths preserves the order of the sequence of arcs. Condition (iii) guarantees that. In terms of superposition of functions, this means that maps preserve the order of the variables used by a function, or equivalently, the maps preserve the names of variables. If T is an ordered tree, then assigning an arc to itself and a vertex to itself is a map from T to T. This assignment is the *identity map on T.* Two ordered digraphs are *isomorphic* if there is a map from the first to the second and a map from the second to the first so that the two compositions, first composed with second and second composed with first, are each the identity map.

Now we can state that there is essentially only one complete ordered r tree. The statement is the following lemma.

Lemma 2.1.3. *The r tree $S[r, N]$ is a complete ordered r tree with r^N leaves and a height of N. If T is a complete r tree of height N, then there are permutations of the sequence of integers* $1, \ldots, r$ σ_v, *one permutation for each branch* *vertex v of $S[r, N]$, such that T is isomorphic to the directed tree $S[r, N]$ with an order function that has at v a value equal to $\sigma_v \circ \Gamma[r, N](v)$.*

A proof of this lemma is in Appendix A.

We have already referred to a complete r tree as an r fan-in. If an elementary class of functions $\mathcal{F}$ consists only of functions of r variables, then an $\mathcal{F}$ network that is represented by an r tree is an $\mathcal{F}$ r fan-in.

An $\mathcal{F}$ network computes functions, and $\mathcal{F}$ networks that are represented by trees compute functions stably. The next step is to relate the computation of a function by an $\mathcal{F}$ network to the computation of the same function by an $\mathcal{F}$ network represented by a tree. If the function can be computed in time t by an $\mathcal{F}$ network, then it can also be computed by a $\mathcal{F}$ network represented by a tree of height t as long as the class of functions $\mathcal{F}$ has enough constants and projections. In this framework, with time as the measure of computational complexity, the analysis of computational complexity is reduced to studying computations represented by superpositions of functions in the collection $\mathcal{F}$. When the functions $\mathcal{F}$ have continuous second derivatives, then there are simple effective criteria to establish lower bounds on the number of superpositions and thus on the time required to compute a given function. These criteria are developed in Chapter 3. The task now is to show that every computation represented by a directed graph can be reduced to one represented by an ordered tree. The replacement of an $\mathcal{F}$ network represented by a digraph with an $\mathcal{F}$ network represented by a tree is called *delooping the digraph*. The precise statement is the following.

Theorem 2.1.4. *If an $\mathcal{F}$ network computes a function $H(y_1, \ldots, y_s)$ in time t, then there is an $\mathcal{F}'$ network represented by a complete r tree, for some r, that computes the function H in time t, where the class of functions $\mathcal{F}'$ consists of the class of functions $\mathcal{F}$, projections, constants, and functions of $\mathcal{F}$ composed with projections.*

The proof that delooping can be achieved is given as Theorem A.0.5 of Appendix A. What follows next is an example of delooping applied to computations that the network $\mathcal{N}$ represented in Figure 2.1.3 carries out in three units of time.[5]

We deloop the graph representing the computation by working backward in time. The network $\mathcal{N}$ computes the function in three units of time, so we begin the analysis at time $t = 3$. At time $t = 3$, when the network $\mathcal{N}$ is in state σ_3, the module F_3 is in state $x^2(2 + y)/(1 + x + y)$; see Table 2.1.1. This state is the

[5] The delooping process is familiar to algebraic topologists as a construction of a simply connected covering space for a one-dimensional finite simplicial complex, and it is certainly no surprise to computer scientists.

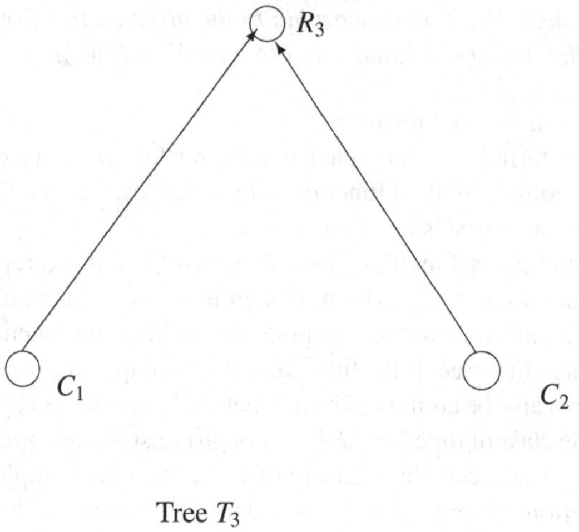

Figure 2.1.5.

next state of F_3 derived from the state $x^2(2+y)$ of F_1 and the state $(1+x+y)$ of F_2 at time $t=2$. We construct an ordered tree T_3 with one vertex labeled R_3 and two leaves labeled C_1 and C_2. The leaf C_j is connected to the vertex R_3 by a single arc c_j. Suppose that the arc $c_j = \overrightarrow{C_j R_3}$ is connected to the variable $[j, R_3]$ (see Figure 2.1.5). This assignment determines the value of the order function at R_3 for the ordered tree we are constructing. Map the tree T_3 to the ordered directed graph that represents the network $\mathcal{N}$, by a map ϕ_3 that carries the root of the tree with label R_3 to the terminal vertex F_3 of $\mathcal{N}$, that carries the leaves labeled C_j to the vertices labeled F_j, that carries the arc $c_1 = \overrightarrow{C_1 R_3}$ to the arc $e = \overrightarrow{F_1 F_3}$, and that carries the arc $c_2 = \overrightarrow{C_2 R_3}$ to the arc $h = \overrightarrow{F_2 F_3}$. If the network represented by the tree T_3 has initial state 1 at vertex F_3, $x^2(2+y)$ at the leaf C_1 and $(1+x+y)$ at the leaf C_2, then one unit of time later, the state of the vertex R_3 in T_3 is $x^2(2+y)/(1+x+y)$.

Construct two new ordered digraphs, one to replace each leaf of the tree T_3. The first of the new networks, denoted by $T_{2,1}$, has a single vertex that is a root labeled $R_{2,1}$ and three leaves labeled $L_{2,1,j}$, $1 \leq j \leq 3$ (see Figure 2.1.6). The leaf $L_{2,1,j}$ is connected to the vertex $R_{2,1}$ of the tree by a single arc $\ell_{2,1,j}$. The order function for the tree $T_{2,1}$ assigns to the vertex $R_{2,1}$ the sequence $\ell_{2,1,1}\ell_{2,1,2}\ell_{2,1,3}$. The second tree $T_{2,2}$ has a single vertex that is a root labeled $R_{2,2}$, two leaves labeled $L_{2,2,1}$ and $L_{2,2,2}$, arc $\ell_{2,2,1} = \overrightarrow{L_{2,2,1} R_{2,2}}$, and arc $\ell_{2,2,2} = \overrightarrow{L_{2,2,2} R_{2,2}}$.

Build a new ordered tree T_2 that has root R_3 and has subtrees $T_{2,1}$ and $T_{2,2}$ associated with the root. The result is represented by the digraph in Figure 2.1.6. The tree T_2 has the module $F_1 = x_1 x_2 x_3$ assigned to the vertex $R_{2,1}$ and has $F_2 = 1 + y_1 + y_2$ assigned to the vertex $R_{2,2}$. The root R_3 still has the function F_3 assigned to it. When the network represented by the graph of Figure 2.1.6

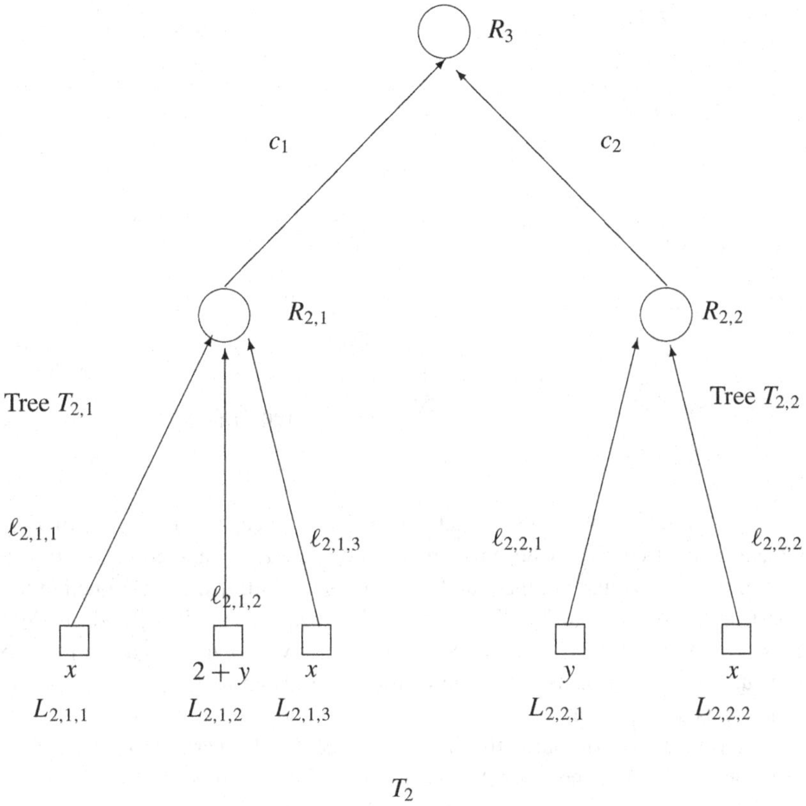

Figure 2.1.6.

has input x at the leaf $L_{2,1,1}$, the value $2 + y$ input at the leaf $L_{2,1,2}$, the value x at each of the leaves $L_{2,2,2}$ and $L_{2,1,3}$, and the value y input at the leaf $L_{2,2,1}$, then in one unit of time the modules associated with the roots of the trees $T_{2,1}$ and $T_{2,2}$ have states $x^2(2 + y)$ and $(1 + x + y)$, respectively. Thus in two units of time the network with tree T_2 computes the same value that the network with tree T_3 computes in one unit of time. Again represent the relation between T_2 and the computation carried out by $\mathcal{N}$ with a map ϕ_2 from the tree T_2 to the graph of $\mathcal{N}$ that carries paths from leaf to root on T_2 to paths of length two in the graph of $\mathcal{N}$ that end at F_3. The map ϕ_2 carries the arc $\ell_{2,1,1}$ to the arc a, the arc $\ell_{2,1,2}$ to the arc b, the arc $\ell_{2,1,3}$ to the empty arc at F_1, $\epsilon(F_1)$, the arc $\ell_{2,2,1}$ to the arc c, and the arc $\ell_{2,2,2}$ to the arc d. The map ϕ_2 carries the vertex $R_{2,j}$ to the vertex F_j. The map ϕ also determines the order function.

The next stage of delooping is to replace each of the leaves of the trees $T_{2,1}$ and $T_{2,2}$ with trees. These trees are illustrated in Figures 2.1.7 and 2.1.8. The

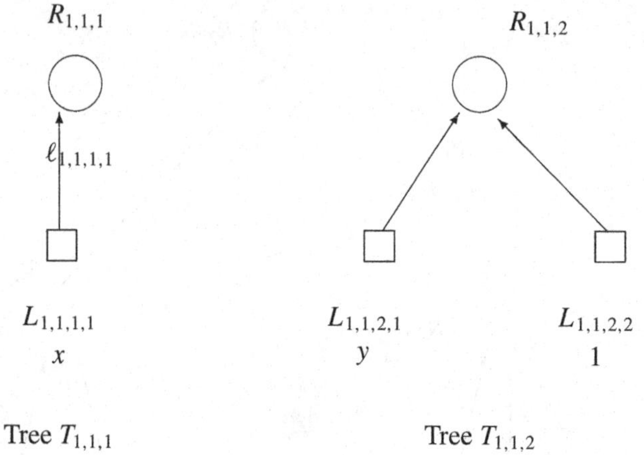

Figure 2.1.7.

tree $T_{1,1,j}$ $1 \leq j \leq 3$ has a terminal vertex that replaces the leaf $L_{2,1,j}$ of $T_{2,1}$. Construct the tree $T_{1,1,1}$ whose root maps to the leaf $L_{2,1,1}$ and computes in one unit of time the value that the leaf $L_{2,1,1}$ has as the initial value assigned in the construction of the tree T_2. Thus the tree $T_{1,1,1}$ has a root $R_{1,1,1}$ and one leaf $L_{1,1,1,1}$ connected to $R_{1,1,1}$ by an arc $\ell_{1,1,1,1}$. The vertex $R_{1,1,1}$ has assigned to it a function that repeats the value of the input at the leaf $L_{1,1,1,1}$. Thus this function is a projection.

The tree $T_{1,1,2}$ computes the input required by the variable $[2, F_1]$. That variable $[2, F_1]$ in the network $\mathcal{N}$ receives input from the module F_2. Therefore, the tree $T_{1,1,2}$ has a root $R_{1,1,2}$ together with two leaves $L_{1,1,2,1}$ and $L_{1,1,2,2}$. We assign the module $F_2 = 1 + y_1 + y_2$ to the root $R_{1,1,2}$. The leaf $L_{1,1,2,1}$ has an input value of y, whereas the leaf $L_{1,1,2,2}$ receives the value that is the initial value of the module F_1; that is, $L_{1,1,2,2}$ receives a value of 1. The tree $T_{1,1,2}$ computes the value $2 + y$. It replaces the leaf $L_{2,1,2}$ in the tree $T_{2,1}$.

The state of the tree $T_{1,1,3}$ after one unit of time is the value of F_1. Therefore, $T_{1,1,3}$ has root $R_{1,1,3}$ and three leaves $L_{1,1,3,j}$, for $1 \leq j \leq 3$. The vertex $R_{1,1,3}$ maps to the module F_1 of $\mathcal{N}$. The leaves $L_{1,1,3,1}$, $L_{1,1,3,2}$, and $L_{1,1,3,3}$ have as inputs the values x, 1, and 1, respectively. There are two trees to be constructed to replace the leaves $L_{2,2,1}$ and $L_{2,2,2}$. The tree $T_{1,2,1}$ has a root $R_{1,2,1}$ and a single leaf $L_{1,2,1,1}$. The root $R_{1,2,1}$ is assigned a module that repeats the value of the leaf $L_{1,2,1,1}$, and that leaf has as input the value y. The tree $T_{1,2,2}$ has root $R_{1,2,2}$ and three leaves $L_{1,2,2,j}$, for $1 \leq j \leq 3$. The root $R_{1,2,2}$ is assigned module F_1. The leaf $L_{1,2,2,1}$ has input x; the remaining two leaves have an assigned value of 1.

Construct the tree T_1 from the tree T_2 by replacing the leaves $L_{2,1,j}$ with the trees $T_{1,1,j}$ and replacing the leaves $L_{2,2,j}$ with the trees $T_{1,2,j}$. In one unit

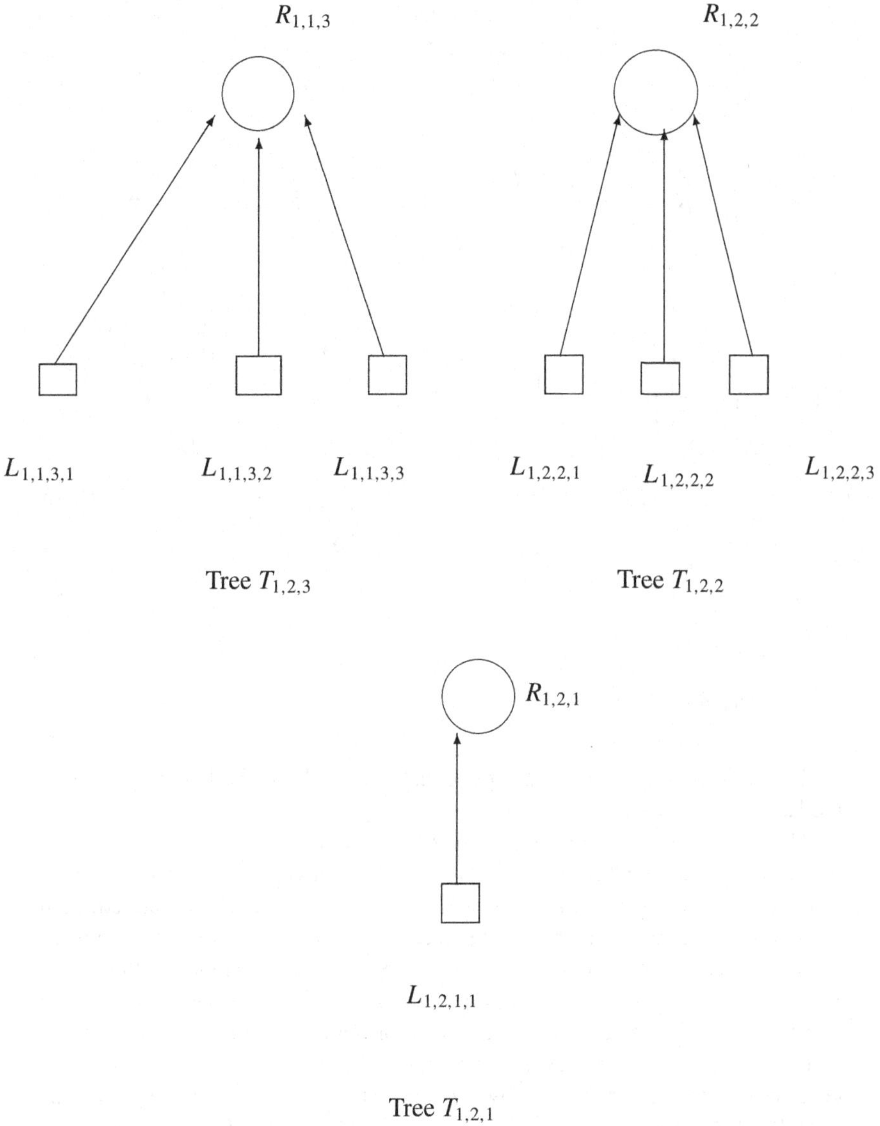

Figure 2.1.8.

of time, the networks constructed from the assignments we have described for the trees $T_{1,j,k}$ compute the inputs required for the tree T_2 to compute in two units of time the value $x^2(2+y)/(1+x+y)$. The final tree T_1 representing the delooped computation is given in Figure 2.1.9. Beneath each of the leaves

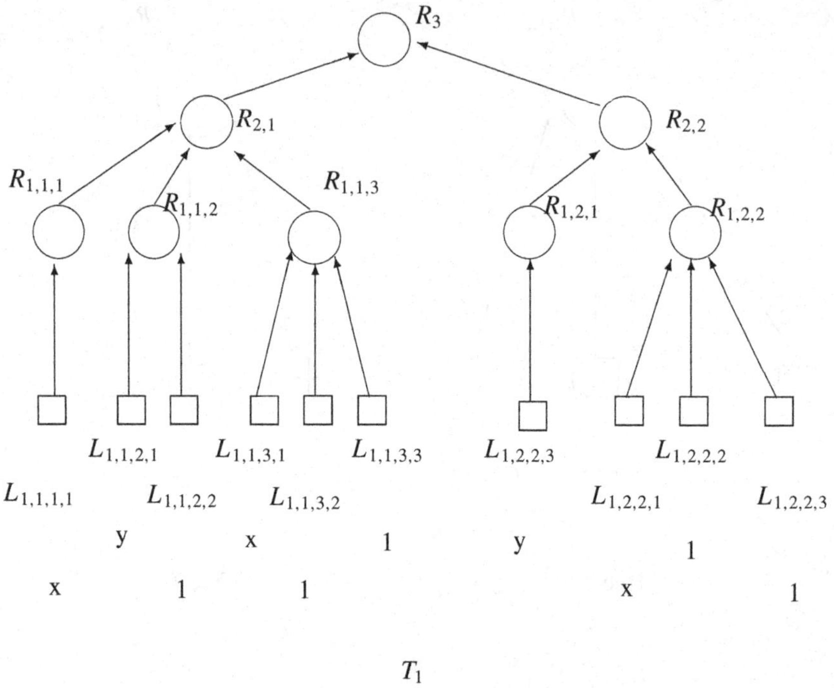

Figure 2.1.9.

we have printed the value to be input constantly to the variable represented by the leaf.

The tree represented in Figure 2.1.9 is not a complete 3-tree. Expand the tree T_1 to a complete tree by adding to each branch vertex a collection of arcs to complete a set of three arcs. If arcs that end at a vertex v are added, then the order function assigns to v a new sequence with the added arcs adjoined (in some order) to the end of the sequence. The module assigned to the vertex v is the composition of a projection composed with the assignment made to that vertex in T_1. The complete tree that represents T_1's computation is given in Figure 2.1.10. The vertex $B_{2,3}$ has been added to the tree T_1. The leaves connected to the vertex $B_{2,3}$ receive an input of (say) x; the vertex $B_{2,3}$ repeats the left value x and sends it to the vertex R_3; and the vertex R_3 has assigned the function $F_3'(A, B, C) = F_3(A, C)$. The vertex $R_{1,1,1}$ in the tree T_1 picks up two new leaves. The new leaves each have the value x as input, but $R_{1,1,1}$ acts as a function of only one of the inputs, say the leftmost input. Similarly, $R_{1,1,2}$ picks up a new leaf and $R_{1,2,1}$ picks up two new leaves. One assigns the inputs to the new leaves arbitrarily. We leave it to the reader to complete the construction of the map ϕ.

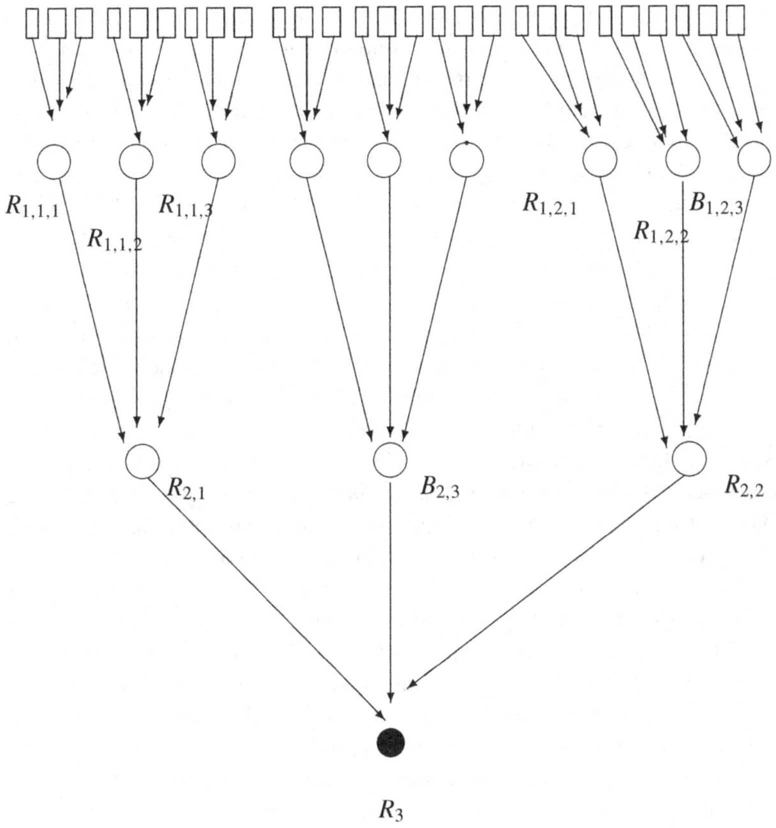

Figure 2.1.10.

2.1.2. Conditional Branching

The examples we have considered above are $\mathcal{F}$ networks for which the functions of $\mathcal{F}$ all have real numbers as values. However, the theory of $\mathcal{F}$ networks does not demand the restriction to functions that are real-number valued. A more general class $\mathcal{F}$ includes functions that have d-dimensional vectors (i.e., d tuples of real numbers) as values and whose domains are r-fold products of d-dimensional vectors. We call such $\mathcal{F}$ networks (r, d) networks. The concept of an (r, d) network is a slight generalization of the (r, d) networks found in Arbib (1960). Conditional branching can be represented in (r, d) networks.

Arbib (1960 p. 69), provides a proof of the proposition that every finite automaton can be simulated by a modular network. A finite state automaton can represent an algorithm in which conditional branching occurs. Arbib also introduces the concept of a *system*, a machine or algorithm that computes with real numbers or vectors. Arbib shows that a system can be simulated by a modular network. One can argue, following Arbib, that an algorithm represented by a system can also be simulated by an (r, d) network. This implies that a system in which conditional branching occurs can be simulated by an (r, d) network. (Arbib also points out that the construction of a network that simulates a given automaton can be grossly inefficient. This is in part the result of restricting himself to the use of (2, 2) modules.) Instead of rehashing proofs given in Arbib, we give a simple example of an (r, d) network that represents an algorithm that uses conditional branching. We take the Newton Machine presented in Blum (et al. 1998) as an example of an algorithm with conditional branching. The algorithm searches for an approximate zero of a differentiable function $f(x)$. That is, the algorithm searches for a value z_0 such that $|f(z_0)| < \epsilon$ for some specified tolerance ϵ. Blum uses the notation $N_f(z)$ for the function $z - f(z)/f'(z)$. The graph labeled A in Figure 2.1.11, taken from Blum, represents the algorithm. At the vertex labeled Branch the value z is tested against the tolerance ϵ. If the condition $|f(z_0)| < \epsilon$ is satisfied the value z is sent to Output. The Output node has an associated linear map to an output space. Otherwise the value z is sent to Input for a new round of a computation.

We construct an (r, d) network, with $r = d = 2$, that simulates the Newton Machine shown in A. This network is shown in the graph labeled B in Figure 2.1.11. Thus, our network is constructed of (2, 2) modules. That is, the modules have at most two inputs where each input is a two tuple of real numbers. One can think of the first coordinate in a two tuple (a, b) as data, and the b coordinate in the tuple as designating an action to be taken. The value of the second coordinate in a two tuple can be one of two distinct real numbers, encoding "Yes" and "No." The labels (u, c) and (v, d) on the arrows into and out of the node $(N_f(u), c)$ indicate the two tuples carried by the arrows. The Output of the (2, 2) network is *accepted* if the two tuple is (v, Yes), otherwise, the tuple is *rejected.* Once the time required to find an approximate zero is determined, then the process of delooping, described on p. 35, produces a loop-free network that computes the same function as the Newton Machine. The delooping process can be applied to this network, resulting in its representation as the tree shown in Figure 2.1.12.

2.1.3. Symmetrical Computation

In the next chapter we assume that a function G of r^N variables $\underline{x}$ is computed by an $\mathcal{F}$ network represented by an r fan-in. We state the conditions that such a function must satisfy for the tree that represents the computation to have height N. The conditions are rank conditions on bordered Hessians associated with G. These conditions were first described by Leontief (1947). In general, functions that satisfy these conditions are rare, and examples of such functions are equally rare in economics. As we have seen, the general class of functions of r^N variables that can be computed in a finite amount of time can be

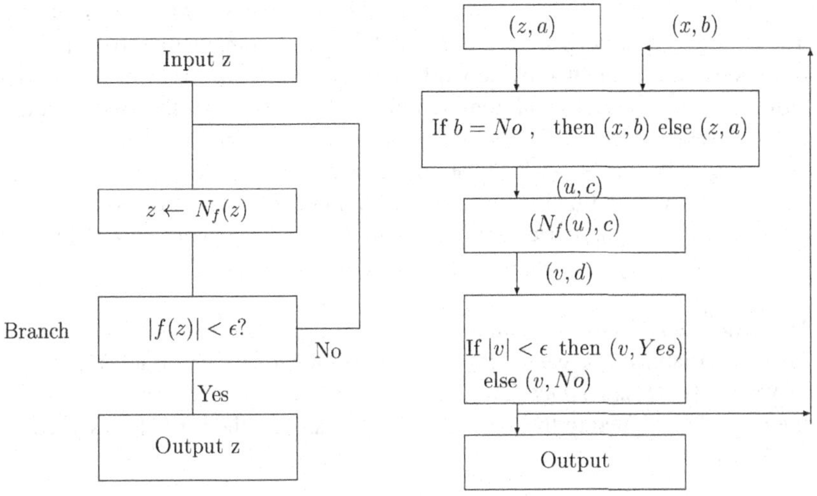

A. B.

Figure 2.1.11.

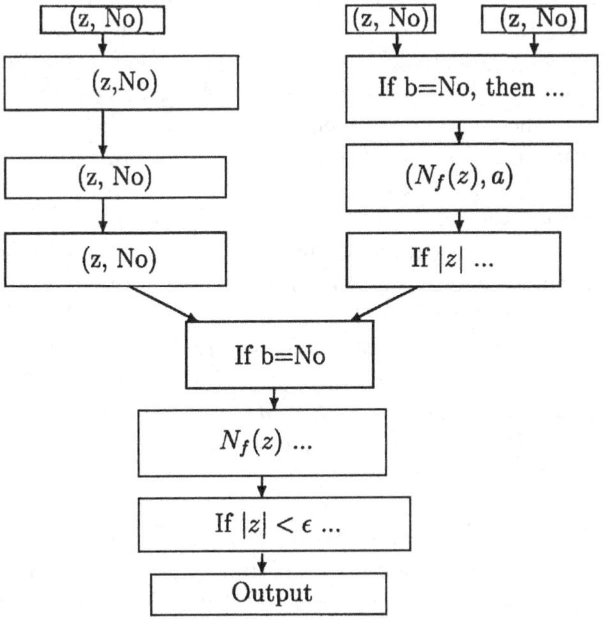

Figure 2.1.12.

computed by networks that are represented by the tree $S[r, M]$, with $M \geq N$. The Leontief conditions do not immediately apply to computations of functions of r^N variables computed by networks represented by $S[r, M]$ when $M > N$. However, the Leontief conditions can be used if we restrict the kind of computation represented by $S[r, M]$ when $M > N$. The restriction is a symmetry condition on the order in which variables are assigned to the leaves of $S[r, M]$. The symmetry conditions are used only in conjunction with bordered Hessians, but because the symmetries are conditions on the assignment of variables to leaves, it seems appropriate to discuss them in this chapter.

Definition 2.1.12. Suppose that $\underline{x} = x_0, \ldots, x_{r^N-1}$ are independent, that is, distinct variables. For each $M \geq N$ an assignment of the variables $\underline{x}$ to the leaves of $S[r, M]$ is *symmetric* if for each $0 \leq j < r^N - 1$ and each $0 \leq k < r^M$ the variable assigned to the leaf (j, M) is the same as the variable assigned to $(kr^N + j,\ M - N)$.

We make a few comments about symmetric assignments. Suppose that $M = N + K$, $K > 0$. At level K of $S[r, M]$ there are r^K vertices, each of which is the root of a tree isomorphic to the tree $S[r, N]$. If (j, K) are the coordinates of such a vertex and we denote by *T(j, K)* the tree that has the vertex at (j, K) as the root, then $T(j, K)$ has the structure of an ordered tree, with its leaves inheriting the lexicographic order that is the order of the leaves of $S[r, M]$. The tree $T(j, K)$ is isomorphic[6] to the tree $S[r, N]$ by a map ϕ_j that preserves the order of the leaves. An assignment of variables $\underline{x}$ to the leaves of $S[r, M]$ is symmetric if there is an assignment of the variables of $\underline{x}$ to the leaves of $S[r, N]$ such that for each j and leaf $\ell \in T(j, K)$ the variable assigned to leaf ℓ is the same as the variable assigned to the leaf $\phi_j(\ell)$. One can also consider symmetric assignments in the following way. Suppose that $\mathcal{L}(v)$ is the set of leaves of $S[r, M]$ that are leaves of the tree with root v. Order the leaves of $\mathcal{L}(v)$ lexicographically. Suppose that $G(M)$ denotes the collection of permutations of the leaves of $S[r, M]$ that preserve the order of the leaves of $\mathcal{L}(v)$ for each v at level K. Symmetric assignments require that for each $g \in G(K)$ the variable assigned to a leaf $\ell \in \mathcal{L}(v)$ is the same as the variable assigned to the leaf $g(\ell)$. Finally, note that if v is a vertex of $S[r, M]$ at level $N + j$, $j \geq 0$, then the assignment of variables to the tree with root v is symmetric if the assignment of variables to $S[r, M]$ is symmetric.

Definition 2.1.13. A function $G(\underline{x})$ of 2^N independent variables $\underline{x} = x_0, \ldots, x_{2^N-1}$ can be $\mathcal{F}$-**symmetrically** computed in time $N + K$, or it can be computed in time $N + K$ by a **symmetric** $\mathcal{F}$ network if G can be computed in time $N + K$ by an $\mathcal{F}$ network represented by the ordered tree $S[2, N + K]$ with a symmetric

[6] We use as the order function $\Gamma[r, N]$.

assignment of variables with variable x_j assigned to the leaf with coordinates $(j, N + K)$.

Note that in the definition, a fixed order has been assumed for the variables of $\underline{x}$. It is generally true that a function that can be computed in time $N + K$ with a symmetric assignment with one ordering of variables cannot be computed in time $N + K$ with variables in a different order.

3 Networks of Real-Valued Functions

3.1. THE LEONTIEF THEOREM

In Chapter 1 we presented the concept of the (time) complexity of a function in an $\mathcal{F}$ network model of computing. In this chapter we analyze the complexity of a function, or obtain bounds on its complexity. It is shown in Chapter 2 that when the class $\mathcal{F}$ of elementary functions consists of Boolean functions the $\mathcal{F}$ network model specializes to the finite-automaton model of computing. The $\mathcal{F}$ network model is also related to an approach to computing and complexity called nomography (Bieberbach, 1922) that was pursued in mathematics from the late 19th into the mid-20th centuries. In this chapter we use some results from that literature to analyze the complexity of functions in the $\mathcal{F}$ network model. Thus, the $\mathcal{F}$ network model serves as a bridge connecting finite-automaton theory to classical mathematics – a connection we will emphasize below, when we consider the complexity of finite approximations of smooth functions (cf. Chapter 5).

A simple case to start with is that of $\mathcal{F}_1$ networks. The class $\mathcal{F}_1$ is the collection of real-valued differentiable functions of one real variable. The class $\mathcal{F}_1$ contains no functions that can be used to reduce the $n(>1)$ variables $\{x_1, \ldots, x_n\}$ to a single real variable. Whether a function G can be computed by an $\mathcal{F}_1$ network can be decided by simply counting the number of variables of G. If $n = 1$, so that G is a function of one variable, and if $\mathcal{G}$ is some subset of $\mathcal{F}_1$, the time required to compute G by a $\mathcal{G}$ network can be very difficult to determine.

For instance, if the class $\mathcal{G}$ consists only of polynomials in one variable of degree at most 2, then the functions x^2, x^4, and $x^2 + 2x^3 + x^4 = (x + x^2)^2$ can be computed in time at most 2, but x^3 cannot be computed in time 2. Indeed, for x^3 to be computable in time 2 by use of only the elements of $\mathcal{G}$, the equation

$$b_0 + b_1(a_0 + a_1x + a_2x^2) + b_2(a_0 + a_1x + a_2x^2)^2 = x^3 \qquad (3.1.1)$$

would have to be satisfied for some choice of the constants $a_0, \ldots, a_2$, $b_0, \ldots, b_2$. Then the coefficient of x^4, that is, the expression $b_2\,a_2^2$, would have to be zero. However, in Equation (3.1.1) the coefficient of x^3 on the left-hand side is $2a_1a_2b_2$. Therefore $a_2 \neq 0$, from which it follows that $b_2 = 0$. Thus Equation (3.1.1) has no solution. We make no general statements about the computability of a function when the class $\mathcal{F}$ is restricted to collections of functions of one variable. This statement means not that there are no such conclusions to be drawn, but only that we have nothing to contribute to that subject.

More can be said when the class $\mathcal{F}$ consists of functions of more than one variable. Nomography studies the question whether a function of several variables can be written as a superposition of functions of fewer variables. One example of the use of nomography is the reduction of the solution of a polynomial equation that depends on several coefficients to a superposition of functions that are solutions of equations that depend on a smaller number of coefficients. For example, a solution of the general quadratic equation $ax^2 + bx + c = 0$ can be considered as the superposition of the solution of the equation $x^2 + Bx + C = 0$ and the two functions b/a and c/a. Furthermore, if a function can be written as a superposition of functions of at most two variables, then the function can also be approximated by graphical methods. More generally, when P is a polynomial of degree at most 6 (see Dehn, 1960), a general solution of the polynomial equation $P = 0$ can be presented as a superposition of functions of at most two variables. However, the classical routines for writing a solution of the equation $P = 0$ as a superposition of functions of two variables fail when P has degree greater than 6. Hilbert's 13th problem (Hilbert, 1900) is precisely the question of whether the solution of a degree 7 polynomial equation $P = 0$ could be written as a superposition of functions of at most two variables. As Hilbert phrased it, the question was whether a solution could be written as a superposition of continuous functions of at most two variables. It is probable (see Lorentz, 1966 or Bierberbach, 1922) that Hilbert meant the question to be whether a solution of the polynomial equation could be written as a finite superposition of power series in at most two variables. Indeed, Hilbert gave an argument to show that there must exist power series in n variables that could not be written as a finite superposition of power series of less than n variables (Hilbert, 1900). He returned to the problem in a subsequent paper (Hilbert, 1927) to show that for the general equation $P = 0$, when P is of degree 9, solutions can be written as superpositions of power series of at most four variables. The classical results on solving polynomial equations by superpositions of functions that are solutions of polynomial equations with a small number of coefficients depend on the identification of a resolvent for the equation. A more modern approach relies on Galois theory. Kolmogorov and Arnol'd abandoned the power series interpretation, and, under the assumption that continuous really means continuous in our modern sense, they showed (Arnol'd, 1963; Kolmogorov, 1961a) that each continuous function of n variables could be written as a superposition of continuous functions of at most two variables. The continuous functions used in the constructions of Arnol'd and Kolmogorov are nondifferentiable. Vitushkin

(1961) and others have shown that whether a function can be written as a superposition of functions of a class $\mathcal{F}$ depends not only on the number of variables, but also on relations between the orders of smoothness of the functions of $\mathcal{F}$ and the functions to be computed.

Leontief took a different tack. In his note (Leontief, 1947) he addressed the problem of deciding whether a differentiable function $F(x_1, \ldots x_n, y_1, \ldots y_m)$ could be written in the form $C[A(x_1, \ldots, x_n), y_1, \ldots y_m]$. From his conditions one can easily derive necessary and sufficient conditions that

$$G(x_1, \ldots x_n, y_1, \ldots, y_m) = C[A(x_1, \ldots, x_n), B(y_1, \ldots, y_m)].$$

When put in the context of the $\mathcal{F}$ network model of computing, nomography theory, the results of Arnol'd and Kolmogorov and those of Leontief are statements about the computability of a function by an $\mathcal{F}$ network for various choices of the class $\mathcal{F}$. In each of those cases, $\mathcal{F}$ contains functions of a bounded number of variables, with some subset of $\mathcal{F}$ that consists of functions of at least two variables.

Of the three types of results about superpositions just mentioned, we make most use of Leontief's Theorem. Leontief's Theorem is a statement about the possibility of writing a function as a superposition in the neighborhood of some point in the space of the variables of the function. The theory we develop following Leontief's approach is a local theory. To facilitate understanding, we first present the gist of the theorem in the context of a function of four variables x, y, z, and w. The theorem is presented formally in Appendix B. We begin with necessary conditions.

3.1.1. Necessary Conditions

Suppose that $F(x, y, z, w)$ can be written as a superposition of three functions of two variables. Thus $F(x, y, z, w) = C[A(x, y), B(z, w)]$, where A, B, C, and F all have continuous second derivatives. Then

$$\frac{\partial^2 F(x, y, z, w)}{\partial x\, \partial z} = \frac{\partial^2 C}{\partial A\, \partial B} \frac{\partial A}{\partial x} \frac{\partial B}{\partial z}, \tag{3.1.2}$$

$$\frac{\partial^2 F(x, y, z, w)}{\partial y\, \partial z} = \frac{\partial^2 C}{\partial A\, \partial B} \frac{\partial A}{\partial y} \frac{\partial B}{\partial z}. \tag{3.1.3}$$

Similarly,

$$\frac{\partial^2 F(x, y, z, w)}{\partial x\, \partial w} = \frac{\partial^2 C}{\partial A\, \partial B} \frac{\partial A}{\partial x} \frac{\partial B}{\partial w}, \tag{3.1.4}$$

$$\frac{\partial^2 F(x, y, z, w)}{\partial y\, \partial w} = \frac{\partial^2 C}{\partial A\, \partial B} \frac{\partial A}{\partial y} \frac{\partial B}{\partial w}. \tag{3.1.5}$$

For functions of four variables, Leontief's necessary conditions are bounds on the ranks of the bordered Hessian matrices $bh_{[(x,y),(z,w)]}(F)$ and $bh_{[(z,w),(x,y)]}(F)$.

Definition 3.1.1. The matrix $bh_{[(x,y),(z,w)]}(F)$ has rows indexed by the variables x and y and columns indexed by F and the variables z, w. The entries in $bh_{[(x,y),(z,w)]}(F)$[1] are as follows. In the F column at row t ($t = x$ or y), enter $[\partial F(x, y, z, w)]/\partial t$. In row u and column v($u = x$ or y and $v = z$ or w), enter $[\partial^2 F(x, y, z, w)]/\partial u\, \partial v$.

That is,

$$bh_{[(x,y),(z,w)]}(F) = \begin{bmatrix} \frac{\partial F}{\partial x} & \frac{\partial^2 F}{\partial x\, \partial z} & \frac{\partial^2 F}{\partial x\, \partial w} \\ \frac{\partial F}{\partial y} & \frac{\partial^2 F}{\partial y\, \partial z} & \frac{\partial^2 F}{\partial y\, \partial z} \end{bmatrix}.$$

The matrix $bh_{[(z,w),(x,y)]}(F)$ has rows indexed by z and w, and columns indexed by F, x, and y. The column labeled F has entries $\partial F/\partial z$ and $\partial F/\partial w$. The entry in row u and column v is $[\partial^2 F(x, y, z, w)]/\partial u\, \partial v$. Thus

$$bh_{[(z,w),(x,y)]}(F) = \begin{bmatrix} \frac{\partial F}{\partial z} & \frac{\partial^2 F}{\partial x\, \partial z} & \frac{\partial^2 F}{\partial z\, \partial y} \\ \frac{\partial F}{\partial w} & \frac{\partial^2 F}{\partial w\, \partial x} & \frac{\partial^2 F}{\partial w\, \partial y} \end{bmatrix}.$$

It follows from Equations (3.1.2)–(3.1.5) that each of the columns indexed by z or w is a multiple of the column indexed by F.

Thus, if F can be written in the form $C[A(x, y), B(z, w)]$ the matrix $bh_{[(x,y),(z,w)]}(F)$ has rank at most 1. Similarly, $bh_{[(z,w),(x,y)]}(F)$ also has rank at most 1.

Note that if one permutes the order of the rows of $bh_{[(x,y),(z,w)]}(F)$, or permutes the order of the columns of $bh_{[(x,y),(z,w)]}(F)$, then there will be no change in rank. Because in what follows it is almost always the case that only the rank of the bordered Hessian is used, we will frequently state an assertion specifying only the sets of variables $\{x, y\}$ and the set of variables $\{z, w\}$ and ignoring the order among the elements of the sets. However, a rank condition on the bordered Hessian $bh_{(\{x,y\},\{z,w\})}(F)$ is quite different from a rank condition on the bordered Hessian $bh_{(\{z,w\},\{x,y\})}(F)$.

We will treat sufficiency in Section 3.1.3 but note here that in the sufficiency part of his theorem, Leontief showed that if the first column of $bh_{[(x,y),(z,w)]}(F)$ is nonzero in a neighborhood of some point $p_0 = (x_0, y_0, z_0, w_0)$, then the necessary conditions are also sufficient to ensure that functions C and A exist and that in a sufficiently small neighborhood of p_0, $F(x, y, z, w) = C[A(x, y), z, w]$. The same conditions on $bh_{[(z,w),(x,y)]}(F)$ ensure the existence of a function B of z and w such that $F(x, y, z, w) = C[A(x, y), B(z, w)]$.

[1] In Appendix B we generalize the concept of a bordered Hessian. There we show that the bordered Hessian is a function that is independent of the choice of coordinates, both in the space of the variables x, y and the space of the variables z, w.

3.1.2. An Example

To show an elementary application of Leontief's necessary conditions, we use them to analyze the computation of certain functions associated with 2×2 matrix (zero-sum) games. Suppose that a matrix for the game G is

$$\begin{bmatrix} x & z \\ y & w \end{bmatrix}.$$

As $x, y, z,$ and w, vary, they sweep out a collection of games. Certain quantities of interest, such as Nash strategies and the value of the game, are functions of these four parameters, $x, y, z,$ and w. We study the computation of these functions by $\mathcal{F}$ networks. For this purpose, suppose that the elementary functions at our disposal are functions of two variables. Specifically, denote by $\mathcal{D}$ the collection of real valued, twice continuously differentiable, nonsingular functions[2] in the neighborhood of the origin of $\Re^2$ (see Definition B.1.4). We avoid games with pure strategy saddle points by assuming that the parameters $x, y, z,$ and w are close to values for a game with no pure strategy equilibria. For example, assume that x and w are near 1 whereas y and z are near zero. If at the Nash equilibrium, player 1 plays row 1 with probability P and player 2 plays column 1 with probability Q, then

$$P(x, y, z, w) = \frac{(w - y)}{(x - y + w - z)},$$

$$Q(x, y, z, w) = \frac{(w - z)}{(x - y + w - z)}.$$

Each of the functions P and Q is a twice continuously differentiable real-valued function with nonzero partial derivatives in each value of $x, y, z,$ and w. We use Leontief's necessary conditions to analyze the $\mathcal{D}$ network computation of P, Q, and the value of the game. As one would expect, the calculations are simple and there are no surprises.

Suppose that a $\mathcal{D}$ network computes P in the shortest time possible by using inputs $x, y, z,$ and w. Each variable must occur as an input to the network because P depends on each of those variables. Chapter 2 shows that if P can be computed by a $\mathcal{D}$ network, then P can also be computed by a network represented by a tree of height equal to the time required to compute P. Any tree T that represents a computation of P must have a least four leaves. The functions of $\mathcal{D}$ are functions of at most two variables; thus the in-degree at each branch vertex of T is at most 2. If a tree T has more than four leaves and is such that the in-degree of each branch vertex is at most 2, then Lemma 2.1.2

[2] By a nonsingular real-valued function we mean a function that has a nonzero Jacobian at each point of its domain. In the language of Golubitsky and Guillemin (1973, p. 94), a nonsingular function is a function such that each point of its domain is a regular point.

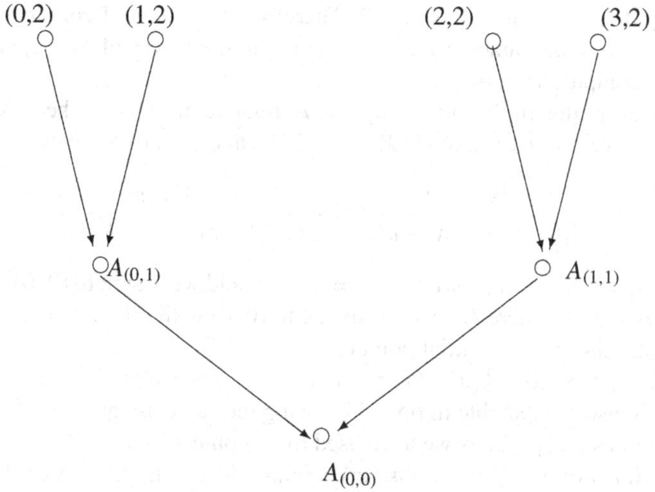

Figure 3.1.1.

states that the computation must take at least three units of time because $\lceil[\log_2(4+\epsilon)] \geq 3\rceil$ when $\epsilon > 0$. Thus the best one can expect, that is, the least computing time one can hope for, is computing time 2. In the case in which the function P can be computed by a $\mathcal{D}$ network in time 2, the computation can be represented by a tree of height 2 with four leaves. The only such trees are isomorphic to $S[2, 2]$ (see Section 2.1.3).

The tree $S[2, 2]$, shown in Figure 3.1.1, has three levels and the seven vertices $(0, 0)$, $(0, 1)$, $(1, 1)$, $(0, 2)$, $(1, 2)$, $(2, 2)$, and $(3, 2)$. The computation of P has graph $S[2, 2]$ with an assignment of x, y, z, and w to each of the leaves $(0, 2)$, $(1, 2)$, $(2, 2)$, and $(3, 2)$, respectively. Each of the vertices $(0, 1)$, $(1, 1)$, and $(0, 0)$ has a function of $\mathcal{D}$ assigned to it. It is very convenient to represent the function assigned to vertex (a, b) by a compact notation.

Notation. *If a tree* $S[r, N]$ *represents the computation of a network, then we denote by* $\langle i, j\rangle$ *the function assigned to the vertex* (i, j). *We shall assume, unless otherwise stated, that the function assigned to the vertex* (i, j) *has variables* $[0, \langle i, j\rangle], \ldots, [r-1, \langle i, j\rangle]$ *and the order function given in Section 2.1.3 for the vertex* (i, j) *assigns the arc* $\overrightarrow{(ri+k, j+1)(i, j)}$ *to the variable* $[k, \langle i, j\rangle]$.

The matrix

$$bh_{[(x,y),(z,w)]}(P) = \begin{bmatrix} \frac{-(w-y)}{(w+x-y-z)^2} & \frac{-2(w-y)}{(w+x-y-z)^3} & \frac{(w-x)-(y-z)}{(w+x-y-z)^3} \\ \frac{-(x-z)}{(w+x-y-z)^2} & \frac{(w-x)-(y-z)}{(w+x-y-z)^2} & \frac{2(x-z)}{(w+x-y-z)^3} \end{bmatrix}.$$

Clearly $bh_{[(x,y),(z,w)]}(P)$ has rank 2. Therefore, the Leontief condition tells us that the given assignment of x, y, z, and w to the leaves of $S[2, 2]$ cannot be used to compute P in time 2.

However, the time complexity of P relative to $\mathcal{D}$ is 2 because if the assignment x to $(0, 2)$, z to $(1, 2)$, y to $(2, 2)$, and w to $(3, 2)$ is used, then

$$P = \frac{(w - y)}{[(x - z) - (y - w)]} = \frac{\langle 1, 1\rangle(y, w)}{[\langle 0, 1\rangle(x, z) + \langle 1, 1\rangle(y, w)]},$$

if $\langle 0, 1\rangle(x, z) = x - z$, $\langle 1, 1\rangle(y, w) = w - y$, and we assign to $(0, 0)$ the function $R/(L + R)$ where L denotes the arc to $(0, 0)$ with initial vertex $(0, 1)$ and R denotes the arc with initial point $(1, 1)$.

That is, $P = \langle 0, 0\rangle[\langle 0, 1\rangle(x, z), \langle 1, 1\rangle(y, w)]$. It is equally easy to see that $1 - P$ is also computable in time 2 by using the same assignment of variables to the leaves of $S[2, 2]$ as we have used to compute P in time 2.

The function $Q(x, y, z, w)$ is very slightly different. The bordered Hessian matrices of Q, $bh_{[(x,y),(z,w)]}(Q)$, and $bh_{[(z,w),(x,y)]}(Q)$ each have rank 1. It is easy to see that Q can be computed in two units of time.

The value of the 2×2 game G is given by the function $V = (xw - yz)/(x + w - y - z)$. The matrix

$$bh_{[(x,y),(z,w)]}(V) =$$

$$\begin{bmatrix} \frac{(-w+y)(-w+z)}{(w+x-y-z)^2} & \frac{(-w+y)(w-x+y-z)}{(-w-x+y+z)^3} & \frac{-2wx+wy+xy-y^2+wz+xz-z^2}{(-w-x+y+z)^3} \\ \frac{(w-z)(x-z)}{(-w-x+y+z)^2} & \frac{w^2+x^2-wy-xy-wz-xz+2yz}{(-w-x+y+z)^3} & \frac{(x-z)(w-x+y-z)}{(-w-x+y+z)^3} \end{bmatrix},$$

whereas

$$bh_{[(x,z),(y,w)]}(V) =$$

$$\begin{bmatrix} \frac{(-w+y)(-w+z)}{(w+x-y-z)^2} & \frac{(-w+z)(w-x-y+z)}{(-w-x+y+z)^3} & \frac{-2wx+wy+xy-y^2+wz+xz-z^2}{(-w-x+y+z)^3} \\ \frac{(w-y)(x-y)}{(-w-x+y+z)^2} & \frac{w^2+x^2-wy-xy-wz-xz+2yz}{(-w-x+y+z)^3} & \frac{(x-y)(w-x-y+z)}{(-w-x+y+z)^3} \end{bmatrix},$$

and

$$bh_{[(x,w),(y,z)]}(V) = \begin{bmatrix} \frac{(-w+y)(-w+z)}{(w+x-y-z)^2} & \frac{(-w+z)(w-x-y+z)}{(-w-x+y+z)^3} & \frac{(-w+y)(w-x+y-z)}{(-w-x+y+z)^3} \\ \frac{(-x+y)(-x+z)}{(w+x-y-z)^2} & \frac{(x-z)(w-x+y-z)}{(-w-x+y+z)^3} & \frac{(x-y)(w-x-y+z)}{(-w-x+y+z)^3} \end{bmatrix}.$$

Each of these bordered Hessians has rank 2. Thus the value V of the game cannot be computed in minimal time $t = 2$ by using the variables x, y, z, and w as inputs to $\mathcal{D}$ networks. However, the function V can be computed in three units of time. Figure 3.1.2 illustrates such a computation. Note that the function V is computed symmetrically, in the sense of Definition 2.1.13, by

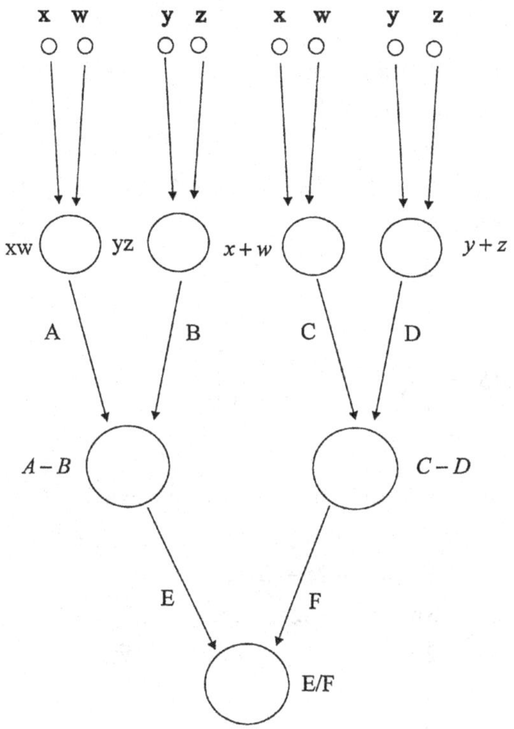

Figure 3.1.2.

the $\mathcal{D}$ network of Figure 3.1.2. Thus symmetry arises naturally in the example. Symmetry appears in a deeper role in the analysis of computational complexity that appears in Chapter 4.

3.1.3. Sufficient Conditions

We turn now to a more general treatment of the sufficient conditions given by Leontief. The functions P and Q are computable in two units of time and they are easy to analyze. However, some functions are not so transparent. For example, it is not immediately clear whether the expression

$$\begin{aligned} S = & -w + 2x - wx + 4y - 2wy + 2xy - wxy + 3z - wz \\ & + 3xz - wxz + 6yz - 2wyz + 3xyz - wxyz + z^2 \\ & + xz^2 + 2yz^2 + xyz^2 \end{aligned} \tag{3.1.6}$$

can be computed in two units of time. We can begin by verifying the necessary conditions, that is, whether the rank conditions on the bordered Hessians are satisfied.

Set

$$
\begin{aligned}
A_{1,1} &= 2 - w + 2y - wy + 3z - wz + 3yz - wyz + z^2 + yz^2,\\
A_{1,2} &= 3 - w + 3y - wy + 2z + 2yz,\\
A_{1,3} &= -1 - y - z - yz,\\
A_{2,1} &= 4 - 2w + 2x - wx + 6z - 2wz + 3xz - wxz + 2z^2 + xz^2,\\
A_{2,2} &= 6 - 2w + 3x - wx + 4z + 2xz,\\
A_{2,3} &= -2 - x - 2z - xz.
\end{aligned}
$$

The 2×2 matrix

$$
bh_{[(x,y),(z,w)]}(S) = \begin{bmatrix} A_{1,1} & A_{1,2} & A_{1,3} \\ A_{2,1} & A_{2,2} & A_{2,3} \end{bmatrix}. \tag{3.1.7}
$$

Set

$$
\begin{aligned}
B_{1,1} &= 3 - w + 3x - wx + 6y - 2wy + 3xy - wxy\\
&\quad + 2z + 2xz + 4yz + 2xyz,\\
B_{1,2} &= 3 - w + 3y - wy + 2z + 2yz,\\
B_{1,3} &= 6 - 2w + 3x - wx + 4z + 2xz,\\
B_{2,1} &= -1 - x - 2y - xy - z - xz - 2yz - xyz,\\
B_{2,2} &= -1 - y - z - yz,\\
B_{2,3} &= -2 - x - 2z - xz.
\end{aligned}
$$

The matrix

$$
bh_{[(z,w),(x,y)]}(S) = \begin{bmatrix} B_{1,1} & B_{1,2} & B_{1,3} \\ B_{2,1} & B_{2,2} & B_{2,3} \end{bmatrix}. \tag{3.1.8}
$$

Each matrix shown in Equations (3.1.7) and (3.1.8) has rank 1; thus the necessary conditions for S to be computable in time 2 are satisfied. Because in each matrix the first column is nonzero in a neighborhood of the origin, Leontief's sufficient conditions are satisfied and hence the sufficiency part of his theorem is applicable in this case. Therefore one can conclude that the function S is computable in time 2.

The next question is: "What is the network?" The proof of Leontief's theorem provides an algorithm for constructing the superposition that computes S in two units of time.

Theorem 3.1.1. *[(From Leontief, 1947)] Suppose that F is a function of the variables $x_1, \ldots, x_m$, $y_1, \ldots, y_n$. Set $F_i = \partial F/\partial x_i$, for $1 \le i \le m$. Assume that $(p, q) = (p_1, \ldots, p_m, q_1, \ldots, q_n)$ is a set of values for the variables $(x_1, \ldots, x_m, y_1, \ldots, y_n)$. A necessary condition that there exist functions $C(w, y_1, \ldots, y_n)$ and $G(x_1, \ldots, x_m)$ such that $F(x, y) = C[G(x), y]$ in a* *neighborhood U of the point (p, q) is that for each $1 \le i, j \le m$ and for each $1 \le k \le n$, $\partial/\partial y_k[F_i/F_j] = 0$. The given necessary condition is also sufficient if for some j, $F_j(x_1, \ldots, x_m)(p, q) \neq 0$.*

Leontief's proof derives from a classical result sometimes referred to as the "General Theorem on Functional Dependence" (see Widder, 1963).

Theorem 3.1.2. *(Functional dependence). Suppose that $x = (x_1, \ldots, x_m)$ and $y = (y_1, \ldots, y_n)$ are sets of real variables and suppose that $F(x, y)$ and $G(x)$ are real-valued C^1 functions defined on a neighborhood U of the point $(p, q) = (p_1, \ldots, p_m, q_1, \ldots q_n)$ that satisfy the following conditions:*

(i)

$$\begin{bmatrix} \frac{\partial F}{\partial x_1} & \cdots & \frac{\partial F}{\partial x_m} \\ \frac{\partial G}{\partial x_1} & \cdots & \frac{\partial G}{\partial x_m} \end{bmatrix}$$

is a matrix of rank at most 1,

(ii) at p, $\partial G/\partial x_1 \neq 0$.

Then there is a function $C(w, y)$, where w is a real variable, such that $F(x, y) = C[G(x), y]$ in some neighborhood of (p, q).

Proof of Theorem 3.1.2. Because of assumption (ii), the equation $w - G(x_1, \ldots, x_m) = 0$ has a unique solution in a neighborhood U' of (p, q). Thus, there is a function $c(w, x_2, \ldots, x_m)$ such that $w = G[c(w, x_2, \ldots, x_m), x_2, \ldots, x_m]$ and such that $c[G(x_1, \ldots, x_m), x_2, \ldots, x_m] = x_1$. Set

$$C(w, x_2, \ldots, x_m, y) = F[c(w, x_2, \ldots, x_m), x_2, \ldots, x_m, y].$$

Then

$$\frac{\partial C}{\partial x_j} = \left(\frac{\partial F}{\partial x_1}\right)\left(\frac{\partial c}{\partial x_j}\right) + \left(\frac{\partial F}{\partial x_j}\right)$$

for $j > 1$. Because $w = G[c(w, x_2, \ldots, x_m), x_2, \ldots, x_m]$, it follows that $0 = (\partial G/\partial x_1)(\partial c/\partial x_j) + (\partial G/\partial x_j)$ for $j > 1$. Further, by condition (i), there is an Ω such that $(\partial F/\partial x_j) = \Omega(\partial G/\partial x_j)$ for $1 \le j \le m$. Therefore, $\partial C/\partial x_j = \Omega[(\partial G/\partial x_1)(\partial c/\partial x_j) + (\partial G/\partial x_j)] = 0$. Hence the function C is independent of the variables $x_2, \ldots x_m$, and we can write $C(w, x_2, \ldots, x_m, y) = C(w, y)$. Then

$$\begin{aligned} C[G(x_1, \ldots, x_m), y] &= F\{c[G(x_1, \ldots, x_m), x_2, \ldots, x_m], x_2, \ldots, x_m, y\} \\ &= F(x_1, \ldots, x_m, y). \end{aligned}$$

□

The proof of Leontief's Theorem is the following.

Proof of Theorem 3.1.1. Form the matrix

$$M = \begin{bmatrix} F_1 & \cdots & F_m \\ F_1^* & \cdots & F_m^* \end{bmatrix}$$

where $F_j^* = [\partial F(x, q)]/\partial x_j$. At the point q, $(\partial F/\partial x_j)(q) = [\partial F(x, q)]/\partial x_j$. Condition (i) implies that the derivative $[\partial(F_i/F_j)]/\partial y_k = 0$. Thus the ratio F_i/F_j is independent of y. Also at (p, q), $F_i^*/F_j^* = F_i(x, q)/F_j(x, q)$. It follows that $F_i^*/F_j^* = F_i/F_j$ for all (x, y). Therefore the matrix M has a rank of at most 1. Further, by assumption, $F_j(p, q) \neq 0$ for some j. The previous theorem shows that we can write $F(x, y) = C[G(x), y]$. □

Returning to the example with the function S of Equation (3.1.6), we show how the proof of Leontief's theorem enables us to write S as a superposition of functions of two variables. The bordered Hessian $bh_{[(x,y),(z,w)]}(S)$ has rank 1; thus Leontief's Theorem says that $S = C[A(x, y), z, w]$. However, it is also easy to see that the bordered Hessian $bh_{[(z,w),A]}(S)$ must have rank 1 because $bh_{[(z,w),(x,y)]}(S)$ has rank 1. A second application of Leontief's Theorem shows that $S = D[A(x, y), B(z, w)]$.

For the particular function $S(x, y, z, w)$ given in Equation (3.1.6), $S(x, y, 0, 0) = 2x + 4y + 2xy$. Set $u = 2x + 4y + 2xy$ and solve for x. Then $x = (u - 4y)/(2 + 2y)$. The result of substituting this expression for x in S is

$$S1 = u - w - (uw/2) + 3z + (3uz/2) - wz - (uwz/2) + z^2 + (u\,z^2/2).$$

Set $u = 0$ in this expression. The result is $-w + 3z - wz + z^2$. Set $v = -w + 3z - wz + z^2$ and solve for w. The solution is $w = (3z + z^2 - v)/(1 + z)$. If this expression for w is substituted in the expression $S1$, the result is $u + v + uv/2$. Therefore

$$\begin{aligned} S = {} & (2x + 4y + 2xy) + (-w + 3z - wz + z^2) \\ & + \frac{(2x + 4y + 2xy)(-w + 3z - wz + z^2)}{2}. \end{aligned}$$

That is,

$$\begin{aligned} & S = D[A(x, y), B(z, w)], \\ & A(x, y) = (2x + 4y + 2xy), \\ & B(z, w) = (-w + 3z - wz + z^2), \\ & D(A, B) = A + B + AB/2. \end{aligned}$$

We have no more to say about 2×2 matrix games, but functions of four variables are interesting for more complicated games: We return to that subject later in this chapter.

3.2. LOCAL CONDITIONS

The previous section's focus is on functions of four variables. In this section we take up the analysis of functions of eight variables computed by $\mathcal{D}$ networks. Recall that $\mathcal{D}$ is the collection of twice continuously differentiable, nonsingular functions of two variables. Functions of eight variables arise naturally in bimatrix games. Suppose that A and B are 2×2 matrices representing a finite two-person general sum game. We study the computation of optimal threat strategies under the assumption that the feasible set S for the game is a section of the first quadrant bounded by the x and y axes and by the line $x + y = 1$. We assume that utility is linearly transferable between the two players. From Owen (1982, p. 137), suppose that utility is transferable at the rate 1:1. We choose A and B close to matrices of diagonal games with no saddle points. Set

$$A = \begin{bmatrix} 2 + a_{(1,1)} & a_{(1,2)} \\ a_{(2,1)} & 2 + a_{(2,2)} \end{bmatrix},$$

$$B = \begin{bmatrix} 1 + b_{(1,1)} & b_{(1,2)} \\ b_{(2,1)} & 1 + b_{(2,2)} \end{bmatrix}.$$

Optimal threat strategies for the bimatrix game (A, B) are the optimal strategies for the matrix game A–B. As we know from Section 3.1, if $(P, 1 - P)$ denotes the optimal mixed strategy for the first player and if $(Q, 1 - Q)$ denotes the optimal mixed strategy for the second player, then

$$P = \frac{\left[1 - a_{(1,2)} + a_{(2,2)} + b_{(1,2)} - b_{(2,2)}\right]}{\left[2 + a_{(1,1)} - a_{(1,2)} - a_{(2,1)} + a_{(2,2)} - b_{(1,1)} + b_{(1,2)} + b_{(2,1)} - b_{(2,2)}\right]}.$$

The function P is a function of eight variables. All the variables are required to evaluate P. P is derived from the solution of a two by two game by simple substitution. The function P can be computed in time 3. A $\mathcal{D}$ network that computes P in time 3 can be represented by the graph $S[2, 3]$. It is an easy matter to construct a $\mathcal{D}$ network that computes P in time 3. The network represented by Figure 3.2.1 computes P in three units of time, where using the notation of 3.1.2 gives

$$\langle 0, 2\rangle = 1 + a_{(2,2)} - b_{(2,2)}, \quad \langle 2, 2\rangle = a_{(1,1)} - b_{(1,1)},$$
$$\langle 1, 2\rangle = a_{(1,2)} - b_{(1,2)}, \quad \langle 3, 2\rangle = a_{(2,1)} - b_{(2,1)}, \quad \langle 0, 1\rangle = L_0 - R_0,$$

and so on.

A more interesting observation is that it is also possible to use Leontief's Theorem to lead one through the construction of the network that computes P. The process illustrates the fact that once the assignment of variables to the leaves of $S[2, 3]$ has been determined, there is essentially only one way (essential uniqueness) that an assignment of functions to the branch vertices of $S[2, 3]$ can be made so that the resulting network computes P. In the next few

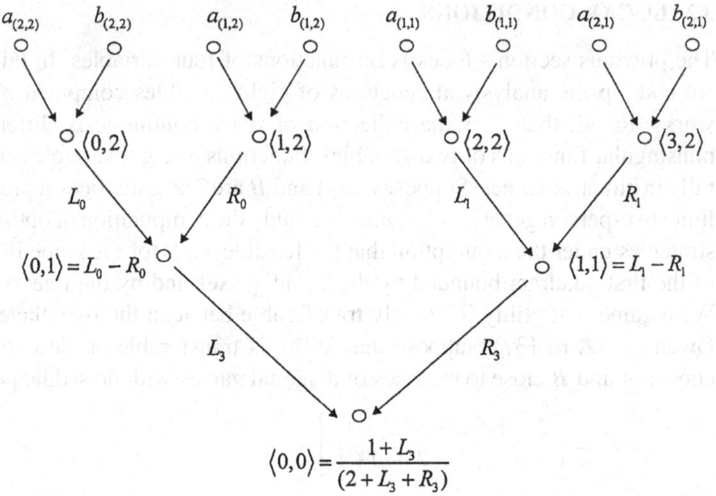

Figure 3.2.1.

paragraphs we carry out that construction. A more general form of the process is included in Appendix B.

The concept of essential uniqueness requires a number of normalizations and assumptions about the function to be computed. To begin, note that if $F(x_0, x_1, x_2, x_3)$ is a function of four variables and if $f(X)$ is a function of a single variable, then the rank of the bordered Hessian $bh_{[(x_0,x_1),(x_2,x_3)]}(F)$ is the same as the rank of the bordered Hessian $bh_{[(x_0,x_1),(x_2,x_3)]}[f(F)]$. Indeed, if we denote df/dx by f', and $\partial F/\partial x_i$ by F_{x_i}, then

$$\partial f(F)/\partial x_i = f'(F)\,F_{x_i}.$$

Furthermore,

$$\partial^2 f(F)/\partial x_i\,\partial x_j = f''(F)\,F_{x_i}\,F_{x_j} + f'(F)\,F_{x_i x_j}.$$

Therefore,

$$bh_{[(x_0,x_1),(x_2,x_3)]}[f(F)] = \begin{bmatrix} f'(F)\,F_{x_0} & f''(F)\,F_{x_0}\,F_{x_2} + f'(F)\,F_{x_0 x_2} & f''(F)\,F_{x_0}\,F_{x_3} + f'(F)\,F_{x_0 x_3} \\ f'(F)\,F_{x_1} & f''(F)\,F_{x_1}\,F_{x_2} + f'(F)\,F_{x_1 x_2} & f''(F)\,F_{x_1}\,F_{x_3} + f'(F)\,F_{x_1 x_3} \end{bmatrix}.$$

This matrix has the same rank as the matrix

$$\begin{bmatrix} f'(F)\,F_{x_0} & f'(F)\,F_{x_0 x_2} & f'(F)\,F_{x_0 x_3} \\ f'(F)\,F_{x_1} & f'(F)\,F_{x_1 x_2} & f'(F)\,F_{x_1 x_3} \end{bmatrix},$$

which has the same rank as the bordered Hessian $bh_{[(x_0,x_1),(x_2,x_3)]}(F)$.

Continuing the discussion of essential uniqueness, we assume that the function is to be computed in an open set of its domain, and that the function has nonzero partial derivatives in each of its variables. We also restrict the class $\mathcal{D}$ to a class $\mathcal{D}_0 \subset \mathcal{D}$ (see Definition B.1.4). The networks we use are $\mathcal{D}_0$ networks. The functions in $\mathcal{D}_0$ are elements of $\mathcal{D}$ that are defined in a neighborhood of the origin of $\Re^2$ and take the value 0 at the origin. The requirement that the functions take value 0 at the origin is restrictive. For example, the function $P(x, y, z, w) = (w - y)/(x - z - y + w)$ of Section 3.1, and the function P in this section cannot be computed by $\mathcal{D}_0$ networks, because neither has value 0 when the variables are all zero. In general, each function F computable by a $\mathcal{D}$ network can be replaced by $F_0 = F-$ {the value of F at the origin} without changing the computing time. It is a quite different restriction that the $\mathcal{D}$ network be replaced with a $\mathcal{D}_0$ network. If a function F does have value 0 at the origin and if F can be computed in time t by a $\mathcal{D}$ network in the neighborhood of the origin, then F can also be computed in the same time by a $\mathcal{D}_0$ network in a neighborhood of the origin. Lemma B.1.1 of Appendix B is a statement of this fact together with a proof. We see that the function P has nonzero derivatives in each parameter in a neighborhood of the origin once P is normalized by subtracting from it the value it has at the origin. The result is the function

$$P_0\left[a_{(1,1)}, a_{(1,2)}, a_{(2,1)}, a_{(2,2)}, b_{(1,1)}, b_{(1,2)}, b_{(2,1)}, b_{(2,2)}\right] =$$

$$\frac{\left[a_{(1,1)} + a_{(1,2)} - a_{(2,1)} - a_{(2,2)} - b_{(1,1)} - b_{(1,2)} + b_{(2,1)} + b_{(2,2)}\right]}{2\left[-2 - a_{(1,1)} + a_{(1,2)} + a_{(2,1)} - a_{(2,2)} + b_{(1,1)} - b_{(1,2)} - b_{(2,1)} + b_{(2,2)}\right]}.$$

Note that each variable occurs with a nonzero coefficient in the linear part of the Taylor series expansion of P_0 at the origin. Therefore, the partial derivative of P_0 with respect to each variable is nonzero in a neighborhood of the origin.

Figure 3.2.2 represents the graph of a $\mathcal{D}_0$ network that computes P_0. If one sets all variables at the leaves of the subtree whose root is (1, 1) equal to zero,

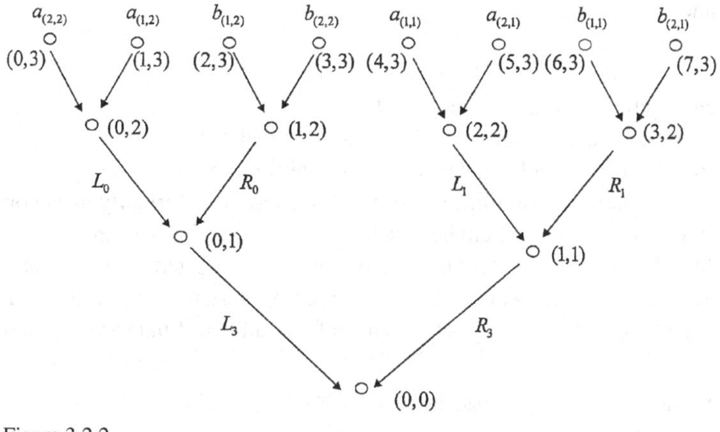

Figure 3.2.2.

then the network computes[3] the function

$$P_0\big[0, a_{(1,2)}, 0, a_{(2,2)}, 0, b_{(1,2)}, 0, b_{(2,2)}\big].$$

The function $\langle 0, 0\rangle(X, Y)$ is a function of two variables. When $Y = 0$, the function $\langle 0, 0\rangle(X, 0) = f(X)$ is a nonsingular function of one variable. The function $f(X)$ is nonsingular, because the network computes P_0, and P_0 is a function that has a nonzero partial derivative in the variable $a_{(2,2)}$. The network whose graph is the subtree with root (0, 1) computes the function

$$f^{-1}\big[P_0(0, a_{(1,2)}, 0, a_{(2,2)}, 0, b_{(1,2)}, 0, b_{(2,2)})\big]$$

in two units of time. As we noted before, composition of the function of four variables with a function of one variable does not change the ranks of the bordered Hessians. Thus composition of

$$P_1 = P_0\big[0, a_{(1,2)}, 0, a_{(2,2)}, 0, b_{(1,2)}, 0, b_{(2,2)}\big]$$

with a nonsingular function of one variable does not change the rank of either the bordered Hessian

$$bh_{\{[a_{(2,2)}, a_{(1,2)}],\ [b_{(1,2)}, b_{(2,2)}]\}}(P_1)$$

or its dual

$$bh_{\{[b_{(1,2)}, b_{(2,2)}],\ [a_{(1,2)}, a_{(2,2)}]\}}(P_1).$$

The function P_1 is computed by the network whose graph is the subtree rooted at (0, 1) in time 2. That is the minimum time possible for the computation of a function of four variables. Thus if P_0 can be computed by the network of Figure 3.2.2, then the bordered Hessian

$$bh_{\{[a_{(2,2)}, a_{(1,2)}],\ [b_{(1,2)}, b_{(2,2)}]\}}(P_0)$$

and its dual

$$bh_{\{[b_{(1,2)}, b_{(2,2)}],\ [a_{(1,2)}, a_{(2,2)}]\}}(P_0)$$

can each have a rank of at most 1.

A similar argument can be made about the network whose graph is the subtree rooted at (1, 1). Thus we have a simple set of necessary conditions that P_0 be computable in time 3. We state the conditions formally in Theorem 3.2.1. Informally we state them here as follows. For each branch vertex v of the graph $S[2, 3]$, set equal to zero the variables that are assigned to leaves not connected to v by a directed path. Split the remaining variables into left and right sets, where the left set is connected to the left arc that has final vertex v, and the right

[3] That is, the network computes the value for all times greater than 3.

set is connected to the right arc that has final vertex v. The resulting function G has a bordered Hessian $bh_{(\text{left, right})}(G)$ of rank at most one in a neighborhood of the origin. Similarly, the bordered Hessian $bh_{(\text{right, left})}(G)$ has a rank of at most 1.

By a direct computation, one can check the assertion that the rank of the bordered Hessian $bh_{(\text{left, right})}(G)$ is at most 1. In order to do so, we simplify some notation. In Figure 3.2.2, label the variables at the leaves $(0, 3), \ldots, (7, 3)$ as $x_0, \ldots, x_7$, respectively. Then for $i \in \{0, 1\}$, abusing notation,

$$\frac{\partial F}{\partial x_i} = \frac{\partial\langle 0,0\rangle}{\partial\langle 0,1\rangle}\frac{\partial\langle 0,1\rangle}{\partial\langle 0,2\rangle}\frac{\partial\langle 0,2\rangle}{\partial x_i}.$$

If $j \in \{2, 3\}$, then

$$\frac{\partial^2 F}{\partial x_j \partial x_i} = \left[\frac{\partial^2\langle 0,0\rangle}{\partial^2\langle 0,1\rangle^2}\frac{\partial\langle 0,1\rangle}{\partial\langle 1,2\rangle}\frac{\partial\langle 0,1\rangle}{\partial\langle 0,2\rangle} + \frac{\partial\langle 0,0\rangle}{\partial\langle 0,1\rangle}\frac{\partial^2\langle 0,1\rangle}{\partial\langle 0,2\rangle\partial\langle 1,2\rangle}\right]\frac{\partial\langle 0,2\rangle}{\partial x_i}\frac{\partial\langle 1,2\rangle}{\partial x_j}.$$

Thus

$$\frac{\partial^2 F}{\partial x_j \partial x_i} = A\,\frac{\partial\langle 0,2\rangle}{\partial x_i}\frac{\partial\langle 1,2\rangle}{\partial x_j},$$

whereas

$$\frac{\partial F}{\partial x_i} = B\,\frac{\partial\langle 0,2\rangle}{\partial x_i}.$$

Then,

$$bh_{[(x_0,x_1),(x_2,x_3)]}(F) = \begin{bmatrix} B\,\frac{\partial\langle 0,2\rangle}{\partial x_0} & A\,\frac{\partial\langle 0,2\rangle}{\partial x_0}\frac{\partial\langle 1,2\rangle}{\partial x_2} & A\,\frac{\partial\langle 0,2\rangle}{\partial x_0}\frac{\partial\langle 1,2\rangle}{\partial x_3} \\ B\,\frac{\partial\langle 0,2\rangle}{\partial x_1} & A\,\frac{\partial\langle 0,2\rangle}{\partial x_1}\frac{\partial\langle 1,2\rangle}{\partial x_2} & A\,\frac{\partial\langle 0,2\rangle}{\partial x_1}\frac{\partial\langle 1,2\rangle}{\partial x_3} \end{bmatrix}.$$

Clearly then, $bh_{[(x_0,x_1),\,(x_2,x_3)]}(F)$ has a rank of at most 1.

The next step is the assignment of the functions $\alpha_{(i,j)}$. The necessity test for computing P_0 by using the graph $S[2, 3]$ derives from putting sets of variables equal to zero. Use the same procedure to ensure that P_0 can be computed in time 3. The function P_0 is to be computed by a $\mathcal{D}_0$ network represented in Figure 3.2.2. Set all the variables except $a_{(2,2)}$ and $a_{(1,2)}$ equal to zero. The $\mathcal{D}_0$ network computes

$$P\big[0, a_{(1,2)}, 0, a_{(2,2)}, 0, \ldots, 0\big] = \frac{\big[a_{(2,2)} - a_{(1,2)}\big]}{2\big[2 + a_{(2,2)} - a_{(1,2)}\big]}.$$

With all variables equal to zero except for $a_{(2,2)}$ and $a_{(1,2)}$, the function $\alpha_{(0,1)}$ receives zero as an output from $\alpha_{(1,2)}$ and acts as a function $g(x)$ of one variable on the value $\alpha_{(0,2)}[a_{(2,2)}, a_{(1,2)}]$. Similarly, the function $\alpha_{(0,0)}$ assigned to the root of the tree $S[2,3]$ receives zero through its right side arc and thus acts as a function $h(y)$ of one variable on the value sent to it by $\alpha_{(0,1)}$. Therefore,

$$\frac{[a_{(2,2)} - a_{(1,2)}]}{2[2 + a_{(2,2)} - a_{(1,2)}]} = h(g\{\alpha_{(0,1)}[a_{(2,2)}, a_{(1,2)}]\}).$$

The functions g and h must be nonsingular at the origin $x = 0$ (or $y = 0$ for h) because $P[0, a_{(1,2)}, 0, a_{(2,2)}, 0, \ldots, 0]$ is nonsingular at the origin. The functions g and h have inverse functions g^{-1} and h^{-1} in a neighborhood of the origin. Thus for some neighborhood of the origin in $\Re^2$,

$$\alpha_{(0,2)} = g^{-1}\left(h^{-1}\left\{a_{(2,2)} - \frac{a_{(1,2)}}{2[2 + a_{(2,2)} - a_{(1,2)}]}\right\}\right).$$

We now know what $\alpha_{(0,2)}$ must be to within composition with a nonsingular function of one variable. Similarly, we know what assignment must be made for the functions $\alpha_{(1,2)}, \ldots, \alpha_{(3,2)}$. That is, to within composition with nonsingular functions of one variable,

$$\alpha_{(1,2)} = b_{(1,2)} - \frac{b_{(2,2)}}{2[2 - b_{(2,2)} + b_{(2,2)}]},$$

$$\alpha_{(2,2)} = a_{(2,1)} - \frac{a_{(1,1)}}{2[2 + a_{(1,1)} - a_{(2,1)}]},$$

$$\alpha_{(3,2)} = b_{(1,1)} - \frac{b_{(2,1)}}{2[2 - b_{(1,1)} + b_{(2,1)}]}.$$

Next we identify the function $\alpha_{(0,1)}$ to within an equivalence class. Set all variables in P_0 equal to zero except for the variables $a_{(2,2)}$ and $b_{(1,2)}$. These two nonzero variables arrive at the (0, 1) vertex unaltered, except for their composition with functions of one variable. That is, $\alpha_{(0,1)}$ receives through the arc L_0 the value of the function $\alpha_{(0,2)}[a_{(2,2)}, 0]$, and it receives from the right arc the value of the function $\alpha_{(1,2)}[b_{(1,2)}, 0]$. The functions $\alpha_{(0,2)}[a_{(2,2)}, 0]$ and $\alpha_{(1,2)}[b_{(1,2)}, 0]$ are nonsingular functions of one variable. The function

$$\alpha_{(0,1)}\{\alpha_{(0,2)}[a_{(2,2)}, 0], \alpha_{(1,2)}[b_{(1,2)}, 0]\}$$

composed with $\alpha_{(0,0)}(X, 0)$, where X is a dummy variable, is

$$P_0[a_{(2,2)}, 0, b_{(1,2)}, 0, 0, 0, 0, 0] = \frac{[a_{(2,2)} + b_{(1,2)}]}{2[2 + a_{(2,2)} + b_{(1,2)}]}.$$

The function assigned to the vertex (0, 1) is determined to within composition with a nonsingular function of one variable and variables composed with nonsingular functions of one variable. We use these conditions as a definition of an equivalence relation hinted at above. We give a more general definition in the sections that follow, but Definition 3.2.1 shows the basic pattern.

Definition 3.2.1. Suppose that F_1 and F_2 are C^2 real-valued functions of two variables defined on neighborhoods of the origin in $\Re^2$ such that $F_i(0, 0) = 0$. The functions F_1 and F_2 are *simply equivalent* at the origin if there are open neighborhoods U_i $(i = 1, 2, 3)$ of $0 \in \Re$ and nonsingular C^2 functions g_i from U_i to a neighborhood of the origin in $\Re$ such that $F_2(x_0, x_1) = g_2\{F_1[g_0(x_0), g_1(x_1)]\}$ in $U_0 \times U_1$.

Simple equivalence is a simplified version of functional equivalence (see Golubitsky and Guillemin, 1973) and it is an equivalence relation.

The analysis of the function P_0 leads to the following theorem. A more general version of uniqueness is given in Appendix B.

Theorem 3.2.1. *Suppose that F is a C^2 function of 2^N real variables $\underline{x} = \{x_0, \ldots, x_{2^N-1}\}$ defined in a neighborhood of the origin of $\Re^{2^N}$. Suppose that (1) F is zero at the origin, (2) F has a nonzero partial derivative with respect to each of the x_i in a neighborhood of the origin, and (3) the variable x_j is assigned to the leaf (j, N) of the tree $S[2, N]$. For each branch vertex v, there are two subtrees T_L and T_R of $S[2, N]$ whose roots are connected to v, each by an arc. Denote by $\underline{x}_L$ the collection of variables that are assigned to the leaves of T_L and denote by $\underline{x}_R$ the collection of variables assigned to the leaves of T_R. Denote by $G(\underline{x}_L, \underline{x}_R)$ the function that is derived from F by setting equal to zero all the variables that are neither in the set $\underline{x}_L$ nor the set $\underline{x}_R$. Then the function F can be computed in time N by a $\mathcal{D}_0$ network represented by the graph $S[2, N]$ and with the given variable to leaf assignment if and only if:*

(i) for each branch vertex v of $S[2, N]$, each of $bh_{(\underline{x}_L, \underline{x}_R)}(G)$[4]*, and*
(ii) $bh_{(\underline{x}_R, \underline{x}_L)}(G)$ has rank 1 in a neighborhood of the origin.

Furthermore, if F can be computed in time N with the given assignment of variables to leaves, then the functions assigned to the branch vertices of $S[2, N]$ are unique to within simple equivalence.

Definition 3.2.2. We say a function is *essentially unique* if it is unique to within simple equivalence.

Note that identifying the equivalence class of the functions at each branch vertex is not sufficient to ensure that the resulting network computes F. If we carry out the construction of a network with the functions derived from P_0 by setting appropriate sets of variables to zero, in general the resulting network

[4] Only ranks are involved, so we need not specify an order for the variables of x_L or x_R.

will not compute P_0. We must choose the "correct" functions of one variable to add to the composition. However, once the equivalence class of functions to be assigned to a vertex is known, then it is easy to find a representative that will suffice to compute the function F. In the next paragraph we show how to choose a correct representative. Beyond the fact that the identification of the equivalence class of functions required at a vertex of the graph $S[r, N]$ simplifies building the network to compute F, we note that identifying the equivalence class makes it easier for us to generalize the Leontief necessary conditions to the case of functions computed by networks represented by $S[r, N]$.

In the case of the function P_0, the following calculations demonstrate how to choose the functions to assign to the vertices of $S[2, 3]$ in order to compute P_0. We know that the functions required can be derived from the function P_0 by setting sets of variables equal to zero and then composing the results with functions of one variable. All we need do is identify the functions of one variable. Assign to the vertex $(0, 2)$ the function $[a_{(2,2)} - a_{(1,2)}]/\{2[2 + a_{(2,2)} - a_{(1,2)}]\}$. Set $x = [a_{(2,2)} - a_{(1,2)}]/\{2[2 + a_{(2,2)} - a_{(1,2)}]\}$. This is an equation nonsingular in (say) $a_{(2,2)}$; thus we can solve this equation for $a_{(2,2)}$ in terms of x. The result is

$$a_{(2,2)} = \frac{\left[a_{(1,2)} - 2a_{(1,2)}x + 4x\right]}{(1 - 2x)}.$$

Similarly, set

$$y = \frac{\left[b_{(2,2)} - b_{(1,2)}\right]}{2\left[-2 - b_{(1,2)} + b_{(2,2)}\right]},$$

$$z = \frac{\left[a_{(2,1)} - a_{(1,1)}\right]}{2\left[-2 - a_{(1,1)} + a_{(2,1)}\right]},$$

$$w = \frac{\left[-b_{(1,1)} + b_{(2,1)}\right]}{2\left[-2 + b_{(1,1)} - b_{(2,1)}\right]}.$$

Solve these equations for $b_{(2,2)}$, $a_{(1,1)}$, and $b_{(1,1)}$, respectively. The solutions are

$$b_{(2,2)} = \frac{\left[b_{(1,2)} + 2yb_{(1,2)} + 4y\right]}{(1 + 2y)},$$

$$a_{(1,1)} = \frac{\left[a_{(2,1)} + 2a_{(2,1)} - 4z)\right]}{(1 + 2z)},$$

$$b_{(1,1)} = \frac{\left[b_{(2,1)} + 2wb_{(1,1)} + 4w\right]}{(1 + 2w)}.$$

If we substitute these expressions in P_0, then $P_0 = L/M$, where

$$L = w + x - y + 4xy + 4wxy + z + 4wz - 4wxz + 4wyz + 4xyz,$$

and

$$M = 1 + 4wx - 4wy + 4xy + 16wxy - 4wz$$
$$+ 4xz + 16wxz - 4yz - 16wyz + 16xyz + 48wxyz.$$

We can check directly that L/M satisfies the Leontief condition, but it is easier just to build a $\mathcal{D}_0$ network that computes it in time 2. We do so by first setting the variables z and w equal to zero. The result is the function

$$\beta_{(0,1)}(x, y) = (x - y + 4xy)/(1 + 4xy).$$

Now set the variables x and y to zero with the result

$$\beta_{(1,1)}(z, w) = w + z.$$

As in the previous paragraph, set

$$X = (x - y + 4xy)/(1 + 4xy),$$
$$W = w + z.$$

Solve these for x and w, respectively, and substitute in L/M. Then

$$x = (X + y)/(1 + 4y - 4Xy),$$
$$w = (W - z)/(1 + 4z + 4Wz).$$

The result of the substitution is

$$(W + X)/(1 + 4WX).$$

A $\mathcal{D}_0$ network that computes P_0 in time 3 is represented in Figure 3.2.3.

3.3. COMPUTABILITY IN EXCESS TIME

Leontief's Theorem and its general form given in Lemma B.2.3 gives necessary conditions and sufficient conditions that a function of 2^N variables can be computed by a $\mathcal{D}$ network in time N. The necessary conditions make it clear that functions of 2^N variables that can be computed in time N by a $\mathcal{D}$ network are rare. In general, a function of 2^N variables has bordered Hessians each of whose rank exceeds 1. What can be said about the complexity of such a function? More specifically, what information about the function's complexity is conveyed if the ranks of its bordered Hessian matrices exceed 1? This question is addressed in this section.

As in the preceding sections, for concreteness and to facilitate understanding, we present the analysis in the context of examples. We compare the times required to compute Nash equilibria in two classes of matrix games. Each class depends on eight parameters.

One class of games characterized by eight parameters is represented by 8×8 diagonal matrices with diagonal entries chosen close to 1. Each specification

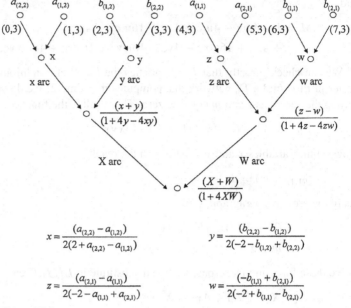

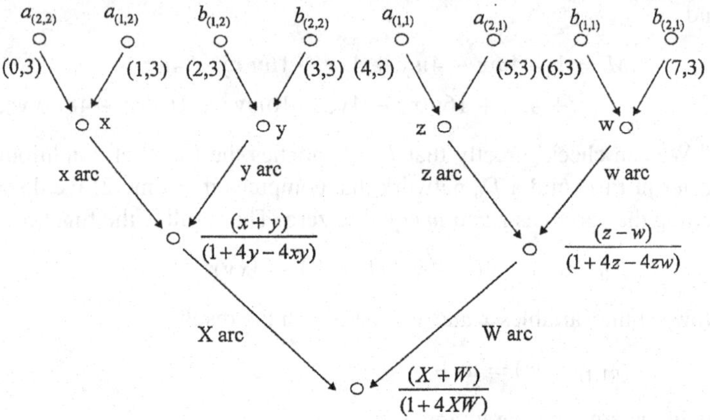

$$x = \frac{(a_{(2,2)} - a_{(1,2)})}{2(2 + a_{(2,2)} - a_{(1,2)})} \qquad y = \frac{(b_{(2,2)} - b_{(1,2)})}{2(-2 - b_{(1,2)} + b_{(2,2)})}$$

$$z = \frac{(a_{(2,1)} - a_{(1,1)})}{2(-2 - a_{(1,1)} + a_{(2,1)})} \qquad w = \frac{(-b_{(1,1)} + b_{(2,1)})}{2(-2 + b_{(1,1)} - b_{(2,1)})}$$

Figure 3.2.3.

of parameters determines a matrix game with optimal mixed strategies near those of the matrix game represented by the 8×8 identity matrix. Denote this class of games by Diag. The parameters for the games in Diag are the variables $d_1, \ldots, d_8$, where the value of each of these variables is close to zero. The game with parameters $d_1, \ldots, d_8$ is represented by the matrix

$$\begin{bmatrix} 1+d_1 & 0 & 0 & 0 & 0 & 0 & 0 & 0 \\ 0 & 1+d_2 & 0 & 0 & 0 & 0 & 0 & 0 \\ 0 & 0 & 1+d_3 & 0 & 0 & 0 & 0 & 0 \\ 0 & 0 & 0 & 1+d_4 & 0 & 0 & 0 & 0 \\ 0 & 0 & 0 & 0 & 1+d_5 & 0 & 0 & 0 \\ 0 & 0 & 0 & 0 & 0 & 1+d_6 & 0 & 0 \\ 0 & 0 & 0 & 0 & 0 & 0 & 1+d_7 & 0 \\ 0 & 0 & 0 & 0 & 0 & 0 & 0 & 1+d_8 \end{bmatrix}. \tag{3.3.1}$$

The Nash optimal mixed strategies for each of these games are easy to find (Owen, 1982, p. 20). The first player should play the jth row with probability

$$\text{pr } D_j = \frac{1}{(1+d_j)} \frac{1}{\sum_{i=1}^{8}[1/(1+d_i)]}. \tag{3.3.2}$$

If all the $d_j = 0$, then the optimal mixed strategy for the first player is to play each row with probability $1/8$.

The second class of games characterized by eight parameters is represented by 3×3 matrices with diagonal entries chosen close to 1. Each specification of parameters determines a matrix game with optimal mixed strategies near those of the matrix game represented by the 3×3 identity matrix. Denote this class of games by Gen. Each game in Gen depends on the nine entries in a 3×3 matrix. We normalize the games so that the entry in the first row and the first column of the matrix of the game is 1. The normalized general element of Gen is given by the matrix

$$\begin{bmatrix} 1 & a_{1,2} & a_{1,3} \\ a_{2,1} & 1 + a_{2,2} & a_{2,3} \\ a_{3,1} & a_{3,2} & 1 + a_{3,3} \end{bmatrix}. \tag{3.3.3}$$

The parameters for the games in Gen are the variables $a_{1,2}, \ldots, a_{3,3}$, where the value of each of these variables is close to zero. The Nash optimal mixed strategies for each of these games are also easy to find (Owen, 1982). The first player should play the jth row with probability

$$\operatorname{pr} G_1 = \frac{\dfrac{1 - a_{3,1} + a_{3,3}}{1 + a_{2,1} - a_{2,3} - a_{3,1} + a_{3,3}} - \dfrac{1 - a_{3,2} + a_{3,3}}{2 + a_{2,2} - a_{2,3} - a_{3,2} + a_{3,3}}}{\dfrac{2 - a_{1,3} - a_{3,1} + a_{3,3}}{1 + a_{2,1} - a_{2,3} - a_{3,1} + a_{3,3}} - \dfrac{1 + a_{1,2} - a_{1,3} - a_{3,2} + a_{3,3}}{2 + a_{2,2} - a_{2,3} - a_{3,2} + a_{3,3}}}. \tag{3.3.4}$$

If all the $a_{i,j} = 0$, then the optimal mixed strategy for the first player is to play each row with probability $1/3$. Recall that in Section 3.2 we showed that to find the minimum computing time required to compute the function pr D_1 by using $\mathcal{D}$ networks in a neighborhood of the origin, it suffices to find the minimum computing time required for $\mathcal{D}_0$ networks to compute the function pr d = pr $D_1 - 1/8$. The partial derivative of pr d with respect to each of the variables d_i is nonzero at the origin. With the use of the given parameters, the evaluation of the function pr d requires input of the values of each of the eight parameters. It follows that a lower bound on the time required to compute pr d by using $\mathcal{D}_0$ networks is 3. It was shown in Chapter 2 that if pr d can be computed in three units of time, it can be computed by a network whose graph is $S[2, 3]$. The assignment of eight variables to the eight leaves of $S[2, 3]$ splits the set of parameters into two sets X and Y, where each set consists of four parameters. The necessary conditions of the Leontief Theorem tell us that if pr d can be computed in time 3 with the given assignment of parameters to the leaves of $S[2, 3]$, then each of the bordered Hessians $bh_{(X,Y)}(\text{pr } d)$ and $bh_{(Y,X)}(\text{pr } d)$ has rank 1 in a neighborhood of the origin. Set $X = \{d_1, \ldots, d_4\}$ and $Y = \{d_5, \ldots, d_8\}$. With a little patience, one can compute the bordered

Hessian $bh_{(X,Y)}(\text{pr } d)$. The value of $bh_{(X,Y)}(\text{pr } d)$ at the origin is

$$\begin{bmatrix} -7/64 & -3/256 & -3/256 & -3/256 & -3/256 \\ 1/64 & 1/256 & 1/256 & 1/256 & 1/256 \\ 1/64 & 1/256 & 1/256 & 1/256 & 1/256 \\ 1/64 & 1/256 & 1/256 & 1/256 & 1/256 \end{bmatrix}.$$

This matrix has rank 2. One could compute the bordered Hessians for each of the possible ways that eight variables can be split into two sets of four elements, but the symmetry of pr d in the variables d_i makes it clear that for each such choice the resulting bordered Hessian has rank 2. We conclude from Leontief's criteria that pr d cannot be computed in three units of time. It is easy to see how to compute pr d in four units of time. The network in Figure 3.3.1 represents such a computation. Each branch vertex of $S[2,4]$ is the final vertex of a left arc L and a right arc R. Represent each function assigned to a branch vertex of $S[2,4]$ as a function of two variables L and R. Table 3.3.1 indicates an assignment to $S[2,4]$ that computes pr d.

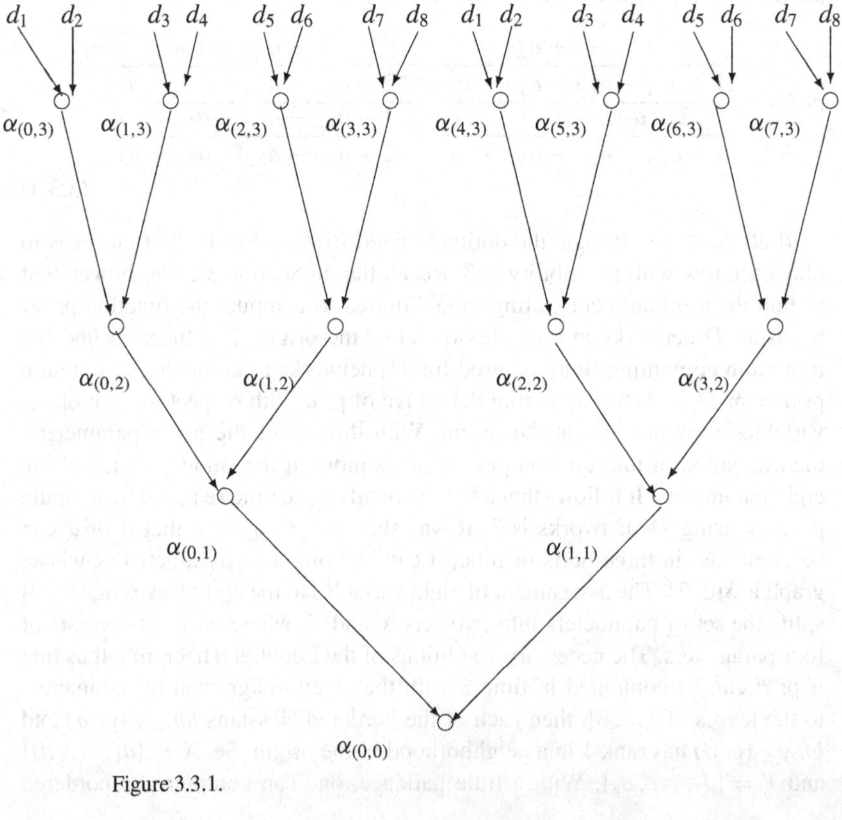

Figure 3.3.1.

Table 3.3.1. Module Assignment to Compile pr *d*.

Vertex	Name in Fig. 3.1.1	Function
(0, 4)	d_1	d_1
⋮	⋮	⋮
(7, 4)	d_8	d_8
(5, 4)	d_1	d_1
⋮	⋮	⋮
(15, 4)	d_8	d_8
(0, 3)	$\alpha_{(0,3)}$	$\frac{1}{(1+d_1)}+\frac{1}{(1+d_2)}-2$
(1, 3)	$\alpha_{(1,3)}$	$\frac{1}{(1+d_3)}+\frac{1}{(1+d_4)}-2$
(2, 3)	$\alpha_{(2,3)}$	$\frac{1}{(1+d_5)}+\frac{1}{(1+d_6)}-2$
(3, 3)	$\alpha_{(3,3)}$	$\frac{1}{(1+d_7)}+\frac{1}{(1+d_8)}-2$
(4, 3)	$\alpha_{(4,3)}$	L
(5, 3)	$\alpha_{(5,3)}$	L
(6, 3)	$\alpha_{(6,3)}$	L
(7, 3)	$\alpha_{(7,3)}$	L
(0, 2)	$\alpha_{(0,2)}$	$L+R$
(1, 2)	$\alpha_{(1,2)}$	$L+R$
(2, 2)	$\alpha_{(2,2)}$	L
(3, 2)	$\alpha_{(3,2)}$	L
(0, 1)	$\alpha_{(0,1)}$	$L+R$
(1, 1)	$\alpha_{(1,1)}$	L
(0, 0)	$\alpha_{(0,0)}$	$\left(\frac{1}{R}\right)\left[\frac{1}{(8+L)}\right]-\frac{1}{8}$

We now take up the analysis of the function pr G_1 for Gen games. This presents more of a challenge than the problem for pr d. Set pr g = pr $G_1 - 1/3$. Then pr g is the normalized version of pr G_1. The function pr $g = U/D$, where

$$\begin{aligned} U = (&a_{1,2} + a_{1,3} - 2\,a_{2,1} + a_{1,2}\,a_{2,1} - a_{1,3}\,a_{2,1} + a_{2,2} + a_{1,3}\,a_{2,2} \\ &+ a_{2,3} - a_{1,2}\,a_{2,3} - 2\,a_{3,1} - a_{1,2}\,a_{3,1} + a_{1,3}\,a_{3,1} - 2\,a_{2,2}\,a_{3,1} \\ &+ 2\,a_{2,3}\,a_{3,1} + a_{3,2} - a_{1,3}\,a_{3,2} + 2\,a_{2,1}\,a_{3,2} - 2\,a_{2,3}\,a_{3,2} \\ &+ a_{3,3} + a_{1,2}\,a_{3,3} - 2\,a_{2,1}\,a_{3,3} + 2\,a_{2,2}\,a_{3,3}), \end{aligned}$$

and

$$\begin{aligned} D = 3\,(3 &- a_{1,2} - a_{1,3} - a_{2,1} - a_{1,2}\,a_{2,1} + a_{1,3}\,a_{2,1} + 2\,a_{2,2} - a_{1,3}\,a_{2,2} \\ &- a_{2,3} + a_{1,2}\,a_{2,3} - a_{3,1} + a_{1,2}\,a_{3,1} - a_{1,3}\,a_{3,1} - a_{2,2}\,a_{3,1} + a_{2,3}\,a_{3,1} - a_{3,2} \\ &+ a_{1,3}\,a_{3,2} + a_{2,1}\,a_{3,2} - a_{2,3}\,a_{3,2} + 2\,a_{3,3} - a_{1,2}\,a_{3,3} - a_{2,1}\,a_{3,3} + a_{2,2}\,a_{3,3}). \end{aligned}$$

The linear term of the numerator U is the expression $a_{1,2} + a_{1,3} - 2\,a_{2,1} + a_{2,2} + a_{2,3} - 2\,a_{3,1} + a_{3,2} + a_{3,3}$. Thus, pr g has nonzero partial derivatives with respect to each of the variables $a_{1,2}, \ldots, a_{3,3}$ in a neighborhood of the origin. As in the case of the function pr d, we use Leontief's criteria to decide whether the function pr g can be computed in time 3. In the case of the function pr d, symmetry implies that the computation time for pr d is insensitive to the order in which variables are assigned to the leaves of $S[2, 3]$. Therefore, to check whether pr d can be written in the form $A(B, C)$, we find it sufficient to check one of the ways to write the set of eight variables as a union of two subsets of four variables. In the case of the function pr g, we see no simple way of choosing such a decomposition. To decide whether the function pr g can be computed in time 3 by using the parameters $a_{i,j}$, we search for a decomposition of the set of variables into two sets X and Y such that each of the bordered Hessians $bh_{(X,Y)}(\text{pr } g)$ and $bh_{(Y,X)}(\text{pr } g)$ has rank at most 1 in a neighborhood of the origin. At the worst, this search could lead to the evaluation of the ranks of $(1/2)\left[\begin{smallmatrix}8\\4\end{smallmatrix}\right] = 35$ bordered Hessians. Each bordered Hessian $bh_{(X,Y)}(\text{pr } g)$ is a 4×5 matrix. A glance at the expression for pr g indicates that computing the rank of a bordered Hessian in a neighborhood of the origin is not an entirely simple task. However, a lower bound on the ranks of bordered Hessians evaluated at the origin is certainly a lower bound on the ranks of the bordered Hessians in each neighborhood of the origin. Rather than computing each of the 35 matrices of functions, we adopt an easier procedure.

Construct a 8×9 matrix $CH(\text{pr } g)$ that whose first column is the derivatives of pr g with respect to each of the variables $a_{i,j}$ ordered lexicographically. Set the remaining 8×8 matrix equal to the Hessian of pr g. The result of evaluating $CH(\text{pr } g)$ at the origin is

$$CH(\text{pr } g)_0 =$$

$$\begin{array}{c} \\ a_{1,2} \\ a_{1,3} \\ a_{2,1} \\ a_{2,2} \\ a_{2,3} \\ a_{3,1} \\ a_{3,2} \\ a_{3,3} \end{array}
\begin{array}{c} \begin{array}{ccccccccc} \text{pr } g & a_{1,2} & a_{1,3} & a_{2,1} & a_{2,2} & a_{2,3} & a_{3,1} & a_{3,2} & a_{3,3} \end{array} \\
\left[\begin{array}{ccccccccc}
1/9 & 2/27 & 2/27 & 2/27 & -1/27 & -1/27 & -4/27 & 2/27 & 2/27 \\
1/9 & 2/27 & 2/27 & -4/27 & 2/27 & 2/27 & 2/27 & -1/27 & -1/27 \\
-2/9 & 2/27 & -4/27 & -4/27 & 5/27 & -1/27 & -4/27 & 5/27 & -1/27 \\
1/9 & -1/27 & 2/27 & 5/27 & -4/27 & -1/27 & -1/27 & -1/27 & 2/27 \\
1/9 & -1/27 & 2/27 & -1/27 & -1/27 & 2/27 & 5/27 & -4/27 & -1/27 \\
-2/9 & -4/27 & 2/27 & -4/27 & -1/27 & 5/27 & -4/27 & -1/27 & 5/27 \\
1/9 & 2/27 & -1/27 & 5/27 & -1/27 & -4/27 & -1/27 & 2/27 & -1/27 \\
1/9 & 2/27 & -1/27 & -1/27 & 2/27 & -1/27 & 5/27 & -1/27 & -4/27
\end{array}\right] \end{array} .$$

Each of the bordered Hessians $bh_{(X,Y)}(\text{pr } g)_0$ is a 4×5 submatrix of $CH(\text{pr } g)_0$ that has the first column chosen from the first column of $CH(\text{pr } g)_0$. It is a tedious computation, best left to software,[5] to compute the ranks of these submatrices. The result of that computation is that each such bordered Hessian has rank either 3 or 4. Therefore pr g cannot be computed in time 3 by using the given parameters. Thus the Leontief criteria are indecisive for the comparison of the functions pr g and pr d. There is a tantalizing difference in the ranks of the bordered Hessians of pr d and pr g. Perhaps the difference in the ranks can

[5] We used Mathematica.

reveal additional information. We will show that for pr g to be computed in four units of time, the bordered Hessians of pr g at the origin must have ranks of at most 2.

Our next objective is to establish that the difference between the ranks of bordered Hessians of pr g and the ranks of bordered Hessians of pr d is significant, at least if one restricts the computations to be symmetrical computations in the sense of Definition 2.1.13. Note that the computation carried out by the network with graph Figure 3.3.1 is a symmetrical computation.

Suppose that a function $f(x_0, \ldots, x_3, y_0, \ldots, y_3)$ of eight variables can be computed symmetrically in four units of time by a $\mathcal{D}_0$ network $\mathcal{N}$ that has graph $S[2, 4]$. We suppose that the variables $\underline{x} = \{x_0, \ldots, x_3\}$ are assigned to the vertices $(0, 4), \ldots, (3, 4)$, respectively, and we suppose that the variables $y_0, \ldots, y_3$ are assigned to the vertices $(4, 4), \ldots, (7, 4)$, respectively. The root $(0, 0)$ of $S[2, 4]$ has a function of two variables $C(L, R)$ assigned to it. Here, L is the variable identified with the left arc that has initial vertex $(0, 1)$ and R is the variable identified with the right arc that has initial vertex $(1, 1)$. The network with a graph that is the subtree of $S[2, 4]$ whose root is the vertex $(0, 1)$ computes a function $A(\underline{x}, \underline{y})$ in three units of time. The subtree of $S[2, 4]$ whose root is the vertex $(1, 1)$ is the graph of a network that computes a function $B(\underline{x}, \underline{y})$ in three units of time. Thus $f(\underline{x}, \underline{y}) = C[A(\underline{x}, \underline{y}), B(\underline{x}, \underline{y})]$. It follows from the necessary conditions of Leontief that the matrices of the bordered Hessians $BH_{(\underline{x}, \underline{y})}A(\underline{x}, \underline{y})$, $BH_{(\underline{y}, \underline{x})}A(\underline{x}, \underline{y})$, $BH_{(\underline{x}, \underline{y})}B(\underline{x}, \underline{y})$, and $BH_{(\underline{y}, \underline{x})}B(\underline{x}, \underline{y})$ each have rank at most 1 in a neighborhood of the origin. In particular, the columns of $BH_{(\underline{x}, \underline{y})}(A)$ are all multiples of a 4×1 column vector C_1, whereas the columns of $BH_{(\underline{x}, \underline{y})}(B)$ are all multiples of a 4×1 column vector C_2.

We can now compute the matrices of the bordered Hessians of the function $f(\underline{x}, \underline{y})$, but for our purposes we separately examine each of the columns of $BH_{(\underline{x}, \underline{y})}(f)$. The column indexed by f is the vector

$$\begin{bmatrix} \frac{\partial C}{\partial A}\frac{\partial A}{\partial x_0} + \frac{\partial C}{\partial B}\frac{\partial B}{\partial x_0} \\ \frac{\partial C}{\partial A}\frac{\partial A}{\partial x_1} + \frac{\partial C}{\partial B}\frac{\partial B}{\partial x_1} \\ \frac{\partial C}{\partial A}\frac{\partial A}{\partial x_2} + \frac{\partial C}{\partial B}\frac{\partial B}{\partial x_2} \\ \frac{\partial C}{\partial A}\frac{\partial A}{\partial x_3} + \frac{\partial C}{\partial B}\frac{\partial B}{\partial x_3} \end{bmatrix}.$$

Note that this vector is a linear combination of the two columns

$$\begin{bmatrix} \frac{\partial A}{\partial x_0} \\ \frac{\partial A}{\partial x_1} \\ \frac{\partial A}{\partial x_2} \\ \frac{\partial A}{\partial x_3} \end{bmatrix}, \quad \begin{bmatrix} \frac{\partial B}{\partial x_0} \\ \frac{\partial B}{\partial x_1} \\ \frac{\partial B}{\partial x_2} \\ \frac{\partial B}{\partial x_3} \end{bmatrix}.$$

Thus the first column of $BH_{(\underline{x},y)}(f)$ is a linear combination of the two column vectors C_1 and C_2. The column of $BH_{(\underline{x},y)}(f)$ indexed by y_j is the sum of the six column vectors:

$$\begin{bmatrix} \frac{\partial^2 C}{\partial A^2}\frac{\partial A}{\partial x_0}\frac{\partial A}{\partial y_0} \\ \frac{\partial^2 C}{\partial A^2}\frac{\partial A}{\partial x_1}\frac{\partial A}{\partial y_0} \\ \frac{\partial^2 C}{\partial A^2}\frac{\partial A}{\partial x_2}\frac{\partial A}{\partial y_0} \\ \frac{\partial^2 C}{\partial A^2}\frac{\partial A}{\partial x_3}\frac{\partial A}{\partial y_0} \end{bmatrix}, \quad \begin{bmatrix} \frac{\partial^2 C}{\partial A\,\partial B}\frac{\partial A}{\partial x_0}\frac{\partial B}{\partial y_0} \\ \frac{\partial^2 C}{\partial A\,\partial B}\frac{\partial A}{\partial x_1}\frac{\partial B}{\partial y_0} \\ \frac{\partial^2 C}{\partial A\,\partial B}\frac{\partial A}{\partial x_2}\frac{\partial B}{\partial y_0} \\ \frac{\partial^2 C}{\partial A\,\partial B}\frac{\partial A}{\partial x_3}\frac{\partial B}{\partial y_0} \end{bmatrix},$$

$$\begin{bmatrix} \frac{\partial^2 C}{\partial A\,\partial B}\frac{\partial A}{\partial y_0}\frac{\partial B}{\partial x_0} \\ \frac{\partial^2 C}{\partial A\,\partial B}\frac{\partial A}{\partial y_0}\frac{\partial B}{\partial x_1} \\ \frac{\partial^2 C}{\partial A\,\partial B}\frac{\partial A}{\partial y_0}\frac{\partial B}{\partial x_2} \\ \frac{\partial^2 C}{\partial A\,\partial B}\frac{\partial A}{\partial y_0}\frac{\partial B}{\partial x_3} \end{bmatrix}, \quad \begin{bmatrix} \frac{\partial^2 C}{\partial B^2}\frac{\partial B}{\partial x_0}\frac{\partial B}{\partial y_0} \\ \frac{\partial^2 C}{\partial B^2}\frac{\partial B}{\partial x_1}\frac{\partial B}{\partial y_0} \\ \frac{\partial^2 C}{\partial B^2}\frac{\partial B}{\partial x_2}\frac{\partial B}{\partial y_0} \\ \frac{\partial^2 C}{\partial B^2}\frac{\partial B}{\partial x_3}\frac{\partial B}{\partial y_0} \end{bmatrix},$$

$$\begin{bmatrix} \frac{\partial C}{\partial A}\frac{\partial^2 A}{\partial x_0\,\partial y_0} \\ \frac{\partial C}{\partial A}\frac{\partial^2 A}{\partial x_1\,\partial y_0} \\ \frac{\partial C}{\partial A}\frac{\partial^2 A}{\partial x_2\,\partial y_0} \\ \frac{\partial C}{\partial A}\frac{\partial^2 A}{\partial x_3\,\partial y_0} \end{bmatrix}, \quad \begin{bmatrix} \frac{\partial C}{\partial B}\frac{\partial^2 B}{\partial x_0\,\partial y_0} \\ \frac{\partial C}{\partial B}\frac{\partial^2 B}{\partial x_1\,\partial y_0} \\ \frac{\partial C}{\partial B}\frac{\partial^2 B}{\partial x_0\,\partial y_0} \\ \frac{\partial C}{\partial B}\frac{\partial^2 B}{\partial x_0\,\partial y_0} \end{bmatrix}.$$

Each of these columns is a linear combination of the columns C_1 and C_2. Thus the rank of the matrix $BH_{(\underline{x},y)}(f)$ is at most 2.

The comparison of pr d and pr g is now relatively simple. The function pr d can be computed in four units of time by the network represented by Figure 3.3.1. If pr g can be computed symmetrically by a $\mathcal{D}_0$ network in time 4, then the network can be represented by the graph $S[2, 4]$. In that case the rank of each bordered Hessian of pr g can be at most 2. However, we have already noted that the ranks of the bordered Hessians of pr g are bounded below by 3. Thus the minimum computing time for pr g by using a symmetric $\mathcal{D}_0$ network is 5. That is, pr g requires a longer computing time than pr d when computations are made by $\mathcal{D}_0$ networks that compute symmetrically.

4 Applications to Economics

4.1. COMPUTATION WITH HUMAN AGENTS

In Chapter 1 we introduced computation with human agents informally. In this section we extend the network model to include human agents.

In many situations it is necessary to evaluate a function F whose domain or range is not a subset of a Euclidean space. The complexity of such a function can be analyzed in the $\mathcal{F}$ network model by converting the computation of F into the computation of a function $F*$ derived from F, whose domain and range are acceptable to a network with modules in $\mathcal{F}$. The conversion is done by using a real-variable version of the concept of computing an encoded version of a function found in Arbib (1960). The idea is that the domain of the function is mapped into a product of Euclidean spaces by encoding functions, and the range of the function to be computed is embedded by one-to-one maps in a product of Euclidean spaces. We also require that the encoding be done so as to preserve the product structure of the domain of F. One reason for this requirement is to accommodate distributed computation of F, or to accomodate a situation often encountered in economic theory in which the value of the function F describes an outcome, for instance an allocation, for a group of agents each of whom is characterized by individual parameters. Then the domain of F is the product of the agents's parameter spaces, which need not be Euclidean. The definition of encoding we use requires that the product structure be preserved; that is, the parameters of each agent must be kept together and associated with the relevant agent. The definition is the following.

Definition 4.1.1. Suppose that $F : X^1 \times \cdots \times X^n \to Y$ is a continuous function from a product of topological spaces X^i to a topological space Y. Suppose $V = \Re \times \cdots \times \Re$ is a d-fold direct product of the real numbers. We say that a $\mathcal{D}^s(r, d)$ network $\mathcal{C}$ *computes an encoded version of F* in time t if

(i) there are Euclidean spaces E^i (E^i is a w_i-fold direct product of copies of V) and continuous functions $g^i : X^i \to E^i$, $1 \le i \le n$, and

(ii) there are continuous functions $h^1, \ldots, h^b$, where $h^j : Y \to V$,

such that the following conditions are satisfied.

1. $h = (h^1, \ldots, h^b)$ is a bicontinuous one-to-one map to a topological subspace of $V \times \cdots \times V$ (h is an embedding).
2. There is a function $D = (D^1, \ldots, D^b) : \prod_1^n E^i \in V \times \cdots \times V$ from (Σw_i)-fold tuples of d vectors to b-fold tuples of d vectors that C computes in time t.
3. The following diagram commutes:

$$\begin{array}{ccc} X^1 \times \cdots \times X^n & \xrightarrow{F} & Y \\ \Pi_i g^i \downarrow & & \downarrow h = (h^1, \ldots, h^b) \\ E^1 \times \cdots \times E^n & \xrightarrow{D=(D^1,\ldots,D^b)} & V \times \cdots \times V. \end{array}$$

The maps g^i encode the domain of F, and the map h encodes the range of F.

The concept of computing an encoded version of a function is useful in modeling computations carried out by human beings, or by humans together with machines. The following two examples illustrate this use.

4.1.1. Example 1: Reading Handwriting

Humans are very good at recognizing visual patterns, whereas this is often a difficult task for a machine. An important example of a computation that humans perform routinely and often easily and that computers have great difficulty with is the reading of handwriting.

"Reading handwriting" can mean several different things. For example, it can mean (1) writing in noncursive form (i.e., print) the (English) expressions that are indicated by a given sample of cursive script; (2) uttering the expressions indicated by the given sample of cursive script; or (3) extracting the "meaning" encoded in the cursive writing sample.

We focus on what may be the simplest of these – translating a sample of cursive writing into printed form. Imagine a typesetter, a person or machine, who has before him (it) a manuscript (cursive statement) and a font of type, and whose task it is to produce a sequence of type elements (upper and lower case letters, punctuation marks, and spaces) that correctly translate the cursive manuscript into printed form.

A cursive writing sample is a plane "curve," a curve that may have discontinuities, perhaps caused by the idiosyncrasies of the handwriting of a particular person, or the normal spaces between words; it may have isolated points, for example, the dot over the letter "i," or the full stop that marks the end of a sentence; it may have crossing strokes, such as in the case of the letter "t." It can be in a variety of positions relative to the paper, blackboard, or other material on which it is written.

We may consider these curves to be concatenations of elements of a space consisting of all conceivable finite samples of cursive script of no more than a given length. Denote this space by C. (Other properties of curves that can be cursive writing samples, such as being of bounded variation, or having uniform upper and lower bounds on the height of letters, could also be considered.) The space C can be made into a topological space, for example, by introducing a metric topology that uses a concept of the distance between curves of finite length.

The space, T, of printed text consists of a null element, and all finite strings of the elements of a type font (or set of fonts). T is a topological space with the discrete topology. The act of reading a cursive statement may be represented by a (continuous) function $\rho : C \to T$. Typically, this function will be many to one. Unreadable cursive samples are mapped to the null element of T. (If it is useful to do so, the function ρ may be assumed to depend on the person who writes, as well as on the person who reads, or both.)

First, however, we consider how a machine might perform this act – read a given cursive writing sample. The curve that constitutes a cursive writing sample must be presented to the computer in a form the computer can accept. This may be done by a device such as a scanner that converts the curve into a string of symbols from the alphabet recognized by the computer, or perhaps by a sensitive tablet on which the sample is written by using some sort of stylus or light pen. The result of either of these input devices is an *encoded representation* of the curve. This may be as a graphic image, or an object specified by the equations that define the curve as a locus in two-space, perhaps relative to some given coordinate system. Another possibility, which, however, involves more information, is to give the curve parametrically, by equations

$$x(\nu) = \phi_1(\nu),\ y(\nu) = \phi_2(\nu), \qquad \nu_1 \leq \nu \leq \nu_2,$$

where (x, y) denotes a point in the plane, and ν is in the interval between ν_1 and ν_2 in the real line. This representation, or a discrete approximation to it, might describe someone writing cursively on a sensitive tablet. Given this input, the computer would require programs to process the input into the ASCII code for the string of font symbols that constitute the output. Because the task is a complex one for a computer, the program is likely to be long and perhaps likely to produce incorrect results on many writing samples. (In the present discussion we may regard an incorrect result as one equivalent to an infinite computing time; i.e., we would have to wait forever for the correct result. A more satisfactory approach would be to measure the degree to which the output approximates the correct result, but this seems too complicated for the present purpose.) The diagram in Figure 4.1.1 represents the situation. In that diagram the function $e : C \to \Re^{l_1} \times \cdots \times \Re^{l_n}$ is an encoding of the elements of C, that is, cursive statements, into elements of $\Re^{l_1} \times \cdots \times \Re^{l_n}$. (Note that if the encoding is done by a device such as a scanner, the encoding may depend on the position of the cursive statement on the screen of the device. In that case the coding would

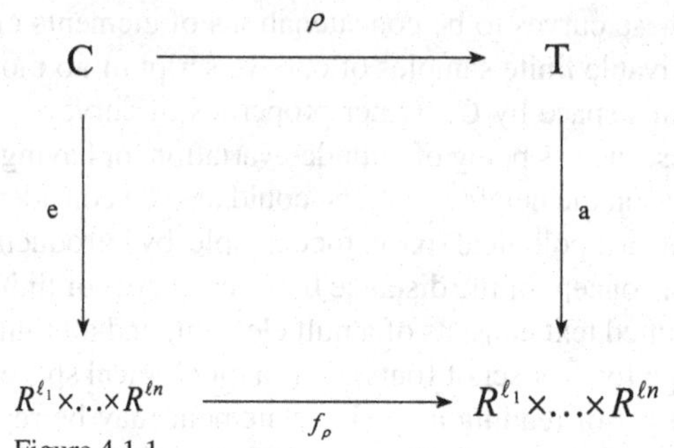

Figure 4.1.1.

not be unique unless the positioning of the cursive sample is standardized. We may either assume that this is the case, or we may define a set of transformations in the plane that leave the cursive sample invariant except for position and define the encoding to be the same for any element of the equivalence class so generated. Evaluating this equivalence relation is something that humans do regularly in stabilizing the visual field; it is a complex task for a machine.) Furthermore, the function, a in the diagram, is an encoding of T in $\mathfrak{R}^{l_1} \times \cdots \times \mathfrak{R}^{l_n}$. The ASCII code for alphanumeric characters is an example. (Here the null element of T is mapped to any element of $\mathfrak{R}^{l_1} \times \cdots \times \mathfrak{R}^{l_n}$ that is not the image of any character.) The inverse of the encoding a, performed by a device such as a printer, would produce the final result, which is the translation of the cursive writing sample into a printed writing sample.

If the computer cannot read a cursive writing sample in one step, then the function f_ρ would not be elementary for that computer; that is, it would not be in the set $\mathcal{F}$ consisting of the operations that are elementary for that computer. There would have to be a program written that computes f_ρ from the inputs using the operations that are elementary for that computer system.

The computation may be represented by an (r, d) network with modules from the class $\mathcal{F}$, which computes f_ρ. The complexity of f_ρ is likely to be very high, if indeed that function is at all computable relative to the modules in $\mathcal{F}$. If, for instance, the elementary operations consist of the arithmetic and logical operations, then a program that can read handwriting is likely to be long and involved, and the time required to compute f_ρ is likely to be long.

Next consider a person reading the cursive writing sample. The fact that a person can read cursive script may be expressed by saying that the evaluation of the function ρ is an elementary operation for that person. That is, the person does it "immediately" or "directly" without any apparent intermediate steps, taking only a small (unit) interval of time per unit length of curve. Another way to say this is that we do not analyze the process into steps internal to the reader.

Although the function ρ is clearly a representation of the act of reading cursive writing, it is not in itself a useful model that meets the criteria stated above; it does not yet connect with any other model of computation, nor does there appear to be a way to use it in the analysis of economic models.

In contrast, in modeling a person reading handwriting, we may consider the function ρ to be equivalent to the composition

$$(\sharp)\quad a^{-1} \circ f_\rho \circ e \equiv \rho$$

in Figure 4.1.1. To say that a person can evaluate ρ in one step can be interpreted as saying that the composition ($\sharp$) can be evaluated in one computational step. This amounts to saying that the function f_ρ cannot take more than one step. Hence it may be included as an elementary operation, that is, a member of $\mathcal{F}$, in any application of the model in which a human being capable of reading cursive writing is among the computational resources. For example, at the local drug store there is a pharmacist who reads the prescription form given to her by the customer, a form written by a physician in long hand. The pharmacist enters the prescription and other relevant information into a desktop computer by typing it on the keyboard. The computer processes this input according to its internal program, a computation representable by an (r, d) network. The act of translating a unit length of the handwritten prescription into type keys is elementary, and in the (r, d) network model it is formally seamless with the rest of the computation.

Note that the time required by a human being to execute an elementary operation is generally not the same as the time required by a machine to execute one of its elementary operations. Therefore the translation of delay in terms of the number of computational steps is done by way of a linear function that gives different weights to steps performed by a human being and steps performed by a machine.

We now take up an example in which the interaction of human and machine is more nearly typical of interactive computations done by economists and other scientists.

4.1.2. Example 2: Chernoff Faces

Human beings are good at seeing patterns. The ability to see patterns seems to depend on the structure and functioning of the human visual apparatus. Consequently, this ability applies to patterns in the space, or space–time, the environment in which the visual system evolved, that is, in at most three or four dimensions. In contrast, situations arise in which we would like to detect patterns in high-dimensional data, say observations represented by points in $\Re^k$, when k is a positive integer much larger than 4. Computers are good at handling data of high dimensionality. Although there are algorithmic processes, such as discriminant analysis or cluster analysis, for detecting patterns or regularities in high-dimensional data, we do not have algorithms for recognizing patterns, particularly subtle ones, that do as well as humans when restricted to low dimensions. Therefore, the idea of combining the power of computers to manipulate data with the ability of humans to see patterns is appealing. Indeed, the practice of making graphical representations of data as a way of bringing human cognitive abilities to bear predates the electronic computer, and it is widely used in physical, biological, and social sciences and mathematics, as well as in business.

Chernoff (1973) introduced the idea of combining human beings and computers to detect patterns in a sample of observations of a relatively large number of variables. Specifically, he introduced the graphical representation of multidimensional data as cartoon faces drawn in two dimensions and illustrated its use by two examples. These are (1) a set of eight measurements made on each of 87 fossils, and (2) a set of 53 observations of 12 variables taken from the mineral analysis of a 4,500 ft. (~1370 m) core drilled from a Colorado mountainside. The data are encoded as faces by a program that provides for up to 18 parameters that govern 18 features of a face. For example, one variable determines the horizontal distance between the eyes; another determines the height of the eyes; another determines the curvature of the arc that forms the mouth, and so on. If the number of variables observed is $k < 18$, then $18 - k$ variables are fixed at some value and the remaining k variables determine the variable features of a face for each point observed. The computer prints out the set of faces, and a human being looks for a pattern in that set. In the example with measurements made on fossils, the pattern sought was a classification of the fossils into groups of similar ones. In the second example, the observations were assumed to be generated by a multivariate stochastic process, and the problem was to detect a point in the time series of observations at which the process changed character.

Let

$$S \subset \Re^k, \qquad S = x^1, \ldots, x^n$$

be the sample of n observations, each a k-dimensional point. Let $\overline{\eta} : \Re^k \to \Re^2$ be a correspondence, where $\overline{\eta}(x^i)$ is the subset of $\Re^2$ that constitutes the visual image encoding the observation x^i. Set $\eta(x^1, \ldots, x^n) = (y^1, \ldots, y^n)$, where $y^i = \overline{\eta}(x^i)$. (It is implicit in this notation that distinct points of S are assumed to be mapped to distinct subsets of $\Re^2$.) Thus, in Chernoff's first example, $k = 8$, x^i is the vector of eight measurements made on the ith fossil, and y^i is the cartoon face that encodes those measurements. Because the problem is to classify the fossils, we seek a partition of the set S, or correspondingly a partition of the set $y^1, \ldots, y^n$. Because S has n elements, the number of nonempty subsets in a partition of S, and *a fortiori* in a partition of Y, is at most n. Therefore a partition of S can be represented by characteristic functions as follows. Let $\xi : S \to \{0, 1\}^n$, where $\xi = (\xi_1, \ldots, \xi_n)$, and $\xi_i : S \to \{0, 1\}$, and define $Q_i = \{x \in S | \xi_i(x) = 1\} = \xi_i^{-1}(1) \subset S$. Then $Q = Q_1, \ldots, Q_n$ is a partition of S, where, possibly after a renumbering of the characteristic functions, Q_i is the ith nonempty subset defined by ξ. Let Y denote the set of all possible n tuples

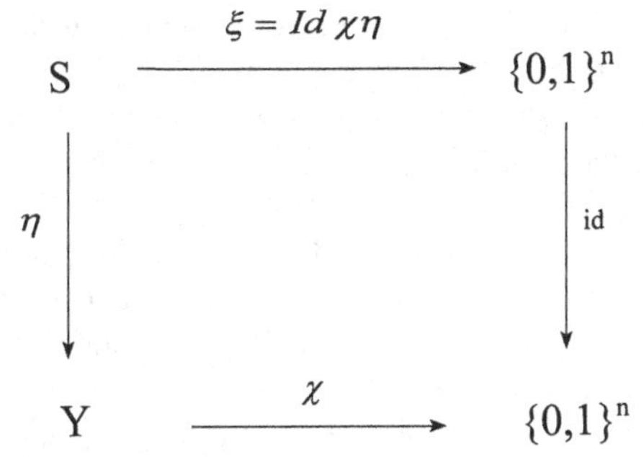

Figure 4.1.2.

of faces. Then, a partition $P = \{P_1, \ldots, P_r\}$ of Y is defined by characteristic functions

$$\chi : Y \to \{0, 1\}^n,$$

where

$$\chi = (\chi_1, \ldots, \chi_n), \quad \chi_i : Y \to \{0, 1\},$$
$$P_i = \{y \in Y | \chi_i(y) = 1\} = {\chi_i}^{-1}(1) \subset Y.$$

Suppose a machine were to execute an algorithm, such as a cluster analysis of S. It would compute a (vectorial) characteristic function, ξ, using some class of elementary operations $\mathcal{F}$ in a computation representable by an $\mathcal{F}$ network. In contrast, a human being looking at the set Y of faces encoding S would compute χ directly. In that case the resulting partition P of Y could be "lifted" to a partition of S by using encoding functions as in Figure 4.1.2. The composition of encoding functions with the mapping χ would be incorporated into the set $\mathcal{F}$ of elementary operations for the computing device that includes the machine and the human being.

For our purpose here, Chernoff's second example differs from the first only in that the sets S and Y are ordered according to the time sequence of the observations and the functions ξ and χ are step functions, with the step at the point at which the stochastic process is judged to change character.

4.2. DECENTRALIZED MECHANISMS

An important motivation for developing the network model of computing is to use it to analyze the computational tasks carried out by economic mechanisms. In particular we wish to study the trade-offs, if any, between the communications requirements and the computational requirements of achieving a given economic performance by a decentralized mechanism. There are, of course, many different mechanisms, and for each there are many computational tasks that could be studied. A particular case is that of a static decentralized mechanism that realizes the Walrasian performance function. In Section 4.3 we apply the network model to analyze an example of this kind, that is, a two-person two-good exchange economy. In this section we provide background for the analysis carried out in Section 4.3, and we define some concepts needed in order to make the model applicable to that and similar examples. The general set-up studied is as follows. There are n agents, $1, \ldots, n$. Each agent has environmental characteristics denoted e^i; the set of possible environments for agent i is E^i. The joint environment $e = (e^1, \ldots, e^n)$ is by assumption an element of $E = E^1 \times \cdots \times E^n$. It is also assumed that agent i initially knows his or her characteristic e^i, and that is all the agent knows directly about the joint environment e. Let A denote the space of joint actions or outcomes. In the case of an exchange environment, these are trades or allocations. There is a function $F : E \to A$ that expresses the goals of economic activity. In our example, $F(e)$ is the (unique) Walrasian trade when the environment is $e \in E$. We consider mechanisms

$$\pi = (\mu, M, h),$$

where

$$\mu : E \to M$$

is a privacy-preserving correspondence, called the message correspondence, M is the message space of the mechanism, and

$$h : M \to A$$

is a function with the property that h is constant on the sets $\mu(e)$ for all e in E.[1] The function h is the outcome function of the mechanism. The mechanism π realizes F on E if, for all $e \in E$,

$$h[\mu(e)] = F(e).$$

The message correspondence μ is privacy preserving if, for each $i = 1, \ldots, n$, there exist correspondences $\mu^i : E^i \to M$ such that

$$\mu(e) = \cap_i \mu^i(e^i).$$

The requirement that μ preserve privacy is that the message of an agent can depend only on that agent's environmental component and on the messages received from other agents. Such a mechanism μ can be given directly, or it can be regarded as the equilibrium form of a dynamic message-exchange process in which the agents exchange messages taken from the space

$$M = M^1 \times \cdots \times M^n$$

[1] More generally, F can be a correspondence, in which case the definition of realizing F must be modified, as in Hurwicz (1986).

according to prescribed rules

$$f^i : M \times E^i \to M^i,$$

where

$$f^i[m(t), e^i] = m^i(t+1),$$

for $i = 1, \ldots, n$ and $t = 1, 2, \ldots,$. The initial message $m(0)$ is given.[2] The stationary messages defined by this system of difference equations are given by

$$0 = g^i(m, e^i) = f^i(m, e^i) - m^i,$$

for all $i = 1, \ldots, n$. We define

$$\mu^i(e^i) = \{m \in M | g^i(m, e^i) = 0\}.$$

We shall focus attention on mechanisms in equilibrium form. Even when abstracting from the dynamics of message exchange, several different computational tasks can be distinguished. One interpretation of decentralized mechanisms in equilibrium form is the verification scenario. In this scenario, a candidate equilibrium message $m \in M$ is "posted" and seen by each agent. Each agent i separately checks the message to see whether it satisfies his or her equilibrium condition. If it does, agent i says "Yes"; if not, agent i says "No". If all agents say "Yes" to a given message, then it is verified to be an equilibrium message. That is, there are individual verifier functions, V^i, for $i = 1, \ldots, n$,

$$V^i(m, e^i) = \begin{cases} 1 & \text{if } g^i(m, e^i) = 0 \\ 0 & \text{otherwise} \end{cases},$$

and a verification function

$$V : \{0, 1\}^n \to [0, 1]$$

given by

$$V(x) = \frac{1}{n} \sum_i x^i,$$

where

$$x^i = V^i(m, e^i), \qquad i = 1, \ldots, n,$$

and $x = (x^1, \ldots, x^n)$. The computational tasks involved in this are (1) to determine whether $g^i(m, e^i) = 0$, for each i, given m; (2) to evaluate V; and (3) to evaluate h. Presumably the V^i's are computed by the individual agents, and the function V by some institution, perhaps personified by an additional agent. In this scenario the origin of the posted message is not considered; nor are the verifying messages (the values of V^i) counted in the message space.

[2] Here privacy preservation is a property of the functions f^i.

Another interpretation is that each agent i transmits the subset $\mu^i(e^i)$ to a central institution that finds the equilibrium, for example, clears the market. Finding equilibrium is most naturally addressed in a dynamic setting, but because much of the research on message space size has been done in the context of equilibrium mechanisms, and because our objective is to illustrate the application of the network model to mechanisms, it is not unnatural to begin by studying trade-offs between communication and computational complexity in that setting. Thus, we adopt the second interpretation of the equilibrium model, one in which the equilibrium is computed from the individual message correspondences. This may be thought of as an iterative dynamic process that finds the equilibrium in one step.

In this interpretation, the computational task is to compute the set $\mu(e)$ from the sets E^i and to evaluate the outcome function h. If we are to model this computation by networks, we must confront the fact that inputs to such a network must be d-dimensional Euclidean vectors.[3] The computational task is then to compute the set $\mu(e)$ and to compute the function h.

The computations of the equilibrium message correspondence and of the outcome function are related. It is possible to shift the burden of computation between them by changing coordinates in the message space. We make the following simplifying assumptions on the mechanisms considered, in effect combining these two tasks.

Assumption 4.2.1. The set M is a p-dimensional submanifold of a Euclidean space, and the sets E^i are Euclidean spaces of dimension q^i, so that E is a Euclidean space of dimension $q = \sum q^i$.

Assumption 4.2.2. First, the message correspondence m is privacy preserving and single valued. Second, the outcome function h is a projection onto a submanifold of M.

We restrict attention to mechanisms satisfying Assumptions 4.2.1 and 4.2.2. Given a goal or performance standard $F : E \to A$, we may consider the class of mechanisms that realize F. For each such mechanism there are two indicators or measures of informational requirements, namely, the dimension, m, of the message space M of the mechanism, and the time, t, required to compute the equilibrium message $\mu(e)$ in M. By Assumption 4.2.2 the time to compute the outcome function is already incorporated in the computation of $\mu(e)$. Thus, each mechanism realizing F and satisfying Assumptions 4.2.1 and 4.2.2 has associated to it a point, (m, t) (with integer coordinates), in $\Re^2$. We

[3] A more general framework is to allow for encoding the message space, the environment space, and the outcome space by real-valued functions, using Definition 4.1.1. We do not include that process here, but assume that it has been carried out, if needed.

may refer to the set of points so defined as the informational image of the set of mechanisms realizing F and satisfying Assumptions 4.2.1 and 4.2.2. The efficient frontier of this informational image describes the available trade-offs between communication and computation in realising F.

4.3. THE EDGEWORTH BOX ECONOMY

In this section we study the efficient frontier, introduced in Section 4.2, for a particular performance function. We consider the case of two agents, each with a two-dimensional parameter space (environment) with, say, coordinates (x, z) for agent 1 and (x', z') for agent 2. The (real-valued) goal function is given by

$$Q(x, z, x', z') = (z - z')/(x - x').$$

Under the assumptions stated next the goal function $Q(x, z, x', z')$ is the Walrasian one for the case of two agents trading two goods. Let (Y, Z) denote the holdings of the two goods. We assume utilities to be quadratic in Y and linear in Z. The initial endowments of the two goods are $w^i(X)$ and $w^i(Y)$, with $i = 1, 2$.

$$u^i(x, z) = \alpha^i Y^i + {}^1\!/\!_2\, \beta^i (Y^i)^2 + Z^i, \qquad i = 1, 2,$$
$$y^i = Y^i - w^i(Y) = (\text{net trade of } i\text{th agent});$$
$$y^1 + y^2 = 0.$$

The equilibrium conditions are as follows.

$$u^i = \alpha^i[y^i + w^i(Y)] + {}^1\!/\!_2\, \beta^i[y^i + w^i(Y)]^2 + Z^i, \qquad i = 1, 2,$$
$$du^i/dy^i = \alpha^i + \beta^i[y^i + w^i(Y)] = p \text{ (the price)}, \qquad i = 1, 2.$$

Let

$$y^1 = y, \quad y^2 = -y,$$

and

$$\alpha^1 + \beta^1[y + w^2(Y)] = p,$$
$$\alpha^2 + \beta^2[-y + w^2(Y)] = p.$$

Let

$$\gamma^i = \alpha^i + \beta^i w^i(Y), \qquad i = 1, 2.$$

Then the equilibrium conditions are written as

$$\gamma^1 + \beta^1 y = p,$$
$$\gamma^2 - \beta^2 y = p.$$

Let

$$(x, z) = (-\beta^1, \gamma^1), (x', z') = (\beta^2, \gamma^2).$$

Then

$$z - xy = z' - x'y$$

or

$$y = (z - z')/(x - x'),$$

which is our goal function. Hurwicz presented essentially the same derivation of this goal function, except for changes in sign, in Hurwicz et al. (1980).

We ask, how long does it take to compute the equilibrium message $\mu(x, z, x', z')$ of a privacy-preserving mechanism that realizes Q at an arbitrary parameter point (x, z, x', z') by using a $\mathcal{D}^2(2, 1)$ network? The question arises from the interpretation of a decentralized mechanism in equilibrium form as a one-step iterative process in which the outcome function is assumed to be a projection (see Assumption 4.2.2 in Section 4.2 and the discussion that precedes it). In this section, no coordinate changes are allowed either in the message space or in the agents's parameter spaces. This restriction makes the analysis of the computation particularly easy. We began by analyzing the mechanism that has as its message correspondence

$$\mu(x, z, x', z') = \left[\frac{(z - z')}{(x - x')}, \frac{(xz' - x'z)}{(x - x')}\right].$$

It is clear that the computation of μ can be done in three units of time by $\mathcal{D}(2, 1)$ networks. The network shown in Figure 4.3.1 computes Q in two units of time, and the network shown in Figure 4.3.2 computes P in three units of time. Therefore, the question of the time required to compute μ is reduced to whether there is a $\mathcal{D}^2(2, 1)$ network $\mathcal{N}$ that computes μ in two units of time. Such a network $\mathcal{N}$ would have the form displayed in Figure 4.3.3, where A, B, C, D, E, and F are real C^2 functions and x, y, z, and w are real variables.

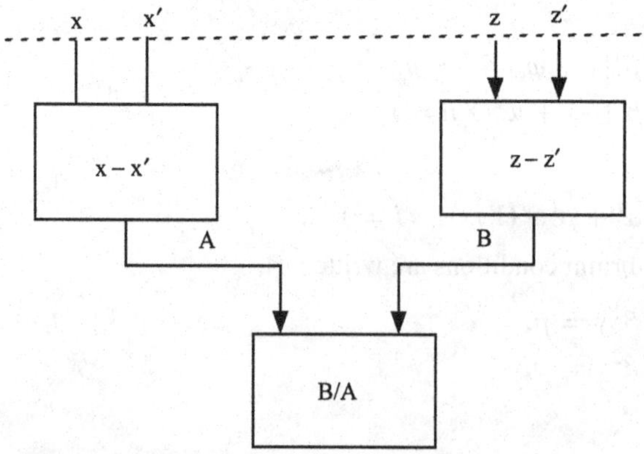

Figure 4.3.1.

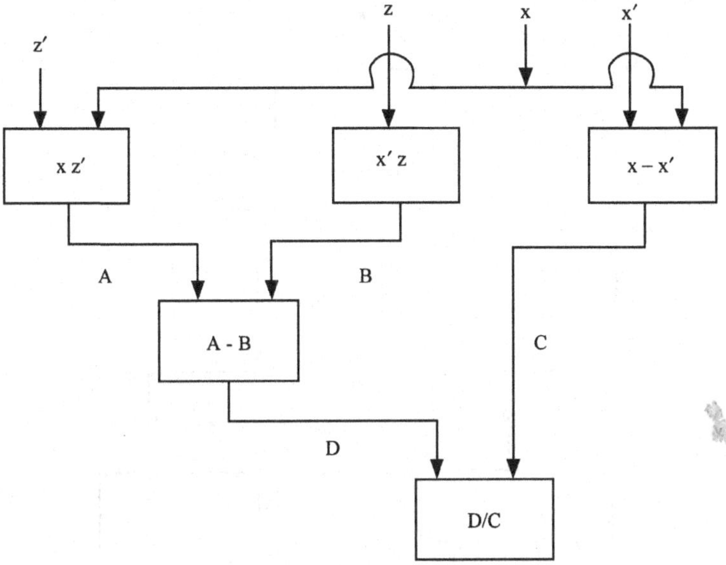

Figure 4.3.2.

Theorem B.2.4 in Appendix B states necessary conditions that a C^2 function $F(x, y, z, w)$ can be written in the form

$$F(x, y, z, w) = C[A(x, y), B(z, w)].$$

We use those conditions to prove that no $\mathcal{D}(2, 1)$ network can compute both components of μ in two units of time.

Notation. *If $T = [f_{ij}(x_1, \ldots, x_n)]$ is a matrix of functions of real variables $(x_1, \ldots, x_n)$, and if $a = (a_1, \ldots, a_n)$ is an n tuple of real numbers, then $T(a)$ denotes the matrix with entries $[f_{ij}(a)]$.*

Theorem B.2.4 states that the time required to compute an encoded version of the message $\mu(x, z, x', z')$ is at least three units of time.

Theorem 4.3.1. *Suppose that X_1 and X_2 are Euclidean spaces of dimension 2 with coordinates (x, z) and (x', z'), respectively. Suppose that Q is the goal function*

$$Q(x, z, x', z') = (z - z')/(x - x'). \tag{4.3.1}$$

Suppose that

$$P(x, z, x', z') = (xz' - x'z)/(x - x'); \tag{4.3.2}$$

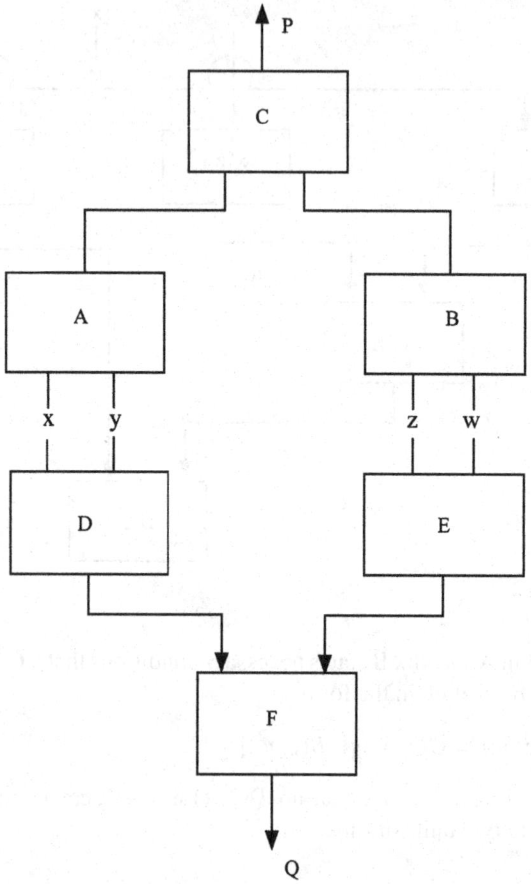

Figure 4.3.3.

suppose that M is the Euclidean space $\Re^2$ with coordinates m^1, m^2; and suppose that h is the projection $h(m^1, m^2) = m^1$. Assume that Q is realized by a mechanism (μ, M, h) where

$$\mu(x, z, x', z') = (Q, P).$$

If $\mathcal{N}$ is a $\mathcal{D}^2(2, 1)$ network that computes an encoded version of μ, where the encodings $g^1 : X_1 \to \Re^2$ and $g^2 : X_2 \to \Re^2$ are the identity functions, then network $\mathcal{N}$ requires three units of time for the computation.

Proof of Theorem 4.3.1. A coordinate change in each X_i that is a translation does not effect computation time. Indeed, suppose that the original network computes a function in time t, and that the computation is represented by a directed graph that is a tree. Suppose that a pair of input vertices have associated variables r and s, and that these variables are connected by edges e_1 and e_2, respectively, to a module $v(e_1, e_2)$. Let the variables r and s be translated to $r' = r + a$ and $s' = s + b$. Then we construct a new network, using the same tree as the original, and we replace the module $v(e_1, e_2)$ by the module $V(e_1, e_2) = g(e_1 - a, e_2 - b)$. If all the modules in the tree other than those connected to input vertices are unchanged, the new network computes the same function as the original network and the new network using the translated coordinates carries out the computation in the same time as the original.

Without loss of generality, we use the coordinates $R = x - 1$, $T = x' + 1$, $S = z$, and $U = z'$. In these coordinates,

$$Q = (S - U)/(2 + R - T),$$
$$P = (S + U + RU - ST)/(2 + R - T).$$

The network in Figure 4.3.4 computes Q in time 2 and the network in Figure 4.3.5 computes P in time 3 by using the inputs R, S, T, and U. In order for a network to compute P in time 3, we must be able to write

$$P(R, S, T, U) = C'[A'(S, T), B'(R, U)],$$

or

$$P(R, S, T, U) = C''[A''(R, T), B''(S, U)],$$

where A, A'', B'', B'', C', and C'' are $\mathcal{D}^2(2, 1)$ functions in the neighborhood of the origin of $\Re^2$. Theorem B.2.4 states that in order for A', B', and C' to

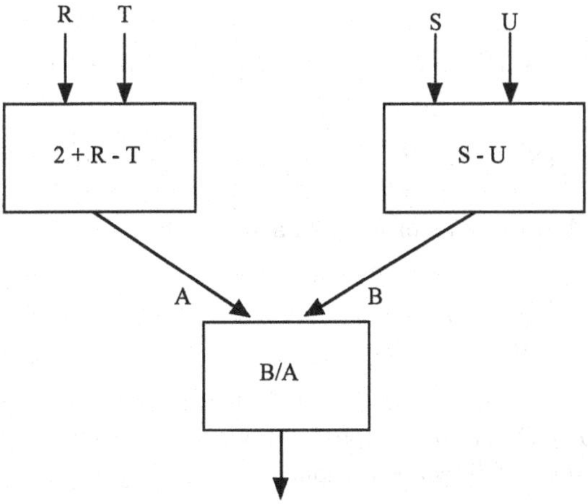

Figure 4.3.4.

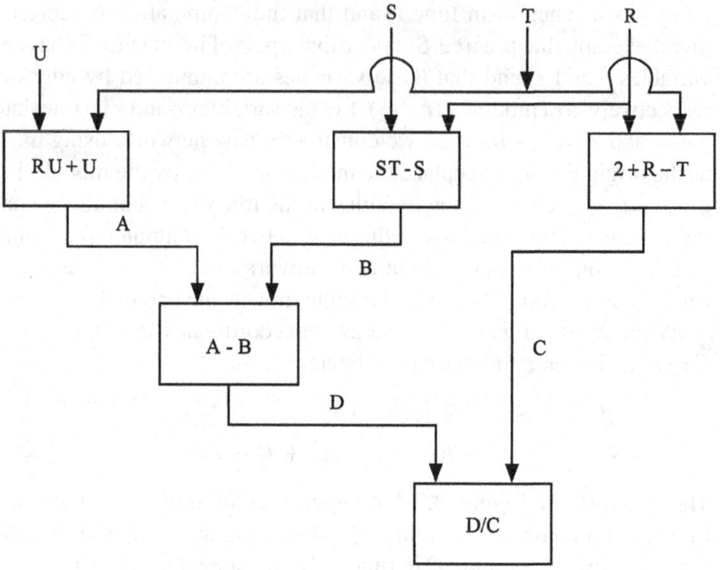

Figure 4.3.5.

exist, the matrix

$$W_1(0,0) = \begin{bmatrix} \frac{\partial P}{\partial S}(0,0) & \frac{\partial^2 P}{\partial R \partial S}(0,0) & \frac{\partial^2 P}{\partial S \partial U}(0,0) \\ \frac{\partial P}{\partial T}(0,0) & \frac{\partial^2 P}{\partial R \partial T}(0,0) & \frac{\partial^2 P}{\partial U \partial T}(0,0) \end{bmatrix}$$

must have a rank of at most 1.

However,

$$P = (S + U + RU - TS)\left[\sum_{j=0}^{\infty}(-1)^j\left(\frac{1}{2}\right)^{j+1}(T-R)^j\right]$$

$$= \left(\frac{1}{2}\right)\left[(S + U + RU - TS) + \frac{(S+U)(T-R)}{2}\right] + \theta,$$

where θ is a sum of monomials in R, S, T, and U with a degree of at least 3. But then,

$$W_1(0,0) = \begin{bmatrix} 1/2 & -1/4 & 0 \\ 0 & 0 & 1/4 \end{bmatrix}$$

has rank 2. Thus the necessary condition of Theorem B.2.4 that $W_1(0,0)$ have a rank of at most 1 if P is to be computed in two units of time by a $\mathcal{D}^2(2,1)$ network is not satisfied. If P can be computed in time 2 by a $\mathcal{D}(2,1)$ network, it must be the case that

$$P(R,S,T,U) = C''[A''(R,T), B''(S,U)].$$

However, in this case, again by Theorem B.2.4, the matrix

$$W_2(0,0) = \begin{bmatrix} \frac{\partial P}{\partial S}(0,0) & \frac{\partial^2 P}{\partial R \partial S}(0,0) & \frac{\partial^2 P}{\partial S \partial T}(0,0) \\ \frac{\partial P}{\partial U}(0,0) & \frac{\partial^2 P}{\partial R \partial U}(0,0) & \frac{\partial^2 P}{\partial T \partial U}(0,0) \end{bmatrix}$$

can have a rank of at most 1, but

$$W_2(0,0) = \begin{bmatrix} 1/2 & -1/4 & -1/4 \\ 1/2 & 1/4 & 1/4 \end{bmatrix}$$

has rank 2. Therefore, P cannot be computed in less than three units of time. The network given in Figure 4.3.5 computes P in three units of time from the inputs R, S, T, and U. □

4.3.1. Linear Coordinate Changes in the Message Space

We examine the task of computing the function

$$\mu(x, z, x', z') = (Q, P)$$

when linear coordinate changes are allowed in the message space $M = \Re^2$. We first show that there is no linear change of coordinates in the message space that reduces the time required for a network to compute μ.

Lemma 4.3.1. *Suppose that X_1 and X_2 are Euclidean spaces of dimension 2 with coordinates (x, z) and (x', z'), respectively. Suppose that Q is the goal function*

$$Q(x, z, x', z') = (z - z')/(x - x').$$

and that

$$P(x, z, x', z') = (xz' - x'z)/(x - x').$$

Suppose that M is the Euclidean space $\Re^2$ with coordinates m^1 and m^2, and assume that Q is realized by the mechanism (μ', M, h') where

$$\mu'(x, z, x', z') = (Q, aP + bQ),$$

where $b \in \Re$ and $a \neq 0$. If N' is a $\mathcal{D}^2(2, 1)$ network that computes an encoded version of μ', where the encodings $g^i : X_i \to \Re^2$ are identity functions, then the network N' requires at least three units of time for the computation.

Proof of Lemma 4.3.2. In order for the network N' to compute $P' = Q + aP$ in two units of time, it must be possible to write

$$P'(R, S, T, U) = C'[A'(S, T), B'(R, U)]$$

or

$$P'(R, S, T, U) = C''[A''(R, T), B''(S, U)],$$

where A', A'', B', B'', C', and C'' are $\mathcal{D}^2(2, 1)$ functions in a neighborhood of the origin of $\Re^2$. Set

$$Y_1 = \begin{bmatrix} \frac{\partial P'}{\partial S} & \frac{\partial^2 P'}{\partial R \partial S} & \frac{\partial^2 P'}{\partial S \partial U} \\ \frac{\partial P'}{\partial T} & \frac{\partial^2 P'}{\partial R \partial T} & \frac{\partial^2 P'}{\partial T \partial u} \end{bmatrix}.$$

If

$$P'(R, S, T, U) = C'[A'(S, T), B'(R, U)],$$

then Y_1 must have a rank of at most 1 in a neighborhood of the origin. However,

$$\left(\frac{\partial^2 P'}{\partial R \partial S}\right)\left(\frac{\partial^2 P'}{\partial R \partial U}\right) - \left(\frac{\partial^2 P'}{\partial R \partial T}\right)\left(\frac{\partial^2 P'}{\partial T \partial U}\right) = \frac{(a + aR - b)(-a - b + aT)}{(2 + R - T)^2}.$$

Because $a \neq 0$, this expression does not vanish identically in the neighborhood of the origin. Therefore,

$$P' = C'[A'(S, T), B'(R, U)].$$

If P' can be computed in two units of time, then

$$P'(R, S, T, U) = C''[A''(R, T), B''(S, U)].$$

Set

$$Y_2 = \begin{bmatrix} \frac{\partial P}{\partial S} & \frac{\partial^2 P}{\partial R \partial S} & \frac{\partial^2 P}{\partial S \partial T} \\ \frac{\partial P}{\partial U} & \frac{\partial^2 P}{\partial R \partial U} & \frac{\partial^2 P}{\partial T \partial U} \end{bmatrix}.$$

If $P'(R, S, T, U) = C''[A''(R, T), B''(S, U)]$, then the determinant formed by the last two columns of Y_2 must be zero. However, we have already seen, in the discussion of Y_1, that the determinant is not zero. Therefore, it follows that no linear change of coordinates in the message space M can reduce the time required to compute μ to two units of time. □

4.3.2. Linear Coordinate Changes in Parameter Spaces

If the agents are allowed to make linear changes of coordinates in their parameter spaces, the problem is considerably more complicated algebraically. Assume that the encoding functions g^i are, as in Theorem 4.3.1, identity functions. Thus a network that computes P and Q must carry out the computation by using the coordinates that the agents send to it. Assume that the first agent, whose coordinates are R and S, introduces new coordinates $A_1 = (r, s)$ given by the linear transformation

$$(A_1): R = ar + bs, \quad S = cr + ds,$$

whereas the second agent uses new coordinates (t, u) given by

$$(A_2) : T = et + fu, \quad U = gt + hu.$$

The elements a, b, c, d, e, f, g, and h are real numbers and the determinants

$$\begin{vmatrix} a & b \\ c & d \end{vmatrix}, \qquad \begin{vmatrix} e & f \\ g & h \end{vmatrix}$$

are both nonzero. The following lemma uses this notation and shows that the new coordinates A_1 and A_2 cannot be chosen to decrease the time required to compute μ. The function Q plays no role in this result.

Lemma 4.3.2. *There is no choice of coordinates A_1 and A_2 for the parameter spaces X_1 and X_2 such that P can be computed in less that three units of time if the encoding functions used to compute an encoded version of P are identity functions.*

The proof, which amounts to no more than a tedious computation, can be found in the proof of Lemma 7.2 in Mount and Reiter (1990).

4.4. THE EFFICIENT FRONTIER

We examine two goal functions and analyze the efficient frontier for each. The two goal functions are each defined on the product of two two-dimensional Euclidean spaces. One goal function is the function $I : \mathfrak{R}^2 \times \mathfrak{R}^2 \to \mathfrak{R}$, given by

$$I(u, v) = uv = I[(x, z), (x', z')] = xx' + zz',$$

which is the inner product. The second goal function is the function

$$Q = (z - z')/(x - x').$$

In the case of the function I, there is a mechanism that realizes I whose message space is of minimum dimension and whose outcome function is a projection. We show that I can be computed in minimum time. In the case of the function Q, we show that if the dimension of the message space is allowed to increase, then the time required to compute the message correspondence μ, of the mechanism π in Section 4.2, can be reduced to two units of time.

We first consider the function I. It is well known (see Hurwicz et al., 1980) that the parameter transfer mechanism (with message space of dimension 3) has a message space of minimum dimension for mechanisms that realize I.

Suppose that $X = \mathfrak{R}^2$, $Y = \mathfrak{R}^2$, that X has coordinates (x, z), and that Y has coordinates (x', z'). Suppose that the message space $\mathfrak{R}^3$ has coordinates (A, B, C). Then set

$$I(x, z, x', z') = xx' + zz'.$$

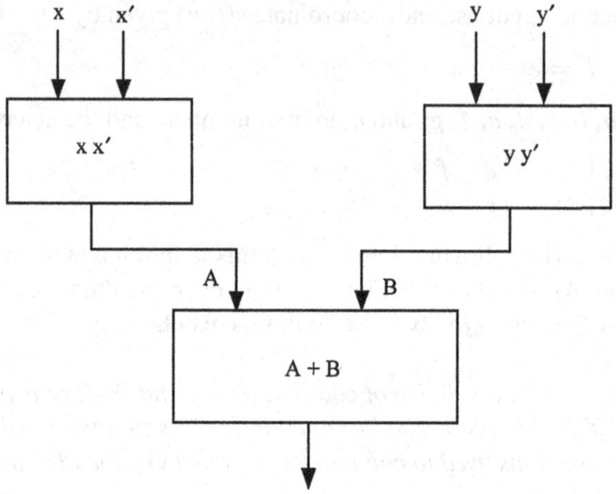

Figure 4.4.1.

A message correspondence for parameter transfer is given by the function

$$\nu(x, z, x', z') = [x, z, I(x, z; x', z')].$$

The agent with parameter space X uses the message correspondence

$$\nu^1(x, z) = \{(x, z, C) : C \in \Re\},$$

whereas the agent with parameter space Y uses the correspondence

$$\nu^2(x', z') = \{(A, B, C) : A, B \in \Re,\ C = I(A, B, x', z')\}.$$

A network that computes the correspondence ν need only compute the function $I(x, z, x, z')$ from the parameters x, z, x', and z'. This function I is a function of four variables that can be computed in two units of time by the network given in Figure 4.4.1. Thus, among mechanisms that realize I with outcome functions that are projections, no increase in the size of the message space will decrease the amount of computing required, because each such computation of a message correspondence must also compute I. It follows that the efficient frontier for the function I is given by the diagram in Figure 4.4.2.

We now turn to the function Q. Note that the function Q can be realized by the parameter transfer mechanism with $\Re^3$ as the message space. In that case, agent 1 has the individual message correspondence

$$\nu^1(x, z) = \{(X, Y, Z) : X = x, Y = z\},$$

whereas agent 2 uses the individual message correspondence

$$\nu^2(x', z') = \{(X, Y, Z) : Z = (Y - z')/(X - x')\}.$$

The message correspondence for the mechanism is then

$$\nu(x, z; x', z') = [x, z, (z - z')/(x - x')].$$

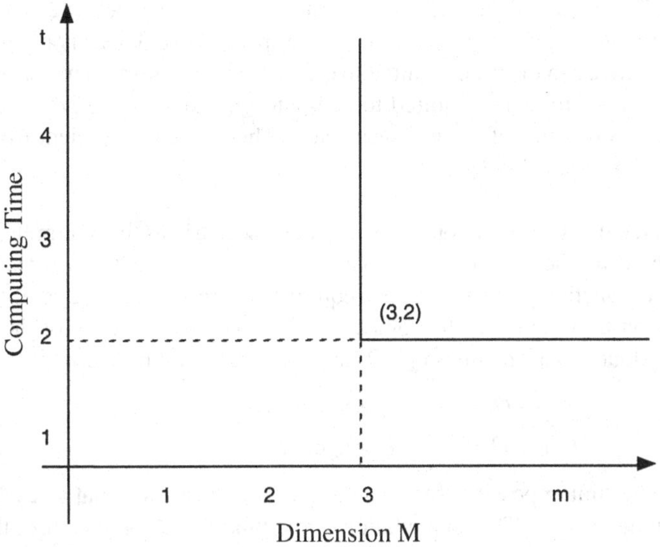

Figure 4.4.2.

Computing the function $(z - z')/(x - x')$, which is the only computation needed, requires two units of time when the network that is given in Figure 4.4.1 is used. Thus we see that increasing the dimension of the message space from 2 to 3 permits a decrease in the time required to compute the message correspondence from three units of time to two units of time. Because the minimum message space for Q is 2, the efficient frontier contains the points $a = (2, 3)$ and $b = (3, 2)$ shown in Figure 4.4.3. Because the minimum dimension for a message space of a privacy-preserving mechanism that realizes Q is known

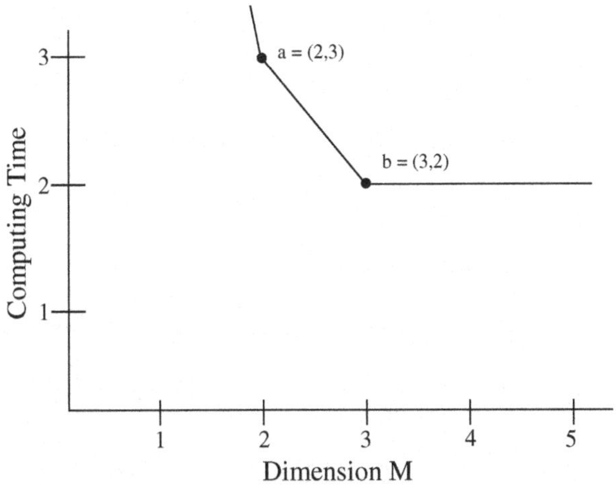

Figure 4.4.3.

to be 2, decreasing the dimension of the message space below 2 is impossible. Increasing the dimension of the message space above 3 does not yield any further decrease in the time required to compute the equilibrium message, because two units of time are required to compute Q, and Q is the projection of one of the coordinates of the message space. Therefore, the efficient frontier is as shown in Figure 4.4.3.

Remark 4.4.1. If we adopt the verification scenario as the interpretation of the mechanism, the computational task is that (1) each agent computes his or her verifier function given a candidate equilibrium message, and (2) the verification function is computed. The computing time required for each of the agents to verify that a pair of values (Q, P) satisfies the equilibrium conditions

$$(i)\ P + xQ = z \qquad \text{(for agent 1)}$$

$$(ii)\ P + x'Q = z' \qquad \text{(for agent 2)}$$

is the minimum possible for a function of four variables; that is, each requires two units of time. The computation of the function (Q, P) requires three units of time.

Although the computational burden of computing the message $(x, z; x', z')$ is decreased by increasing the dimension of the message space, this decrease is at the expense of an increased computational burden on the second agent. To check the equation $Z = (z - z')/(x - x')$, the agent must compute the function $Z - (z - z')/(x - x')$, and this is a function of five variables. The minimum computing time for such a function is $\text{Int}[\log_2(5)] = 3$. This increase in computing time for agents is a feature of all the mechanisms we have examined.

5 Applications to Games

5.1. BARGAINING GAMES

5.1.1. Bargaining Games with Quadratic Boundaries

In this section we continue the analysis and comparison of the computational complexity of functions. Recall that in some cases, for example, the case of two-person zero-sum games analyzed in Chapter 3, Section 3.1, Leontief's criteria give unambiguous comparisons of solution functions. The comparison of diagonal games and 3×3 matrix games of Chapter 3, Section 3.3 cannot be made by a direct application of the Leontief criteria. In that chapter an added restriction, the symmetrical computation restriction, is imposed on the networks that represent the computation. That restriction can be interpreted as a simplicity requirement on the structure of the network. With this restriction we are able to apply Leontief's criteria to obtain unambiguous comparisons of the solution functions for the two classes of games.

However, it remains the case that when the number of variables is small, without imposing additional restrictions, the methods of Chapter 3 can be used to distinguish between the computational complexities of members of only a small class of functions.

In this chapter we extend the applicability of Leontief's criteria by introducing another type of restriction on the networks that represent computations. As in the preceding chapters, we do this in the setting of examples. We seek to compare the complexities of two different solutions in a class of two-agent bargaining problems. Specifically, we compare the Nash solution and the Kalai–Smorodinsky solution. Direct application of Leontief's criteria to the payoff functions for the Nash and Kalai–Smorodinsky solutions is not decisive. We assume that the computations are carried out by $\mathcal{D}$ networks, and we impose a restriction on them that leads to an unambiguous comparison of their complexities. The restriction is, as we shall see, a natural one. The result is that the Nash solution is more complex than the Kalai–Smorodinsky solution in the class of bargaining problems we consider.

A bargaining problem consists of a pair $(\mathbf{F}, v)$, where $\mathbf{F}$ is a closed convex subset of $\Re^2$, $v = (v_1, v_2)$ is a point in $\Re^2$, and the set

$$\mathbf{F} \cap \{(x_1, x_2) \mid x_1 \geq v_1 \quad \text{and} \quad x_2 \geq v_2\}$$

is nonempty and bounded (see Myerson, 1991, p. 370).

We consider a class of bargaining problems such that the set $\mathbf{F}$ is the intersection of the first quadrant of $\Re^2$, denoted $\Re^2_+$, with the interior of an ellipse. The disagreement point v is in $\Re^2_+$ and in the interior of the ellipse. The class of problems we consider can be represented by four parameters, as follows. The general form of a quadratic equation in two variables is

$$A'x'^2 + B'x'y' + C'y'^2 + 2D'x' + 2E'y' + F' = 0.$$

We suppose that the bargainers are capable of multiplying by parameter values. Indeed, they can do so by using one unit of computing time, because a product is the value of a function of two variables. Assume the values A' and C' are positive. Replace the variable x' with $x/\sqrt{A'}$ and replace y' with $y/\sqrt{C'}$. Because the analysis of computation is easiest for us when parameters are chosen close to zero, we apply a translation and set

$$\sqrt{B'/A'} = B+1, \quad D'/\sqrt{A'} = C+1, \quad E'/\sqrt{C'} = D+1, \quad F' = -4(F+1).$$

The result is the equation

$$x^2 + (B+1)xy + y^2 + 2(C+1)x + 2(D+1)y - 4(F+1) = 0. \qquad (5.1.1)$$

Denote by $\mathbf{E}(B, C, D, F)$ the elliptic region in $\Re^2$ described by the inequality

$$x^2 + (B+1)xy + y^2 + 2(C+1)x + 2(D+1)y - 4(F+1) \leq 0.$$

We suppose that the values B, C, D, and F are close to zero. The set $\mathbf{E}(B, C, D, F)$ is a nonempty convex set close to the region in $\Re^2$ described by the inequality $x^2 + xy + y^2 + 2x + 2y \leq 4$. The boundary of this set, that is, the boundary of $\mathbf{E}(0, 0, 0, 0)$, is given by the equation

$$x^2 + xy + y^2 + 2x + 2y - 4 = 0. \qquad (5.1.2)$$

Set

$$\mathbf{F}(B, C, D, F) = \mathbf{E}(B, C, D, F) \cap \Re^{+2}.$$

The bargaining problems we examine are the pairs $[\mathbf{F}(B, C, D, F), (0, 0)]$. These are not too far removed from the general bargaining problem in which $\mathbf{F}$ is the interior of some generic ellipse and v is a point in the interior of the ellipse. In our case the disagreement point is the origin, because we presume that each change in disagreement point is absorbed in the translation terms

$2(C+1)x + 2(D+1)y$ of Equation (5.1.1). The parameters for the problem are the variables $B, C, D,$ and F.

The Nash solution maximizes the function xy on the boundary of the set $\mathbf{F}(B, C, D, F)$. With the restriction on the domain of the variables (B, C, D, F) we have imposed, that is, that they are close to zero, this reduces to maximizing xy on the intersection of the first quadrant and the ellipse with Equation (5.1.1).

The Kalai–Smorodinsky solution[1] to the bargaining problem is given as follows. Suppose the ellipse that is the boundary of the set $\mathbf{F}(B, C, D, F)$ intersects the x axis at $(x_0, 0)$ and intersects the y axis at the point $(0, y_0)$. The Kalai–Smorodinsky solution is the intersection of the line through the points $(0, 0)$ and (x_0, y_0) with the boundary of the set $\mathbf{F}(B, C, D, F)$. The Nash solution

$$[x_N(B, C, D, F), y_N(B, C, D, F)]$$

and the Kalai–Smorodinsky solution

$$[x_{\mathrm{KS}}(B, C, D, F), y_{\mathrm{KS}}(B, C, D, F)]$$

each are pairs of functions of the four parameters $B, C, D,$ and F. The problem we pose is to compare the computational complexity of the functions $x_N(B, C, D, F)$ and $x_{\mathrm{KS}}(B, C, D, F)$ in the neighborhood of the point

$$(B, C, D, F) = (0, 0, 0, 0).$$

5.1.2. The Kalai–Smorodinsky Solution for Quadratic Boundaries

It is a simple matter to check that for the parameter values $(0, 0, 0, 0)$, the Kalai–Smorodinsky solution and the Nash solution have values $x_{\mathrm{KS}} = y_{\mathrm{KS}} = x_N = y_N = 2/3$.

We first find the function x_{KS}. Set $s_C = x_0(B, C, D, F) = -(C+1) + \sqrt{(C+1)^2 + 4(F+1)}$, and set $s_D = y_0 = -(D+1) + \sqrt{(D+1)^2 + 4(F+1)}$. Then $x_{\mathrm{KS}}(B, C, D, F)$ is a solution of the quadratic equation

$$\left[1 + (B+1)\frac{s_D}{s_C} + \left(\frac{s_D}{s_C}\right)^2\right]x^2 + \left[2(C+1) + 2(D+1)\frac{s_D}{s_C}\right]x - 4(F+1) = 0.$$

If U and V are variables, then a solution $X(U, V)$ of the quadratic equation $X^2 + 2(U+1)X - V = 0$ is $[-(U+1) + \sqrt{(U+1)^2 + V}]$, which is a function of the two variables U and V. The solution $X(U, V)$ has a Taylor series expansion around the origin. The function $X(U, V)$ is nonsingular in the variables U and V at the origin; thus $X(U, V) \in \mathcal{D}$ and the function $X(U, V) - 1$ is in $\mathcal{D}_0$.

[1] This solution was proposed by Howard Raiffa in an unpublished report (Raiffa, 1951); it later appeared in published form in Raiffa (1953) and in Luce and Raiffa (1958, p. 136). Raiffa does not characterize his solution by axioms. However, Luce and Raiffa (1958) do remark that it satisfies all of Nash's axioms except for independence of irrelevant alternatives. Kalai and Smorodinsky do give an axiom system for the solution.

Set

$$S = \frac{s_D}{s_C}, \quad P = \frac{(1+C)+(D+1)S}{1+(B+1)S+S^2}, \quad Q = \frac{4(F+1)}{1+(B+1)S+S^2}.$$

The function $x_{\mathrm{KS}}(B, C, D, F)$ is the solution of the equation

$$x^2 + 2Px - Q = 0.$$

Thus

$$X_{\mathrm{KS}} = (-P + \sqrt{P^2 + Q}).$$

For values of the parameters B, C, D, and F close to zero, the expression $\sqrt{P^2 + Q}$ is close to 2/3, so the function $\sqrt{P^2 + Q}$ has a Taylor series expansion around the origin. It is awkward to write the expression for x_{KS} directly in terms of the parameters B, C, D, and F. As in the discussion of the function $\Pr G_1$ of Chapter 3, Section 3.3, we compute the matrix $CH(x_{\mathrm{KS}})_0$ that has rows indexed by the variables B, C, D, and F and that has columns indexed by x_{KS} and the variables B, C, D, and F. The entry in row B at column x_{KS} is the value of the partial derivative $\partial x_{\mathrm{KS}}/\partial B$ at the origin. The entry at row B and column C is the value at the origin of the second partial derivative $\partial^2 x_{\mathrm{KS}}/\partial B\, \partial C$. Therefore,

$$CH(x_{\mathrm{KS}})_0 =$$

$$\begin{array}{c} \\ B \\ C \\ D \\ F \end{array}
\begin{array}{c}
\begin{array}{ccccc} x_{\mathrm{KS}} & B & C & D & F \end{array} \\
\left[\begin{array}{ccccc}
-\frac{1}{18} & \frac{7}{432} & \frac{-45+29\sqrt{5}}{720(-1+\sqrt{5})} & \frac{-5+21\sqrt{5}}{720(-1+\sqrt{5})} & -\frac{1}{16} \\
\frac{15-7\sqrt{5}}{-30+30\sqrt{5}} & \frac{-45+29\sqrt{5}}{720(-1+\sqrt{5})} & \frac{2055-1069\sqrt{5}}{1800(-1+\sqrt{5})^2} & \frac{27+23\sqrt{5}}{360(-1+\sqrt{5})^2} & \frac{-365+159\sqrt{5}}{600(-1+\sqrt{5})^2} \\
\frac{5+3\sqrt{5}}{30-30\sqrt{5}} & \frac{-5+21\sqrt{5}}{720(-1+\sqrt{5})} & \frac{27+23\sqrt{5}}{360(-1+\sqrt{5})^2} & \frac{375-61\sqrt{5}}{1800(-1+\sqrt{5})^2} & \frac{85+9\sqrt{5}}{1200(-3+\sqrt{5})} \\
\frac{1}{2} & -\frac{1}{16} & \frac{-365+159\sqrt{5}}{600(-1+\sqrt{5})^2} & \frac{85+9\sqrt{5}}{1200(-3+\sqrt{5})} & \frac{-3}{16}
\end{array}\right]
\end{array}.$$

Let $\{\{X\}, \{Y\}\}$ be a partition of the variables $\{B, C, D, F\}$ into two sets of two elements each, and denote by $bh_{(X,Y)}(x_{\mathrm{KS}})_0$ the bordered Hessian $bh_{(X,Y)}(x_{\mathrm{KS}})$ evaluated at the origin. It is straightforward to read $bh_{(X,Y)}(X_{\mathrm{KS}})_0$ from $CH(x_{\mathrm{KS}})_0$. Note that the first partial derivatives of the function x_{KS} are all nonzero at the origin. Also note that for each partition $\{X, Y\}$ of the set of variables, either $bh_{(X,Y)}(x_{\mathrm{KS}})_0$ or $bh_{(Y,X)}(x_{\mathrm{KS}})_0$ has rank 2. Leontief's criteria tell us that at least three units of time are required to compute x_{KS}. The symmetrical computation assumption allows us to conclude something new about computation only if the result of computing a bordered Hessian is a matrix with a rank that is intermediate between a rank of 1 and the number of rows in the bordered Hessian. Thus, the symmetrical computation assumption yields no new information.

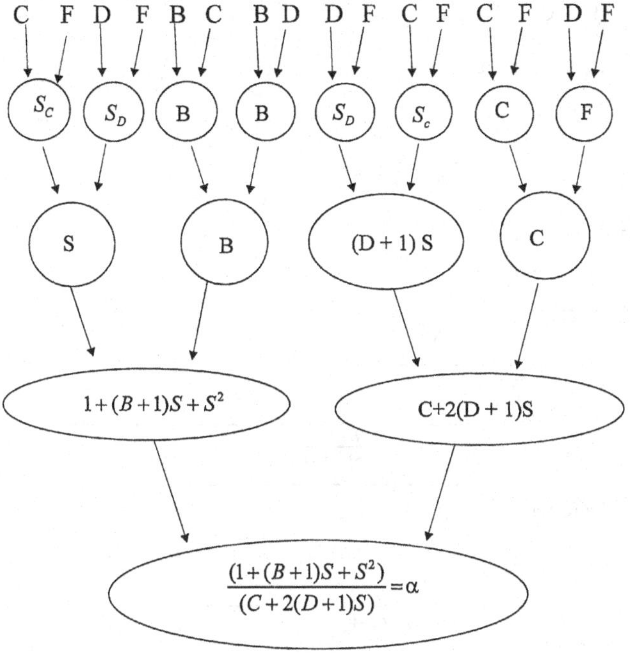

Figure 5.1.1.

However, we can build a $\mathcal{D}$ network $\mathcal{K}$ that computes x_{KS}. This places an upper bound on the time required to compute x_{KS}. The function x_{KS} is the solution of a quadratic equation $x^2 + 2\alpha x - \beta = 0$. A solution to this equation can be computed from the values of α and β in one unit of time. The diagram in Figure 5.1.1 computes the function α in four units of time and the diagram in Figure 5.1.2 computes the function β in four units of time. In each of these diagrams, a vertex is not labeled with the function that $\mathcal{K}$ assigned to that vertex; a vertex is labeled with the function computed by the network with that vertex as the terminal vertex. Once the function to be computed at a vertex is known, then the function assigned by $\mathcal{K}$ to that vertex is easily inferred. It follows that x_{KS} can be computed in five units of time.

5.1.3. The Nash Solution for Quadratic Boundaries

Next we analyze the function $x_N(B, C, D, F)$. The Lagrange multiplier solution of the Nash optimization problem leads to the pair of equations (5.1.1) and

$$x^2 - y^2 + (C + 1)x - (D + 1)y = 0.$$

Near the origin the values of x and y must be close to $^2/_3$; thus we can solve

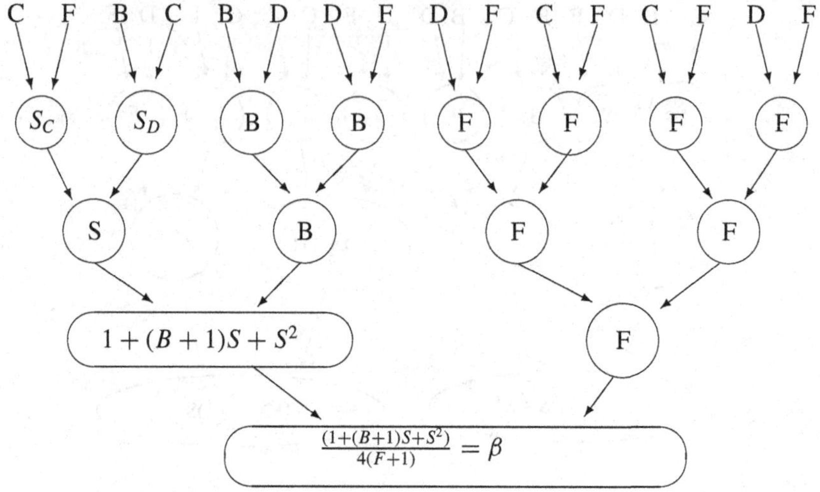

Figure 5.1.2.

for y by using the root

$$y = \frac{\{-(D+1) + \sqrt{(D+1)^2 + 4[x^2 + (C+1)]}\}}{2}.$$

Substitute this value into Equation (5.1.1) and clear the radicals. The result is the quartic equation

$$\begin{aligned}
&(80 + 32\,D + 16\,D^2 + 144\,F + 32\,D\,F + 16\,D^2\,F + 64\,F^2) \\
&+ (-96 + 16\,B - 112\,C - 16\,D + 16\,B\,D - 32\,C\,D - 16\,D^2 \\
&- 16\,C\,D^2 - 80\,F + 16\,B\,F - 96\,C\,F + 16\,D\,F + 16\,B\,D\,F)x \\
&+ (-60 - 20\,B + 52\,C - 20\,B\,C + 36\,C^2 - 44\,D - 20\,B\,D \\
&- 20\,C\,D - 20\,B\,C\,D - 12\,D^2 - 64\,F)x^2 + (28 - 24\,B - 4\,B^2 \\
&+ 44\,C - 8\,B\,C - 4\,B^2\,C - 16\,D - 16\,B\,D)x^3 \\
&+ (12 - 8\,B - 4\,B^2)x^4 = 0.
\end{aligned} \tag{5.1.3}$$

Set

$$\begin{aligned}
C_0 &= 12 - 8\,B - 4\,B^2, \\
C_1 &= (28 - 24B - 4B^2 + 44C - 8\,B\,C - 4\,B^2\,C - 16\,D - 16\,B\,D), \\
C_2 &= (-60 - 20\,B + 52\,C - 20\,B\,C + 36\,C^2 - 44\,D - 20\,B\,D \\
&\quad - 20\,C\,D - 20\,B\,C\,D - 12\,D^2 - 64\,F), \\
C_3 &= (-96 + 16\,B - 112\,C - 16\,D + 16\,B\,D - 32\,C\,D - 16\,D^2 \\
&\quad - 16\,C\,D^2 - 80\,F + 16\,B\,F - 96\,C\,F + 16\,D\,F + 16\,B\,D\,F), \\
C_4 &= (80 + 32\,D + 16\,D^2 + 144\,F + 32\,D\,F + 16\,D^2\,F + 64\,F^2).
\end{aligned} \tag{5.1.4}$$

We argue now that the evaluation of the function $x_N(B, C, D, F)$ in the neighborhood of the origin requires at least six units of time.

The general quartic equation is

$$x^4 + Q_1x^3 + Q_2x^2 + Q_3x + Q_4 = 0. \tag{5.1.5}$$

The Nash solution of the bargaining problem is the point that maximizes xy on the frontier. When $B = C = D = F = 0$, the frontier of the bargaining problem satisfies Equation (5.1.2); that is, $x^2 + xy + y^2 + 2x + 2y - 4 = 0$. The x coordinate x_N of the Nash solution of the bargaining problem with $B = C = D = F = 0$ is the solution of the quartic

$$80 - 96\,x - 60\,x^2 + 28\,x^3 + 12\,x^4 = 0.$$

The coefficients are obtained by substituting zero for each of the parameters B, C, D, and F in Equation (5.1.3). Normalize this equation by dividing the coefficients by the coefficient of x^4. The result is the equation

$$x^4 + 7/3x^3 - 5x^2 - 8x + 20/3 = 0.$$

Recall that for this problem, the Nash solution has $x_N = 2/3$. Solving the Nash problem in the neighborhood of $B = C = D = F = 0$ is equivalent to solving the quartic Equation (5.1.3) in the neighborhood of $(Q_1, Q_2, Q_3, Q_4) = (7/3, -5, -8, 20/3) = \underline{0}$. We require the solution that has value 2/3 when $B = C = D = F = 0$.

Suppose that a $\mathcal{D}$ network $\mathcal{N}$ computes the solution $Z(Q_1, Q_2, Q_3, Q_4)$ of the general quartic Equation (5.1.5). We show that the computation requires at least three units of computation time. We show this by computing each of the bordered Hessians $bh_{(X,Y)}(Z)$ for each partition X, Y of the set $\{Q_1, Q_2, Q_3, Q_4\}$ into two disjoint subsets of two variables and by evaluating each bordered Hessian at the point $\underline{0}$. The computations show that for each partition, the associated bordered Hessian has a rank of 2.

We use implicit differentiation to compute $\partial Z/\partial Q_k$.

$$(4Z^3 + 3Q_1Z^2 + 2Q_2Z + Q_3)\,\partial Z/\partial Q_k = -Z^{(4-k)}. \tag{5.1.6}$$

Set $d(x, Q_1, Q_2, Q_3) = (4x^3 + 3Q_1x^2 + 2Q_2x + Q_3)$. Therefore, at $\underline{0}$,

$$\frac{\partial Z}{\partial Q_k} = \frac{-1}{d(2/3, 7/3, -5, -8)} Z\left(\frac{7}{3}, -5, -8, \frac{20}{3}\right)^{(4-k)}.$$

Next compute $\frac{\partial^2 Z}{\partial Q_k\,\partial Q_\ell}$ from Equation (5.1.6). The second partial derivative is the solution of the equation

$$(4Z^3 + 3Q_1Z^2 + 2Q_2Z + Q_3)\frac{\partial^2 Z}{\partial Q_k\,\partial Q_\ell} + \frac{\partial Z}{\partial Q_k}\frac{\partial Z}{\partial Q_\ell}(12Z^2 + 6Q_1Z + 2Q_2)$$
$$+ (4-\ell)Z^{(3-\ell)}\frac{\partial Z}{\partial Q_k} = -(4-k)Z^{(3-k)}\frac{\partial Z}{\partial Q_\ell}. \tag{5.1.7}$$

Set $f(x, Q_1, Q_2, Q_3, Q_4) = (12x^2 + 6Q_1x + 2Q_2)$, set $\Phi = f(Z, Q_1, Q_2, Q_3)$, and set $\Delta = d(Z, Q_1, Q_2, Q_3)$. Thus

$$\Delta \frac{\partial^2 Z}{\partial Q_k \, \partial Q_\ell} + F \frac{\partial Z}{\partial Q_k} \frac{\partial Z}{\partial Q_\ell} + (4 - \ell) Z^{(3-\ell)} \frac{\partial Z}{\partial Q_k} = -(4 - k) Z^{(3-k)} \frac{\partial Z}{\partial Q_\ell}.$$

Substitute the expressions obtained from Equation (5.1.6) into Equation (5.1.7) and solve for $\partial^2 Z / \partial Q_k \partial Q_\ell$. Then

$$\frac{\partial^2 Z}{\partial Q_k \partial Q_\ell} = \frac{1}{\Delta^3} \left[(4 - k - \ell) \Delta Z^{(7-k-\ell)} - F Z^{(8-k-\ell)} \right]. \tag{5.1.8}$$

Now construct the Hessian of Z (not the bordered Hessian) multiplied by Δ^3. The result is

$$H(Z)(\Delta, \Phi, Z)$$

$$= \begin{array}{c} \\ Q_1 \\ Q_2 \\ Q_3 \\ Q_4 \end{array} \begin{array}{c} \begin{array}{cccc} \quad Q_1 \quad & \quad Q_2 \quad & \quad Q_3 \quad & \quad Q_4 \quad \end{array} \\ \begin{bmatrix} 6\Delta Z^5 - \Phi Z^6 & 5\Delta Z^4 - \Phi Z^5 & 4\Delta Z^3 - \Phi Z^4 & 3\Delta Z^2 - \Phi Z^3 \\ 5\Delta Z^4 - \Phi Z^5 & 4\Delta Z^3 - \Phi Z^4 & 3\Delta Z^2 - \Phi Z^3 & 2\Delta Z - \Phi Z^2 \\ 4\Delta Z^3 - \Phi Z^4 & 3\Delta Z^2 - \Phi Z^3 & 2\Delta Z - \Phi Z^2 & \Delta - \Phi Z \\ 3\Delta Z^2 - \Phi Z^3 & 2\Delta Z - \Phi Z^2 & \Delta - \Phi Z & -\Phi \end{bmatrix} \end{array}.$$

Set $X = \{Q_1, Q_2\}$ and set $Y = \{Q_3, Q_4\}$. When the 2×2 submatrix of $H(Z)(\Delta, \Phi, Z)$ with rows indexed by $\{Q_1, Q_2\}$ and columns indexed by $\{Q_3, Q_4\}$ is multiplied by Δ^3, the result is the 2×2 submatrix of the bordered Hessian $bh_{(X,Y)}(Z)$ that has columns labeled Q_3 and Q_4. The determinant of the 2×2 submatrix of $H(Z)(\Delta, \Phi, Z)$ whose rows are indexed by X and whose columns are indexed by Y is $-\Delta^2 Z^4$. Similarly, the subdeterminant of $H(Z)(\Delta, \Phi, Z)$ with rows $\{Q_1, Q_3\}$ and columns $\{Q_2, Q_4\}$ is $-4\Delta^2 Z^4$, and the subdeterminant of $H(Z)(\Delta, \Phi, Z)$ with rows $\{Q_1, Q_3\}$ and columns $\{Q_2, Q_3\}$ is $-\Delta^2 Z^4$. At the point $\underline{0}$, $Z = 2/3$ and $\Delta(\underline{0}) = (280/27)$. Thus each of the 2×2 subdeterminants has a rank of 2. It follows that the bordered Hessian of Z for each choice of partition of the set $\{Q_1, Q_2, Q_3, Q_4\}$ has a rank of 2. This shows that the computation of the solution $Z(Q_1, Q_2, Q_3, Q_4)$ of the quartic Equation (5.1.5) requires three units of time.

The list given in Equation (5.1.4) is a catalog of the coefficients, C_i, of Equation (5.1.3). Next we show that if

$$\Gamma(B, C, D, F)$$
$$= [C_1(B, C, D, F), C_2(B, C, D, F), C_3(B, C, D, F), C_4(B, C, D, F)],$$

then Γ carries a neighborhood of $(B, C, D, F) = (0, 0, 0, 0)$ to a neighborhood of the point $\underline{0}$. The Jacobian of Γ evaluated at the point (0, 0, 0, 0) is

$$\begin{array}{c} \\ \frac{C_1}{C_0} \\ \frac{C_2}{C_0} \\ \frac{C_3}{C_0} \\ \frac{C_4}{C_0} \end{array} \begin{array}{c} \begin{array}{cccc} Q_1 & Q_2 & Q_3 & Q_4 \end{array} \\ \begin{bmatrix} -4/9 & 11/3 & -4/3 & 0 \\ -5 & 13/3 & -11/3 & -16/3 \\ -4 & -28/3 & -4/3 & -20/3 \\ 40/9 & 0 & 8/3 & 12 \end{bmatrix} \end{array}.$$

The Jacobian of Γ has rank 4. Thus Γ maps a neighborhood of the origin to a neighborhood of the point $\underline{0}$.

Using the ranks of bordered Hessians, we verify that the function C_3/C_0 requires three units of computing time in a neighborhood of the origin. As in the case of the function Z we compute the matrix $CH(C_3/C_0)$ evaluated at the origin. The result is the matrix

$$\begin{array}{c} \\ B \\ C \\ D \\ F \end{array} \begin{array}{c} \begin{array}{ccccc} \left(\frac{C_3}{C_0}\right) & B & C & D & F \end{array} \\ \begin{bmatrix} -4 & -32/3 & -56/9 & 4/9 & -28/9 \\ -28/3 & -56/9 & 0 & -8/3 & -8 \\ -4/3 & 4/9 & -8/3 & -8/3 & 4/3 \\ -20/3 & -28/9 & -8 & 4/3 & 0 \end{bmatrix} \end{array}.$$

It is now simple to check that the bordered Hessians $bh_{(\{Q_1,Q_2\}),(\{Q_3,Q_4\})}(C_3/C_0)_{(0,0,0,0)}$, $bh_{(\{Q_1,Q_3\}),(\{Q_2,Q_4\})}(C_3/C_0)_{(0,0,0,0)}$, and $bh_{(\{Q_1,Q_4\},\{Q_2,Q_3\})}(C_3/C_0)_{(0,0,0,0)}$ each have a rank of 2. Therefore, under the restrictions we have placed on the order of computation, the Nash solution requires six units of computing time whereas the Kalai–Smorodinsky solution requires only five units of time.

5.1.4. Bargaining Games with Cubic Boundaries

In the previous section we showed that the Nash solution is computationally more complex than the solution of Kalai–Smorodinsky. Although that analysis is suggestive, the question remains whether the same comparison holds for bargaining games whose feasible sets are more complicated. In this section we comment on the comparison of the two solutions for bargaining games whose set of feasible payoff pairs is contained in the first quadrant and is bounded by the coordinate axes and one of a class of cubic curves. The Leontief criteria are not sufficiently fine to be able to distinguish between the Nash solution and the Kalai–Smorodinsky solution.[2] The Kalai–Smorodinsky solution requires finding the coordinates of the point of intersection of a line with the frontier. The

[2] The classes, $\mathcal{F}$, of functions we consider here are the collection of complex analytic functions of two variables and subsets of that collection.

x coordinate of the intersection is the solution of a cubic equation whose coefficients are themselves rational functions of solutions of cubic equations. It is straightforward to build a network of complex analytic functions that computes solutions of such cubic equations by using Cardano's formulas (see Dummit and Foote, 1991; p. 543). The result is a network that computes the x coordinate of the Kalai–Smorodinsky solution in ten units of time by using complex analytic functions of two variables. We believe that the Nash solution cannot be computed in ten units of time. Indeed, we believe that the Nash solution cannot be computed. That is, we believe no $\mathcal{F}$ network can compute the Nash solution when $\mathcal{F}$ is the collection of complex analytic functions of two variables. Our reason is that for the class of cubics we discuss, the x coordinate of the Nash solution is the solution of a polynomial equation of degree 7. Hilbert's 13th problem (Hilbert, 1900) is to decide whether the solutions of generic polynomials of degree 7 can be expressed as a finite superposition of "continuous functions" of at most two variables. That the Nash solution leads to a polynomial of degree 7 is at least suggestive. We can show that the polynomial that results, which, for lack of a better term we call the Nash polynomial, is irreducible.[3] There is a sequence of Tschirnhaus transformations (see Dehn, 1960) that reduce the solution of a general polynomial of degree 7 to the solution of a polynomial equation $W^7 + R'W^3 + S'W^2 + T'W + 1 = 0$. Our attempt to apply Tschirnhaus transformations to the Nash polynomial led to calculations that we were unable to complete. We did find it possible to apply Tschirnhaus transformations to the Nash polynomial and reduce it to the solving of a polynomial equation of the form

$$Z^7 + DZ^4 + EZ^3 + FZ^2 + GZ + H = 0. \tag{5.1.9}$$

Even these calculations are so intractable that we do not include them in this book. The computations that we were able to carry out for these calculations led to the conclusion that D, E, F, G, and H are functions of the five game parameters for the class of cubic boundaries we chose and that the Jacobian of the map from the game parameters to the coefficients D, E, F, G, and H has a rank of 5 at an appropriate point. Thus we conjecture that the Nash solution with cubic boundary is not computable in finite time by superpositions of real analytic functions of at most two variables.

The class of cubic curves that bound the bargaining sets we choose are those given by the equations

$$Y^2 + \frac{1}{3}\left(\frac{X+Y}{1+A}\right)^3 + \left(p - \frac{1}{2}\right)\left(\frac{X+Y}{1+A}\right) + q - 1 = 0. \tag{5.1.10}$$

Here the coefficients A, p, and q and the coordinates (a, b) for the disagreement point are the parameters for the bargaining problem. Parameter values are

[3] A polynomial is irreducible if it is not the product of nonconstant polynomials of lower degree.

chosen in a neighborhood of $p = A = a = b = q = 0$. For the values of the parameters we chose, these curves, together with the coordinate axes, bound convex sets in the first quadrant.

To simplify the equations that result from solving the Lagrange multiplier problem for the function $h(X, Y)$ with the constraint given by Equation (5.1.10), we apply a coordinate change to the XY plane. Set $x = (X + Y)/(1 + A)$ and $y = Y$. This change of coordinates transforms Equation (5.1.10) into the equation

$$y^2 + 1/3x^3 + (p - 1/2)x + q - 1 = 0. \tag{5.1.11}$$

In the x, y coordinate system, the function $(X - a)(Y - b)$ is given by the expression $h^*(x, y) = [(1 + A)x - y - a](y - b)$. Thus the Nash solution requires the maximization of $h^*(x, y)$ on the curve with Equation (5.1.11). We obtain the Nash solution by solving the Lagrange multiplier problem for the objective function $h^*(x, y)$ and the constraint given by Equation (5.1.11). The Lagrange multiplier calculations for the Nash solution can be found in Appendix C.

5.2. COMPUTATIONAL SUPERIORITY AND STRATEGIC ADVANTAGE

Suppose the players in a two-person game have different computational abilities. Does it follow that the player with superior abilities has an advantage? We investigate this question supposing that each player i computes with $\mathcal{F}^i$ networks for some class $\mathcal{F}^i$ of elementary functions.

Definition 5.2.1. We say that a class of $\mathcal{F}$ networks is superior to the class of $\mathcal{G}$ networks if the class $\mathcal{F}$ properly contains the class $\mathcal{G}$.

Note that superiority does not linearly order the collection of networks, because for two classes $\mathcal{F}$ and $\mathcal{G}$ it is possible that neither class contains the other. Furthermore, it can happen that a class of $\mathcal{F}$ networks is superior to a class of $\mathcal{G}$ networks, yet every function that can be computed by a $\mathcal{F}$ network can also be computed by a $\mathcal{G}$ network. For instance, suppose $\mathcal{F}$ consists of all rational functions of two variables, and $\mathcal{G}$ consists of constants, $x + y$, xy, and x/y. Then $\mathcal{F}$ networks are superior to $\mathcal{G}$ networks, but each function computable by an $\mathcal{F}$ network can be computed by a $\mathcal{G}$ network. In contrast, we know that there are classes of functions $\mathcal{F}$ and $\mathcal{G}$ such that $\mathcal{F}$ contains $\mathcal{G}$, and there are functions in $\mathcal{F}$ that no $\mathcal{G}$ network can compute in finite time. A simple example of this is as follows. Let $\mathcal{G} = \mathcal{L}$ where $\mathcal{L}$ consists of constants and linear functions of two variables. Each $\mathcal{L}$ network computes an affine function as a superposition of linear functions and constant functions. Suppose that the class $\mathcal{F}$ contains $\mathcal{L}$ and the function $\sqrt{x}$. No $\mathcal{G}$ network can compute $\sqrt{x}$ in finite time. More generally, suppose that $\mathcal{F}$ consists of functions of n variables that are s times continuously differentiable, and that $\mathcal{G}$ consists of functions of n' variables that are s' times continuously differentiable. Vitushkin (1961) has shown that if $n/s > n'/s'$, then there are functions in $\mathcal{F}$ that cannot be computed as superpositions of functions in $\mathcal{G}$.

Next we explore examples of games in which the players have different computational abilities.

Example 5.2.1. First we consider a class of two-person zero-sum games that are played under a time constraint. The games we consider have payoff functions given by matrices whose entries are real numbers.

$$A[a, b, c, d] = \begin{bmatrix} a & b \\ c & d \end{bmatrix}. \tag{5.2.1}$$

We assume that the matrix $A[a, b, c, d]$ has a nonzero determinant, and the game has no saddle point. The players first see the matrix $A[a, b, c, d]$ when play begins. Player X (X is either I or II) has a class of elementary functions $\mathcal{F}_X$. Each player X builds an $\mathcal{F}_X$ network by using the class of elementary functions $\mathcal{F}_X$. The numbers a, b, c, d are the values of their variables; these networks compute the (mixed) strategy of each player. The players have finitely many units of time to build networks. Once the networks are completed, the players are told the values of the parameters. The time restriction is that play must begin, using the computed strategies, in one unit of time. The play is simultaneous. The mixed strategy optimum for the first player is

$$\left[\frac{d-c}{a+d-(b+c)}, \frac{a-b}{a+d-(b+c)}\right],$$

whereas the mixed strategy optimum for the second player is

$$\left[\frac{d-b}{a+d-(b+c)}, \frac{a-c}{a+d-(b+c)}\right].$$

Suppose that $\mathcal{F}_{\text{I}}$ is the class of rational functions of four variables, and that $\mathcal{F}_{\text{II}}$ is the class of rational functions of two variables. Player I can construct a network that computes the optimal mixed strategy in one unit of time. It is simple to check that the function $(d-c)/[a+d-(b+c)]$ cannot be computed in one unit of time by an $\mathcal{F}$ network when the functions of $\mathcal{F}$ are real-valued rational functions (and therefore have continuous first- and second-order derivatives) of two variables. Player II has only the elements of the class $\mathcal{F}_{\text{II}}$ to construct networks; thus he is incapable of computing the optimal mixed strategy in one unit of time. If Player II is forced to play, he is forced to choose his strategy to be something he can compute in one unit of time. For instance, he could arbitrarily fix the values of two of the four entries in the payoff matrix and thereby reduce the expression for his mixed strategy to a function of two variables and constants. He could compute the resulting candidate for his mixed strategy in one unit of time. Player I has an advantage because Player II cannot find, and therefore cannot play, the optimal strategy, except by chance. Indeed, in this game Player II is fairly helpless.

Next we consider an example of a two-player zero-sum game on the unit square with one pure optimal strategy. The payoff function for the first player is known to each player. Each player knows that the payoff function is a concave–convex function and therefore that the game has an optimal pure strategy.[3]

The payoff to Player I is

$$P(x, y) = dx - 3x^2 - x^3 - y + x^2y + 3y^2 + xy^2 + y^3.$$

When the parameter d is in the interval (0.5, 1.5), this is a concave–convex game with optimal pure strategies. The quadratic formula applied to $\partial P/\partial y = 0$ yields a function that has values between 0 and 1 for values of x between 0 and 1 when $d \in (0.5, 1.5)$. The same is true for the solutions of the equation $\partial P/\partial x = 0$ when $d \in (0.5, 1.5)$ and y is between 0 and 1. Thus it is easy to compute a mini-max solution of the game with payoff $P(x, y)$.

Each player builds an $\mathcal{F}$ network in order to compute his strategy.

We make the following assumptions about the players and the game.

1. Each player knows the payoff function $P(x, y)$, and for each pair of real numbers r_1, r_2, each can evaluate $P(x, y)$ in one unit of time.
2. Player I, with strategy x, computes with $\mathcal{L}$ networks where $\mathcal{L}$ is the class of rational functions of a finite number of variables together with a function that computes the maximum component of a 2-tuple. Thus Player I can approximate the game by an $N \times N$ matrix game found by evaluating the function $P(x, y)$ at points (a, b), where a and b are real numbers. He can use a linear programming or "saddle point" solution of the approximating game as his strategy. However, he need not use this method of deciding on a strategy.
3. Player II, whose strategy is y, uses $\mathcal{M}$ networks where $\mathcal{M} \supset \mathcal{L}$ and $\mathcal{M}$ also contains functions that return real-valued solutions between 0 and 1 that solve (when possible) the equations $x^n - a = 0$ for n equal to 2 or 3.
4. Each elementary function that is a function $\mathcal{M}$ requires one unit of computing time.

The assumptions listed above clearly give Player II superior networks. We argue that Player II with superior networks can consistently do better than the payoff at the optimal pure strategy equilibrium of the game.

[3] See Owen (1982).

To complete the argument, we show that the x coordinate of the optimal point is not a rational function of d, and that the second player can compute his optimal strategy.

The x coordinate of the optimal point is

$$x = \frac{1}{5808}\left(-4752 - \sqrt{22}\,\mathrm{Sqrt}\left(\frac{1}{F5^{1/3}\sqrt{F6}}\mathrm{Sqrt}\,(-1965312 + 696960\,d\,F5^{1/3} \right.\right.$$
$$+ 38016F1F5^{1/3} - 1212^{2/3}F2\sqrt{F6} + 2052864F5^{1/3}\sqrt{F6}$$
$$\left.\left. - 15488F1F5^{1/3}\sqrt{F6} - 38722^{1/3}F5^{2/3}\sqrt{F6} + 2904\sqrt{F6}\right)\right),$$

where

$$F1 = (65 - 17\,d),$$
$$F2 = 380224 + 186688\,d + 18880\,d^2,$$
$$F3 = 1896943 + 1343958\,d + 301026\,d^2 + 20264\,d^3,$$
$$F4 = 3004265473 + 1936930532\,d + 272031648\,d^2 - 23427688\,d^3 - 2691740\,d^4 + 186288\,d^5 - 1584\,d^6,$$
$$F5 = F3 + 9\sqrt{F4},$$
$$F6 = \frac{324}{121} - \frac{2F1}{99} + \frac{F2}{15842^{1/3}F5^{1/3}} + \frac{2^{1/3}F5^{1/3}}{99},$$
$$F7 = \frac{2^{1/3}F5^{1/3}}{99} + F6.$$

The y coordinate of the optimal point can be computed by the second player, but the formula for that coordinate is significantly more complicated than that for x. We give the expression for y in Appendix C.

In conclusion, if the second player has the capacity to solve for the y coordinate of the Nash solution of the game, and if her opponent has the capacity only to carry out rational operations on rational numbers, then she can always do better in this game than minus the value of the game. Even though Player I can approximate the Nash solution, he can never find the x coordinate of it, because its x coordinate is irrational.

We now take up another class of two-person games specified as follows. The strategy domain of each player is a compact subset of R^n. Let X be the strategy domain of Player I, and Y be the strategy domain of Player II. For simplicity we suppose that the two domains have the same dimension. That is, for each player a strategy is specified by choosing the values of n (real) variables, $x = (x_1, \ldots, x_n)$ for Player I, $y = (y_1, \ldots, y_n)$ for Player II. The payoff function of player i is denoted by V^i, $i = 1, 2$. Thus, when the players choose strategies x and y, respectively, then the payoff are $V^1(x, y)$ to Player I, and $V^2(x, y)$ to Player II. The strategy domains and payoff functions are common knowledge among the players. A player's process of reasoning, leading to his choice of strategy, is made explicit. Each player must compute his choice of strategy from his knowledge of the game, and the common knowledge of rationality. We focus attention on a class of games that we call "Ready-or-Not" games. These games are played in time. At time $t = 0$, the players acquire common knowledge of the game and of rationality. They begin deciding on their strategies. The first player to decide on his strategy puts it into effect immediately. For instance, if the game models introduction of a new product, or other "physical action," that action takes place as soon as the player has chosen it. We model this abstractly by supposing that when a player decides on his strategy, he reports it to a referee who reports it to the other player. We assume that transmission of these reports takes no time. We assume that once a choice is reported it cannot be changed in that play of the game. We suppose that each agent has a class $\mathcal{F}^i, i = 1, 2$ of elementary functions and that each player calculates by means of $(r^i, 1)$ networks with modules $\mathcal{F}^i$. If $\mathcal{F}^2 \subseteq \mathcal{F}^1$, then the set of networks of Player I is superior to that of Player II. Does this give Player I a strategic advantage? The answer can go either way, depending on the details of the game. It is possible that the calculations that the players must make involve modules from $\mathcal{F}^2$ only. In that case there is no advantage from having elementary functions that are redundant. We strengthen the assumption by assuming that $\mathcal{F}^2 \subset \mathcal{F}^1$, and also that $r^1 > r^2$. If the game has a unique Nash equilibrium, then there might or might not be an advantage to being the first to move, and therefore might or might not be an advantage to having computational superiority. We next consider games that have multiple equilibria. Let $V^i(x, y, \alpha)$, $i = 1, 2$ be the payoff function of Player i when the strategies x and y are played and the game is characterized by parameters α. Player II's best response (assumed to be a function) to each of Player I's possible actions is given by the mapping $\eta(x, \alpha)$ whose value at x in game α is the set of maximizers of $V^2(x, y, \alpha)$ with respect to $y \in Y$. Note that for each y in $\eta(x, \alpha)$, the payoff to Player II is the same, whereas the payoff to Player I can vary with y. Player I would be prudent to expect that his payoff will be the minimum attainable when y is constrained to be a member of $\eta(x, \alpha)$. Then, we can assume for simplicity that $\eta(x, \alpha)$ is single valued, that is, a function. Similarly, Player I's best response is $\xi(y, \alpha)$, which is the set of maximizers of $V^1(x, y, \alpha)$ with respect to x. As in the case of Player II, we assume that $\xi(y, \alpha)$ is a function. In a Ready-or-Not game in which the players have perfect information about the game, but have neither knowledge nor beliefs about the other player's computational powers, the players would seek to be the first to select their actions. Thus, Player I maximizes the function $V^1[x, \eta(x, \alpha), \alpha] = W^1(x, \alpha)$ with respect to x. Player II does the corresponding thing, computing the set $\xi(y, \alpha)$ of maximizers of $V^2(x, y, \alpha)$ with respect to x for each y and α, and then maximizing $V^2[\xi(y, \alpha), y, \alpha] = W^2(y, \alpha)$ with respect to $y \in Y$. The results of these two maximizations can be written as $\phi^1(\alpha)$, and $\phi^2(\alpha)$. (Generally ϕ^1 and ϕ^2 are correspondences. We assume that they are functions.)

Suppose for definiteness that $\mathcal{F}^1$ consists of C^2 functions of four variables and $\mathcal{F}^2$ consists of C^2 functions of two variables, that is, $r^1 = 4$ and $r^2 = 2$. Then Player I can compute a function of four variables in one unit of time, whereas Player II requires two units of time to compute that function. In a case like that, Player I has a strategic advantage. This is because when Player I selects her action first, Player II is no longer playing the original game. He is effectively constrained so that the best he can do is to choose the action given by $\eta[\phi^1(\alpha), \alpha]$, that is, to maximize his payoff given the action of Player I. In a game with multiple Nash equilibria, it is advantageous to move first. Do the players know at the start of the game that Player I has computational powers that give him a strategic advantage? If so, is Player II behaving rationally when he, in effect, waits to see what Player I does? In this situation Player II cannot figure out what Player I's action will be in time to do anything effective about it. Perhaps Player II might find a preemptive action that would give him a higher payoff than what he gets by passively responding to the action of Player I. The preemptive action would have to be one that he could calculate before Player I completes her calculation, and would also have to be one that can be justified as rational *in the game including knowledge of computing abilities*. Suppose Player II somehow arrived at a choice $y*$ that he could announce before Player I's announcement. Rationality of Player II would require that he do better by choosing $y*$ than by waiting, and playing his best response to Player I's action. That is, $y*$ must satisfy

$$V^2[\xi(y*, \alpha), y*, \alpha] \geq V^2\{\phi^1(\alpha), \eta[\phi^1(\alpha), \alpha], \alpha\}.$$

In order to verify this inequality, Player II must calculate Player I's best response function at the point $y*$, and the action Player I will submit to the referee. Player II cannot carry out that calculation in less time than Player I would take to do it. Therefore, he cannot rationally announce $y*$ early enough to beat Player I's announcement. Unless a different concept of rationality is imposed, Player II is faced with the same calculation independent of how his choice is made. It seems that this problem would not be avoided if the players were assumed to have beliefs, or knowledge, about the other players' computational abilities, as long as the concept of rationality remained the same. It seems that further exploration of concepts of rationality would be useful in situations in which computational powers of agents are explicit.

6 Lower Bounds and Approximations

6.1. REVELATION MECHANISMS

This section establishes an elementary lower bound on the computational complexity of smooth functions between Euclidean spaces (actually, smooth manifolds).

Our lower bound generalizes a bound given by Arbib (1960) and Arbib and Spira (1967) for the complexity of functions between finite sets. The Arbib–Spira bound is based on the concept of *separator sets* for a function. This concept corresponds to the number of (Boolean) variables that the function actually depends on. In the finite case the number of variables can easily be counted, but a counting procedure is too crude to be used for functions between infinite sets. Instead, our analysis uses an equivalence relation that corresponds to separator sets in the finite case, and it also applies to functions with infinite domains and ranges. The counting procedure is replaced with the construction of a *universal object in a category*, namely the category of *encoded revelation mechanisms* that realize the function F, or ERM(F), whose complexity is under analysis. The universal object is a minimal encoded revelation mechanism called an *essential revelation mechanism.* The dimension (when it exists) of the message space of the universal object is the number of variables on which F really depends.[1]

In addition to this abstract characterization of the number of variables that must be used in order to compute the function F, we give a characterization in terms of conditions on the ranks of the bordered Hessian matrices of F.

The formal presentation of this material is organized as follows. Subsection 6.1.1 contains the set theoretic constructions used subsequently. Definitions of

[1] Although we use a concept from category theory, our analysis is self-contained and does not require knowledge of category theory other than the concept of a universal object in a category, which is explained in the paper. This concept is not new to economic theory; Sonnenschein (1974) and Jordan (1982) have used it in analyzing economic mechanisms.

F-equivalence, of encoded and essential revelation mechanisms are given. It is established (Lemma 6.1.1 and Theorem 6.1.2) that the essential revelation mechanism for a given function, F, is the smallest encoded revelation mechanism that serves as a universal object in the category ERM(F) of encoded revelation mechanisms for F. Subsection 2 deals with the case in which the domain of F is a product of smooth manifolds, and F is smooth. Simple conditions are given that ensure that the quotient sets (under F equivalence) are topological manifolds and therefore have dimensions.

When the domain of a function F is a smooth manifold, the number of variables on which F depends is not obvious. Suppose that F is a real-valued function with partial derivatives defined on the Euclidean space $E^1 = \Re^2$, where the Euclidean space has specified coordinates, x and y. Then the number of coordinates required to compute F is usually easy to estimate by computing the number of nonzero partial derivatives. For example, the function $F(x, y) = x + y^2$ has partial derivatives in x and y that are both nonzero. One might be tempted to think that $F(x, y)$ is a function more complex than, say, the function x. However, if we view $\Re^2$ as a differentiable manifold, where smooth coordinate changes are allowed, then the function $F(x, y)$ can be introduced as a coordinate function on $\Re^2$, so that $\Re^2$ has coordinates $F(x, y)$ and y. Having done that, one finds that $F(x, y)$ is a function of the one parameter F, and is no more complex than x. Thus, the possibility of making unrestricted (smooth) coordinate changes invalidates the use of the number of nonzero partial derivatives of F, that is, the number of variables on which F apparently depends, as an indicator of its complexity.

Another view of this is as follows. Define an equivalence relation according to which two points a and a' in $\Re^2$ are equivalent if F takes the same value at a and a'. The level sets of F are the equivalence classes of this equivalence relation. This set of equivalence classes is a one-dimensional family (indexed by the values of F), and hence it is no more complex than the level sets of the function x.

Beyond that, when F is defined on a product space, there is a natural restriction on coordinate changes allowed in the product $E^1 \times \cdots \times E^n$. The restriction is to allow only coordinate changes that are the product of individual coordinate changes in the separate spaces E^i. This is especially clear when the space E^i is the parameter space of an agent i. Although there may be nothing intrinsic about the coordinate system used in E^i, because agent i's parameters are private to i, coordinate transformations that depend on parameters in E^j with $j \neq i$ should certainly be ruled out. Moreover, even when the spaces E^i are not parameter spaces of agents, such transformations should be ruled out, because computations helpful in evaluating F could be carried out by means of such transformations, but in a form concealed from the analysis. With this restriction we seek a lower bound on the number of parameters from coordinate systems in E^i needed to compute F.

For example, if $X = \Re^2$ with coordinates x_1 and x_2 and $Y = \Re^2$ with coordinates y_1 and y_2 and if $G(x_1, x_2, y_1, y_2) = x_1 y_1 + x_2 y_2$, then the restriction that a coordinate change is allowable only if it is the product of a coordinate change in X and a coordinate change in Y leads to the conclusion that all four of the parameters x_1, y_1, x_2, and y_2 are required for the evaluation of G. To see this, one can describe the level sets of the function $G(x_1, x_2, y_1, y_2)$, with the restriction that two points α and β in X are equivalent only if $G(\alpha, \eta) = G(\beta, \eta)$ independent of the point η chosen in Y. Then α and β are equivalent only if $\alpha = \beta$. Indeed, if $\alpha = (\alpha_1, \alpha_2) \neq \beta = (\beta_1, \beta_2)$ where $\alpha_1 \neq \beta_1$, then there exists η_1 such that $G(\alpha_1, \alpha_2, \eta_1, 0) \neq G(\beta_1, \beta_2, \eta_1, 0)$. A similar argument applies if $\alpha_2 \neq \beta_2$. Thus, to compute G one needs sufficiently many parameters to distinguish between each two points of X; that is, we need two parameters from X. Similarly, we need two parameters from Y. Suppose we regard the space X as associated with agent 1 and Y with agent 2, and that the value of the function G is computed by a third entity. Then the first step in computing the value of G is that agent 1 reveals the value of his parameters, and so does agent 2. We call this a revelation mechanism, because the step in which each agent fully reveals his parameters to a central agent defines a revelation mechanism in the field of mechanism design.

We extend the concept of a revelation mechanism to allow for partial revelation of parameters in any allowable coordinate system in the space E. We refer to a mechanism of this type as an *encoded revelation mechanism.* (Note that although these mechanisms form a larger class than do revelation mechanisms, that class does not include all privacy-preserving mechanisms, or game forms, with the given structure of private information.) Our formulation of the concept of separator sets for the function F is in terms of an equivalence relation induced on each of the sets E^i by F. To begin with this is stated set theoretically without topological or smoothness conditions on the set E^i. The quotient constructions are quite elementary. Additional smoothness conditions can be imposed, when the E^i are differentiable manifolds, the set theoretic constructions are used to establish the existence of certain required functions, for which the required smoothness conditions can then be verified.

The procedure used to construct the quotients that describe the number of variables on which the function F depends is a natural generalization of the argument used in the discussion of the function $G(x_1, x_2, y_1, y_2) = x_1 y_1 + x_2 y_2$. The quotient object so constructed has the natural set theoretic structure of a universal object. The remaining task is to show that in the case of differentiable functions, a set of rank conditions on certain matrices associated with the function under analysis ensures that the quotient object has the structure of a differentiable manifold. The manifold structure on the quotient object allows us to conclude that the dimension of the quotient exists as a topological concept and that the dimension of the quotient is the number of variables required to compute the function. The universality condition guarantees that the quotient object is a space with the least number of variables sufficient to compute the function.

Specifically, for a function $F : E^1 \times \cdots \times E^n \to Z$ we establish the existence of a collection of sets (E^i/F), where $1 \leq i \leq n$, functions $q^i : E^i \to (E^i/F)$, and a function $F^* : (E^1/F) \times \cdots \times (E^n/F) \to Z$ that together satisfy the following conditions.

First, the composition

$$F^* \circ (q^1 \times \cdots \times q^n) = F.$$

Second, if there are functions

$$p^i : E^i \to X^i$$

and

$$H : X^1 \times \cdots \times X^n \to Z$$

for which

$$H \circ (p^1 \times \cdots \times p^n) = F,$$

then there are (one can construct) unique functions

$$r^i : X^i \to (E^i/F), \qquad 1 \leq i \leq n,$$

such that

$$r^i \circ p^i = q^i,$$
$$H = F^* \circ (r^1, \ldots, r^n).$$

These conditions state that the quotient object $(E^1/F) \times \cdots \times (E^n/F)$ is *universal*, a concept to be discussed further. (The term "universal object" is used in category theory to describe objects that allow each object of the category to be specified by identifying a mapping to (or from) the universal object; see MacLane, 1971.)

If the sets E^i are finite, then the cardinality of the set (E^i/F) is an upper bound on the cardinality of the corresponding Arbib–Spira separator set. Furthermore, each separator set in E^i is the image of a subset of (E^i/F) under some thread of q^i. By a thread of q^i we mean a function t from (E^i/F) to E^i such that $q^i \circ t$ is the identity function.

Next we assume that each E^i is a differentiable manifold with appropriate smoothness. If in some coordinate system $(x_1, \ldots, x_t)$ around a point, in (say) E^1, it were possible to ignore the coordinate x_t and still to evaluate F, then knowledge of the coordinates $(x_1, \ldots, x_{t-1})$ would be adequate, at least locally. That is, F would depend on no more than the first $t-1$ variables. In this case the manifold E^i can be replaced, locally, with the quotient induced by the equivalence relation $(\chi_1, \ldots, \chi_{t-1}, \chi_t) \approx (\chi_1, \ldots, \chi_{t-1}, \chi_t')$ if and only if for

$\chi_i \in E^i$ and $\chi_t' \in E^t$

$$F(\chi_1, \ldots, \chi_{t-1}, \chi_t) = F(\chi_1, \ldots, \chi_{t-1}, \chi_t').$$

However, it is possible that even if in a given coordinate system no variable can be eliminated, a change of coordinates can be introduced that leads to a reduction of the number of variables required to compute F. Therefore, we seek a "good" coordinate system by looking for a "good" quotient. The equivalence relation we use is the approximately equal sign, $\approx$.

In the case of smooth manifolds, the quotient using the $\approx$ relation may not have the structure of a smooth manifold for which the quotient map is differentiable. In contrast, when such a structure does exist, then separator sets are again the image of subsets of the quotient under threads of the quotient map.

Conditions are imposed that ensure that $(E^1/F) \times \cdots \times (E^n/F)$, the quotient object, is a topological manifold. In that case, the dimension of the quotient manifold counts the number of variables required.

When we assume the existence of certain local threads, this quotient object satisfies the universality conditions. Whether there is a universal object that is as smooth as the original product $E^1 \times \cdots \times E^n$ is not known. Possibly Godement's Theorem (Serre, 1965, p. LG 3.27) might resolve this difficulty.

If the quotient map is one to one, then no reduction in the number of variables is possible no matter what coordinate system is used. A characterization of the number of variables required to compute a given function F is obtained from the Leontief theorem given in Theorem B.2.4.[2]

The conditions we use for the construction of a "good" quotient of E^1, where $F : E^1 \times \cdots \times E^n \to \mathfrak{R}$, are rank conditions on the bordered Hessians $bh_{(E^i, \prod_{j \neq i} E^j)}(F)$. Because F is a real-valued function, the matrix $BH_{(.,.)}(F)$ of the bordered Hessian with respect to a choice of coordinates (., .) consists of an array of rows where each row is indexed by a coordinate variable of E^i. The columns of the array are indexed by the (dummy) variable Z and the coordinates of the product $\prod_{i \neq j} E^j$. The Hessian, $H_{(.,.)}(F)$, is the submatrix of the bordered Hessian matrix (B.2) that consists of the columns other than column Z.

Suppose that E^i has coordinates $\underline{x}$ and that the space $\prod_{i \neq j} E^j$ has coordinates $\underline{y}$. We use conditions on the matrix $BH_{(\underline{x}, \underline{y})}(F)$ to guarantee the existence of a manifold structure on the quotient objects (E^i/F). If at each point α of E^1 and $\beta \in \prod_{j \neq i} X^j$ the matrix $BH_{(\underline{x}, \underline{y})}|_{(\alpha, \beta)}$ has rank r and $H_{(\underline{x}, \underline{y})}|_{(\alpha, \beta)}$ also has rank r at each point α of E^1 and each point β of $\prod_{j \neq i} E^j$, then the quotient of E^i under the equivalence relation $\approx$ is a manifold of dimension r.

[2] Abelson (1980) used this result to construct a lower bound on the communication complexity of F in a distributed system. In Abelson's paper, communication complexity is the number of real variables that must be transmitted among the processors in order to compute F. This is essentially the same as the size of the message space as analyzed in the economics literature [see Hurwicz, 1986 and the references therein].

As an example, consider the function

$$K(x, x', y, y') = xy + x'^2y + 2xy'^2 + 2x'^2y'^2 = (y + 2y'^2)(x + x'^2)$$

where the variables are all scalars. No variable can be eliminated and still permit the function to be evaluated in terms of the remaining variables. Indeed, no linear change of coordinates can reduce the number of variables required. This is indicated by the fact that the Hessian $H_{(x,y)}(K)$, of K, with rows and columns indexed by all variables x, x', y, y', has rank 4. However, the (nonlinear) change of coordinates given by

$$z = (x + x'^2),\ w = (y + 2y'^2)$$

permits K to be written in terms of only two variables, namely,

$$K(x, x', y, y') = zw.$$

The matrices $H_{z,w}K$ and $BH_{(z,w)}K$ both have rank equal to 1.

Using the basic setup and notation introduced in Chapter 4, Section 4.2. We focus now on the case in which the characteristics of the agents are given by real parameters. It has been shown (see Hurwicz, 1986, and the references therein) that the inverse image of a point m in the message space M is a rectangle, that is, a product of subsets of the spaces $E^1, \ldots, E^n$ contained in the level set $F^{-1}[h(m)]$. This fact, in the presence of appropriate smoothness conditions, allows us to compute a lower bound on the dimension of the message space of a privacy-preserving mechanism that realizes F (see Hurwicz et al., 1980 or Hurwicz, 1986). A *revelation mechanism* is one in which each agent transmits his or her parameter value to the message space. (If the mechanism realizes F, then the outcome function h is F itself.) Formally this can be represented as a mechanism in which the message space M is a product $M = M^1 \times \cdots \times M^n$. If $M^i = E^i$, and if the individual message correspondence of agent i maps the parameter vector e^i in E^i to

$$\mu^i(e^i) = M^1 \times \cdots \times M^{i-1} \times \{e^i\} \times M^{i+1} \times \cdots \times M,$$

then the mechanism is a *direct revelation mechanism.*

When μ^i is given by equilibrium equations, we may write it as $m^i - e^i = 0$, and we may define $g^i : E^i \to M^i$ by

$$g^i(e^i) = m^i \quad \text{if and only if } m^i - e^i = 0.$$

The mechanism realizes F if the outcome function h satisfies the condition that

$$F(e^1, e^2, \ldots, e) = h[g^1(e^1), g^2(e^2), \ldots, g^n(e^n)].$$

If we permit M^i to be any space obtained from E^i by allowable coordinate transformations, then the mechanism

$$(M^1, \ldots, M^n,\ g^1, \ldots, g^n,\ h)$$

is an *encoded revelation mechanism.*

Let ERM(F) denote the class of encoded revelation mechanisms that realize F. If the mechanisms in ERM(F) have a universal object, then we call it the *essential revelation mechanism for F*. An essential revelation mechanism is unique to within isomorphism. The universal object exists when certain conditions on bordered Hessian matrices of F, including smoothness assumptions, are satisfied. The universal object is the product $(E^1/F) \times \cdots \times (E^n/F)$, with a differentiable manifold structure on each of the factors (E^i/F). The dimension of (E^i/F) is a lower bound on the number of variables agent i must reveal to the computing network for F to be computed; the sum of these numbers over the agents is a lower bound on the number of variables on which F really depends, and therefore it determines a lower bound on the computational complexity of F. The computational complexity of F is an indicator of the costs of computation that are incurred by any mechanism that realizes F. It also indicates the computational costs of implementing F by game forms, because to each equilibrium of a game form that implements F there corresponds a privacy-preserving mechanism that realizes F (see Reichelstein and Reiter, 1988).

Let PPM(F) denote the class of all privacy-preserving mechanisms that realize F. The construction of ERM(F) shows that it is a subset of the class PPM(F). Although the dimension of the manifolds of the universal object is a lower bound on the dimensions of message spaces of encoded revelation mechanisms, and therefore determines a lower bound on computational complexity, it is not a lower bound on the dimension of messages spaces of mechanisms in PPM(F). In general, the bound on the dimension of message spaces is lower than the bound on computational complexity.

6.1.1. Constructions

Notation. *If X^j, with $1 \le j \le n$, are sets and $\overline{X} = \prod_{j=1}^{n} X^j$, then $\overline{X}_{\langle -j \rangle}$ denotes the set*

$$X^1 \times \cdots \times X^{j-1} \times X^{j+1} \times \cdots \times X^n.$$

If $\chi \in X^j$ and if $\zeta = (\zeta^1, \ldots, \zeta^{j-1}, \zeta^{j+1}, \ldots, \zeta^n) \in \overline{X}_{\langle -j \rangle}$, then $\chi \int_j \zeta$ denotes the element

$$(\zeta^1, \ldots, \zeta^{j-1}, \chi, \zeta^{j+1}, \ldots, \zeta^n) \text{ of } \overline{X}.$$

Similarly, suppose that for each $1 \le i \le n$, X^i is a manifold of dimension d_i and $[x_{(i,j)}]$, $1 \le j \le d_i$ is a (local) coordinate system on X^i. If $\underline{x}_i = [x_{(i,1)}, \ldots, x_{(i,d_i)}]$ and $\underline{x} = (\underline{x}_1, \ldots, \underline{x}_n)$, then for each $1 \le j \le n$, $\underline{x}_{\langle -j \rangle} = (\underline{x}_1, \ldots, \underline{x}_{j-1}, \underline{x}_{j+1}, \underline{x}_n)$. For coordinate systems, we use a similar extension of notation for the symbol $\underline{y}_i \int (\underline{z}_1, \ldots, \underline{z}_{j-1}, \underline{z}_{j+1}, \ldots, \underline{z}_n)$.

Definition 6.1.1. Suppose that X^i, $1 \le i \le n$, Y are sets; suppose that $F : \overline{X} = \prod_{i=1}^{n} X^i \to Y$ is a function; and suppose that $1 \le j \le n$. Two points

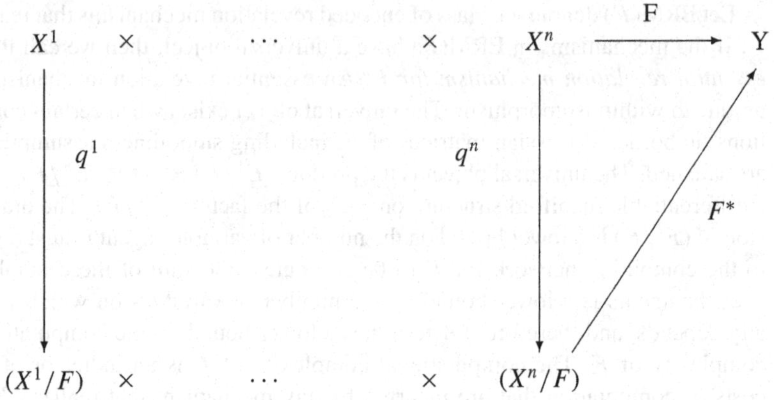

Figure 6.1.1.

χ and χ' in X^j are F equivalent in X^j if for each $\zeta \in \overline{X}_{\langle -j \rangle}$, $F(\chi \int_j \zeta) = F(\chi' \int_j \zeta)$.

It is elementary that F equivalence in X^j is an equivalence relation on points of X^j. Denote by (X^j/F) the collection of F equivalence classes of X^j. Set q^j equal to the quotient map from X^j to (X^j/F).

The following lemma establishes the sense in which the set $(X^1/F) \times \cdots \times (X^n/F)$ is the smallest product set through which F factors.

Lemma 6.1.1. *Suppose that* $X^1, \ldots, X^n$ *and* Y *are sets and suppose that* $F : \overline{X} = X^1 \times \cdots \times X^n \to Y$ *is a function. There is a unique function* $F^* : (X^1/F) \times \cdots \times (X^n/F) \to Y$ *that makes Figure 6.1.1 commute. Furthermore, if* $Z^1, \ldots, Z^n$ *are sets, and if there are functions* $g^i : X^i \to Z^i$, $1 \leq i \leq n$, *and a function* $G : \overline{Z} = Z^1 \times \cdots \times Z^n \to Y$ *that makes Figure 6.1.2 commute, then there are uniquely determined maps* $g^{*1}, \ldots, g^{*n}$, $g^{*i} : Z^i \to (X^i/F)$, *that make Figure 6.1.3 commute.*

We now prove Lemma 6.1.1.

Proof of Lemma 6.1.1. We first show that if $g^i : X^i \to Z^i$ and $G : \prod_1^n Z^i \to Y$ are functions that make Figure 6.1.1 commute, then we can factor the map $\prod_1^n g^i$ through the product $\prod_1^n (X^i/F)$. If $\zeta \in Z^i$, choose $\chi, \chi' \in X^i$ such that $g^i(\chi') = g^i(\chi) = \zeta$. For each $\omega \in \overline{X}_{\langle -i \rangle}$, set

$$g(\omega) = [g^1(\omega^1), \ldots, g^{i-1}(\omega^{i-1}),\ g^{i+1}(\omega^{i+1}), \ldots, g^n(\omega^n)] \in \overline{Z}_{\langle -i \rangle}.$$

Then

$$F\left(\chi \underset{i}{\int} w\right) = G\left[g^i(\chi) \underset{i}{\int} g(\omega)\right] = G\left[g^i(\chi') \underset{i}{\int} g(\omega)\right] = F\left(\chi' \underset{i}{\int} \omega\right).$$

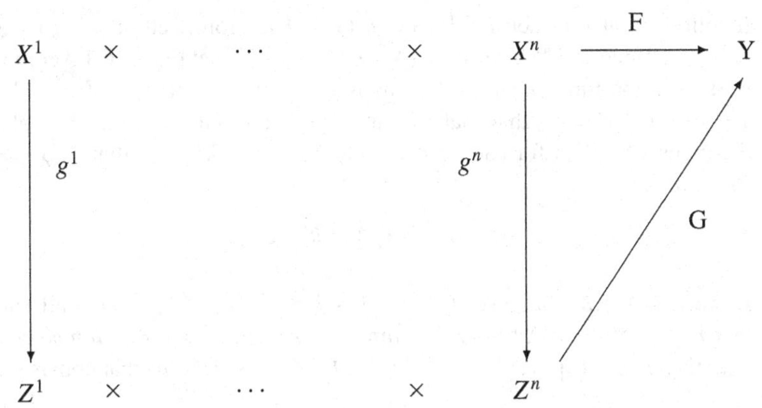

Figure 6.1.2.

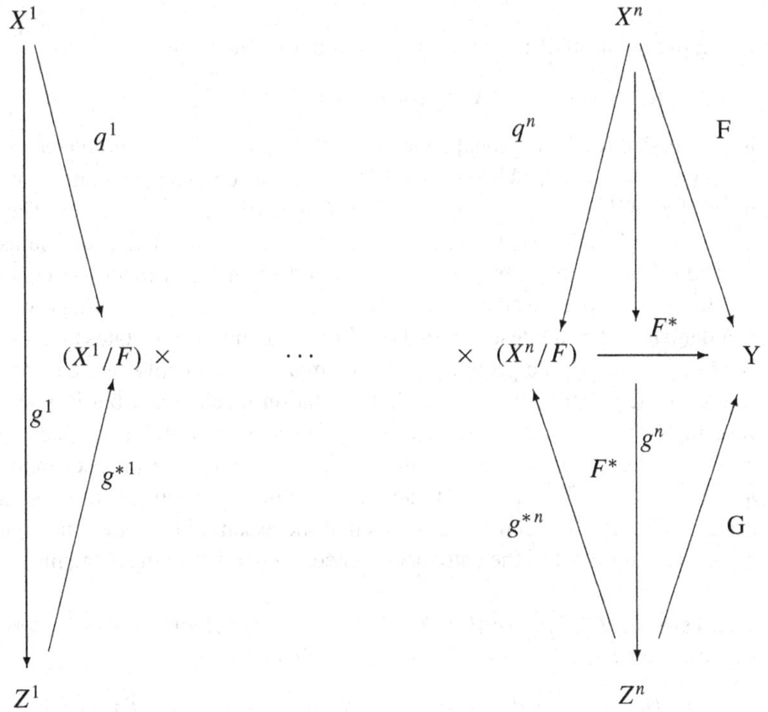

Figure 6.1.3.

It follows that for each i, $q^i(\chi) = q^i(\chi')$. Therefore, setting $g^{*i}(\zeta) = g^i(\chi)$ defines a function g^{*i} from Z^i to (X^i/F). It is clear that Figure 6.1.3 commutes.

To see the uniqueness of the maps g^{*i}, note that if $h^{*i} : Z^i \to (X^i/F)$, $1 \le i \le n$, are maps that make Figure 6.1.3 commute when used in place of the maps g^{*i}, then for each $\zeta \in Z^i$ and each $\chi \in X^i$ such that $g^i(\chi) = \zeta$, it follows that

$$g^{*i}(\zeta) = g^{*i}[g^i(\chi)] = q^i(\chi) = h^{*i}[g^i(\chi)] = h^{*i}(\zeta). \qquad \square$$

Definition 6.1.2. Suppose that X^i, $1 \le i \le n$, and Z are sets and suppose that $F : X^1 \times \cdots \times X^n \to Z$ is a function. An *encoded revelation mechanism realizing* F is a triple $(g^1 \times \cdots \times g^n,\ M^1 \times \cdots \times M^n,\ h)$ that consists of:

(i) a product of sets $M^1 \times \cdots \times M^n$,
(ii) a collection of functions $g^i : X^i \to M^i$, $1 \le i \le n$, and
(iii) a function $h : M^1 \times \cdots \times M^n \to Z$, such that for each

$$(\eta_1, \ldots, \eta_n) \in X^1 \times \cdots \times X^n, \quad F(\eta_1, \ldots, \eta_n) = h[g^1(\eta_1), \ldots, g^n(\eta_n)].$$

Using the notation of Lemma 6.1.1, we find that the triple

$$[q^1 \times \cdots \times q^n, (X^1/F) \times \cdots \times (X^n/F), F^*]$$

is an encoded revelation mechanism called the *essential revelation mechanism.*

If $(g^1 \times \cdots \times g^n,\ M^1 \times \cdots \times M^n,\ h)$ is an encoded revelation mechanism, then $M^1 \times \cdots \times M^n$ is an *encoded revelation message space.* The map $g^1 \times \cdots \times g^n$ is the *message function* of the encoded revelation mechanism.

The following theorem is a restatement of Lemma 6.1.1 in terms of encoded revelation mechanisms. It establishes the sense in which the essential revelation mechanism is the smallest encoded revelation mechanism. It states that not only is $M^1 \times \cdots \times M^n$ the product with the smallest cardinality that can be used as the message space for an encoded revelation mechanism, but it is also the case that for every other product space that acts as a message space for an encoded revelation mechanism that realizes F, there is a product map onto $M^1 \times \cdots \times M^n$. This is a characteristic of a universal object in the sense of category theory. Theorem 6.1.2 states that the essential revelation mechanism is a universal object in the category of encoded revelation mechanisms.

Theorem 6.1.2. *Suppose that X^i, $1 \le i \le n$, and Z are nonempty sets and suppose that $F : X^1 \times \cdots \times X^n \to Z$ is a function.*

1. *The triple*[3] *$[q^1 \times \cdots \times q^n,\ (X^1/F) \times \cdots \times (X^n/F),\ F^*]$ is an encoded revelation mechanism that realizes F.*

[3] The notation F^* denotes that unique function described in Lemma 6.1.1 that makes Figure 6.1.1 commute.

2. *The message function for any other encoded revelation mechanism factors through* $(X^1/F) \times \cdots \times (X^n/F)$.
3. *The set* $(X^1/F) \times \cdots \times (X^n/F)$ *is the smallest set in cardinality that can be used as an encoded revelation message space for a mechanism that realizes* F.
4. *Finally, the essential revelation mechanism is the unique encoded revelation mechanism (to within isomorphism) through which all encoded revelation mechanisms that realize* F *factor.*

When the X^i are topological manifolds and when F is continuous, it is generally not true that the sets (X^i/F) are manifolds. Even a high degree of smoothness of F is insufficient to guarantee that (X^i/F) is a topological manifold. However, when the (X^i/F) are Hausdorff, a fairly simple condition on the Jacobian of F coupled with a global separation condition stated in Definition 6.1.3 does imply that the (X^i/F) are manifolds. When these conditions are satisfied, the essential revelation mechanism has the structure of a manifold, and the dimensions of the (X^i/F) can be used to establish a lower bound on the number of variables, that is, the number of functions in a coordinate system, that must be passed to a central processor in order to compute F. This number determines a lower bound for the complexity of the function F.

Next we introduce the concept of differentiable separability. We then give simple global conditions on the function F to ensure that the sets (X^i/F) are topological manifolds. We begin with some concepts from differential geometry (see Golubitsky and Guillemin, 1973).

Definition 6.1.3. Suppose $X^1, \ldots, X^n$ are differentiable manifolds, where for each $1 \le i \le n$, X^i has dimension d_i. Suppose that $p_i \in X^i$, $1 \le i \le n$, and suppose that for each i, $[x_{(i,1)}, \ldots, x_{(i,d_i)}]$ is a coordinate system in an open neighborhood U^i of p_i. Suppose that $F : \prod_{i=1}^n X^i \to \mathfrak{R}$ is a C^2 function. Assume that for $1 \le i \le n$, $\underline{x}_i = \prod_j x_{(i,j)}$ maps U^i into an open neighborhood V^i of the origin 0_i of a Euclidean space $E^i = \mathfrak{R}^{d_i}$ and that $\underline{x}_i$ carries p_i to 0_i. The function F is said to be *differentiably separable of rank* $(r_1, \ldots, r_n)$ *at the point* $(p_1, \ldots, p_n)$ *in the coordinate system* $[x_{(1,1)}, \ldots, x_{(n,d_n)}]$ if for each $1 \le i \le n$, the matrices

$$BH_{(\underline{x}_i, \underline{x}_{(-i)})}\left[F \circ \left(\prod \underline{x}_t\right)^{-1}\right]$$

and

$$H_{(\underline{x}_i, \underline{x}_{(-i)})}\left[F \circ \left(\prod \underline{x}_t\right)^{-1}\right][\underline{x}_i, 0_{(-i)}]$$

have rank r_i in a neighborhood of $(0_1, \ldots, 0_n)$. If F is differentiably separable of rank $(r_1, \ldots, r_n)$ at $(p_1, \ldots, p_n)$, and if $r_i = \dim(X^i)$ for each $1 \le i \le n$, then we will say that F is *differentiably separable at* $(p_1, \ldots, p_n)$.

It follows in Appendix B, p. 211, from the discussion that the ranks of the Hessians used in the previous definition are unchanged by coordinate changes.

We can now define the term *differentiably separable* for a function defined on a differentiable manifold.

Definition 6.1.4. If $X^i, 1 \leq i \leq n$ are C^2 manifolds, the function $F : X^1 \times \cdots \times X^n \to \mathfrak{R}$ is differentiably separable of rank $(r_1, \ldots, r_n)$ at the point $(p_1, \ldots, p_n)$ if there is a coordinate system $[x_{(i,j)}]$ at the point $(p_1, \ldots, p_n)$ such that F is differentiably separable of rank $(r_1, \ldots, r_n)$ at the point $(p_1, \ldots, p_n)$ in the coordinate system $[x_{(1,1)}, \ldots, x_{(n,d_n)}]$.

If $F : X^1 \times \cdots \times X^n \to \mathfrak{R}$ is differentiably separable of rank $(r_1, \ldots, r_n)$ at a point $(p_1, \ldots, p_n)$, then it is possible to write F as a function of variables $[y_{(1,1)}, \ldots, y_{(1,r_1)}, \ldots, y_{(n,1)}, \ldots, y_{(n,r_n)}]$. This assertion, Lemma 6.1.3, is a restatement of Theorem 3.2.1.

Lemma 6.1.3. *Suppose that for* $1 \leq i \leq n$, X^i *is a* C^2 *manifold. Assume that (1)* $F : X^1 \times \cdots \times X^n \to \mathfrak{R}$ *is a* C^2 *function, (2)* $(p_1, \ldots, p_n)$ *is a point on* $X^1 \times \cdots \times X^n$*, and (3)* X^i *has coordinates* $\underline{x}_i$*. A necessary condition that in a neighborhood of the point* $(p_1, \ldots p_n)$*,* F *can be written in the form*

$$G\left[y_{(1,1)}, \ldots, y_{(1,r_1)}, \ldots, y_{(n,1)}, \ldots, y_{(n,r_n)}\right],$$

where $[y_{(i,1)}, \ldots, y_{(i,d_i)}]$ *is a coordinate system on* X^i*, is that the matrix*

$$BH_{(\underline{x}_i, \underline{x}_{(-i)})}(G)$$

has rank at most r_i *for each i. Furthermore, a sufficient condition for* F *to be written in the form* $G[y_{(1,1)}, \ldots, y_{(1,r_1)}, \ldots, y_{(n,1)}, \ldots, y_{(n,r_n)}]$*, for a* C^2 *function* G *in a neighborhood of a point* $(p_1, \ldots, p_n)$*, is that* F *is differentiably separable of rank exactly* $(r_1, \ldots, r_n)$ *at* $(p_1, \ldots, p_n)$*.*

Lemma 6.1.3 suggests that in the case of a differentiable function F satisfying the rank conditions stated in the lemma, it is possible to construct an essential revelation mechanism whose message space is a topological manifold. We now carry out the construction suggested by the lemma. The main result is given in Theorem 6.1.5 and in Corollary 6.1.6.

Definition 6.1.5. Suppose that $X^i, 1 \leq i \leq n$, and Z are C^2 manifolds and suppose that $F : X^1 \times \cdots \times X^n \to Z$ is a differentiable function. The triple $[g^1, \ldots, g^n, M^1 \times \cdots \times M^n, h]$ that consists of spaces $M^1 \times \cdots \times M^n$, maps $g^1, \ldots, g^n, g^i : X^i \to M^i, 1 \leq i \leq n$, and function $h : M^1 \times \cdots \times M^n \to Z$ is an encoded C^2 revelation mechanism that realizes F if

(i) each of the spaces M^i is a C^2 manifold;
(ii) each of the functions $g_i, 1 \leq i \leq n$, and h is C^2 differentiable;

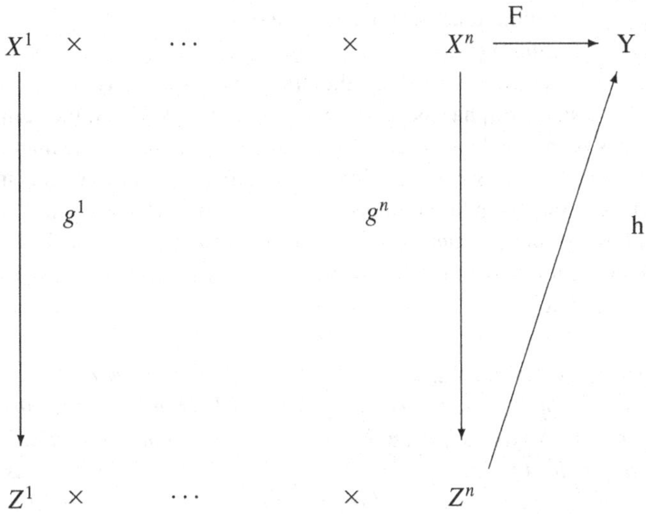

Figure 6.1.4.

(iii) each g^i, $1 \leq i \leq n$, has a local thread at each point of M^i; and
(iv) $h \circ (\prod_i g^i) = F$.

Definition 6.1.6. Suppose that $F : X^1 \times \cdots \times X^n \to Z$ is a differentiable map from a product of differentiable manifolds $X^1, \ldots, X^n$ to a differentiable manifold Y. The function F *factors through a product of manifolds* $Z^1 \times \cdots \times Z^n$ if there are submersions $g^i : X^i \to Z^i$, and a differentiable mapping $h : Z^1 \times \cdots \times Z^n \to Y$ such that Figure 6.1.4 commutes.

It has not yet been established that the essential revelation mechanism is an encoded C^2 revelation mechanism, because the construction given in Theorem 6.1.2 ignores all topological and differentiable structure.

The method we use to put a structure on the (X^i/F) is straightforward. The general outline of the method is as follows. The space X^i has coordinates $\underline{x}_i = [x_{(i,1)}, \ldots, x_{(i,d_i)}]$. We first show that when the rank of $BH_{(\underline{x}_i, \underline{x}_{\langle -i \rangle})}(F)$ is the same as the dimension of X^i, then for each two points a and a' in X^i, there is an element $b \in X_{\langle -i \rangle}$ such that $F(a, b) \neq F(a', b)$. Therefore, the set (X^i/F) is X^i. We next appeal to the generalization of the theorem of Leontief given in Lemma 6.1.3. That lemma shows that if $\overline{X} = \prod_j X^j$ and the rank of $bh_{(X^i, \overline{X}_{\langle -i \rangle})}(F)$ at a point is r_i, then in a neighborhood of the point there is a coordinate system $\underline{x}_i = [x_{(i,1)}, \ldots, x_{(i,d_i)}]$ and a function G such that

$$F(\underline{x}_1, \ldots, \underline{x}_n) = G\left\{\left[x_{(i,1)}, \ldots, x_{(i,r)}\right] \int_i \underline{x}_{\langle -i \rangle}\right\}.$$

We can use the remaining set of coordinates in X^i to determine a subspace S of X^i by setting $x_{(i,r+1)} = 0, \ldots, x_{(i,d_i)} = 0$. The set S is a submanifold of X^i and the restriction of F to the space $S \times \overline{X}_{\langle -i \rangle}$ has the property that $bh_{(X^i, \overline{X}_{\langle -i \rangle})}[\text{restrict}(F)]$ has as rank the dimension of S. On S, the restriction of F separates points (at least in a neighborhood) and therefore the map from S to (X^i/F) is one to one. Some technical yoga with quotient topologies makes the quotient map, locally, a homeomorphism. Therefore, at least locally, the space (X^i/F) has the same structure as S. The rest of the proof consists of adding enough restrictions to ensure that the local argument can be carried out globally on $X^1 \times \cdots \times X^n$.

Theorem 6.1.4. *Suppose that X^i, $1 \leq i \leq n$, is a Euclidean space of dimension $d_i \geq 1$. Suppose that for each $1 \leq i \leq n$, U^i is an open neighborhood of the origin 0_i of X^i and suppose that F is a C^3 function differentiably separable at each point $(p_1, \ldots, p_n) \in \overline{U} = U^1 \times \cdots \times U^n$. Then there is an open neighborhood U of $\underline{p_i}$ such that for each pair of points a and a' in U, $a \neq a'$, there is a point $b \in \overline{U}_{\langle -i \rangle}$ such that $F(a, b) \neq F(a', b)$.*

Proof of Theorem 6.1.4. The matrix $H(F)_{(x,y)}[0, 0]$ has rank d_i, by assumption. Denote the product $\prod_j X^j$ by $\overline{X}$. Set $X = X^i$, set $\overline{X}_{\langle -i \rangle} = Y$, set $\dim(X_{\langle -i \rangle}) = N$, and set $m = d_i$. We can change coordinates in X and Y separately to coordinates z in X and w in Y so that the new matrix $H(F)(z, w)[0, 0]$ has a 1 in the $z_j \times w_j$ position, $1 \leq j \leq m$, and a zero in all the other positions. The Taylor series expansion for $F(z_1, \ldots, z_m, w_1, \ldots, w_N)$ then has the form

$$F(z, w) = F(0, 0) + u \circ z + v' \circ w + w \circ z + z^T Qz + w^T Q'w$$
$$+ P(z^*, w^*)[z, w],$$

where Q and Q' are square matrices; u and v' are vectors in $\mathfrak{R}^m$ and $\mathfrak{R}^N$, respectively; $v' \circ w$ denotes inner product; z^T denotes the transpose of the column vector z; and where $P(z^*, w^*)[z, w]$ is a cubic polynomial in the variables $(z_1, \ldots, z_m, w_1, \ldots, w_N)$ with coefficients that are continuous functions on $U \times V$ evaluated at some point $z^* \in U$ and $w^* \in V$. These coefficients of P are bounded on a ball that is a compact neighborhood of $(0, 0) \in U' \times V'$, $U' \subseteq U$, and $V' \subseteq V$. Then for z, $z' \in U'$, and $w \in V'$,

$$|F(z, w) - F(z', w)| = |u \circ (z - z') + w \circ (z - z') + z^T Qz'$$
$$+ P(z'^*, w'^*)[z', w] - P(z^*, w^*)[z, w]|.$$

The vector $(z - z') \neq 0$ and the w is to be chosen in the set V'. Set $z'^T Qz' - z^T Qz = K$, set $u \circ v = L$, and set $(z - z') = v$. To complete the proof, we find that it will suffice to show that the function

$$w \circ v + P(z^*, w^*)[z', w] + P(z^*, w^*)[z, w] + K + L$$

is not constant on the ball V'. For this it will suffice to show that the function

$$G = w \circ v + P(z^*, w^*)[z', w] - P(z^*, w^*)[z, w]$$

is not constant on the ball V'. The function $P(z^*, w^*)[z', w] - P(z^*, w^*)[z, w]$ is a homogeneous cubic $\Sigma_{\alpha,\beta} a_{\alpha,\beta} z^\alpha w^\beta$ in the variables $w_1, \ldots, w_N$ with coefficients $\{a_{\alpha,\beta}(z, z', w, w')\}$ that are functions bounded on $U' \times V'$. Set $w = tv$. The powers of the constants $z_1, \ldots, z_m$ can be combined with the coefficients $a_{\alpha,\beta}$ and therefore $G = t \mid v \mid^2 + a(t)t^3$, where the $a(t)$ is also bounded as a function of t. If $a(t) = 0$ identically in t, then because $v \neq 0$, different values of t produce different values of G. If $a(t) \neq 0$, and $\mid v \mid^2 + a(t)t^2 = c$ (a is constant), then $a(t) = (c - \mid v \mid^2)/t^2$, and therefore $a(t)$ is not bounded as t approaches zero. Therefore G is not a constant. □

We now give conditions on a function F that is differentiably separable of rank $(r_1, \ldots, r_n)$, that imply that each of the sets (X^i/F), with the quotient topology, has the structure of a C^0 manifold of dimension r_i. Under these conditions the set theoretic essential revelation mechanism is a topological essential revelation mechanism.

Definition 6.1.7. If X^i, $1 \leq i \leq n$, are topological spaces, then a real-valued function $F : X^1 \times \cdots \times X^n \to \mathfrak{R}$ *induces strong equivalence* on X^i, if the following condition is satisfied for each $\chi, \chi' \in X^i$, such that $\chi \neq \chi'$; there is an open neighborhood U of a point $\eta \in X_{\langle -i \rangle}$, such that if $F(\chi \int_i \omega) = F(\chi' \int_i \omega)$ for each $\omega \in U$, then $F(\chi \int_i \zeta) = F(\chi' \int_i \zeta)$ for all $\zeta \in X_{\langle -i \rangle}$.

It is relatively easy to find classes of functions that induce strong equivalence. Suppose the X^i are Euclidean spaces with coordinates $x_{i,j}$, $1 \leq i \leq n, 1 \leq j \leq d_i$. If for each $1 \leq i \leq n$, $\beta(i) = [\beta(i, 1), \ldots, \beta(i, d_i)]$ is a sequence of nonnegative integers, denote by $\underline{x}_i^{\beta(i)}$ the monomial $x_{(i,1)}^{\beta(i,1)}, \ldots, x_{(i,d_i)}^{\beta(i,d_i)}$, and denote by $\underline{x}_1^{\beta(1)}, \ldots, \underline{x}_n^{\beta(n)}$ the product of the monomials $\underline{x}_i^{\beta(i)}$. Write

$$F(\underline{x}_1, \ldots, \underline{x}_n) = \sum\nolimits_{\beta(1),\ldots,\beta(n)} A_{\beta(1),\ldots,\beta(n)} \underline{x}_2^{\beta(2)}, \ldots, \underline{x}_n^{\beta(n)},$$

where $A_\beta(\underline{x}_1)$ are polynomials in $\underline{x}_1$. Then for $\chi_1, \chi_1' \in X^1$, $F(\chi_1, \chi_{\langle -1 \rangle}) = F(\chi_1', \chi_{\langle -1 \rangle})$ for $\chi_{\langle -1 \rangle}$ in an open set in $X^{\langle -1 \rangle}$, if and only if $[A_\beta(\chi_1) - A_\beta(\chi_1')]\, \chi_2^{\beta(2)}, \ldots, \chi_n^{\beta(n)} = 0$ for the $\chi_2, \ldots, \chi_n$ chosen arbitrarily in an open set in $X^2 \times \cdots \times X^n$. However, a polynomial vanishes in an open set if and only if each of its coefficients is zero. Therefore if $F(\chi_1, \chi_{\langle -1 \rangle}) = F(\chi_1, \chi_{\langle -1 \rangle})$ for the $\chi_{\langle -1 \rangle}$ chosen in some open set, it follows that for each β, $A_\beta(\chi_1) - A_\beta(\chi_1') = 0$. That is, F induces a strong equivalence relation on X^1.

Theorem 6.1.5. *Suppose that X^i, $1 \le i \le n$ are C^4 manifolds of dimensions $d_1, \ldots, d_n$, respectively. Suppose $F : X^1 \times \cdots \times X^n \to \mathfrak{R}$ is a C^4 function that is differentiably separable on $X^1 \times \cdots \times X^n$ of rank $(r_1, \ldots, r_n)$ where each $r_i \ge 1$. Assume that F induces strong equivalence in X^i for each i. If (i) the spaces (X^i/F) are all Hausdorff, then (ii) quotient map $q^i : X^i \to (X^i/F)$ is open for each $1 \le i \le n$. Then, for each $1 \le i \le n$, the space (X^i/F), with quotient topology, is a topological manifold (i.e., a C^0 manifold). Furthermore, the quotient map $q^i : X^i \to (X^i/F)$ has a local thread in the neighborhood of each point.*

Proof of Theorem 6.1.5. Suppose that $p_i^* \in (X^i/F)$, $1 \le i \le n$. Set $\overline{X} = \prod_j X^j$. Choose a point $p_i \in X^i, 1 \le i \le n$, such that $q^i(p_i) = p_i^*$. Because the function F is differentiably separable of rank $(r_1, \ldots, r_n)$ at the point $(p_1, \ldots, p_n)$, it follows from Leontief's Theorem B.2.4 that for $1 \le i \le n$, there is an open neighborhood $\overline{U}_{\langle -i\rangle}$ of $p_{\langle -i\rangle}$ in $\overline{X}_{\langle -i\rangle}$, an open neighborhood U^i of the point p_i, and a coordinate system $\underline{x}_i = \{x_{(i,1)}, \ldots, x_{(i,d_i)}\}$ in X^i such that $\underline{x}_i(p_i) = (0, \ldots, 0)$ and a C^3 function G defined in a neighborhood of the origin, such that for each $(\underline{\chi}_1, \ldots, \underline{\chi}_n) \in \overline{U}$,

$$F(\underline{\chi}_1, \ldots, \underline{\chi}_n) = G\left\{\left[\chi_{(i,1)}, \ldots, \chi_{(i,r_i)}\right] \underset{i}{\int} \zeta\right\}$$

for each $\zeta \in \overline{U}_{\langle -i\rangle}$. Denote by S^{*i} the set of elements $\{\chi_{i,1}, \ldots, \chi_{i,r_i}, 0, \ldots, 0\}$ that lie in U^i. Choose a compact neighborhood S^i of $(0, \ldots, 0)$ in S^{*i} (in the induced topology on S^{*i}). The map q^i carries the set U^i to an open set of (X^i/F) because we have assumed that q^i is an open map. We have assumed that the equivalence relation induced on $\overline{X}_{\langle -i\rangle}$ by F is strong; therefore the equality

$$F\left[\chi_{(i,1)}, \ldots, \chi_{(i,r_i)}, \beta_1, \ldots, \beta_{d_i - r_i} \underset{i}{\int} \zeta_{\langle -i\rangle}\right] = F\left\{\left[\chi_{(i,1)}, \ldots, \chi_{(i,r_i)}, 0, \ldots, 0\right] \underset{i}{\int} \zeta_{\langle -i\rangle}\right\}$$

implies that

$$q^i\left[\chi_{(i,1)}, \ldots, \chi_{(i,d_i)}\right] = q^i\left[\chi_{(i,1)}, \ldots, \chi_{(i,r_i)}\right]$$

for each $[\chi_{(i,1)}, \ldots, \chi_{(i,d_i)}]$ in U^i. Therefore, $q^i(U^i) = q^i(S^{*i})$. The set S^{*i} was constructed so that q^i is one to one on S^{*i}. By assumption, the space (X^i/F) is Hausdorff; therefore the restriction of q^i to S^i is a homeomorphism from S^i to a neighborhood N^i of p_i^*. Denote by s^i the inverse of q^i on N^i. It follows that the point $p_i^* \in X^i$ has a neighborhood N^i that is homeomorphic to a neighborhood of the origin of the space $\mathfrak{R}^{r_i}$. Furthermore, the function s^i is a thread of q^i on the set N^i. □

The following corollary states that the essential revelation mechanism is a C^0 essential revelation mechanism. In this case, under the assumptions made about F, each C^0 encoded revelation mechanism factors through the C^0 essential revelation mechanism.

Corollary 6.1.6. *Suppose that X^i, $1 \leq i \leq n$ are C^4 manifolds and that X^i has dimension d_i. Assume that $F : X^1 \times \cdots \times X^n \to \mathfrak{R}$ is a real-valued function on F that satisfies the following conditions.*

1. *There are integers $(r_1, \ldots, r_n)$, $1 \leq r_i \leq d_i$, such that at each point $(p_1, \ldots, p_n) \in X^1 \times \cdots \times X^n$, F is differentiably separable of rank $(r_1, \ldots, r_n)$.*
2. *For each i, the map $q^i : X^i \to (X^i/F)$ is open and (X^i/F) is Hausdorff.*
3. *For each i, F induces a strong equivalence relation on X^i.*

Then the triple

$$[q^1 \times \cdots \times q^n, (X^1/F) \times \cdots \times (X^n/F), F^*]$$

where (1) each (X^i/F) is given the quotient topology, (2) the map $q^i : X^i \to (X^i/F)$ is the quotient map, and (3) $F^* : (X^1/F) \times \cdots \times (X^n/F) \to \mathfrak{R}$ is such that

$$F^*[q^1(\chi_1), \ldots, q^n(\chi_n)] = F(\chi_1, \ldots, \chi_n),$$

for each $(\chi_1, \cdots, \chi_n) \in X^1 \times \cdots \times X^n$, is an encoded C^0 revelation mechanism that realizes F.

The space (X^i/F) has dimension r_i. Furthermore, if a triple

$$(g^1 \times \cdots \times g^n, Z^1 \times \cdots \times Z^n, G)$$

is such that $g^i : X^i \to Z^i, G : Z^1 \times \cdots \times Z^n \to \mathfrak{R}$, and the triple is an encoded revelation mechanism that realizes F, then there are continuous maps $g^{*i} : Z^i \to (X^i/F)$ such that the diagram in Figure 6.1.3 commutes, with $Y = \mathfrak{R}$.

Proof of Corollary 6.1.6. Set $\overline{X} = \prod_j X^j$. We have already shown in Theorem 6.1.5 that the triple

$$[q^1 \times \cdots \times q^n, (X^1/F) \times \cdots \times (X^n/F), F^*]$$

is an encoded revelation mechanism that realizes F. Suppose that $\zeta *_i \in Z^i$. For each $\omega \in \overline{X}_{\langle -i \rangle}$, denote $[g^1(\omega), \ldots, g^{i-1}(\omega), g^{i+1}(\omega), \ldots, g^n(\omega)]$ by $g_{\langle -i \rangle}(\omega)$.

Choose an element $\chi_i^* \in X^i$ such that $g^i(\chi_i^*) = \zeta_i^*$. Suppose that $\chi_i^{**}, \chi_i^* \in X^i$, such that $g^i(x_i^*) = g^i(\chi **_i) = z_i^*$. Then for each $\omega \in \overline{X}_{\langle -i \rangle}$,

$$F\left(\chi^{*i} \underset{i}{\int} \omega\right) = G\left[g^i(\chi^{*i}) \underset{i}{\int} g_{\langle -i\rangle}(\omega)\right] = G\left[g^i(\chi_i^{**}) \underset{i}{\int} g_{\langle -i\rangle}(\omega)\right] = F\left(\chi_i^{**} \underset{i}{\int} \omega\right).$$

Therefore, $q^i(\chi_i^*) = q^i(\chi_i^{**})$. Set $g^{*i}(\zeta_i^*) = q^i(\chi_i^*)$. Because the map $g^i : X^i \to Z^i$ has a thread in the neighborhood of each point, there is a neighborhood N of the point ζ_i^* and a thread $s^i : N \to X^i$ such that $g^i[s^i(\zeta_i^*)] = g^i(\zeta_i^*)$ for each $\zeta^* \in N$. Then $g^{*i}(\zeta^{*i}) = q^i[s^i(\zeta^{*i})]$. Because both q^i and s^i are continuous, it follows that the map g^{*i} is continuous. □

6.2. FINITE APPROXIMATIONS

Here we analyze the time needed to compute a C^s function F by $\mathcal{D}^s(2, 1)$ networks as a limit of times taken by finite networks, that is networks whose modules use finite alphabets, that compute finite approximations to F. In the limiting process studied here, the structure of the approximating networks remains fixed while the size of the alphabet is allowed to vary. This may be interpreted to say that the same algorithm is used to compute the finite approximating functions and the limiting function, while increasingly many symbols are used to encode the finer approximations as we pass to the limit, much as the number of digits in a rational approximation of a real number increases as we consider progressively finer measurements.

Theorem 6.2.1 states the result of interest, a result that helps to justify the use of $\mathcal{D}^0(2, 1)$ or $\mathcal{D}^s(2, 1)$ networks to represent computing. The assumption used in Lemmas 6.2.2 and 6.2.3, which are part of the hypotheses of Theorem 6.2.1, can be satisfied, for instance, by using polynomials for the approximating functions. Before we can state and prove these propositions, we must introduce some definitions, in particular the definition of the lattice of a rectangular decomposition of a Euclidean space, an ϵ approximation of a function and some related notions. We do this next.

6.2.1. Lattice Decomposition of $\mathfrak{R}^n$

We will define an approximation of a continuous function by finite functions defined on a lattice. We begin by introducing concepts associated with the lattices to be used.

Definition 6.2.1.

1. A *rectangular decomposition* of $\mathfrak{R}$ is a countable collection of half-open intervals $[a_i, b_i)$ that form a partition of $\mathfrak{R}$, that is, such that $\mathfrak{R} = \bigcup_i [a_i, b_i)$, and $[a_i, b_i) \cap [a_j, b_j) = \emptyset$, unless $i = j$.

2. Let V be a Euclidean space with standard basis $(e_1, \ldots, e_n)$. A rectangular decomposition of V along the basis $\{e_i\}$ is a family of n rectangular decompositions of $\mathfrak{R}$,

   $$\{[a_{(k,i)}, b_{(k,i)})\},$$

   such that

   $$V = \bigcup_{i_1,\ldots,i_n} \{[a_{(1,i_1)}, b_{(1,i_1)}) \times [a_{(2,i_2)}, b_{(2,i_2)}) \times \cdots \times [a_{(n,i_n)}, b_{(n,i_n)})\}.$$

   A rectangular decomposition of V is the partition of V formed by the product of the rectangular decompositions that partition the lines

   $$\Lambda(e_i) = \{v \in V : v = \lambda e_i \text{ for some } \lambda \in \mathfrak{R}\}.$$

   A rectangular decomposition of V is of course a covering of V. Therefore every point of V is contained in some rectangle of the decomposition. Because the covering is a partition, that rectangle is unique.
3. Let D be a rectangular decomposition of V along the basis $(e_1, \ldots, e_n)$, and let

   $$d = [a_{(1,i_1)}, b_{(1,i_1)}) \times \cdots \times [a_{(n,i_n)}, b_{(n,i_n)})$$

   be a rectangle of the decomposition. The point $[a_{(1,i_1)}, \ldots, a_{(n,i_n)}]$ is called the *principal vertex of* d.
4. The set of principal vertices of rectangles in a rectangular decomposition of V form a lattice, called the *lattice of the decomposition.*
5. If L is the lattice of a decomposition of V, and $v \in L, v = (v_1, \ldots, v_n)$, then $B(v) = \{[v_1, b_1) \times \cdots \times [v_n, b_n)\}$ is the rectangle of the lattice with principle vertex v. Each $[v_i, b_i)$ is called a *side of* $B(v)$.
6. For $x \in V$, and L the lattice of a decomposition of V, $l(x)$ is defined to be that point of L such that $x \in B(\ell(x))$.

Definition 6.2.2. Let V_i $i = 1, \ldots, p$, be Euclidean spaces, and let F: $V_1 \times \ldots \times V_p \to \mathfrak{R}$. Let L_i $i = 1, \ldots, p$ be the lattice of a rectangular decomposition of V_i, and let

$$f : L_1 \times \cdots \times L_p \to \mathfrak{R}.$$

For $\epsilon > 0$, the function f is called an ϵ *approximation* of F if for each $(v_1, \ldots, v_p) \in \prod_{i=1}^{p} L_i$ and each $(\chi_1, \ldots, \chi_p) \in \prod_{i=1}^{p} B(v_i)$,

$$|f(v_1, \ldots, v_p) - F(\chi_1, \ldots, \chi_p)| < \epsilon.$$

Definition 6.2.3. The lattice of a rectangular decomposition of a Euclidean space is *uniform* if, for some real number s, the length of each side of each rectangle of the lattice is s.

6.2.2. A Limit Theorem

Theorem 6.2.1. *(Limit Theorem) Let* $F : V_c \to \mathfrak{R}$, $V_c = \mathfrak{R}_c \times \cdots \times \mathfrak{R}_c$, *where* $\mathfrak{R}_c$ *is a compact neighborhood of zero in* $\mathfrak{R}$ *and* V_c *is a compact neighborhood of zero in the Euclidean space V, be a function satisfying* $F(0) = 0$ *that is computed by a* $\mathcal{D}^0(2, 1)$ *[resp.* $\mathcal{D}^s(2, 1)$*] network in time* t*. Suppose further that if a* $\mathcal{D}^0(2, 1)$ *[resp.* $\mathcal{D}^s(2, 1)$*] network computes F in time* t'*, then* $t' \geq t$*. For* $j = 1, 2, \ldots$*, let* $\epsilon_j > 0$ *be such that* $\epsilon_j > \epsilon_{j+1}$*, and* ϵ_j *and* ϵ_{j+1} *tend to 0 as* $j \to \infty$*. Let* $\{\mathbf{C}^j\}$ *be a sequence of finite* $(2, d_j)$ *networks with graphs that are trees such that* C^j *computes an* ϵ_j *approximation to F in a bounded neighborhood of 0, in time* t_j*.*[4] *Suppose further that the modules of* $\mathbf{C}^j$ *can be approximated at lattice points by* $\mathcal{D}^0(2, 1)$ *[resp.* $\mathcal{D}^s(2, 1)$*] functions, as described in the hypotheses of Lemma 6.2.2. Then* $\tau = \liminf\{t_j\}$ *satisfies the inequality* $\tau \geq t$*.*

Proof of Theorem 6.2.1. Let $\{\epsilon_j\}_{j=1}^{\infty}$ be a sequence of real numbers where $\epsilon_j > 0$, $\epsilon_j > \epsilon_{j+1}$, and $\epsilon_j \to 0$ as $j \to \infty$. Let $F : L_j \times \cdots \times L_j$ be an $\epsilon/2$ approximation of F, where L_j is the lattice of a rectangular decompostion of $\mathfrak{R}_c$. For each j, and ϵ_j, let C^j be a $(2, d_j)$ network with alphabet L_j that computes F_j in time τ_j. Because $\tau_j > 0$, it follows that $\tau = \liminf\{\tau_j\}$ ≥ 0.

If $\tau \geq t$, there is nothing left to prove. So, suppose $\tau < t$. Because τ_j and hence τ are integers, there is an infinite subsequence $\{C^{j^q}\} \subseteq \{C^j\}$ of networks that compute F_{j^q} in time τ.

For given τ, the number of binary trees of depth τ is finite. Therefore, there must be an infinite subsequence $\{C^{j^{q^r}}\} \subseteq \{C^{j^q}\}$ of $(2, d_j)$ networks, each of which computes F_{j^q} and all of which have the same graph. To simplify notation, let us call this subsequence $\{C_j\}$ and the corresponding sequence of approximations $\{F_j\}$. Thus, $\{C_j\}$ is an infinite sequence of $\{2, d_j\}$ networks, each with the same graph, that compute F_j in time τ.

Because all the networks C_j have the same graph, we can unambiguously identify modules in the same position in different networks. Let G^i_j be the module (function) in position i in network j.

Given the functions $G^i_j : L_j \times L_j \to L_j, i = 1, \ldots, q$ and $\epsilon_j > 0$, under the hypotheses of Lemma 6.2.2 there exist $\mathcal{D}^0(2, 1)$ [resp. $\mathcal{D}^s(2, 1)$] functions

[4] By Theorem A.0.5 we can, without loss of generality, confine attention to networks with graphs that are trees.

$P_j^i : \mathfrak{R}_c \times \mathfrak{R}_c \to \mathfrak{R}_c$ such that

$$\left|P_{n(\epsilon_j)}^i(l) - G_j^i(l)\right| < \epsilon_j/4$$

for $l \in L_j \times L_j$.

Under the hypotheses of Lemma 6.2.2, for each $i = 1, \ldots, q$, the sequence of $\mathcal{D}^0(2,1)$ [resp. $\mathcal{D}^s(2,1)$] functions $\{P_{n(\epsilon_j)}^i(l)\}_{j=1}^{\infty}$ has a uniform limit that is continuous (resp. C^n). Thus, the sequence of networks C_j converges to a network C' whose graph is the same as the common graph of all the C_j, and whose modules are the limits of the functions P_j^i as $j \to \infty$. Thus, the network C' is a $\mathcal{D}^s(2,1)$ network.

Furthermore, the network C' computes F. To see this, let C_j' be the network that results from substituting the function P_j^i in place of the function G_j^i in the network C_j. Let $F_j' : V_c \to \mathfrak{R}$ denote the function computed by C_j'. Because for each ϵ_j we have chosen the functions P_j^i such that

$$\left|P_j^i(l) - G_j^i(l)\right| < \epsilon_j/4,$$

it follows from Lemma 6.2.3 that for k sufficiently large,

$$|F_k' - F_k| < \epsilon_j/2.$$

Then,

$$|F_k' - F| \leq |F_k' - F_k| + |F_k - F| < \epsilon_j/2 + \epsilon_j/2 = \epsilon_j.$$

Finally, the limiting network C' computes F in time τ, because its graph is that of a network with graphs that are trees whose delay is τ.

Thus, the limiting network C is a $\mathcal{D}^0(2,1)$ [resp. $\mathcal{D}^s(2,1)$] network that computes F in time $\tau < t$. But this is impossible, because, by hypothesis, t is the minimum delay among all such $\mathcal{D}^0(2,1)$ [resp. $\mathcal{D}^s(2,1)$] networks that compute F. This concludes the proof. □

In the proof of Theorem 6.2.1 we have used a sequence of $\mathcal{D}^0(2,1)$ [resp. $\mathcal{D}^s(2,1)$] functions that approximate the modules of the finite networks at lattice points. Lemma 6.2.2 gives conditions under which the values of such an approximating function cannot differ much from the finite function everywhere on the rectangles of the lattice decomposition.

Lemma 6.2.2. *Let $\{\epsilon_j\}$ be a sequence of positive numbers decreasing to zero as j tends to infinity. For each ϵ_j let L_j be a lattice decomposition of $\mathfrak{R}_c$ (a compact neighborhood of zero in $\mathfrak{R}$) such that, (a) for $\ell \in L_j \times L_j$, $|P_j(\ell) - G_j(\ell)| < \epsilon_j/4$, where the functions $P_j : \mathfrak{R}_c \times \mathfrak{R}_c \to \mathfrak{R}_c$ form a sequence of $\mathcal{D}^0(2,1)$ [resp. $\mathcal{D}^s(2,1)$] functions that converge equicontinuously to a $\mathcal{D}^0(2,1)$ [resp. $\mathcal{D}^s(2,1)$] function $P : \mathfrak{R}_c \times \mathfrak{R}_c \to \mathfrak{R}_c$, and*

$$G_j : L_j \times L_j \to L_j$$

is a (finite) function for each $j = 1, 2, \ldots,$ *and (b) the mesh of the lattice* L_j *decreases to zero as* j *tends to infinity. Then, for* j *sufficiently large,* G_j *is an* ${}^{\epsilon_j}/_2$ *approximation to* P_j*. That is, for all* $x \in \mathfrak{R}_c \times \mathfrak{R}_c$,

$$|P_j(x) - G_j[l(x)]| < \epsilon_j/2.$$

Proof of Lemma 6.2.2. To show that for j sufficiently large G_j is an ${}^{\epsilon_j}/_2$ approximation to P_j on $\mathfrak{R}_c \times \mathfrak{R}_c$, we find that it suffices to show that if $x \in D_j[l(x)]$, then

$$|P_j(x) - G_j[l(x)]| < \epsilon_j/2.$$

Now,

$$|P_j(x) - G_j[l(x)]| \leq |P_j(x) - P_j[l(x)]| + |P_j[l(x)] - G_j[l(x)]|.$$

By hypothesis,

$$|P_j[l(x)] - G_j[l(x)]| < \epsilon_j/4$$

for all j. Therefore it remains to show that the other term is small. Because P_j is uniformly continuous on $\mathfrak{R}_c \times \mathfrak{R}_c$, for every $\eta_j > 0$, there exists $\gamma_j(\eta_j) > 0$ such that

$$|x - l(x)| < \gamma_j(\eta_j)$$

implies

$$|P_j(x) - P_j[l(x)]| < \eta_j.$$

Under assumption (a) of the Lemma, P_j converges equicontinuously to a $\mathcal{D}^0(2,1)$ [resp. $\mathcal{D}^s(2,1)$] function $P : \mathfrak{R}_c \times \mathfrak{R}_c \to \mathfrak{R}_c$. Because P is also uniformly continuous on $\mathfrak{R}_c \times \mathfrak{R}_c$, there is a function $\gamma : \mathfrak{R} \to \mathfrak{R}$ such that for every $\eta > 0$, $|x - y| < \gamma(\eta)$ implies $|P(x) - P(y)| < \eta$. Now,

$$\begin{aligned}|P_j(x) - P_j[l(x)]| = |P(x) - P[l(x)] - P(x) + P_j(x) + P[l(x)] \\ - P_j[l(x)]| \leq |P(x) - P[l(x)]| + |P(x) \\ - P_j(x)| + |P[l(x)] - P_j[l(x)]|.\end{aligned}$$

Given η, there exists an integer $J({}^{\eta}/_3)$ such that $j > J({}^{\eta}/_3)$ implies

$$|P(x) - P_j(x)| < {}^{\eta}/_3,$$
$$|P[l(x)] - P_j[l(x)]| < {}^{\eta}/_3.$$

Furthermore,

$$|x - l(x)| < \gamma({}^{\eta}/_3)$$

implies

$$|P(x) - P[l(x)]| < {}^{\eta}/_3.$$

Now, let $\eta_j = \epsilon_j/4$ and let $J_j = J(\eta_j/3) + J(\eta_j/12)$. Further, define $\sigma : N \to N$ by the condition that $\sigma(j)$ is the smallest integer, k, such that $\gamma(\eta/3) > \delta_k$, where $\delta_k = |D_k|$ is the mesh of the lattice $L_{k.}$ Thus, corresponding to the sequences $j = 1., 2, \ldots$, and $\{\epsilon_j\}$, there are the sequences $\{J_j\}$ and $\{\sigma(j)\}$ such that for all $k > \max\{J_{j,}\sigma(j)\} = K(j)$,

$$|P_k(x) - P_k[l(x)]| < \epsilon_j/4.$$

Hence for each j and all $k > K(j)$,

$$\begin{aligned}|P_k(x) - G_k[l(x)]| &\leq |P_k(x) - P_k[l(x)]| + |P_k[l(x)] - G_k[l(x)]|\\ &\leq \epsilon_j/4 + \epsilon_j/4 = \epsilon_j/2.\end{aligned}$$

This completes the proof. □

We turn now to Lemma 6.2.3. The sequence of finite networks generated by the construction in the proof of Theorem 6.2.1 computes a sequence of finite functions. The sequence of $\mathcal{D}^0(2, 1)$ [resp. $\mathcal{D}^s(2, 1)$] networks generated by approximating the finite modules of the first sequence by $\mathcal{D}^0(2, 1)$[resp. $\mathcal{D}^s(2, 1)$] modules also computes a sequence of functions. Lemma 6.2.3 establishes that these two sequences of functions converge to a common limit.

Lemma 6.2.3. *Let $\{\epsilon_j\}$ be a sequence of positive numbers decreasing to zero as j tends to infinity. For each ϵ_j, let L_j be a lattice decomposition of $\mathfrak{R}_c$, and let c_j be a finite $(2, d_j)$ network with alphabet L_j, modules*

$$G_j^i : L_j \times L_j \to L_j \; i = 1, 2, \ldots, q,$$

and for all j, a common tree as digraph that computes a (finite) function[5] *$F_j : L_j \times \cdots \times L_j \to L_j$. Let C_j' be a $\mathcal{D}^0(2, 1)$ [resp. $\mathcal{D}^s(2, 1)$] network with the same digraph as C_j, whose module in position i is*[6] *$P_j^i : \mathfrak{R}_c \times \mathfrak{R}_c \to \mathfrak{R}_c$*

[5] Let L be the lattice of a rectangular decomposition of a compact neighborhood of zero in $\mathfrak{R}$, denoted $\mathfrak{R}_c$, and let $F : L \times L \to L$ be a finite function. There is a $(2, d)$ network C that computes F, where d is equal to the number of points in L. In that case the alphabet used by C can be identified with the lattice L and the modules of C with functions from $L \times L$ to L. If C uses an alphabet A such that $g : L \to A$ is a one-to-one encoding of L onto A, both sets having d elements, and if $\hat{G}^\nu$ denotes a module of C, then the function

$$G^\nu(l_1, l_2) = \hat{G}^\nu[g(l_1), g(l_2)]$$

is the corresponding module of the corresponding $(2, d)$ network that uses the alphabet L. It is straightforward to show that if $\alpha : A \times A \to A$ is everywhere computed by the network C, and if $F : L \times L \to L$ is computed by the network with modules G^ν and the same digraph as C, then F and α satisfy the relation $g[F(l_1, l_2)] = \alpha[g(l_1), g(l_2)]$. The generalization to the case in which the domain of F is a product of more copies of L is straightforward.

[6] The module in position i in the network C_j is well defined, because all networks are finite and have the same digraph.

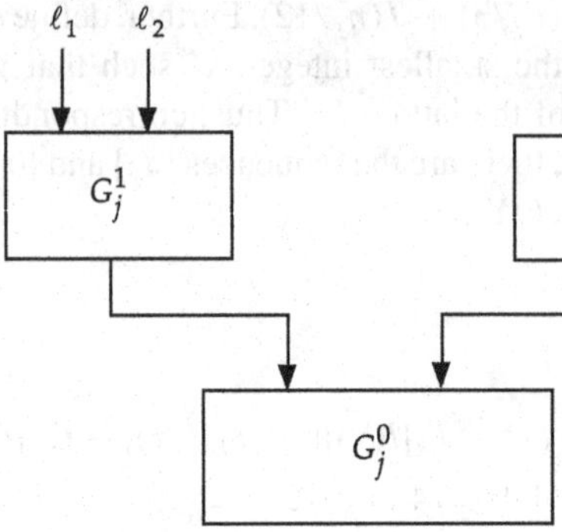

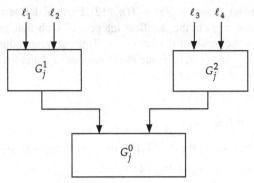

Figure 6.2.1.

in place of G_j^i, *where for* $i = 1, \ldots, q$, P_j^i *and* G_j^i *satisfy the hypotheses of Lemma 6.2.2, and where* C_j' *computes a function* $F_j' : \mathfrak{R}_c \times \cdots \times \mathfrak{R}_c \to \mathfrak{R}_c$. *For each* ϵ_j *there exists an integer* $K(j) = K(\epsilon_j)$, *such that for all* $k > K(j)$, *and for all* $x \in \mathfrak{R}_c \times \cdots \times \mathfrak{R}_c$,

$$|F_k'(x) - F_k[l(x)]| < \epsilon_k/2.$$

We present the argument for the case of a network with a tree as its graph and with delay 2. The same argument applies in general, but the notation is less complicated and the argument is easier to follow in the case of a delay 2 network. In that case the domain of F_j is (at least) four dimensional. Then let $x = (x_1, x_2, x_3, x_4)$, and let $l(x) = [l(x_1), l(x_2), l(x_3), l(x_4)]$. We shall also write $l^i(x) = l(x_i)$, for $i = 1, 2, 3, 4$ so that $l(x) = [l^1(x), l^2(x), l^3(x), l^4(x)]$. We suppose the network for F_j to be as shown in Figure 6.2.1 and similarly for F_j' to be as shown in Figure 6.2.2.

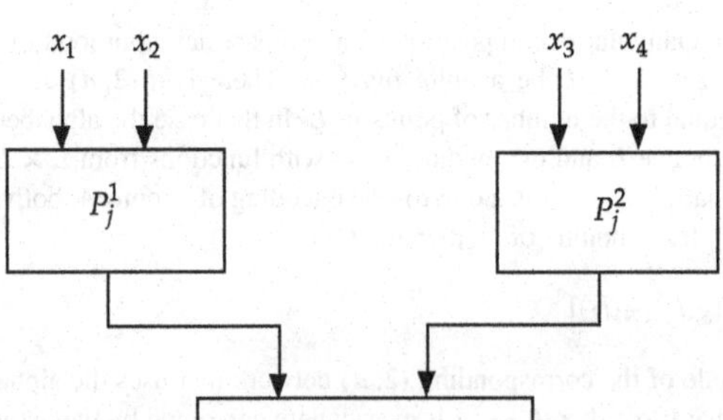

Figure 6.2.2.

Abbreviating still further, we shall write $l_1(x) = [l^1(x), l^2(x)]$, and $l_2(x) = [l^3(x), l^4(x)]$, and $x^1 = (x_1, x_2)$, $x^2 = (x_3, x_4)$. With these notations we may write $F'_j(x) = P^o_j[P^1_j(x^1), P^2_j(x^2)]$ and

$$F_j[l(x)] = G^o_j\{G^1_j[l^1(x)],\ G^2_j[l^2(x)]\}.$$

Thus,

$$\begin{aligned}|F'_j(x) - F_j[l(x)]| &= \left|P^o_j\left[P^1_j(x^1), P^2_j(x^2)\right] - G^o_j\{G^1_j[l^1(x)],\ G^2_j[l^2(x)]\}\right| \\ &= \left|P^o_j(u_j, v_j) - G^o_j(w_j, z_j)\right| \leq \left|P^o_j(u_j, v_j) - P^o_j(w_j, z_j)\right| \\ &\quad + \left|P^o_j(w_j, z_j) - G^o_j(w_j, z_j)\right|,\end{aligned}$$

where

$$\begin{aligned}(u_j, v_j) &= \left[P^1_j(x^1), P^2_j(x^2)\right], \\ (w_j, z_j) &= \left\{G^1_j[l^1(x)], G^2_j[l^2(x)]\right\}.\end{aligned}$$

Because $G^i_j : L_j \times L_j \to L_j$, for $i = 1, 2$, it follows that

$$l(w_j, z_j) = (w_j, z_j) \in L_j \times L_j.$$

Hence P^o_j and G^o_j are defined at (w_j, z_j). By hypothesis,

$$\left|P^o_j(w_j, z_j) - G^o_j(w_j, z_j)\right| < \epsilon_j/4 < \epsilon_j/2,$$

for all j. It remains to show that

$$\left|P^o_j(u_j, v_j) - P^o_j(w_j, z_j)\right| < \epsilon_j/4.$$

Because P^o_j is uniformly continuous on $\mathfrak{R}_c \times \mathfrak{R}_c$, for every $\eta_j > 0$ there exists $\delta_j(\eta_j) > 0$ such that

$$|(u_j, v_j) - (w_j, z_j)| < \delta_j(\eta_j),$$

which implies

$$\left|P^o_j(u_j, v_j) - P^o_j(w_j, z_j)\right| < \eta_j.$$

Hence it suffices to show that

$$|(u_j, v_j) - (w_j, z_j)| < \delta_j(\epsilon_j/4).$$

Now,

$$\begin{aligned}|(u_j, v_j) - (w_j, z_j)|^2 &= (u_j - w_j)^2 + (v_j - z_j)^2 \\ &= \left\{P^1_j(x^1) - G^1_j[l^1(x)]\right\}^2 + \left\{P^2_j(x^2) - G^2_j[l^2(x)\right\}^2.\end{aligned}$$

It follows from Lemma 6.2.2 that for each $k \geq K(j)$, G_j^i is an $\epsilon_j/4$ approximation of P_j^i on $\mathfrak{R}_c \times \mathfrak{R}_c$ for each i, by taking

$$\frac{\delta_j(\epsilon_j/4)}{(2)^{1/2}}$$

in place of $\epsilon_j/4$ in that proof.[7]

[7] Since q is finite, a standard argument shows that there is a value of $K(j)$ that works for all $i = 1, \ldots, q$. Then, for $i = 1, 2$,

$$\left|P_k^i(x) - G_k^i[l(x)]\right| < \frac{\delta_j(\epsilon_j/4)}{(2)^{1/2}}.$$

Hence,

$$\left|P_k^1(x) - G_k^1[l^1(x)]\right|^2 + \left|P_k^2(x) - G_k^2[l^2(x)]\right|^2 < \delta_j(\eta_j)^2/2 + \delta_j(\eta_j)^2/2 = \delta_j(\eta_j)^2.$$

It follows that

$$|(u_k, v_k) - (w_k, z_k)| = \left\{\left|P_k^1(x) - G_k^1[l^1(x)]\right|^2 + \left|P_k^2(x) - G_k^2[l^2(x)]\right|^2\right\}^{1/2} < \delta_j(\epsilon_j/4).$$

Thus, it follows that for each j and hence each ϵ_j, there is an integer $K(j) = K(\epsilon_j)$ such that $k > K(\epsilon_j)$ implies

$$|F_k'(x) - F_k[l(x)]| < \epsilon_j/4$$

uniformly in x.

7 Organizations

7.1. COORDINATION PROBLEMS

In this chapter we use the $\mathcal{F}$ network model of computing as the basis for a computational approach to the organization of economic activity, especially to coordination of production. Physical laws, including limitations on the productive capacities of people and machines, underlie the necessity for, and the benefits from, division of labor and specialization. In turn, division of labor and specialization create the need for coordination. Just as physical limitations constrain productive activity, information-processing limitations constrain the possibilities of coordination. The modular network model provides formal entities that can express these limitations. More specifically, relevant information is typically dispersed among economic agents, and the information-processing capacity of any one agent is typically limited. These limitations generally demand that the computations required to achieve coordinated action must be distributed among the agents.

The $\mathcal{F}$ network model as presented earlier is a model of algorithms. It is made into a model of the *execution* of algorithms by requiring that each module of a given network be evaluated by a computational agent subject to constraints specified later in this chapter. For a given network, assigning its modules to agents, and scheduling their execution in time, changes the initially given graph that represents the algorithm, and it also determines certain performance measures associated with carrying out the computation. A concept of efficiency can be defined for assigned networks such that the structure of an (efficient) assigned network can be interpreted as representing aspects of organizational structure.

In this chapter the notion of a *coordination problem* is defined in the context of production, and so is an efficient coordination mechanism. Production units are introduced, and we discuss the possibility of combining them in larger organizations.

We apply the *extended* $\mathcal{F}$ network model to three examples. The first is motivated by a classic question: "Which economic activities are (or should be) coordinated by markets, and which by other means?" Note that "other means" usually refers to administrative or bureaucratic mechanisms; sometimes the word "hierarchies" is used. The example has two cases, differing in their demand conditions. In Case 1 it is shown that the market mechanism cannot achieve efficient coordination, even though there are market equilibria and the First Welfare Theorem (see Debreu, 1959) is valid. There are alternative mechanisms, especially one called a direct mechanism, that do achieve efficient coordination. In Case 2 both types of mechanism achieve efficient coordination, but the market mechanism has higher informational costs. The second example illustrates a case in which some parameter values lead to an assigned modular network that suggests that the organizational structure consists of one unit whose parts are connected by direct channels; other parameter values suggest three units coordinated by markets. In the third example the network suggests that the organization consists of two distinct parts coordinated by direct channels.

Questions about how economic activity should be coordinated have usually been addressed in the context of "theory of the firm." However, to us that does not appear to be a useful setting in which to study choice among coordinating mechanisms. A mechanism of coordination that is used within a firm may also be used across firms. One can observe a variety of coordinating mechanisms, each commonly and persistently used in the economy, especially in the production sector, between, across, and within firms. This phenomenon is not likely to be understood by way of theories in which the only coordinating mechanisms are firms and markets. The concept of firm currently prevalent is essentially legal; a firm is seen as a collection of assets with an owner – an agent who has the legal right to control the use of the assets, and the right to the residual income. A firm that has more than one person in it generally has a mechanism for coordinating its internal activities, and generally a firm is a participant in external mechanisms that coordinate its actions with the actions of other economic units. A given firm can change its internal coordination mechanisms without changing its identity as a firm; the mechanisms that coordinate a firm's actions with those of others might also change without changing the identities of the firms involved.

An organization is sometimes likened to an organism that exists in a complex changing environment to which it must adapt its behavior. However, in this analysis we take a static design approach. An organization exists in any one of a class of possible environments. The designer knows the class of environments and what behavior would be desired in each environment, but not which specific environment prevails. In each environment the organization "computes" its desired behavior from inputs arising from that environment. The problem of design is to structure the organization so that it attains its goals efficiently no matter which member of the class of environments prevails. The desired actions can be expressed by a (decision) function whose domain is the information that the organization receives from the environment, and whose range is the set of possible actions. Sometimes the decision function can be derived from a goal function (more generally a correspondence) whose domain is the set of environments and whose range is the set of outcomes of action, or the payoff or utility associated with the outcomes of action. Generally several people are needed to acquire and process information from the environment, and several people are needed to carry out actions. Thus, the goal function defines a *coordination problem*. The nature of the coordination problem affects the structure of organizations that can solve it efficiently.

Distribution of information and action among several people creates private information and possibly hidden action. The analysis of the consequences of private information and hidden action has been the focus of much recent research on organizational design in economic theory. In that line of research the focus is on incentives; constraints on information processing and computing are generally ignored. Although many important phenomena of both the structure and behavior of organizations are best understood in terms of incentives, other important issues are not. For instance, the wave of restructuring of business organizations seen in the decade of the 1990s is more plausibly understood as arising from changes in the technology of information processing than from changes in incentives. Here we focus on information processing.

The term *coordination* commonly refers to a situation in which several actions *fit well together* or *match*. For instance, several musicians play together in time and tune. In another example, the quarterback throws the football to a running receiver in such a way that the ball is caught in full stride. To capture these phenomena more abstractly, we say that there are two or more variables specifying actions, and only a certain subset of the feasible combinations of the values of those variables leads to the desired outcomes. More formally, there is a function whose domain is the product of the domains of two or more variables. Fixing a value of this function defines a locus in the product domain, a level set of the function. A vector of variable values is called *coordinated* if it lies in the specified locus. An alternative formulation is that the value of the function defines a *degree of coordination*, which in a sense measures the "distance" of a point representing the joint decision or action from the locus that defines fully coordinated action.

As we stated earlier, we use the $\mathcal{F}$ network model to represent algorithms for computing the decision function. It was shown that if the goal or decision function being computed satisfies the conditions prescribed in Theorem 3.2.1 then it can be computed in minimal time for the given the number of parameters. It was also shown that the goal function determines the $\mathcal{F}$ network that computes it up to simple equivalence of the modules. Thus, in that case, the decision function determines both the algorithm, and the network up to simple equivalence.

Next, we suppose that agents are needed to carry out the computations, specifically to evaluate the modules of the network. The term "agent" is a primitive of our model. It can be interpreted as a person or a machine, or a person–machine combination, or a group of people with or without machines. It is the entity that carries out the computational steps that are taken to be elementary. For a given decision function a different assignment of the modules to agents generally results in a different performance of the algorithm, and therefore may suggest a different organizational structure. The dimensions of performance where important differences may appear include the following:

(i) the time it takes to compute the decision;
(ii) the amount of communication used in computing the decision;
(iii) the amount of memory used in computing the decision; and
(iv) the number of agents employed in the computation.

Time required to acquire the inputs and accuracy of the results should also be included, but they are not taken account of here. It is assumed that transmission of inputs is without delay, and that communication and computation are without error.

Agents have limited powers to observe, encode, and store information. Limits may be due to physical constraints, such as the impossibility of being in two places at once, or constraints on the rate at which information can be absorbed, or to other factors. Communication between agents is also constrained. The constraints can depend on the relationships between the agents. For instance, agents who are close together in stable, persistent relationships can come to share information, and to be able to exchange information at a much higher rate than those who are at arm's length, say, in different organizational units. We present next a formal extension of the modular network model to incorporate these elements in preparation for analyzing organizational structure. We also define efficient assignments of modules to agents, and the relation of efficiency to the cost of information processing.

7.1.1. Costs of Information Processing and Efficient Assignments

Suppose the function to be computed is $P : X \to Y$, where X and Y are Euclidean spaces. We suppose that the algorithm must be executed by agents. We seek to organize the required computation so that the "cost" of carrying it out is a minimum. Even if the algorithm to be used is fixed, it is possible to organize the computation in different ways. Minimum cost is achieved by choosing among efficient organizations of computing, given cost weights or prices, which allow the different dimensions of cost factors to be combined into a single cost figure.[1]

Using the $\mathcal{F}$ network model to represent algorithms, we suppose that there is an (r, d) network with modules in a class $\mathcal{F}$ that computes P in time t^*. If t^*

[1] If deviations from optimal decisions can be weighed against costs of computation, then "optimal" could mean "maximization of net performance."

is minimal for (r, d) networks with modules in $\mathcal{F}$, then t^* is the computational complexity of P relative to $\mathcal{F}$. We suppose that the $\mathcal{F}$ network $\mathcal{N}$ achieves the minimum delay t^*. As seen in Chapter 2, a network can be represented by a directed graph. Although that graph may have loops, it is shown in Chapter 2 that for each such graph there is an equivalent loop-free graph – a directed acyclic graph (dag) G such that:

(i) G has the same modules as $\mathcal{N}$, possibly with the addition of constants, projections, and compositions of projections with elements of $\mathcal{F}$; and
(ii) G computes P in time t^*.

For the computation to be carried out, the modules of G must be assigned to agents. Let the set of available agents be $\{1, 2, \ldots, N\}$. An agent is characterized by the set of modules in $\mathcal{F}$ that he can evaluate, and by restrictions on the set of inputs that he can observe directly.[2] We assume for simplicity that each agent can evaluate any module in $\mathcal{F}$.

Let a denote an assignment of the modules of G to agents; thus, a is a function from the set of vertices of G to $\{1, \ldots, N\}$. The value of a at the vertex v is the agent assigned to evaluate the module v. The same element of $\mathcal{F}$ may be associated with another vertex of G and may be assigned to any agent to evaluate, subject to the following constraints.

1. A module assigned to an agent must be one of her elementary operations.
2. A module representing the observation of an input variable must satisfy the given restrictions on observation, that is, the restriction of a to the leaves of G must agree with given restrictions on who may observe what.
3. There is a parallel constraint, that is, each agent is capable of carrying out at most one elementary operation in a unit of time.

Even if the algorithm allows two particular operations to be carried out in parallel, and therefore both could in principle be executed in the same unit of time, that can be done only if those operations are assigned to different agents.

An assignment of modules to agents determines several quantities of interest. First is the number of sequential steps required to compute the value of P in the assignment, a. Because the network G (or $\mathcal{N}$) expresses only the logical restrictions imposed by the algorithm, and because any assignment of the modules to agents must respect those precedence relations, t^* is a lower bound on the delay

[2] We present a formal model of technology and production in Section 7.3. Anticipating that model, we also assume that an agent who works for a given manager can directly observe those inputs, and only those inputs, that enter the leaves of the subgraph corresponding to the process her manager is in charge of.

resulting from an assignment of the modules of G to agents. Often the lower bound is not attained. Second, an assignment determines the communication that takes place in carrying out the computations required. Communication is itself a multidimensional matter that calls for recognizing distinctions among different types of communication channels. This will be discussed in more detail below. Finally, an assignment determines the number of different agents used to carry out the computation. Typically, agents are costly.

Communication between agents takes place by means of channels. An agent can remember something she already knew, that is, make a retrieval from memory. An agent can communicate with another agent with whom she is in close and regular contact, such as someone who works in the same organizational unit. An agent can communicate with someone with whom she is not in close contact, perhaps someone in another unit. Another possibility is that the agent can communicate with another by means of an anonymous channel, such as communication through a market. To begin to capture distinctions of this kind, we first distinguish two classes of channels – *direct* and *market* channels. A direct channel links two agents who know one anothers' identity. The message transmitted over the channel can be the output value of any module. The message transmitted over a market channel is required to be anonymous, and it must have the form prescribed by the market's institutional rules. For instance, messages transmitted from a buyer or seller to (or from) an intermediary in an organized market are required to have a specific form. Thus, a market channel arises only within a graph that models a market algorithm, for instance, one that models profit (or utility) maximizing behavior as prescribed by perfect competition. Within the class of direct channels we distinguish two types of links – selflinks and crosslinks.[3] A *selflink* is an arc of the graph G that goes between two vertices that are assigned to the same agent. A *crosslink* goes between two vertices assigned to different agents. In some cases we would want to distinguish different types of crosslinks to capture the idea that communication between agents in close proximity is less costly or more efficient than communication between agents who are in some sense distant from one another. Ideas such as "learning curves," "organizational learning," "organizational culture," and "organizational memory" all suggest mechanisms of communication internal to an organization that do not operate across boundaries between organizations.[4]

[3] We confine our attention here to two types of direct channels. In Subsection 7.4.1 we consider more than two types to capture distinctions among links between agents in different organizational units.

[4] A sample of references from the literature concerned with these ideas includes Schein (1985), Arrow (1974), and Levitt and March (1988). In a more recent unpublished paper, Kachingwe (1997) discusses the idea of "learning by watching." He summarizes the idea that "necessarily shared experiences will lead to shared knowledge within the firm, or 'corporate knowledge'." This concept, he says, provides the basis for a notion of organizational memory. He also assumes that learning by watching is costless, in contrast to learning by doing. Our assumption about

These authors in one way or another take it for granted that agents inside an organization can transfer information in ways that agents in different organizations cannot.

In situations in which close, stable, persistent interactions among agents allow them to observe one another's behavior closely and repeatedly in different situations, agents can internalize much of what would have to be communicated at length in arm's length dealings. In this respect, intraorganizational communication calls to mind a practice used in telegraph transmissions, according to which certain messages are precoded in a table of standard messages. In these circumstances a transmission between agents in the same organization is more like a retrieval from memory than it is like a message exchange between strangers.

Given a goal or decision function and an algorithm, in the form of an (r, d) network that computes that function, an assignment of the modules of the network to agents determines cost. Let

$$\overline{\chi}(a) = \chi[\varsigma(a), \nu(a), \tau(a), n(a)]$$

denote the cost function, a real-valued function of the number of selflinks, ς, the number of crosslinks, ν, the delay, τ, and the number of agents, n, in the assignment, a. We assume that χ is monotone increasing in each of its arguments. Because of monotonicity, an efficient assignment is one such that the resulting vector of cost factors satisfies

$$(\varsigma^*, \nu^*, \tau^*, n^*) \leq (\varsigma, \nu, \tau, n)$$

for all $(\varsigma, \nu, \tau, n)$ satisfying Assumption 7.1.1 in the following paragraph.

Next we show that finding efficient assignments reduces to finding efficient pairs $[\nu(\cdot), \tau(\cdot)]$ for each fixed value of $n(\cdot)$. To see this, consider a network $\mathcal{N}$ with graph G. To lighten notation we drop explicit reference to a where it is possible to do so without confusion, and we indicate the effects of different assignments by other notation. The graph G has a fixed number c of arcs. Each arc is either a selflink or a crosslink. Thus, $\varsigma + \nu = c$. It follows that $\chi(\varsigma, \nu, \tau, n) = \chi(c - \nu, \nu, \tau, n)$. We make the following assumption.

Assumption 7.1.1.

$$\begin{aligned} &|\chi(c - \nu + 1, \nu - 1, \tau, n) - \chi(c - \nu, \nu - 1, \tau, n)| \\ &\quad < |\chi(c - \nu, \nu - 1, \tau, n) - \chi(c - \nu, \nu, \tau, n)|. \end{aligned}$$

channels can be interpreted to say that learning by watching is an example of the existence of a channel for conveying information from one agent to another when they are in close organizational proximity, a channel that would not be available to them if they were not in close organizational proximity (Kachingwe, 1997).

Proposition 7.1.1. *Given a network N and a monotone increasing cost function satisfying Assumption 7.1.1, if* (ν, τ, n) *is not efficient, then* $(c - \nu, \nu, \tau, n)$ *does not minimize cost.*

Proof of Proposition 7.1.1. If (ν, τ, n) is not efficient, then there exists (ν', τ', n') such that

$$(\nu', \tau', n') \leq (\nu, \tau, n),$$

with equality ruled out. If $\nu' = \nu$, then either $\tau' < \tau$, or $n' < n$, or both. In that case, monotonicity of χ yields the conclusion that $(c - \nu, \nu, \tau, n)$ does not minimize cost. Suppose next that $\nu' < \nu$. It suffices to consider the case where $\nu' = \nu - 1$. Then,

$$\begin{aligned} &\chi(c - \nu + 1, \nu - 1, \tau', n') - \chi(c - \nu, \nu, \tau', n') \\ &\quad = \chi(c - \nu + 1, \nu - 1, \tau', n') - \chi(c - \nu, \nu - 1, \tau', n') \\ &\qquad + \chi(c - \nu, \nu - 1, \tau', n') - \chi(c - \nu, \nu, \tau', n') \end{aligned}$$

It follows from monotonicity that the difference of the first two terms is positive, and the difference of the second two terms is negative. By Assumption 7.1.1, the second term is larger in absolute value than the first; therefore the reduction in the number of crosslinks from ν to $\nu - 1$ reduces cost, which means that cost is not minimized at (ν, τ', n') and hence not at (ν, τ, n) either. □

Remark 7.1.1. It is obvious that for a given assignment a, if (ν, τ) is not efficient in the space of crosslinks and delays, then neither is (ν, τ, n) in its space.

Let $a^*(n)$ be a cost-minimizing assignment to n agents, for each n, and let $[\nu^*(n), \tau^*(n)]$ be the number of crosslinks and the delay resulting from that assignment. That is, for each n and each assignment $a^*(n)$,

$$\begin{aligned} &\chi[c - \nu^*(n), \nu^*(n), \tau^*(n), n] \\ &\quad = \chi\{c - \nu^*[a^*(n)], \nu^*[a^*(n)], \tau^*[a^*(n)], n\} \\ &\quad \leq \chi\{c - \nu[a(n)], \nu[a(n)], \tau[a(n)], n\} \\ &\quad = \chi[c - \nu(n), \nu(n), \tau(n), n] \end{aligned}$$

Now let n^* minimize $\chi\,[c - \nu^*(n), \nu^*(n), \tau^*(n), n]$ with respect to n. Then $[\nu^*(n^*), \tau^*(n^*), n^*]$ minimizes cost over all feasible assignments. It follows from Proposition 7.1.1 that $[\nu^*(n^*), \tau^*(n^*), n^*]$ is efficient. Hence the assignment of modules to n^* agents that results in the pair $[\nu^*(n^*), \tau^*(n^*)]$ is an efficient assignment. Thus, the search for efficient assignments can be confined to the search for efficient assignments in the space of crosslinks and delay for each value of n. It should be noted that constructing efficient assignments involves both assigning modules at vertices to agents and scheduling their execution in time, subject to the parallel constraint and the precedence relations in the given network $\mathcal{N}$. Examples and procedures for calculating assignments and schedules can be found in Appendices I and II of Reiter (1995). More generally, graph-coloring algorithms that apply to various cases of our assignment and scheduling problem can be found in the Operations Research literature.[5]

7.2. TWO EXAMPLES

We turn next to two examples. Each example conforms to the formal model presented in Section 7.3. We present them here because they motivate and illustrate the formal model, but are self contained and simple enough to be understood on their own.

7.2.1. Example 1

This example has two parts. The first is a case in which the coordination of production specified by the performance criterion cannot be achieved by using a market channel, whereas it can be achieved by using a direct channel. Therefore, according to our lexicographic criterion for comparing coordination mechanisms, explained in Section 7.2, the first step is decisive; there is no need to go on to a comparison of information costs.

The second part is a variation of the first in which the desired coordination can be achieved by using either a market channel or a direct channel, hence bringing the comparison of costs of the two mechanisms into play.

Suppose the technology T consists of two processes, P_1 and P_2, each with two states, S_1^i and S_2^i, where $i = 1, 2$. In state S_1^1, P_1 produces one unit of good W(hite) by using one unit of input B(lue) and uses the services of one unit of facility F_1 for half a week. In state S_2^1, processor P_1 produces one unit of G(reen) from one unit of R(ed), using the same facility for half a week.

For example, the facility F_1 consists of machines for manufacturing tractors. There are two types of tractor: a large, heavy tractor that requires a heavy-duty gear train, and a smaller, light tractor that uses a light-duty gear train. To set up the machinery to produce a heavy tractor requires a period of time, and once the machinery is so configured it is not possible to produce light tractors until the machinery is reconfigured.

In state S_1^2, processor P_2 produces one unit of B(lue) from a unit of raw material, using the services of one unit of facility F_2 for half a week, and in state S_2^2, processor P_2 produces one unit of R(ed) from raw material, using one

[5] I am indebted to my colleague Rakesh Vohra for guidance to this literature, which includes his own work on coloring graphs.

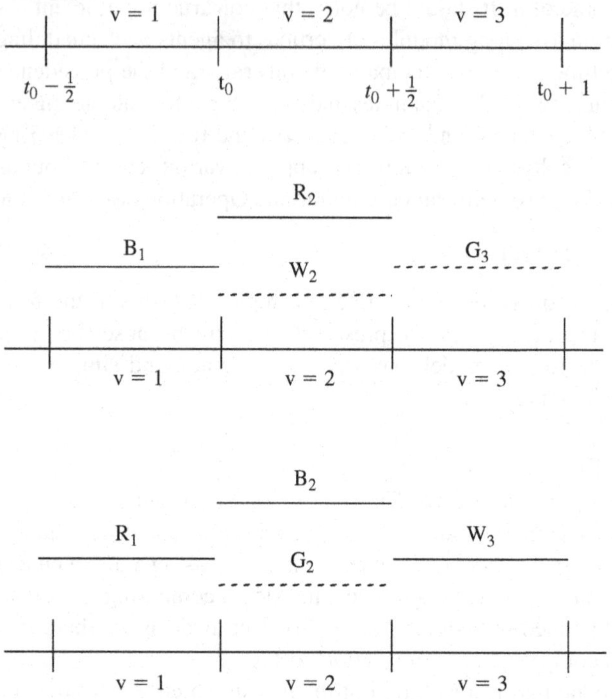

Figure 7.2.1. Two just-in-time production plans.

unit of facility F_2 for half a week. To avoid cluttering up the calculations without adding generality, we assume that the raw material is free. There is one unit of each facility available. W and G are final products; B and R are intermediate products. There are two production units, one operating P_1 and the other P_2.

This technology operates in time. We assume that the unit of time is a half-week. Each process can operate in each half-week, and correspondingly, commodities are dated; the date is the half-week in which they become available. For purposes of exposition, fix a time t_0 and consider the periods shown in Figure 7.2.1. These are $(t_0 - 1/2, t_0)$, $(t_0, t_0 + 1/2)$, and $(t_0 + 1/2, t_0 + 1)$, which we relabel $v = 1$, $v = 2$, and $v = 3$, respectively. Then a typical commodity vector has the form $[W(2), W(3), G(2), G(3), B(1), B(2), R(1), R(2)]$. The commodity space is further restricted by requiring the amount of each commodity to be a nonnegative integer. (Thus, we abuse the notation by using the same symbol for the name of the commodity and its quantity, and we rely on the context to make clear which is intended.) When a market channel is used, prices are introduced; the price vector corresponding to the commodity subspace is

$$[w(2), \omega(3), \gamma(2), \gamma(3), p(1), p(2), q(1), q(2)].$$

The space of attainable states is

$$S^A(t_0) = \{s_j^i(v), i, j \in \{1,2\}, v \in \{1,2,3\}\}.$$

A profile of states for the time period under consideration has the form

$$s(t_0) = [s^1(1), s^1(2), s^1(3), s^2(1), s^2(2), s^2(3)],$$

where

$$s^i(v) \in \{s_j^1, i, j = 1, 2\}.$$

We suppose that there is a representative end user who receives the final products. The end user can absorb at most two units of product in a given week. He pays $\omega(2)$ for a unit of $W(2)$ delivered at time $t_0 + 1/2$ and $\omega(3)$ for a unit of $W(3)$ delivered at time $t_0 + 1$. The end user can refuse delivery of items he did not order and pay nothing. Because only one unit of each commodity is possible, when the final commodities have prices, the payments $\omega(j)$, and $\gamma(j)$, $j = 2, 3$ coincide with those prices. We distinguish two cases, each leading to a different conclusion.

Case 1

The end user does not distinguish time periods shorter than a week. In this case, periods 2 and 3 together make up one time period in which the end user does not distinguish $W(2)$ from $W(3)$ nor $G(2)$ from $G(3)$. The effect of this will be to require $\omega(2) = \omega(3)$ and $\gamma(2) = \gamma(3)$.

Case 2

The end user recognizes half-weeks, and thus distinguishes $W(2)$ from $W(3)$ and $G(2)$ from $G(3)$. The effect will be to allow $\omega(2) \neq \omega(3)$ or $\gamma(2) \neq \gamma(3)$.

In Case 1 the demand parameters are $\Theta = \{\theta_1, \theta_2, \theta_3\}$. Buyers of W (resp. G) do not distinguish between units of W (resp. G) delivered at any time within the week for which they are desired. Demand for W and G is determined for each week independently, and the demand for week $(t, t+1)$ beginning at t is known at time $t - \frac{1}{2}$.

Demand for final products delivered in any period is shown in Table 7.2.1 in terms of θ.

In Case 2 the demand parameters are as shown in Table 7.2.2.

Table 7.2.1. Demand for Final Products, Case 1

Demand	Description
$\theta(t) = \theta_1$	1 unit each of W and G in week $(t, t+1)$
$\theta(t) = \theta_2$	2 units of W and 0 units of G in week $(t, t+1)$
$\theta(t) = \theta_3$	0 units of W and 2 units of G in week $(t, t+1)$

Table 7.2.2. Demand for Final Products, Case 2

Demand	Description
$\theta(t) = \theta_{11}$	1 unit of W and 0 units of G in period $(t, t+1/2)$, or 0 units of W and 1 unit of G in period $(t+1/2, t+1)$.
$\theta(t) = \theta_{12}$	0 units of W and 1 unit of G in period $(t, t+1/2)$, or 1 unit of W and 0 units of W in period $(t+1/2, t+1)$.
$\theta(t) = \theta_2$	2 units of W and 0 units of G in week $(t, t+1)$.
$\theta(t) = \theta_3$	0 units of W and 2 units of G in week $(t, t+1)$.

We focus on the actions of a manager M_1 of process P_1 and a manager M_2 of process P_2. We can think of these managers as representative of managers of their types.

Recall from the specification of the technology that to produce one unit of W in week $(t, t+1)$ requires either one unit of B delivered by time t, in which case one unit of W can be produced in the interval $(t, t+{}^1\!/_2)$, or one unit of B delivered by time $(t+{}^1\!/_2)$, in which case one unit of W can be produced in the interval $(t+{}^1\!/_2, t)$; the case is similar for G and R. Satisfaction of demand in the time period indexed by t_0 is expressed by the condition that

$$W^d(t_0) = W^s(2) + W^s(3),$$
$$G^d(t_0) = G^s(2) + G^s(3),$$

where the superscript d indicates a quantity required or demanded and the superscript s indicates a quantity supplied. Demand quantities for the periods corresponding to t_0 are the functions shown in Table 7.2.1 in Case 1 and in Table 7.2.2 in Case 2. Supplies are the functions of $S(t_0)$ defined above.

To avoid an unnecessarily tedious exposition of the performance criterion and an equally tedious analysis of the example, we take note of two points.

1. If inventories can be kept, then any pattern of demand can be met, provided initial inventories are suitable.
2. If carrying inventories is costly, and if every admissible pattern of demand can be met without inventories, then no production plan that involves carrying inventories can be *efficient*.

The three patterns of demand shown in Table 7.2.1 can be met by M_1, the manager of the producer using process P_1, by choosing from the following:

If	Then
$\theta(t) = \theta_1$	$s^1(2) = s_1^1;\ s^1(3) = s_2^1$; or $s^1(2) = s_2^1;\ s^1(3) = s_1^1$
$\theta(t) = \theta_2$	$s^1(2) = s_1^1;\ s^1(3) = s_1^1$
$\theta(t) = \theta_3$	$s^1(2) = s_2^1;\ s^1(3) = s_2^1$,

provided that the inputs are available in time. This can be ensured by the following rule for the producer using P_2:

If	**Then**
$s^1(2) = s_1^1$	$s^2(1) = s_1^2$
$s^1(2) = s_2^1$	$s^2(1) = s_2^2$
$s^1(3) = s_1^1$	$s^2(2) = s_1^2$
$s^1(3) = s_2^1$	$s^2(2) = s_2^2$

These are the desired actions derived from the performance criterion implied by the two simplifying points made above; that is, these actions optimize the outcome on the feasible set.

We turn now to comparison of the coordination mechanisms under consideration, and we compare two mechanisms, $\mathcal{D}$ and $\mathcal{M}$, for coordinating the actions of the managers of the two processes. The first mechanism uses a direct channel between the two managers; the second uses a market channel between the two managers.

We assume that transmission over each channel is instantaneous and costless. This simplification avoids having to keep track of transmission delays and the accounting that goes with them. With this simplification, we shall see that in Case 1 the comparison of mechanisms reduces to verifying that the mechanism using a direct channel is *efficient*, and that the market mechanism is not. Therefore the need to compare information-processing costs does not arise. In Case 2, both mechanisms are *efficient*; therefore the need to compare information-processing costs does arise.

In the case of direct channels at time $t_0 - \tau$, manager M_1 learns the demand for the final products in period t_0. With that information, M_1 can decide on her actions $s^1(2)$, $s^1(3)$, thereby determining $W^s(2)$, $W^s(3)$, $G^s(2)$, $G^s(3)$, and therefore also determining the input requirements $B^d(2)$, $B^d(3)$, $R^d(2)$, $R^d(3)$. Availability of a direct channel whose capacity is sufficient to carry four one-digit numbers allows M_1 to communicate these requirements directly to M_2, who can then determine his actions $s^2(1)$, $s^2(2)$ and, if necessary, communicate them to M_1.

The availability of a direct channel allows the managers to achieve just-in-time delivery of intermediate products, and therefore to meet demand without carrying inventories of intermediate or final products, thus attaining the efficient outcome.

In the case of market channels, transactions between the managers of processes of type P_1 and those of type P_2 are mediated by a competitive market. (We do not model the transactions between producers of the final products and consumers of them explicitly, but these could also be mediated by a competitive market.) Using competitive market channels as the coordinating mechanism prescribes the behavior of the managers; each manager of a process must determine her action as the solution of a profit-maximization problem.

Consider first the profit $\pi^{M_1} = \pi^1$ of the manager of process P_1 when the coordination mechanism is the market mechanism.

$$\pi^1 = \omega(2)W(2) + \omega(3)W(3) + \gamma(2)G(2) + \gamma(3)G(3)$$
$$-[p(1)B(1) + p(2)B(2) + q(1)R(1) + q(2)R(2)].$$

To derive the demand for $B(1)$, $B(2)$, $R(1)$, $R(2)$, we maximize π^1 subject to the technological constraints

$$W(2) = B(1), \quad W(3) = B(2), \quad G(2) = R(1), \quad G(3) = R(2),$$
$$W(j)G(j) = 0 = B(i)R(i), \quad j = 2, 3; \quad i = 1, 2,$$

and

$$W(j), G(j), B(i), R(i) \in \{0, 1\}$$

for

$$i \in \{1, 2\}, \quad j \in \{2, 3\}.$$

In addition there is the resource constraint

$$0 \leq W(2) + W(3) + G(2) + G(3) \leq 2.$$

Using the technological constraints, we can write the profit function in the form

$$\pi^1 = [\omega(2) - p(1)]B(1) + [\omega(3) - p(2)]B(2) + [\gamma(2) - q(1)]R(1)$$
$$+ \{[\gamma(3) - q(2)]R(2)\} \qquad (7.2.1)$$

with the constraints

$$0 \leq B(1) + B(2) + R(1) + R(2) \leq 2,$$

and

$$B(j)R(j) = 0,$$

for $j = 1, 2$, and

$$B(j), R(j) \in \{0, 1\}. \qquad (7.2.2)$$

The technological and resource constraints define the feasible set in the four-dimensional subspace whose coordinates are $B(1)$, $B(2)$, $R(1)$, $R(2)$. This set consists of the origin and the eight points whose coordinates have exactly one coordinate different from zero, and the four points that have exactly two coordinates different from zero.

Table 7.2.3. Demand for Inputs

	$\omega - p(2) > \gamma - q(2)$	$\omega - p(2) < \gamma - q(2)$	$\omega - p(2) = \gamma - q(2)$
$\omega - p(1) > \gamma - q(1)$	(B, B)	(B, R)	$(B, R), (B, B)$
$\omega - p(1) < \gamma - q(1)$	(R, B)	(R, R)	$(R, R), (R, B)$
$\omega - p(1) = \gamma - q(1)$	$(R, B), (B, B)$	$(R, R), (R, B)$	$(R, R), (R, B), (B, R), (B, B)$

We assume that demand is not satiated which implies that, the points having only one coordinate different from zero are not *efficient*. Then we can confine attention to the four points that have two coordinates different from zero, and, of course, those coordinates are each equal to one.

Because of formula (7.2.2), two of the coordinates in the demand vector for inputs $[B(1), B(2), R(1), R(2)]$ must be zero. Therefore we can abbreviate the notation, letting (B, R) represent demand for a unit of B in the first period and a unit of R in the second and (R, B) represent demand for a unit of R in the first period and a unit of B in the second, and so on. The demand correspondence for inputs of a manager of type 1 is shown in Table 7.2.3 as a function of certain intervals of prices.

Recalling that the prices $p(i), q(i)$ are net of the cost of the input to process P_2, which we assumed to be zero, we find that the profit function of the second type of manager is

$$\pi^2 = p(1)B(1) + p(2)B(2) + q(1)R(1) + q(2)R(2).$$

The constraints are the same as those displayed for process P_1 above. Then supply correspondence for the manager of process P_2 is shown in Table 7.2.4.

For the coordination mechanism using the market channel to be efficient, it must have an efficient equilibrium for every state of demand θ. For the sake of the argument, suppose π^2 is maximized at the point $[B(1), B(2), R(1), R(2)] = (1, 0, 0, 1)$, which we also write (B, R), indicating that a unit of B is produced in the period $v = 1$, and a unit of R is produced in the period $v = 2$. Then the profit of M_2 at (B, R) is

$$\pi^2(B, R) = p(1) + q(2)\cdot$$

Table 7.2.4. Supply of Inputs

	$p(2) > q(2)$	$p(2) < q(2)$	$p(2) = q(2)$
$p(1) > q(1)$	(B, B)	(B, R)	$(B, R), (B, B)$
$p(1) < q(1)$	(R, B)	(R, R)	$(R, R), (R, B)$
$p(1) = q(1)$	$(R, B), (B, B)$	$(R, R), (B, R)$	$(R, R), (R, B), (B, R), (B, B)$

If this maximizes π^2 on the feasible set, then the following three inequalities must hold.

$$p(1) + q(2) \geq p(1) + p(2),$$
$$p(1) + q(2) \geq q(1) + p(2),$$
$$p(1) + q(2) \geq q(1) + q(2).$$

It follows that (1a) $p(1) \geq q(1)$; (1b) $q(2) \geq p(2)$; and (1c) $p(1) + q(2) \geq q(1) + q(2) \geq q(1) + p(2)$.

If (B, R) is to be an equilibrium, it must also maximize π^1 on the feasible set.

In Case 1,

$$\omega(2) = \omega(3) = \omega,$$
$$\gamma(2) = \gamma(3) = \gamma.$$

If (B, R) maximizes π^1 on the feasible set, then the following three inequalities must hold.

$$\omega + \gamma - [p(1) + q(2)] \geq 2\omega - [p(1) + p(2)],$$
$$\omega + \gamma - [p(1) + q(2)] \geq 2\gamma - [q(1) + q(2)],$$
$$\omega + \gamma - [p(1) + q(2)] \geq \gamma + \omega - [p(1) + p(2)].$$

These can be written as (2a) $\gamma - [p(1) + q(2)] \geq \omega - [p(1) + p(2)]$; (2b) $\omega - [p(1) + q(2)] \geq \gamma - [q(1) + q(2)]$; and (2c) $-[p(1) + q(2)] \geq -[q(1) + p(2)]$.

Thus, inequalities (1a)–(1c) and (2a)–(2c) must hold. Together they imply

$$p(1) + q(2) = q(1) + q(2) = q(1) + p(2)$$

and hence

$$p(1) = q(1), \quad p(2) = q(2).$$

Then it follows from inequality (2a) that

$$\omega = \gamma.$$

Substituting in the expression for π^1 gives

$$\pi^1 = [\omega - p(1)][B(1) + R(1)] + [\omega - p(2)][B(2) + R(2)].$$

Thus, π^1 takes the same value $2\omega - [p(1) + p(2)]$ at each of the four nonzero feasible actions, that is, those that produce (1, 0, 0, 1), (0, 1, 1, 0), (1, 1, 0, 0), and (0, 0, 1, 1) in the subspace with coordinates $B(1)$, $B(2)$, $R(1)$, and $R(2)$.

Turning now to π^2, after substitution, we find

$$\pi^2 = p(1)[B(1) + R(1)] + p(2)[B(2) + R(2)].$$

This function takes the same value at every nonzero feasible action of M_2.

Because not every pair consisting of a feasible action of M_1 and a feasible action of M_2 is *efficient*, it follows that the mechanism using a market channel does not ensure *efficient* performance in Case 1.

Note that there are competitive equilibria in this example. The price vector

$$\begin{aligned}&[p(1), p(2), q(1), q(2), \gamma(1), \gamma(2), \omega(1), \omega(2)]\\&\quad = [p(1), p(2), p(1), p(2), \gamma(1), \gamma(2), \gamma(1), \gamma(2)],\end{aligned}$$

and either of the two commodity vectors

$$[W(1), W(2), G(1), G(2), B(1), B(2), R(1), R(2)] = (1, 0, 0, 1, 1, 0, 0, 1)$$

or

$$[W(1), W(2), G(1), G(2), B(1), B(2), R(1), R(2)] = (0, 1, 1, 0, 0, 1, 1, 0)$$

form competitive equilibria. In each case, the markets for final goods and for intermediate goods clear. Both equilibria are efficient.

However, if manager M_1 chooses $(1, 0, 0, 1)$ whereas M_2 chooses $(0, 1, 1, 0)$, the market for final goods clears, but the market for intermediate goods does not. The same conclusion holds if the managers choose $(0, 1, 1, 0)$ and $(1, 0, 0, 1)$, respectively. In neither of these cases do we have a competitive equilibrium. Therefore the hypothesis of the First Welfare Theorem (see Debreu, 1959, p. 94) is not satisfied, and hence the theorem is vacuously true.

In Case 2 the profit function of M_2 remains the same as in Case 1. Hence inequalities (1a)–(1c) remain valid. However, it is not required that $\omega(2) = \omega(3)$ or that $\gamma(2) = \gamma(3)$; in general neither of these equalities will hold. The profit function of M_1 in Case 2 is

$$\begin{aligned}&[\omega(2) - p(1)]\, B(1) + [\omega(3) - p(2)]\, B(2) + [\gamma(2) - q(1)]\, R(1)\\&\quad + [\gamma(3) - q(2)]\, R(2),\end{aligned}$$

which is to be maximized subject to the constraints

$$\begin{aligned}&B(1)R(1) = 0 = B(2)R(2),\\&0 \le B(1) + R(1) + B(2) + R(2) \le 2,\end{aligned}$$

where all variables are nonnegative integers.

In this case for each of the four possible states of final demand there is a competitive equilibrium with a unique associated production plan for each production unit. For example, the price vector

$$[\omega(2), \omega(3), \gamma(2), \gamma(3), p(1), p(2), q(1), q(2)] = (8, 4, 5, 6, 3, 2, 1, 3)$$

is part of the competitive equilibrium that leads to the commodity vector

$$(1, 0, 0, 1, 1, 0, 0, 1).$$

The price vector

$$[\omega(2), \omega(3), \gamma(2), \gamma(3), p(1), p(2), q(1), q(2)] = (8, 7, 4, 4, 3, 3, 1, 2)$$

is part of a competitive equilibrium with commodity vector

$$(1, 1, 0, 0, 1, 1, 0, 0).$$

To summarize, in Case 1, because each producer of a given type has no information with which to distinguish among profit-maximizing production plans, each could choose any of them. Thus, there is no guarantee of efficient equilibrium. Even when there are several producers of each type, and the number of producers of each type is the same, and even if all producers of a given type choose the same production plan, equilibrium would not be ensured. This is, of course, the case when there is just one producer of each type. Thus, the mechanism using a market channel cannot be guaranteed to achieve just-in-time production, and consequently it cannot coordinate production without inventories. This result may be anticipated whenever the supply and demand correspondences are not single valued at equilibrium. This in itself might not be considered too serious a difficulty,[6] except for the fact that in this case the multiplicity of values arises not from linearity in the technology, but from relations of timing. These are likely to be prevalent in the economy, and that prevalence indicates that the example is more typical than its simplified form might suggest. The practices associated with just-in-time production in the automobile industry provide a good example. There are many other important examples that attest to the prevalence in the economy of coordination mechanisms that use direct channels. Because the market mechanism cannot ensure just-in-time production, the criteria specified for comparing mechanisms tell us that informational costs, or informational efficiency properties, do not come into play.

In contrast, in Case 2 the market mechanism is in the class of efficient mechanisms. Therefore, a comparison of the cost or informational efficiency properties of the two mechanisms is in order.

A comparison of the informational cost or efficiency of the two mechanisms requires that we construct the two networks that represent the computations to be carried out. For this we must specify the class $\mathcal{F}$ of elementary functions. For our example it is natural to consider the binary operations of arithmetic, together with the two unary functions, the identity, Id, and the sign function, sgn. Thus, the networks used are (2, 1) networks, where $\mathcal{F} = \{\text{add, subt, mult, Id, sgn}\}$.

To begin, we consider the informational tasks under the assumption that the relevant networks are given, and that the communication channels exist.

[6] When multiple maximizers of profit arise because of linearity in the underlying technology, the slightest displacement from linearity would result in unique maximizers. However, linearity itself is a kind of razor's edge phenomenon.

In the direct mechanism the computational task of a manager of type M_1 is to observe the demand vector for final products, and having done so, to select from the four feasible plans a production plan that meets the demand. The computation involved is to choose a vector $[W(2), W(3), G(2), G(3)]$, to translate that choice into demand for inputs $[B^d(1), B^d(2), R^d(1), R^d(2)]$, and then to communicate that vector to M_2. This amounts to evaluating a (vector) identity function at the given demand point and sending the result to the other manager. This computation has delay two, and it requires at most four crosslinks; that is, there are four one-dimensional direct channels over which these messages are transmitted.

The task of M_2 is also to evaluate identity functions at the points communicated to her by M_1. Because communication is assumed to be instantaneous and computation of the identity function has delay one this computation has delay two.

In the mechanism $\mathcal{M}$, a manager of type M_1 must find a profit-maximizing production plan, and hence her demand for the intermediate products, given all the prices. From Equation (7.2.1) we see that finding the profit-maximizing demands for intermediate products reduces to the following computation. M_1 must first compute the four differences

$$\begin{aligned}
&\omega(2) - p(1) = a,\\
&\omega(3) - p(2) = b,\\
&\gamma(2) - q(1) = c,\\
&\gamma(3) - q(2) = d.
\end{aligned}$$

In addition, M_1 must compute the signs of the expressions:

$$\begin{aligned}
&a + d - b + c,\\
&d - b,\\
&a - c,\\
&a + b - c + d.
\end{aligned}$$

That is, in addition to computing four differences, M_1 must compute two sums and make the comparisons indicated among the eight resulting quantities. Verifying that the maximum profit is nonnegative follows from the signs of the differences and sums. With the use of (2, 1) networks it follows that if the manager carries out the computation alone, the delay would be eleven units of time; with an additional agent it would be six units of time; and with three additional agents, the minimum attainable delay is three units of time. The calculation of M_2 is similar.

The calculation of the market agent, M_0, is to receive the excess demands of M_1 and M_2, and to select the eight prices to make excess demand equal to zero. When, as is usually the case, there are replications of the producers, M_0 must first aggregate excess demand, which involves executing $2(N - 1)$

additions when there are N managers of each type. Finally, the prices must be communicated from the market agent to all the managers. This could be done by broadcast channels, in effect posting the prices.

It is clear from these comparisons that in this example, the direct mechanism is informationally more efficient than the market mechanism. This seems to be in conflict with the conventional wisdom that market mechanisms are informationally more efficient than alternatives.

However, the calculation we made is based on the assumption that the communication channels exist. In the case of a direct mechanism, each direct channel must be created. In industrial practice this usually involves activities of a purchasing agent, or team of them for the unit that is buying, and a sales agent or group of them for the producing unit that is selling. Typically each side invests resources to create and maintain a long-term relationship. Negotiation between the two units often takes place repeatedly, even when a long-term relationship is established between them, because contracts are usually for a specified period of time. Thus, although once a direct channel is established the cost of using it may be very small, the cost of setting it up and maintaining it can be significant.

Market channels exist in different institutional forms, including organized markets, such as the Chicago Board of Trade, or in more decentralized manifestations, which combine informational functions with other service functions. An organized market may be costly to set up, but the costs of creating the market are usually borne by the market intermediaries, and only indirectly by the buyers and sellers. In organized markets, buyers and sellers typically pay for each use.

As remarked above, it sometimes happens that two producing units, one a supplier to the other, are in the same firm. It is often remarked that the firm could, if it wished, introduce an internal market channel between the units. It would be interesting to know how frequently coordination of the two units is done by market channels. When the two units are in the same firm, it is likely that the cost of setting up and maintaining a direct channel between them is relatively small, whereas the cost of creating a genuine market channel is relatively large. Furthermore, to create and maintain an internal market may be more difficult in light of incentive issues when the channel is internal to a single firm. It should also be noted that the use of internal transfer prices is in itself not sufficient to constitute an internal market. A mechanism that looks like a competitive market can be modified so that it becomes a central planning mechanism that uses prices and competitive behavior rules. The modification needed is to allow the market agent to communicate prices and *quantities* to each producing unit directly. In Case 1 that extension of the market agent's function would allow him to select one of the equilibria from the excess demand correspondence and communicate each manager's part of that equilibrium to that manager, in effect communicating the production plan. In the example a direct mechanism would bring about efficient coordination more cheaply. Thus, if the example were typical, except for incentive reasons, we should not expect to observe price-coordinated central mechanisms in such cases. Indeed, casual observation suggests that we do not see such mechanisms very often. Usually incentive schemes are tacked on to direct coordination mechanisms in such cases. However, if the computations required to operate the direct mechanism were sufficiently more complex than the calculations involved in figuring out profit-maximizing actions, the comparison might go the other way.

7.2.2. Example 2

There are three processes, ρ_1, ρ_2, and ρ_3. Each process produces "objects," each of which is characterized by a vector of properties or attributes. The attributes are represented by a vector of dimension q. To facilitate understanding, it helps to have a specific situation in mind.

Suppose that ρ_1 produces gears, ρ_2 produces pinions, and ρ_3 produces assemblies, each consisting of one gear and one pinion. The gear and pinion are designed to mesh to form a power-transmission mechanism. The attributes of a gear include its dimensions, the geometry and measurements of its tooth structure, its metallurgical properties, and the like. Similar attributes exist for pinions and for assemblies. We can imagine that a gear is produced by a sequence of operations. Each finished gear can be labeled, say, $1, 2, \ldots, n^1$. The properties of the ith gear produced are represented by its attribute vector, $a^i = (a^i_1, \ldots, a^i_q)$, which is a q-dimensional vector of real numbers. The sequence of operations is determined by the precise configurations and settings of the machines that carry out the operations. We indicate these settings by the value of a parameter denoted $\widehat{\alpha} = (\widehat{a}_1, \ldots, \widehat{a}_q)$. The parameter $\widehat{\alpha}$ is the attribute vector of the target gear (that is, a gear with the desired attributes) to be produced by the operations. However, the process is not perfect. Given a particular configuration and setup, the process produces gears with properties only approximately equal to the vector of attributes that the process is designed to produce.

To enable the specification of the tolerance in gear production, we introduce in R^q a norm $||x|| = \max_{j=1,\ldots,q}\{|x_j|\}$. The tolerances associated with that process are represented by a scalar $\varepsilon^1 \geq 0$; it is the case that every gear, i, produced by ρ_1 at the setting $\widehat{\alpha}$ for all $i = 1, \ldots, n^1, a^i$ satisfies

$$||a^i - \widehat{\alpha}|| \leq \varepsilon^1. \tag{7.2.3}$$

The tolerance ε^1 is independent of the setting $\widehat{\alpha}$. A gear produced by process ρ_1 with setting $\widehat{\alpha}$, and therefore with a tolerance ε^1, is identified as a commodity – a gear of type $(\widehat{a}, \varepsilon^1)$. The setting $\widehat{\alpha}$ also determines the time t^1

that it takes to produce a single gear. The state of the process ρ_1 can be identified with the value of $\widehat{\alpha}$, and the number n^1 of units of output to be produced; thus, $s^1 = (\widehat{\alpha}, n^1)$. The output of process ρ_1 is $f^1(s^1) = (a^1, \ldots, a^{n^1}; \varepsilon^1, n^1 \times t^1)$, where for each $1 \leq i \leq n^1$ the vector a^i satisfies inequality (7.2.3). The time it takes to produce n^1 gears is included because the gears are not explicitly dated. If commodities were dated, the date of a batch of n^1 type $(\widehat{\alpha}, \varepsilon^1)$ gears would be $t_0 + n^1 \times t^1$, where t_0 is the time when production of this batch begins.

We suppose that a pinion is characterized by a vector that describes the gears to which it best fits. Thus a typical pinion has an attribute vector $(b_1, \ldots, b_q)$, which indicates not only the attributes of the pinion, but also the attributes of the gear to which it should be fitted. As in the case of gear production, when a target vector $\widehat{\beta} = \widehat{b} = (\widehat{b}_1, \ldots, \widehat{b}_q)$ is set for pinion production and a set of n_2 pinions $b^1 = (b^1_1, \ldots, b^{n_2}_q) = [(b^1_1, \ldots, b^1_q), \ldots, (b^{n_2}_1, \ldots, b^{n_2}_q)]$ is manufactured, then for each i,

$$||\widehat{\beta} - b^i|| < \varepsilon^2. \tag{7.2.4}$$

The scalar ε^2 is a specification of the tolerance of the process. As in the case of gears, the tolerance is independent of the specification $\widehat{\beta}$.

In the same way as in gear production, a state of ρ_2, denoted $s^2 = (\widehat{b}, n^2)$, determines its output $f^2(s^2) = (b^1, \ldots, b^{n^2}; \varepsilon^2, n^2 \times t^2)$. As in process ρ_1, if $\widehat{\beta} = \widehat{b}$, then, for $i = 1, \ldots, q$,

$$||b^i - \widehat{\beta}|| \leq \varepsilon^2. \tag{7.2.5}$$

Process ρ_3 forms pairs of gears and pinions to form an assembly. We suppose to start with that this process has only one state, s^3_0, and requires t^3 units of time per assembly. The attribute of an assembly is a pair of vectors, $c^{i,k} = (a^i, b^k)$, where the attribute (a^i, b^k) represents gear i, $i \in \{1, \ldots, n\}$ mated to pinion k, $k \in \{1, \ldots, \widehat{n}\}$, $\widehat{n} = \min(n^1, n^2)$. The measure of quality of an assembly is the closeness of the attributes of pinion and gear; the better the match, the smoother the operation of the assembly, and the longer its useful life. Thus, if process ρ_1 is set up to produce gears of type $(\widehat{a}, \varepsilon^1)$, then the best setting of ρ_2 is $\widehat{\beta} = \widehat{b} = \widehat{a}$, and conversely. For simplicity, without loss of generality, we rename gears so that the gear paired with pinion i in an assembly is gear i. It follows from inequalities (7.2.3) and (7.2.4) that if a gear from process ρ_1 and a pinion from process ρ_2 are assembled, for $i \in \epsilon\{1, \ldots, \widehat{n}\}$, we have

$$||a^i - b^i|| \leq \varepsilon^1 + \varepsilon^2. \tag{7.2.6}$$

A user of assemblies has a requirement (demand) for a number n of assemblies of a specified quality expressed by a scalar $\eta \geq 0$, and the condition that for all $i \in \{1, \ldots, n\}$,

$$||a^i - b^k|| \leq \eta. \tag{7.2.7}$$

There are three managers, M_k, the manager of process ρ_k, $k = 1, 2, 3$. Manager M_1 knows his own technology ρ_1, including the value of ε^1, chooses the value of α, and of n^1, and observes the vector of attributes of the product of his process resulting from his choice. Similar knowledge exists for manager M_2, who knows ρ_2 and ε^2, and chooses $\widehat{\beta}$ and n^2, and observes[7] the vector b of attributes of each unit produced by her process with configuration $\widehat{\beta}$. Manager M_3 knows the value of η and chooses n^3.

Efficient production in this technology means, given n and η, to choose $\widehat{\alpha}, \widehat{\beta}, n^1$, and n^2 such that the assemblies meet the quality requirement (7.2.7), and the time to complete production of the required assemblies is minimum among all programs that meet the required quality level η. Here we are taking time as a proxy for all resource requirements, that is, cost elements. Efficient production in this technology depends on the quality standard η for assemblies. It follows from inequalities (7.2.4) and (7.2.6) that if for Case 1,

$$\varepsilon^1 + \varepsilon^2 \leq \eta,$$

and the demand is for type $(\widehat{a}, \widehat{a})$ assemblies, then for any n, it is possible to achieve efficient production by setting $n^3 = n$, $\widehat{\alpha} = \widehat{a}$, $n^1 = n^3$; $\widehat{\beta} = \widehat{a}$, $n^2 = n^3$. The minimum time to produce the assemblies is $n(\max\{t^1, t^2\} + t^3)$. This is clearly the minimum possible. Among the coordination mechanisms that can achieve efficient coordination in Case 1 is one that uses market channels. Manager M_3 sells assemblies to the outside users, who are not modeled explicitly, and buys gears from M_1, and pinions from M_2 in two separate markets, one for gears of type $(\widehat{\alpha}, \varepsilon^1)$ and the other for pinions of type $(\widehat{\alpha}, \varepsilon^2)$. The assemblies are type $(\widehat{\alpha}, \widehat{\alpha}, \varepsilon^3)$. The types define commodities. These are common knowledge among managers and buyers. It is easy to verify that these arrangements define a coordination mechanism, and that it results in efficient production in Case 1.

For Case 2,

$$\eta < \varepsilon^1 + \varepsilon^2.$$

This case has two subcases of interest. We make the assumption that $\varepsilon^1 < \varepsilon^2$. (It is often the case that the pinion is smaller – less massive – than the gear, and that most of the variation in a pinion's attributes are due to distortion arising from hardening by heat treating, whereas the corresponding distortion of the gear is smaller. For future reference we note that it is generally the case that variation in the composition of the metal from which the pinions are made also contributes to the distortion resulting from heat treating.) For Case 2.1,

$$\varepsilon^1 < \eta < \varepsilon^1 + \varepsilon^2.$$

[7] It would be more realistic to suppose that the manager observes an approximation to the attribute vector of each unit produced by her process. For simplicity, we assume that she observes the attributes precisely.

For Case 2.2,

$$\eta < \varepsilon^1.$$

In Case 2.1 there are several coordination mechanisms that can achieve efficient production. Because each manager's optimal decisions are so simple, the algorithms for calculating them are trivial, amounting to setting one variable equal to another. Therefore, we describe the mechanisms in an informal way, focusing on the information channels used.

First, we consider a coordination mechanism that can achieve efficient production when $\eta = \varepsilon^1$, hence *a fortiori* when $\eta \geq \varepsilon^1$. Manager M_3 transmits $n^3 = n$, and the desired value of $\widehat{\beta} = \widehat{b}$ to M_2. Manager M_2 chooses $\widehat{\beta} = \widehat{b}$, and hence the state $s^2 = (\widehat{b}, n)$, and produces n pinions $b^1, \ldots, b^n$. This takes $n \times t^2$ units of time. Manager M_2 sends the array $b^i = (b^i_1, \ldots, b^i_q)$, $i = 1, \ldots, n$ to M_1, and she sends the pinions to M_3. Then M_1 chooses a sequence of values of $\widehat{\alpha}$, namely $\widehat{\alpha}_1, \ldots, \widehat{\alpha}_n$, where $\widehat{\alpha} = b^i$, $i = 1, \ldots, n$. Each term of this sequence satisfies inequality (7.2.3). Therefore, $\|a^i - b^i\| \leq \varepsilon^1 = \eta$ for $i = 1, \ldots, n$. Clearly the same conclusion holds for $\eta \geq \epsilon^1$. The additional time in general depends on the sequence of settings; the transition from state s to state s' depends on the states, and it is not necessarily the same as the transition from s' to s. Therefore M_1 would have to solve a complex combinatorial problem to determine an efficient order in which to produce gears that match the pinions individually. This might be worthwhile if setup transitions can be done quickly. If setup transitions are costly, it is possible for a closer match of gears to pinions to be achieved by having M_2 transmit the vector b^1 to M_1, thereby enabling M_1 to produce all n gears with the setting $\alpha = b^1$. That is, M_2 produces one finished pinion, which takes time t^2, observes its attributes, and transmits them to M_1. This permits M_1 to set his process to match those attributes. If, as noted above, there is a source of variation that applies to the entire batch of n pinions, this may result in a quality variation of gear and pinion between ε^1 and $\varepsilon^1 + \varepsilon^2$. A coordination mechanism capable of carrying out individual matching, or the more limited approximation that matches a sample of one finished pinion, would use direct channels between the managers. To achieve the same quality by using market channels would require defining each gear, each pinion, and each assembly as a commodity, and it would also require that the demand for each of those commodities be substantial in relation to the capacities of possible suppliers.

In Case 2.2, where $\eta < \varepsilon^1$, it may be possible for a coordination mechanism with market channels, or one with direct channels, to achieve the desired quality level, η, by having M_3 inspect the final assemblies, sorting them into those that satisfy inequality (7.2.7) and those that do not. This would in general require that n^3 and therefore n^1 and n^2 be greater than the required number of final assemblies. If there is demand for assemblies of various qualities, this might be the efficient coordination mechanism. (This appears to be the way computer chips are produced.) If not, and if the yield of acceptable assemblies is low relative to the cost of producing them, then coordination mechanisms using direct channels would be preferable. It should be noted that in a more complex setting where a variety of objects is being produced with the same machinery, the timing of production becomes a more significant issue, as it is in the first example in this chapter.

The examples show that the measures of performance, especially delay and the number of crosslinks in the assigned graph, play a central role in distinguishing among coordination mechanisms. They also have a part in determining whether it pays to internalize crosslinks by combining basic units in a larger organizational structure. In Case 1 of Example 1 the failure of the competitive mechanism to achieve the desired coordination is due to an insufficient number of independent price variables. The equations characterizing equilibrium reduce the size of the set of equilibrium prices to the point where there are not enough prices to distinguish possible equilibria from one another.

In Case 1 of Example 2, a coordination mechanism using (competitive) market channels does bring about coordination. We saw that when the parameter η expressing the desired precision of matching of gear and pinion is sufficiently large (greater than $\varepsilon^1 + \varepsilon^2$), the function giving the desired actions in terms of the parameters is independent of the attributes of gear and pinion, respectively. The decision reduces to how many gears and pinions of the standard type should be produced. In the remaining cases of Example 2, it is clear that delay, the number of crosslinks, and the number of agents depend sensitively on the number of parameters in the function to be computed, and on the initial distribution of information about the environment – on what each manager can observe directly. When a coordination mechanism using market channels is used, the number of such channels reflects the number of different commodities, and the number of variables needed to specify each one, and depends on the number and distribution of underlying parameters of the function to be computed.

Example 3, presented later, illustrates the fact that the communication required (number of crosslinks) depends on the initial distribution of information, and on the way the function to be computed depends on the underlying parameters.

When the function to be computed is given, along with the initial distribution of information about its arguments, and an algorithm in the form of a $\mathcal{F}$ network is specified, it is in principle a straightforward exercise to construct the assigned graphs and find the efficient assignments, and their associated delays, number of crosslinks, and number of agents. These factors are determined by the function to be computed, and by the initial distribution of information among the basic units. In Example 2 a straightforward analysis based on counting parameters shows that when (2, 1) modules are used, a lower bound on delay is $\log_2(n)$, and the the number of variables that agents M_1 and M_2 must transmit is at least $2n$. The lower bound on delay can be attained by employing enough agents. In general this increases the number of crosslinks, but the increase comes in the form of internal crosslinks, whereas the number of external ones remains constant at n for each basic unit.

In contrast, in Example 3 below, each manager can send the other the values a_1 and b_1, respectively, and if necessary, one of them can send his calculated decision to the other. If, as the efficient graph Figure 7.4.7 suggests, the units are regarded as separate, then there is no need to compute the sum. The decision function depends on all the variables; that number cannot be reduced.

7.3. A FORMAL MODEL

7.3.1. Technology and Production

Here we present a model of technology and production designed to provide a formal framework that can capture the essential features of Examples 1 and 2. Technology is modeled by *processes*. A process produces objects or services described by *attributes*, or *properties* or *characteristics*. A specification of characteristics is a vector in the space $\underline{C}$ of characteristics or attributes. We assume that $\underline{C}$ is a subset (finite dimensional and closed under addition) of a real vector space $\mathbb{A}$. Although in principle an object has infinitely many properties, we consider only a finite number of relevant ones. The subset being closed under addition permits us to consider discrete as well as continuous properties. A *commodity* is a subset of the space $\underline{C}$. All objects (services) whose vector of characteristics lie in the given subset are instances of the same commodity. For example, in Example 2, all gears whose vector of attributes $a = (a_1, \ldots, a_q)$ satisfies $|a - \widehat{a}| < \varepsilon^1$ are instances of the commodity designated $(\widehat{a}, \varepsilon^1)$. The quantity of that commodity is a real number or an integer; in Example 2 it is an integer. When the commodity $(\widehat{a}, \varepsilon^1)$ is named, say, c, then x_c is the quantity of that commodity.

Technology consists of knowledge of how to produce things – goods or services. This is represented by *processes*. A process consists of a function that maps *states* into the set of characteristics $\underline{C}$. A state of a given process designates a way of operating that process. In Example 2 there is a process that produces gears. That process can be configured, or set up, or controlled, to produce gears intended to meet given specifications. The process can produce gears to meet any of a variety of specifications. Each possible configuration of the process is a possible state. If the process is in state s, the resulting vector of attributes produced is $f(s) \in \underline{C}$. Thus, a process ρ is defined by a function f_ρ whose domain is the set of states S_ρ and whose range is the set of possible attributes. That is, $\rho = (S_\rho, f_\rho)$, where $f_\rho : S_\rho \to \underline{C}$. The available technology $\mathcal{T}$ is a set of known processes.

Production is carried out in *production units*. A production unit consists of a collection of processes – a subset of $\mathcal{T}$ – and a manager who is in charge of that unit. A manager is in charge of at most one production unit. The role of a manager is to choose the state of his production unit. When there is more than one production unit, say there are N of them, there are correspondingly N managers. Formally there is a correspondence that associates with each production unit, i, and hence with manager, i, the set $\mathcal{T}_i \subseteq \mathcal{T}$ of processes that manager i is in charge of.

A given process can be used by different production units. Because a process used in several production units can be in different states, those "copies" of the process must be distinguished from one another. Formally, we label the process with the name of the unit, or the manager who is uniquely associated with the unit. If the process ρ is in both unit j and unit j', then we write ρ^j and $\rho^{j'}$, where $\rho^j = \rho^{j'} = \rho$. A *profile of states* is an array of the states of processes in the sets $\mathcal{T}_1, \ldots, \mathcal{T}_N$ in order within each set. For simplicity we assume that each production unit, i, consists of just one process. Then a profile $s = (s^1, \ldots, s^N)$, where s^i is the state of the process ρ^i in production unit i. Define the function $T : S \to \underline{C}$, where S is the set of profiles of states, by $T(s) := H[f^1_{\rho^1}(s^1_{\rho^1}), \ldots, f^N_{\rho^N}(s^N_{\rho^N})]$. When all inputs and outputs of these processes are commodities, and there are no externalities, the value of the function H is the sum of its arguments; the value $T(s)$ is the input–output vector associated with the profile s, and $T(S)$ is the set of all technologically feasible input–output vectors in the commodity space. Other feasibility constraints, such as the availability of resources, determine a subset of the commodity space consisting of all technologically feasible commodity bundles that also satisfy resource constraints. Correspondingly, there is a set of attainable profiles of states, denoted S^A. The set $T(S^A)$ is the *attainable production set* in the commodity space.

Because we are interested in mechanisms for coordinating the actions of the group of managers, the simplest case to consider is that in which the technology of each production unit consists of exactly one process, in which case no problem of coordination internal to a production unit arises. One consequence of the assumption that each manager is in charge of a single process is that when a process appears in two different production units, then the units have identical technologies.[8]

The purpose of production is to satisfy some outside requirements, such as demands of economic agents outside the particular sector of production

[8] It is also possible to make the number and types of production units endogenous. For the present purpose we do not do this, because our focus is on mechanisms for coordinating the actions of a given set of producers.

under consideration. We model these demands or requirements in terms of parameters that characterize them, such as parameters of utility or demand functions of consumers or of other producers outside the sector of production under consideration. If the outside demands are specific requirements rather than functions, the parameters identify those specific requirements. In either case we take them as exogenous. Denote the parameter space by Θ. An environment is a pair $(\mathcal{T}, \theta)$, where $\mathcal{T} = (\mathcal{T}_1, \ldots, \mathcal{T}_N)$ is the given, known technology distributed among the existing production units, and $\theta \in \Theta$ is a possible parameter value characterizing demand. We assume here that the technology is fixed and known, but that the outside environment is not known – only the set of possible outside environments is known. (It can be the case that the technology itself depends on parameters and that the organizational design must be determined by knowing only the set of possible values of those parameters as well, rather than a particular value.)

7.3.2. Efficient Production

A *performance criterion* is a characterization of the desired joint action in each possible environment. The characterization may be given by a goal function or a correspondence that identifies the profile(s) of states that are desired, or result in the outcomes that are preferred, in each possible environment. In this way goals such as "productive efficiency," or Pareto optimality, or "corporate profitability," or "meeting specified requirements" can be represented. In Example 2 the characterization of desired actions is given by functions determining the values of $\widehat{\alpha}$ and $\widehat{\beta}$, and by inequalities involving $\widehat{\alpha}$, $\widehat{\beta}$, ε^1, ε^2, and ε^3. In general, the formal element characterizing desired action is a relation (or system of relations) that can be written as $\Gamma(s, \theta; \mathcal{T}) = 0$. Given a characterization of desired joint action, the task of a designer of organization is to construct coordination mechanisms that can achieve the desired joint actions in the given class of environments. The first step in this direction is to specify the information that each manager has.

7.3.3. Information, Communication, and Coordination

The initial information of a manager consists of:

- knowledge of the processes assigned to her; thus, the manager assigned process ρ knows (S_ρ, f_ρ);
- a subset of Θ_j of Θ for manager j, possibly empty, consisting of the parameters that j can observe directly.

In addition to initial information, a manager may acquire information through communication. Each manager can send and receive messages to or from other managers, using communication channels. We consider two types of channels, called direct channels and market channels, respectively. Channels are directed;

the channel used by manager A to send a message to manager B is different from the one used by B to send a message to A.

A direct channel carries addressed messages from one specific agent to another. The sender and receiver are known to one another in the sense that for each message, the sender knows who the receiver is and vice versa. As with any communication channel, sender and receiver share the language in which messages are expressed. The structure and content of messages is otherwise restricted only by channel capacity. An agent who communicates with several other agents by means of direct channels can use her knowledge of who is at the other end to send a different message to each of the other agents. She can receive different messages from each of them.

The concept of a market channel requires some discussion. The term "market" is ubiquitous in economics. It has many different meanings. One can speak of the wheat market in Chicago, or the real estate market in Chicago, or the advertising market in Chicago, though these are very different things. If the term "market" can be used in a way that suggests that it applies to any situation in which two or more economic agents exchange something, or agree on a joint economic action, then the question we started with, that is, Which economic activities are, or should be, coordinated by markets and which by something else?, has only one possible answer. For this question to make sense, we need a class of things, which we call coordination mechanisms, with (at least) two elements, one of which is called market and one of which is not. Before introducing coordination mechanisms formally, we further explain the motivation for the formal concepts introduced in the next section.

It seems desirable to require that a coordination mechanism called the market mechanism should cover the case of a competitive market mechanism as it appears in general equilibrium models, such as the classical Arrow–Debreu model. It seems slightly ironic that there is no formal entity called "market" in that model; there is only "commodity," "price," and the actions of agents. Nevertheless, this model suggests that all communication among agents in a market mechanism should be by means of messages restricted to the commodities in the given list of commodities and their prices.

The most familiar formal specification of a competitive market is the one in terms of the Walrasian auctioneer. It is also suggestive to think about examples of markets, such as the local supermarket for groceries, or a hardware store, or some types of farmers' market or flea market. The supermarket stands ready to sell a variety of commodities to buyers, and buys what it has to sell from sellers. A buyer who goes to the supermarket can expect to buy what he wants, if he is willing to pay the posted market price. A seller who supplies the supermarket can offer to the buying agency of the supermarket what he wants to sell at a given price. There is no direct communication between those who buy from the supermarket and those who sell to the supermarket. The price at which goods are offered to buyers is the same for all buyers. Similarly, in a competitive situation, the price paid for a given product is the same to all sellers of that product. Furthermore, the supermarket cannot tell any buyer what to buy at the posted prices, nor can it instruct a seller what to sell. However, a supermarket or hardware store provides economic services that are not just informational. Conceptually we can separate these functions from the purely informational function of acting as a communication link between buyers and sellers, concentrating our attention on only the latter function. With these suggestive remarks in mind, we give the following concept of "market channel," a concept that combines the device of the Walrasian auctioneer with the informational role of the supermarket.

A market is personified as an agent, called the "market agent." Messages flow only between individual managers and the market agent. The form of messages is prescribed. In the case of a perfectly competitive market, a message from a manager to the market agent is a supply or demand function, whereas a message from the market agent to a manager is a vector of prices, the same for each manager. This is a static formulation. If, as in Example 1, several time periods are involved, the market is viewed as finding a multiperiod equilibrium at the beginning of the relevant time period, as in Debreu's formulation (Debreu, 1959).

In some institutional situations that we would naturally think of as markets, buyer and seller do meet directly. For example, in a farmers' market or a flea market, this is usually the case. The basic distinction we draw here is whether or not there is bargaining between buyer and seller. In our local farmers' market, where buyer and seller meet, the prices of the items for sale are posted. If a price is changed in the course of a market day, the new price is posted. This market can be described as one in which the seller – the farmer – is represented by an agent who merely transmits information – the price and specification of each item for sale – from seller to buyer, and also accumulates information about the demands of buyers. In fact, it is often the case that the sales booth is not manned by the supplier of the items offered for sale, but by an agent who is not authorized to change the posted prices in response to individual buyers. Furthermore, the identity of buyers or sellers is not used in determining the market agent's response to messages received. In the case of a competitive market, as modeled here, the market agent's message is obtained by aggregating the messages of managers to obtain the aggregate demand correspondence, and finding a price (if there is one) such that the aggregate excess demand at that price is not positive. If so, that price is the message sent from the market agent to all managers, that is, posted.

There is another aspect of markets that should be addressed, which we may call its scope. Consider a somewhat idealized flea market in which the items offered for sale at each booth are unique to that booth. In other words, the commodity vector is partitioned into subvectors that are each associated with a subset of sellers, in this case a unique seller. Although buyers (and possibly also sellers) might consider the entire vector of prices in calculating their decisions to supply or demand commodities, in this situation it may be the case that there is a different market agent for each segment of the market corresponding to the partition of the commodity vector – in the simplified flea market, a single market agent for each booth. The case in which the subvectors of the commodity vector corresponding to different "local" markets can overlap is more complicated. We do not treat it here.

We can also consider cases in which the market is not perfectly competitive but is still a market; that is, it is still the case that communication between buyers and sellers is mediated in a way that does not constitute direct personalized communication between an individual buyer and an individual seller. For example, a market agent might communicate to each seller the demand function for that seller's product as a function of the prices of the products of certain other sellers, without naming the buyers, or permitting the offered terms of sale to be different for different buyers. This would fit the case of nondiscriminating duopolists, for example.

When the interaction between agents is direct, as in bilateral bargaining, we do not speak of a market between them. Thus, a farmers' market, or a flea market in which the price of an item for sale is not posted but can change from one buyer to another, is not a market channel.

As we have said, the task of a manager is to choose the state of her process. The group of managers compute their decisions about actions in a joint distributed computation, each using his initial information, including the results of observation, and the information obtained as a result of communication. The joint computation, including the algorithm that it uses and the assignment of resources used to carry out the computation, constitutes the coordination mechanism.

The algorithm used to compute the desired actions is represented by an $\mathcal{F}$ network, as described especially in Chapter 3.

It was noted above that the assignment of processes to managers determines a partition of the set of (possibly replicated) processes. Therefore, certain subnets of the assigned $\mathcal{F}$ network that expresses the algorithm can be associated with the manager whose actions are being computed. Furthermore, because the network's inputs are determined by the initial information, and the structure of the initial information is also associated with the managers, the connections between subnetworks associated with different managers consist exclusively of communication channels. To facilitate exposition, suppose that there are two managers who have been assigned processes; correspondingly there are two subnets $\mathfrak{N}_1$, $\mathfrak{N}_2$ that compute the states of the two processes involved, associated with manager M_1 and with manager M_2, respectively. The (directed) arcs of the graph G that connect the graph G_1 with the graph G_2 carry communications between the two managers. These arcs are direct channels.

Alternatively, if a market agent were introduced between the two managers, two things would be different.

First, all communication between the managers would take place through the market agent. In the case of a competitive market, messages from managers to the market agent would be about commodity vectors, for example, supply or demand functions, and messages from the market agent would be prices. That is, communication between the managers would be indirect by means of a market channel.

Second, the nets $\mathfrak{N}_1$, $\mathfrak{N}_2$ would be replaced by nets that compute the messages required by the market channel, but the class $\mathcal{F}$ of elementary operations would be the same as in the case of an $\mathcal{F}$ network with direct channels. When there is a competitive market agent between the two managers, each manager would compute her excess demand by maximizing her profit, taking the prices transmitted by the market agent parametrically. Her action would be a state of her process that would result in a commodity vector yielding the maximum possible profit to her production unit, given all the data and the prices.

In a market with other structure, the behavior of the managers would be determined by the equilibria of the game that models the market. In either case, the task of manager M_i, which is to compute her action from the inputs to her subnetwork, is represented by a subnetwork. The inputs are the variables whose values come into the subnetwork either from the environment or by means of communication lines into the subnetwork.

The use of a competitive market channel usually, but not necessarily, entails the assumption that there are many production units that use the same process, with a different manager in charge of each unit. When several managers are in charge of replicas of a given process, or set of processes, we say they are the same *type*. In that case, all managers of the same type carry out the same computation. In contrast, when the channels between subnetworks corresponding to different managers are direct channels, then the algorithm embodied in the network specifies the computations to be carried out by each manager, which might be different for each manager. Generally these computations will be different from those required when the channel is a market channel.

An *information technology* consists of the set of $\mathcal{F}$ networks available, the restrictions on observation as expressed above, and the channels available for communication. In operating an $\mathcal{F}$ network, a manager can use *agents* who, under her supervision, carry out the elementary steps of the computation specified by the network. The manager herself may be one of those agents. Each agent works for only one manager. An agent supervised by a given manager is subject to the same constraints on initial information as her manager. Thus, the vertices of the graph of the network are assigned to agents under certain restrictions described earlier in Subsection 7.1.1. A network whose vertices are assigned to agents is called an *assigned $\mathcal{F}$ network*. The simplest case is that in which all computations of a manager are carried out by that manager.

A coordination mechanism is an assigned $\mathcal{F}$ network. For a given technology $\mathcal{T}$ and a given class of environmental parameters, a coordination mechanism computes the actions of each manager. Specification of the $\mathcal{F}$ network includes specification of the messages sent between managers. Messages generally depend on the parameter θ. Manager M may receive a message from another manager at any stage of computation, depending on the algorithm expressed by their two subnetworks. For a given coordination mechanism, the network is given. We may therefore describe the message received by manager M from other managers by the notation $m^{-M} = m^{-M}(\theta^{-M})$, where θ^{-M} refers to the components of θ observed by the managers other than M, reflecting dependence of their messages on the parameters they observe. The notation refers to the entire ordered array of messages received by M in the course of the computation. Thus, for fixed $\mathcal{T}$ and θ, the computation of manager M can be represented by the mapping $\zeta^M (m^{-M}, \theta^M)$. In general, ζ^M is not single valued. In that case, in order for the coordination mechanism to be well defined, that is, to determine a particular action of manager M, it is necessary that she be able to choose an element of $\zeta^M (m^{-M}, \theta^M)$ arbitrarily. This must be the case for every manager. Thus, if the coordination mechanism is to result in outcomes that are Γ *efficient*, then every manager must be able to choose an arbitrary element of the set of actions determined for him by his computation. To express this, we say that a coordination mechanism $\mathfrak{C}$, consisting of an assigned $\mathcal{F}$ network, is Γ *satisfactory* if and only if for every $\theta \in \Theta$, and for every manager $i = 1, \ldots, N$, and every state $s^{M_i} \in \zeta^{M_i} (m^{-M_i}, \theta^{M_i})$, the profile $s = (s^{M_1}, \ldots, s^{M_N})$ satisfies the relation $\Gamma(s, \theta; \mathcal{T}) = 0$.

We saw that in Case 1 of Example 1, competitive equilibria do not necessarily satisfy this condition.

Given an environment, a performance criterion, a set of production units, and an information technology, we find that the question How should economic activity be coordinated? becomes "Which coordination mechanisms should be used?," To address this question, we must specify the criteria by which alternative organizations are to be compared.

If a coordination mechanism, $\mathfrak{C}$, is applied to a class of environments, the mechanism determines the actions of the managers in each possible environment, including the observations, the communications, and the computations that are carried out in arriving at those actions. Generally, resources are used in observing, communicating, and computing. Resources include those used to set up and to operate the facilities needed to carry out the information processing. Resources used in information processing are not available for use in production. Ideally, the net result of using each mechanism could be determined for the class of environments, and choice among them would be guided by maximizing the "utility" of net performance. However, we are not yet able to deal adequately with criteria for comparing alternative mechanisms at this level of generality. Instead we require that the mechanism compute actions that meet the performance criterion, and among those mechanisms we look for ones that are efficient in the space of the cost determinants. This amounts to a lexicographic principle according to which we first require meeting the specified goal, Γ, and second that the mechanism be *cost efficient* in the set of all Γ – satisfactory mechanisms.

7.4. STRUCTURE OF ORGANIZATIONS

7.4.1. Larger Organizations

In the discussion so far, the basic organizational unit is the production unit, with its manager. We now consider the possibility of combining production units – basic units – to form larger organizations. The structure of organization is, we suppose, the result of (rational) choice; we ask, How does the structure of an efficient coordination mechanism bear on the choice of organization? To address this question, we suppose that a coordination problem is given, and so is at least one efficient coordination mechanism for that problem. When the coordination mechanism uses market links exclusively, the larger organization that basic units form is part of a market economy or structure.[9] When basic units are coordinated by a mechanism with direct channels, it is possible either to combine several basic units in a larger organizational structure that is not a market structure, or to leave them as separate units coordinated by the given mechanism. Two related considerations bear on this choice. First, referring to our earlier discussion of cost of communication, we say that the cost of a crosslink can depend on whether or not that link is between agents who are in close and persistent contact. To express this distinction formally, we introduce two kinds of crosslinks, which we call *internal crosslinks* and *external crosslinks*, respectively. An internal crosslink is one that goes between agents who belong to production units in the same organization; an external crosslink is one that goes between agents in production units in different organizations. Given a coordination mechanism – an assigned graph – combining production units represented in the graph into a single organizational unit converts all crosslinks between those units from external crosslinks to internal crosslinks. The conversion results in changing the cost of communication among those units.

7.4.2. Revised Cost Model

The model of cost presented earlier is modified to include internal and external crosslinks as follows. Let the number of external crosslinks be ν_ϵ, and the number of internal crosslinks be ν_ι, where $\nu_\epsilon + \nu_\iota = \nu$. We suppose as before that the cost of communicating by means of an external crosslink is increasing in ν_ϵ and is 0 for $\nu = 0$. In contrast, the cost of communicating by means of an internal crosslink has a fixed cost, so that the cost of $\nu_\iota = c > 0$ and is increasing in ν_ι, but at a significantly lower rate than the cost of ν_ϵ. Consequently there is a critical value ν^0, such that if ν is less than ν^0 it is cheaper to set $\nu_\epsilon = \nu$, whereas if ν is greater than ν^0, it is cheaper to set $\nu_\iota = \nu$ (see Figure 7.4.1). That is, if the assigned graph requires a lot of communication among the production units in order to execute the algorithm efficiently, then it is better to bring the managers of those units into a larger organization and pay the cost of creating the necessary

[9] It is not ruled out that a number of those units have the same owner.

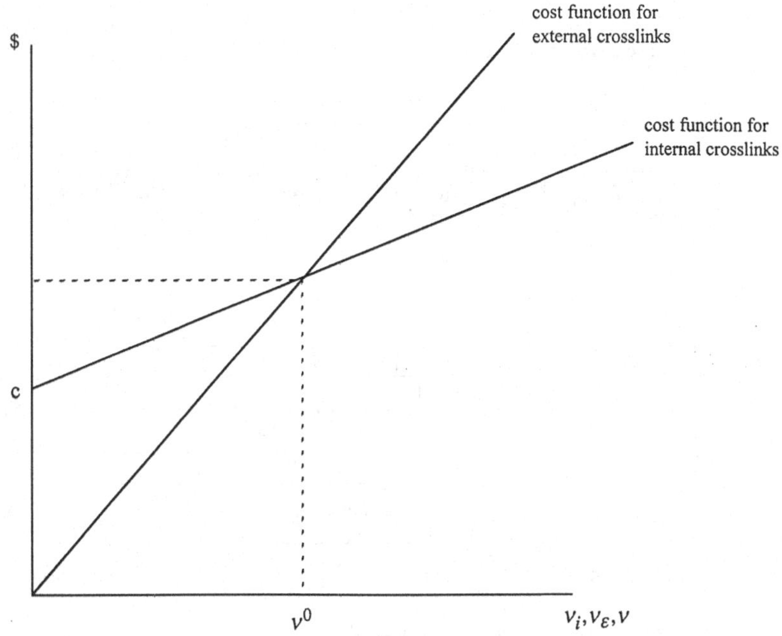

Figure 7.4.1.

infrastructure, whereas if relatively little communication is required, then is is better to use external crosslinks, that is, to leave the basic units organizationally separate.

Example 3

We consider the question whether to combine basic production units into a larger organization in the context of Example 3, a variant of Example 2. In this variant, processes ρ_1 and ρ_2 each have just one setting, $\widehat{\alpha} = a$ with resulting attribute vector $a = (a_1, \ldots, a_q)$, and $\widehat{\beta} = b$ with resulting attribute vector $b = (b_1, \ldots, b_q)$, such that a and b vary in some set. We suppose that there are three production units, each with its own manager, corresponding to the three processes in Example 2, where ρ_3 assembles the products of ρ_1 and ρ_2. Suppose the quality of an assembly is measured by

$$D = \sum_{j=1}^{q} (a_j - b_j)^2.$$

Suppose further that it is possible by application of effort in the assembly stage to improve the match between two items being assembled. Let the value of a perfectly mated assembly be $Y \geq 0$, and let the effort applied in correcting a mismatch be z, where $0 \leq z$. Suppose that the "cost" of applying effort z is wz measured in the same units as Y. Suppose further that the net value of a unit

q=4

The unassigned F network

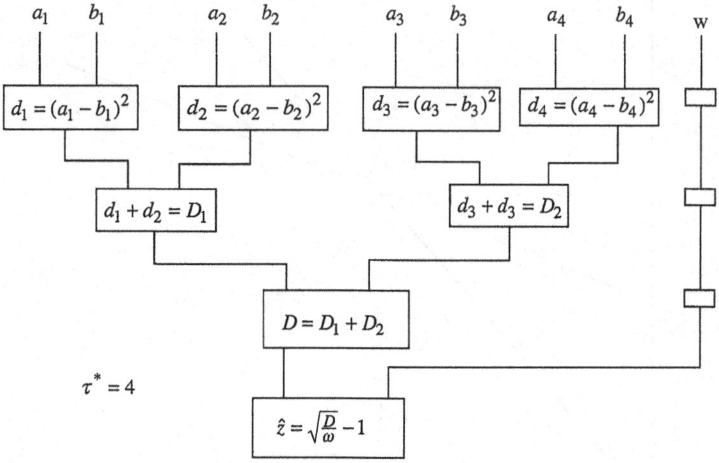

Figure 7.4.2.

of the assembled product as a function of z is

$$V(z) = Y - [D/(1+z)] - wz.$$

Thus,

$$V(0) = Y - \sum_{j=1}^{q}(a_j - b_j)^2.$$

The manager of process ρ_3 observes Y and $w \geq 0$, and he chooses the value of z. He should choose z to maximize V subject to $0 \leq w$. This maximization leads to

$$\hat{z} = +\sqrt{D/w} - 1 = \phi(D, w).$$

The basic production units labeled with the names of their managers are M_1, operating process ρ_1; M_2, operating process ρ_2; and M_3, operating process ρ_3. Suppose that manager M_1 observes the vector a; M_2 observes b, and M_3 observes Y and w and chooses the value of z – the amount of corrective effort to be done in process ρ_3.

There are several algorithms available for computing the desired action $\hat{z}$. We consider these algorithms when the dimensions of vectors a and b are both q, and when $q = 4, 5, 6$. We begin with the algorithm defined by the unassigned network shown in Figure 7.4.2.[10] Beginning with $q = 4$, we see

[10] The obvious alternative algorithm for this problem is inefficient.

Algo I. Assignment 2: M_1 sends a_3 and a_4 to M_2
M_2 sends b_1 and b_2 to M_1
M_1 computes $d_1 + d_2 = D_1$; M_2 computes $d_3 + d_4 = D_2$
M_1 and M_2 send D_1 and D_2 resp. to M_3 who computes $\hat{z}$.

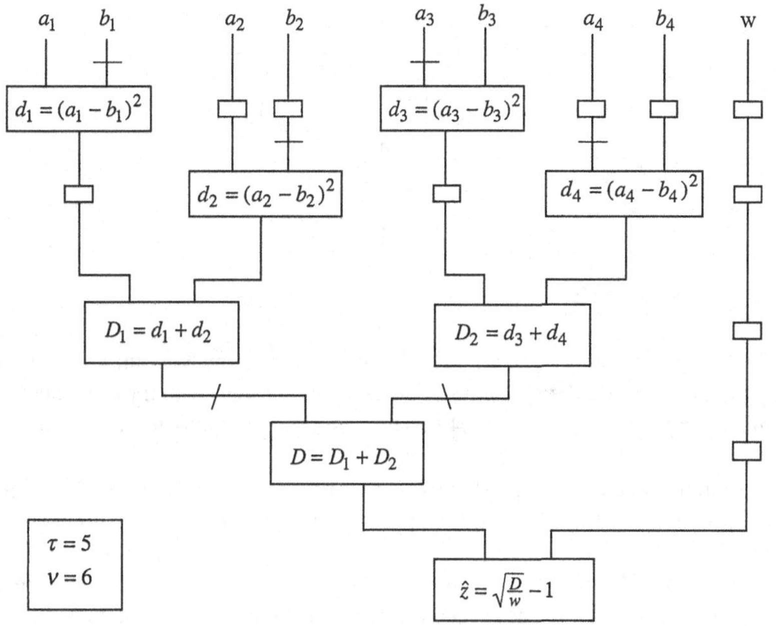

Figure 7.4.3.

that the efficient assignment with three agents (the three managers) is shown in Figure 7.4.3.

It results in delay $\tau = 5$ and crosslinks $\nu = 6$. The assigned graph in Figure 7.4.3 breaks up into three subgraphs, as shown in Figure 7.4.4, where $\mathbf{M_1}$ is the subgraph that represents the computation of M_1, $\mathbf{M_2}$ is the subgraph of M_2, and $\mathbf{M_3}$ is the subgraph of M_3.

Combining any two or all three of these units into a single larger organizational unit would permit each manager to participate in any of the computations, perhaps increasing efficiency. However, in this case doing so does not decrease the delay, but does increase the number of crosslinks. Given that the assignment shown in Figure 7.4.3 is efficient, if the critical value ν^0 is at least 6, it does not pay to combine the three basic units.

Consider next the case $q = 6$. The assigned graph that has the same structure as the one shown in Figure 7.4.4 is shown in Figure 7.4.5.

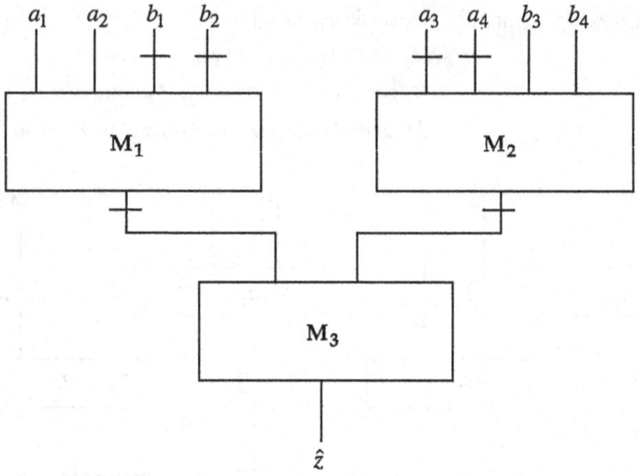

Figure 7.4.4.

It results in delay $\tau = 7$, and crosslinks $\nu = 8$. However, unlike in the case $q = 4$, in this case there is another efficient assignment with three agents (three managers) shown in Figure 7.4.6. This assignment results in delay $\tau = 6$ and crosslinks $\nu = 10$.

Which assignment turns out to be preferable depends on the value of a reduction in delay from 7 to 6 compared with the cost of an increase in crosslinks from 9 to 10.[11] Figure 7.4.5 shows the same organizational structure as in Figure 7.4.4. The assignment shown in Figure 7.4.6 is a little different in that the unit supervised by M_3 receives inputs from M_1 and M_2 at two stages of computation. Whether or not to internalize crosslinks by forming a larger organizational unit depends on the critical value of ν_0.

The preceding examples make it clear that the measures of performance, delay, amount of communication, and the number of agents required to operate the coordination mechanism depend on the number q of parameters. The second consideration bearing on the structure of organization of basic units is the effect of increasing values of q. In general, increases in q result in increases in the number of crosslinks ν and in the delay τ for a given number of agents. However, there are cases in which increasing the number of parameters does not increase the number of crosslinks in an efficient assignment. The following example illustrates this phenomenon.[12] In this example there are two production units, one with parameters $a = (a_1, \ldots, a_q)$ and the other with parameters $b = (b_1, \ldots, b_{q'})$, where q and q' need not be equal. Manager M_1 observes a and chooses the state s_1 of his process; manager M_2 observes b, and

[11] For $q = 5$, the values are $\tau = 6$ and $\nu = 8$. The structure of the graph is an adjusted version of that shown in Figure 7.4.6.

[12] See Abelson (1980).

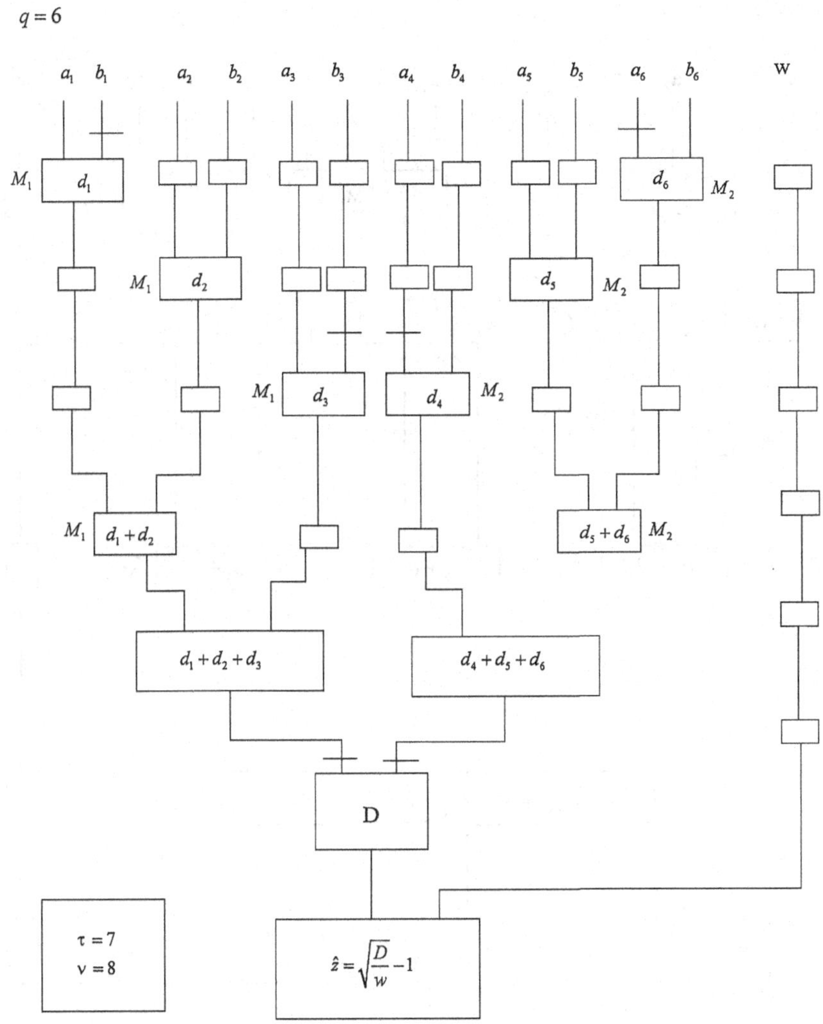

Figure 7.4.5.

chooses the state s_2 of her process. The functions that define coordinated action are

$$\hat{s}_1 = \sum_{i=1}^{q} b_1^i a_i,$$

$$\hat{s}_2 = \sum_{j=1}^{q'} a_1^j b_j.$$

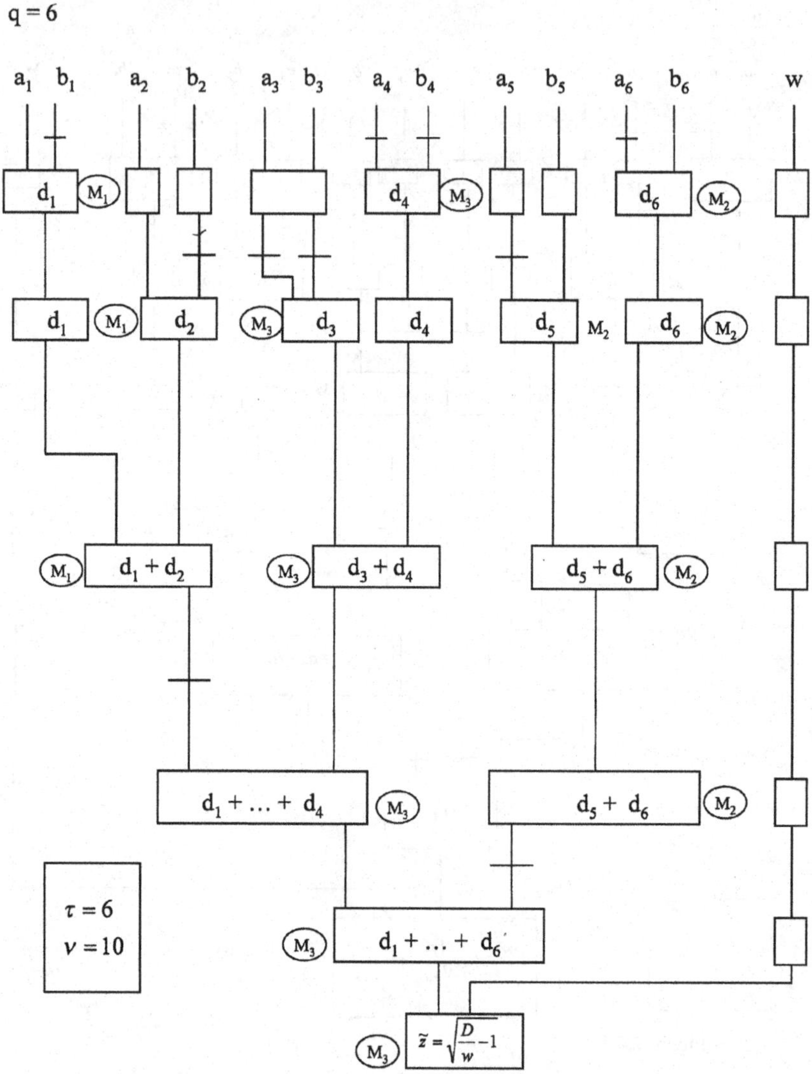

Figure 7.4.6.

Assuming the same class of elementary operations as in the preceding examples, we find that the obvious assignment of operations is to assign the entire computation of $\hat{s}_1$ to M_1, and the computation of $\hat{s}_2$ to M_2. Figure 7.4.7 shows the resulting computation on the assumption that the number of agents employed by each manager is sufficient to allow every set of modules that the algorithm

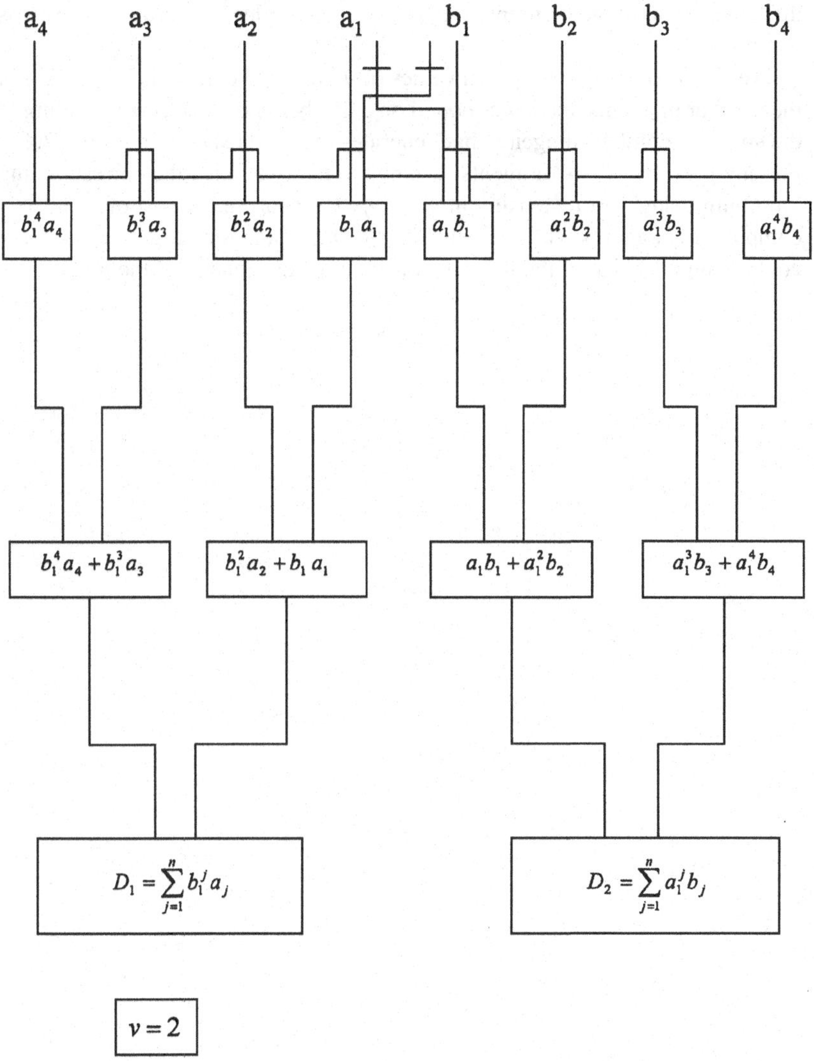

Figure 7.4.7.

permits to be computed in parallel is so computed. For the present purpose, this simplification allows the point to be made without irrelevant complexity.

It is obvious from Figure 7.4.7 that the number of crosslinks is 2; M_1 sends the value of a_1 to M_2, and M_2 sends the value of b_1 to M_1. It is also evident that the number of crosslinks is the same for every value of q and of q'. That is, independent of the number of parameters, it is better to have two separate units than to combine them into one larger one in order to internalize the cross communication.

We can also see that for given values of q and q', the delay is decreasing in the number of agents, the lower bound on delay being the one corresponding to the smallest number of agents that generates the graph shown in Figure 7.4.7. For any given numbers of agents assigned to the two units, the corresponding minimum delays are increasing in q and q'. Comparing the cost of additional computational agents with the value of the corresponding reductions in delay could bound the size of the information-processing capacity of the units.

Appendix A Appendix to Chapter 2: Graph Theory

In Chapter 2 we stated that the concept of an $\mathcal{F}$ network and the concept of an automaton are closely related. We referred the reader to this appendix for a more detailed discussion of that relation. We begin this appendix with that topic. A d-**modular network** is an $\mathcal{F}$ network such that for some finite set Y of cardinality d (a finite alphabet), each function of $\mathcal{F}$ has a finite product of copies of Y as its domain and the range of the function is Y.[1]

We repeat the notation of Chapter 2.

Notation. *If X is a finite set, then X^* denotes the set of finite sequences, or strings, of empty elements and elements of X. If x, $x' \in X^*$, then xx' denotes the concatenation of the strings x and x'.*

Definition A.0.1. (Arbib, 1960). An *automaton* is a quintuple $M = (\mathcal{X}, \mathcal{Y}, Q, \delta, \lambda)$, where

$\mathcal{X}$ is a finite set, the set of *inputs*;
$\mathcal{Y}$ is a finite set, the set of *outputs*;
Q is a set, the set of *states*;
$\delta : Q \times \mathcal{X} \to Q$ is the *next-state function*; and
$\lambda : Q \times \mathcal{X} \to \mathcal{Y}$ is the *next-output function.*

An automaton M is a *finite automaton* if Q is finite.

Of special interest are automata such that for some function $\beta : Q \to \mathcal{Y}$, $\lambda(q, x) = \beta[\delta(q, x)]$ for each $(q, x) \in Q \times \mathcal{X}$. Automata for which such a function β exists are called *state-output machines*, and the function β is called the *present-output function.*

[1] When $\mathcal{F}$ contains functions other than those defined on finite sets, then the network is a *system* in the sense of Arbib (1960, p. 54).

If an automaton is a state-output machine, the functions δ and λ extend to functions on the set $Q \times \mathcal{X}^*$. One does this by setting

(i) $\delta(q, \Lambda) = q$, for Λ an empty element;
(ii) $\lambda(q, \Lambda) = \beta(q)$;
(iii) for all x and $x' \in \mathcal{X}^*$, (a) $\delta(q, xx') = \delta[\delta(q, x), x']$ and (b) $\lambda(q, xx') = \beta[\delta(q, xx')]$.

If $M = (\mathcal{X}, \mathcal{Y}, Q, \delta, \lambda)$ is a state-output machine and if σ is a state of M, then for each $x \in \mathcal{X}^*$ set $M_\sigma(x) = \lambda(\sigma, x)$. The function M_σ is the *function computed by the automaton* on $\mathcal{X}^*$ given the initial state σ.

We have noted that an $\mathcal{F}$ network composed of functions defined on products of a finite alphabet whose cardinality is d is a d-modular network or *circuit*. Definition 2.1.6 of Chapter 2 defines the concept of an $\mathcal{F}$ network computing a function in time t. Next, we specify the input, output, state, next-state function, next-output function, and present-value function required to make a circuit into an automaton. The specifications determine the sense in which a circuit is a state-output machine.

Suppose Y is a nonempty finite set and suppose $f : Y \times \cdots \times Y \to Y$ is a function of r variables that has Y as its range. We interpret the function f as an automaton by defining states for f, a next-state function, and a next-output function. The inputs of f are elements of $Y \times \cdots \times Y$ (an r-fold product) and the outputs of f are elements of Y. The set of states of f is the set Y. The next-state function and the next-output function determine the next state and next output of f one unit of time later than the time at which an input is presented to f. For a state σ of f and $(y_1, \ldots, y_r) \in Y \times \cdots \times Y$, the value of the next-state function δ is $\delta[\sigma, (y_1, \ldots, y_r)] = f(y_1, \ldots, y_r)$. The value of the next-output function λ is $\lambda[\sigma, (y_1, \ldots, y_r)] = f(y_1, \ldots, y_r)$. If Y is a finite set with d elements and if each function of $\mathcal{F}$ has as domain $Y \times \cdots \times Y$ (an a-fold product $1 \leq a \leq r$) and range Y, then the next-state function and next-output function make each $\mathcal{F}$ module a finite automaton. A module that uses a finite alphabet is a state-output machine, because we can define a present-output function β by setting $\beta(y) = y$ when the module is in state y.

Suppose the elements of $\mathcal{F}$ are functions interpreted as finite state-output automata, and suppose that an $\mathcal{F}$ network $\mathcal{N}$ is represented by an ordered directed graph N (see Definition 2.1.3). Think of the arcs of the graph as representing wires between the modules of the network. A wire carries values without delay from one module to a variable of a second (not necessarily different from the first) module. At time t, once an initial state for the network is known and the value at each network input line is given, the state of each module of the network is known at time $t + 1$.[2] Suppose that the network $\mathcal{N}$ has q modules, r input lines, and s output lines. The set of inputs of the network is the product

[2] Because the wires, or arcs, of the network have no delay, the state of a module would be undefined if the modules also computed without delay.

$\mathcal{X} = Y \times \cdots \times Y$ (an r-fold product). The set of outputs of the network is $\mathcal{Y} = Y \times \cdots \times Y$(an s-fold product). The state of the network is an element of the q-fold product $Q = Y \times \cdots \times Y$, where the components of the product are indexed by the vertices of the directed graph that represents the network. If v is a vertex, then the vth entry in the product is the state of the module assigned to v. If $y \in \mathcal{Y}$ is an input of the network and if σ is a state of the network, then the next-state function $\delta_{\mathcal{N}}$ is determined by the next state of each of the modules of the network. If f is a module of the network with t variables $[1, f], \ldots, [t, f]$, then a variable $[j, f]$ of the module is either an input line of the network, which has an assigned value determined by the input $x = (x_1, \ldots, x_r)$, or the variable $[j, f]$ is in the domain of the connection function C (see Definition 2.1.5) of the network. Then $C([j, f])$ is a module of the network. Suppose that $[j, f]$ receives the value γ_j. The next-state function of the module f converts the state of f to the next state $f(\gamma_1, \ldots, \gamma_t)$. The next-output function of the network, $\lambda_{\mathcal{N}}$, has as value the tuple that has as entry at each output line the state of that output line of the network.

A modular network $\mathcal{N}$ can be considered to be a state-output automaton using as the present-output function for $\mathcal{N}$ the function that projects the state of $\mathcal{N}$ to the product of the states of the output modules. These definitions make an $\mathcal{F}$ network an automaton. That automaton is *the automaton associated with* $\mathcal{N}$, and it is denoted by $\widetilde{\mathcal{N}}$. If σ is a state of the automaton $\widetilde{\mathcal{N}}$ associated with $\mathcal{N}$, the function $\widetilde{\mathcal{N}}_\sigma$ is *the function computed by the network* given the initial state σ.

Definition 2.1.6 defines what it means for an $\mathcal{F}$ network to compute a function F in time t. We will state an equivalent formulation of what it means for the associated automaton $\widetilde{\mathcal{N}}$ to compute a function F in time t. Suppose the domain of F is $\mathcal{Y}$, an r-fold product of copies of Y, and assume that F has an s-fold product of copies of Y as its range. The automaton $\widetilde{\mathcal{N}}$ computes F in time t if there is a state σ of $\widetilde{\mathcal{N}}$ such that for each $\overline{y} \in \mathcal{Y}$ and string $\overline{y}^\sharp$ that consists of t copies of $\overline{y}$,

$$\widetilde{\mathcal{N}}_\sigma(\overline{y}^\sharp) = F(\overline{y}).$$

As we have seen, a modular network has a natural expression as a state-output automaton. There is a converse for this assertion (Arbib, 1960, p. 69). Suppose that $M = (\mathcal{X}, \mathcal{Y}, Q, \delta, \lambda)$ is a state-output finite automaton. There is a modular network $\mathcal{N}$ with an associated finite automaton $\widetilde{\mathcal{N}} = (\mathcal{X}, \mathcal{Y}, Q, \delta, \lambda)$ and three functions (h_1, h_2, h_3) such that:

(i) $h_1 : (\mathcal{X}')^* \to \mathcal{X}^*$ that carries $\mathcal{X}'$ into $\mathcal{X}$ and carries an empty element to an empty element;
(ii) h_1 carries each sequence $a_1, \ldots, a_r$ to the sequence $h_1(a_1), \ldots, h_1(a_r)$;
(iii) $h_2 : Q' \to Q$; and
(iv) $h_3 : \mathcal{Y} \to \mathcal{Y}'$

such that $\widetilde{\mathcal{N}}_{q'}(x') = h_3\{M_{h_2(q')}[h_1(x')]\}$.

$$\begin{array}{ccc} (\mathcal{X}')^* & \xrightarrow{\tilde{N}_{\sigma'}} & \mathcal{Y}' \\ {\scriptstyle h_1}\downarrow & & \uparrow{\scriptstyle h_3} \\ \mathcal{X}^* & \xrightarrow{M_{h_2}(\sigma')} & \mathcal{Y} \end{array}$$

Figure A.0.1.

That is, Figure A.0.1 is a commuting diagram.

Thus, there is a modular network that *simulates* the state-output finite-automaton M. It follows that in the case of finite automata, whatever a state-output finite automata can compute can also be computed by a modular network.

We next give the proof of Lemma 2.1.2 of Chapter 2.

Lemma A.0.1. *Suppose* $r \geq 2$ *and suppose that* T *is a directed tree with* N *leaves such that each vertex has an in-degree of at most* r*. There is a path in* T *of length* $\geq \lceil log_r N \rceil$.

Proof of Lemma A.0.1. We show that if the path of maximum length in T has length L, then the number of leaves of T is at most r^L.[3] The proof is by induction on the length L. Suppose that $L = 1$. Each path must start at a leaf and end at the root. The root has an in-degree of α, where α is the number of leaves. But $\alpha \leq r$; thus the number of leaves is at most r^L. Assume, as an inductive hypothesis, that each directed tree with maximum path length L has at most r^L leaves. Suppose that T is a directed tree with maximum path length $L + 1$. The root R of T has an in-degree of α, $\alpha \leq r$. Suppose that $a_1, \ldots, a_\alpha$ denote all of the arcs of T that have R as the final vertex. Assume that a_i has an initial vertex v_i. If p is a path from a leaf $\mathcal{L}$ to v_i, then $\langle p, a_i \rangle$ is a path from a leaf in T to R. Therefore the length of $\langle p, a_i \rangle$ is at most $L + 1$. Thus the length of the path p is at most L. Denote by T_i the subtree of T that has as the root the vertex v_i. Then T_i is a directed tree with root v_i and T_i has leaves that form a subset of the leaves of T. Each path in T_i has a length of at most L. Indeed, if a path in T_i has a length larger than L, then it is possible to extend that path by one more arc in T and produce a path in T whose length is greater than $L + 1$. By the inductive hypothesis, T_i has at most r^L leaves. Because each leaf of T is a leaf of T_i for some i, it follows that the total number of leaves in T is $\leq r(r^L) = r^{L+1}$. For a tree with N leaves and maximum path length L, we have shown that $N \leq r^L$. Therefore $L \geq \lceil \log_r N \rceil$. □

[3] Note that a directed tree has no cycles; therefore, a path can have no repeated arcs.

Next we give the proof of Lemma 2.1.3 of Chapter 2.

Lemma A.0.2. *There is a complete ordered tree $S[r, N]$ of height N with r^N leaves. Each complete ordered r tree with r^N leaves is isomorphic to the ordered r tree $S[r, N]$.*

Proof of Lemma A.0.2. Denote by $V[r, N]$ the set of points in $\Re^2$ of the form (i, j), where $0 \leq i < r^j$ and $0 \leq j \leq N$. Say that j is the level of the point (i, j) and i is the abscissa of the point (i, j). We will build a tree whose vertices are the points in $v[r, N]$ and whose root is the point $(0, 0)$ at level 0. The arc from a vertex at level $j + 1$ to a vertex at level j is determined by the *roll right map.* Express each abscissa as a decimal expansion in base r. The point $(d_n, \ldots, d_0, j + 1)$ is connected by an arc to the vertex $(d_n, \ldots, d_1, j)$. Thus, the point (i, j), $j \geq 0$ is the final vertex of an arc with initial vertex $(ir + b, j + 1)$, $0 \leq b < r$. Note that each point on the line at level j is the final vertex of exactly r arcs with initial vertices on the line at level $j + 1$. Denote the arc from $(ir + b, j + 1)$ to (i, j) by $\overrightarrow{(ir + b,\ j + 1), (i, j)}$. Denote by $S[r, N]$ the digraph with vertices $V[r, N]$ and arcs that are determined by the roll right map. The digraph $S[r, N]$ is connected because each point at level $j < N$ is the final vertex of an arc whose initial vertex is at level $j + 1$. Each vertex of $S[r, N]$ is connected by a path to $(0, 0)$. Each path from a leaf to the vertex $(0, 0)$ has a length equal to N. Furthermore, $S[r, N]$ has no cycles, because each path passes through a sequence of vertices with levels that form a monotone decreasing sequence. We define an order function on the vertices of $S[r, N]$ by setting $\Gamma(i, j) = \overrightarrow{(ri,\ j + 1)(i, j)} < \cdots < \overrightarrow{[ri + (r - 1),\ j + 1](i, j)}$; that is, we use lexicographic order.

We show that if T is a complete ordered r-tree of height L, then T is isomorphic to $S[r, L]$. We proceed by induction on L. If $L = 1$, then each path from leaf to root in T has a length of one. Because each leaf is connected to the root, which has an in-degree of r, it follows that T has exactly r arcs. Each arc connects a leaf to the root. Suppose the leaves of T are $\mathcal{L}_0, \ldots, \mathcal{L}_{r-1}$ and suppose the arcs are $a_0, \ldots, a_{r-1}$, where a_i has initial vertex $\mathcal{L}_i$ and final vertex R, the root of T. Define a map θ (see Definition 2.1.11) from T to $S[r, 1]$ by setting the vertex map v_θ to have values $v_\theta(\mathcal{L}_i) = (i, 1)$, $v_\theta(R) = (0, 0)$. Set the value of the arc map at a_i to be $v_\theta(a_i) = \overrightarrow{(i, 1)(0, 0)}$.

The maps v_θ and a_θ are clearly one-to-one and onto. Assume, as the inductive hypothesis, that for each complete order r tree with $r^{(L-1)}$ leaves, there is an isomorphism from that tree onto $S[r, L - 1]$. Note that the subtree of $S[r, L]$ that has the vertex $(i, 1)$ as its root, is isomorphic to the tree $S[r, L - 1]$. The inductive hypothesis states that for each $0 \leq i \leq r - 1$, there is an isomorphism θ_i from T_i to $S[r, L - 1]$. For each $0 \leq i \leq r - 1$, follow the map θ_i by the map from $S[r, L - 1]$ to the subtree of $S[r, L]$ whose root is the vertex $(i, 1)$. We then map the root of T to the vertex $(0, 0)$. Because each arc of $S[r, L]$ is uniquely determined by its initial and final vertices, the assignment of vertices we have described also determines a map of arcs from the tree T to the tree $S[r, L]$. Denote this map from T_i to $S[r, L]$ by μ_i. We define a map μ from T to $S[r, L]$ as follows. For each i, the map μ_i is the restriction of μ to T_i. We suppose that the map v_μ from T to $S[r, L]$ carries the root of T to the root (0, 0) of $S[r, L]$. The map of arcs a_μ is the map a_{μ_i} on the tree T_i. The map a_μ carries the arc a_i to the arc in $S[r, L]$ whose initial vertex is $v_{\mu_i}(b_i)$ and whose final vertex is the root (0, 0) of $S[r, L]$. The map a_μ extends naturally to a map defined on sequences of arcs by setting $a_\mu(b_1 \dots b_s) = a_\mu(b_1) \dots a_\mu(b_s)$. Thus the order function of the tree T maps to the order function of $S[r, L]$. □

If an $\mathcal{F}$ network $\mathcal{N}$ computes a function in time t, then that function can also be computed by an $\mathcal{F}'$ network $T_t(\mathcal{N})$ represented by a tree $T_t(\mathcal{N})$. The set $\mathcal{F}'$ is the union of functions of $\mathcal{F}$, functions of $\mathcal{F}$ composed of projections, and a collection of constants and projections. The next paragraphs describe the construction of the tree $T_t(\mathcal{N})$ that represents $T_t(\mathcal{N})$. We carry out the steps of the construction and illustrate them by using as an example the network $\mathcal{E}$ whose associated graph is given by the diagram in Figure A.0.2. As a way to keep the

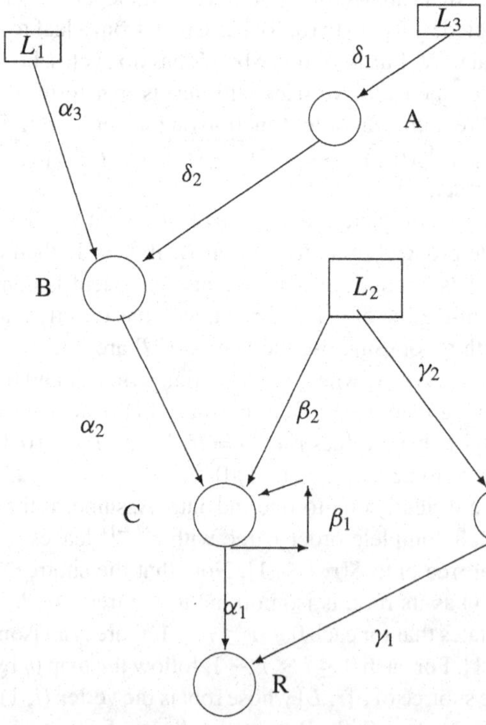

Figure A.0.2.

general construction separate from the illustrative example, a paragraph marked "(General)" is matched by a paragraph marked "(Example)" that illustrates the general step. If the step is obvious for the example, then we omit the (Example) paragraph. We prove the following assertion.

Lemma A.0.3. *Assume that N is the finite-ordered directed graph of an $\mathcal{F}$ network $\mathcal{N}$. Suppose that N has a single terminal vertex at a vertex R and suppose that N has input vertices $\mathcal{L}_1, \ldots, \mathcal{L}_r$ where $r > 0$. For a positive integer t, denote by $\mathcal{P}_t(\mathcal{N})$ the collection of paths in N that have R as the final vertex and either have length t or have a length of at most t and have as the initial vertex an input vertex for N. Then:*

- *(i) there is a tree $T_t(\mathcal{N})$ of height t and a map of directed graphs ϕ from $T_t(\mathcal{N})$ to N that carries the paths of maximum length in $T_t(\mathcal{N})$ onto the elements of $\mathcal{P}_t(\mathcal{N})$;*
- *(ii) each path from leaf to root of the tree $T_t(\mathcal{N})$ has length t;*
- *(iii) the map from paths of maximum length in $T_t(\mathcal{N})$ to $\mathcal{P}_t(\mathcal{N})$ is one to one and onto; and*
- *(iv) the tree $T_t(\mathcal{N})$ is an ordered direct digraph and ϕ is a map of directed ordered graphs.*

(Example) Figure A.0.2 represents the graph, E, of an $\mathcal{F}$ network $\mathcal{E}$. The network $\mathcal{E}$ has inputs at the vertices L_1, L_2, and L_3. The functions of the network are $A(x)$, $B(x, y)$, $C(x, y, z)$, $D(x)$, and $R(x, y)$. We assume that the variables x, y, and z take elements of some set Y as values. To complete the specification of E as an ordered graph ordered with the arcs at each of the vertices A, B, D, and R from left to right. The order at C is $\alpha_2\beta_1\beta_2$. To illustrate the general construction of $T_t(\mathcal{N})$, we will build $T_3(\mathcal{E})$. That is, we are interested in the computation that is carried out in three units of time.

(General) The $\mathcal{F}$ network $\mathcal{N}$ is represented by a digraph N. We suppose that N has at least one arc. Assume that $\mathcal{N}$ has a single output line at a module represented in N by a vertex R. One can think of the computations made by $\mathcal{N}$ as flows of computations along paths in N. For a function computed in time t, the flows that affect the value of the output are along paths of length t that begin at inputs of the network and end at R. This picture is not complete because some of the flows that end at R do not begin at input vertices of the network. A variable presented to the module at R can be the result of carrying out computations on a constant introduced in the initial state of the network. Such a value can be the result of a flow along a path of length less than t. A complication of the construction of $T_t(\mathcal{N})$ is the elongation of such short paths. Nevertheless, in general the paths of length t that end at R are the major concern in the construction of $T_t(\mathcal{N})$. Because $\mathcal{N}$ is an $\mathcal{F}$ network, where $\mathcal{F}$ is a collection of functions, with each function defined on a product of copies of

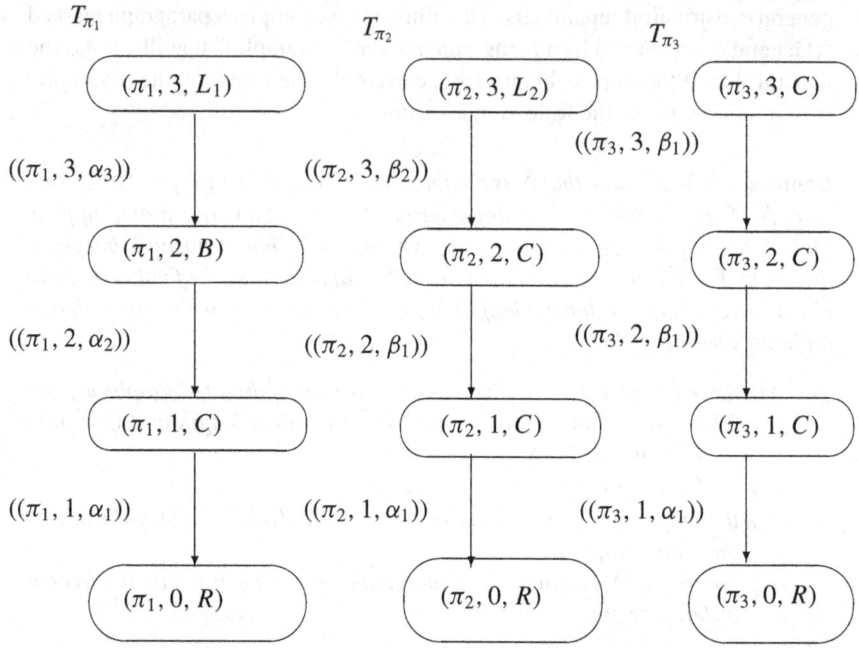

Figure A.0.3.

the nonempty set Y, then the only vertices with an in-degree of zero are inputs to the network.[4]

(Example) For the network of Figure A.0.2, the set $\mathcal{P}_3$ has seven entries. The paths are $\pi_1 = \langle \alpha_3, \alpha_2, \alpha_1 \rangle$, $\pi_2 = \langle \beta_2, \beta_1, \alpha_1 \rangle$, $\pi_3 = \langle \beta_1, \beta_1, \alpha_1 \rangle$, $\pi_4 = \langle \alpha_2, \beta_1, \alpha_1 \rangle$, $\pi_5 = \langle \delta_2, \alpha_2, \alpha_1 \rangle$, $\pi_6 = \langle \gamma_2, \gamma_1 \rangle$, and $\pi_7 = \langle \beta_2, \alpha_1 \rangle$. Because the time of computation chosen for $\mathcal{E}$ is 3, the value input to $\mathcal{E}$ at the input line L_3 does not affect the function computed by $\mathcal{E}$ because the shortest path from L_3 to R has a length of 4.

(General) For each path π in $\mathcal{P}_t(\mathcal{N})$ of length t, we build a tree $T(\pi)$. Suppose $\pi = \langle \pi_t \cdots \pi_1 \rangle$ is such a path. The vertices of $T(\pi)$ are triples $[\pi, j, b(\pi_j)]$. Each j is a nonnegative integer, $1 \leq j \leq t$, and $b(\pi_j)$ is the initial vertex of the jth arc, π_j, of the path π. Adjoin a vertex $(\pi, 0, R)$ to $T(\pi)$. Because π is a path that terminates at R, the final vertex of π_1 is R. The tree $T(\pi)$ has a single path from the vertex $[\pi, t, b(\pi_t)]$ at level t to the root of the tree $(\pi, 0, R)$ at level 0.

(Example) For the network $\mathcal{E}$ the elements of $\mathcal{P}_3(\mathcal{E})$ that have length 3 are the paths $\pi_1, \ldots, \pi_5$. These paths can be found easily by reversing the arrows in Figure A.0.2. It suffices to catalog sequences of three reversed arrows starting at the vertex R. The trees $T_{\pi_1}, \ldots, T_{\pi_5}$ are represented in Figure A.0.3 and Figure A.0.4.

[4] We do not allow empty functions.

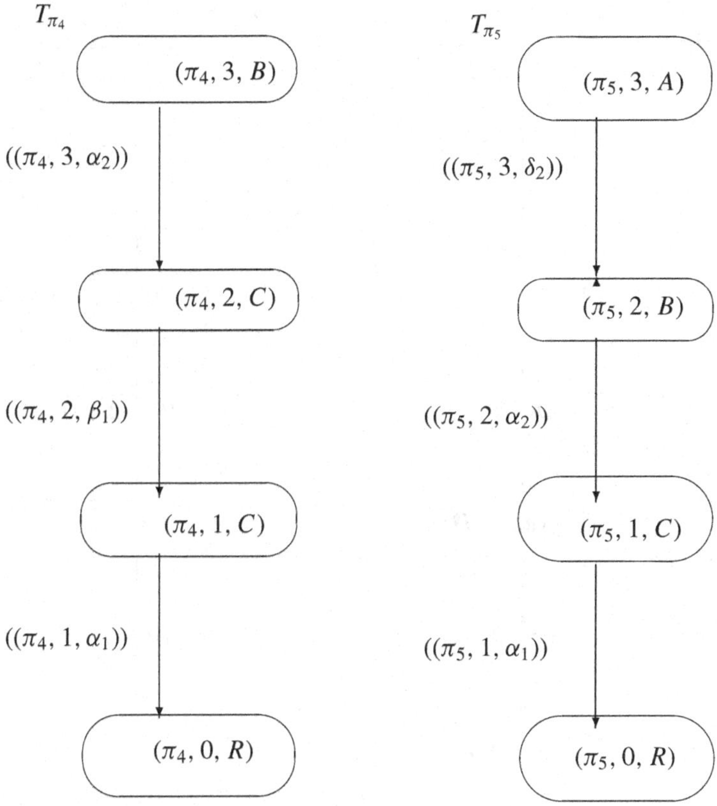

Figure A.0.4.

It is possible that there are paths of $\mathcal{P}_t(\mathcal{N})$ of length less than t. We also build a tree for such short paths. If a path $\rho = \langle \rho_\tau, \ldots, \rho_1 \rangle$ in $\mathcal{P}_t(\mathcal{N})$ has length $\tau < t$, then the vertices of a tree $T(\rho)$ are triples (ρ, j, v_j) for $1 \leq j \leq t$. If $j \leq \tau$, then $v_j = b(\rho_j)$. For $j > \tau$, $v_j = b(\rho_\tau)$. As we did in the case of paths of length t, we add a vertex $(\rho, 0, R)$. The arcs of $T(\rho)$ are triples $[(\rho, j, a_j)]$, where a_j is an arc or an empty arc. If $j \leq \tau$, then $a_j = \rho_j$. If $j > \tau$, then a_j is the empty arc at $b(\rho_\tau)$.[5]

(Example) Figure A.0.5 represents the trees T_{π_6} and T_{π_7}. The two paths π_6 and π_7 each have a length of 3.

(General) Denote by $\text{For}_t(\mathcal{N})$ the *forest*[6] that is the union of the $T(\pi)$ for all π in $\mathcal{P}_t(\mathcal{N})$.

(Example) For the example $\mathcal{E}$, the forest $\text{For}_3(\mathcal{E})$ is the collection of trees in Figure A.0.3, Figure A.0.4, and Figure A.0.5.

[5] For the case $j > \tau$, the arc $[(\rho, j, a_j)]$ at (ρ, j, v_j) is not an empty arc; only the "third coordinate" a_j is empty.

[6] A forest is a set of zero or more disjoint trees (see Knuth, 1973a, p. 306).

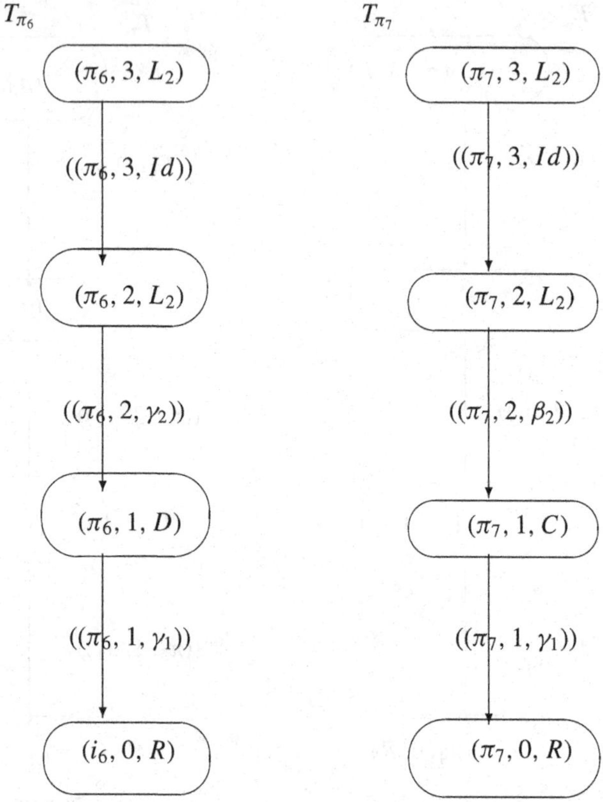

Figure A.0.5.

(General) The vertices of the tree $T_t(\mathcal{N})$ that deloops (see Chapter 2) the network $\mathcal{N}$ are equivalence classes of vertices of the forest $\mathrm{For}_t(\mathcal{N})$. If $\pi = \langle \pi_\tau, \ldots, \pi_1 \rangle$ is an element of $\mathcal{P}_t(\mathcal{N})$, and $\rho = \langle \rho_\sigma, \ldots, \rho_1 \rangle \in \mathcal{P}_t(\mathcal{N})$, $\sigma \leq \tau$, then the vertex (π, j, u_j) is equivalent to the vertex (ρ, k, v_k) if $j = k \leq \sigma$ and if $u_\ell = v_\ell$ for each $\ell \leq j$. Denote by $[\pi, j, v_j]$ the equivalence class of (π, j, v_j).

(Example) The result of applying the equivalence relations to the forest $T_3(\mathcal{E})$ is represented in Figure A.0.6. In the trees $T_{\pi_1}, \ldots, T_{\pi_5}$ and T_{π_7}, the vertices at level 1 are $(\pi_1, 1, C), \ldots, (\pi_5, 1, C)$ and $(\pi_7, 1, C)$, respectively. These six vertices form one equivalence class that is denoted by $[\pi_1, 1, C]$ in Figure A.0.6. Thus the trees $T_{\pi_1}, \ldots, T_{\pi_5}$ and T_{π_7} are glued together to form the vertex $[\pi_1, 1, C]$ in $T_3(\mathcal{E})$. Furthermore, each tree T_{π_j} in the forest $\mathrm{For}_3(\mathcal{E})$ has a root at $(\pi_j, 0, R)$. These roots form a second equivalence class $[\pi_1, 0, R]$.

(General) If $\pi = \langle \pi_\tau, \ldots, \pi_1 \rangle$ and $\rho = \langle \rho_\sigma, \ldots, \rho_1 \rangle$, where $\sigma \leq \tau$ are two elements of $\mathcal{P}_t(\mathcal{N})$, then the arc $[(\pi, j, \pi_j)]$ is equivalent to the arc $[(\rho, k, \rho_k)]$ if $j = k \leq \sigma$ and if for each $\ell \leq j$, $\pi_\ell = \rho_\ell$. Denote by $[[\pi, j, \pi_j]]$ the equivalence class of the arc $[(\pi, j, \pi_j)]$.

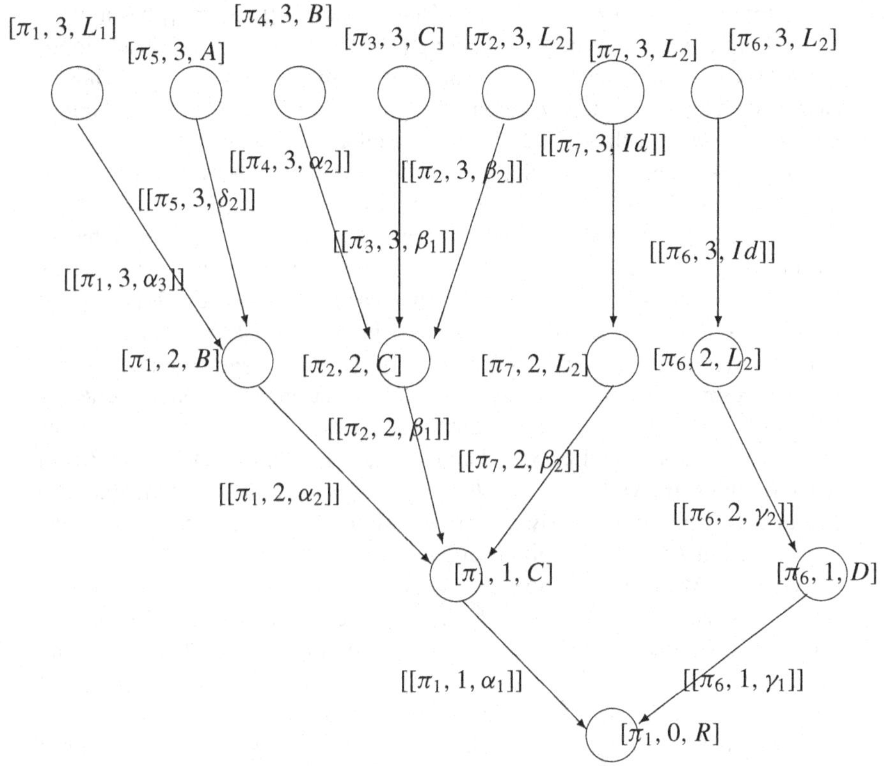

Figure A.0.6.

(Example) In each of the trees $T_{\pi_1}, \ldots, T_{\pi_5}$ and T_{π_7}, the vertex at level 1 is connected to the root of the tree by an arc $[(\pi_j, 1, \alpha_1)]$. Thus these arcs form one equivalence class $[[\pi_1, 1, \alpha_1]]$. The vertex $(\pi_7, 2, L_2)$ of T_{π_6} is not equivalent to the vertex $(\pi_6, 2, L_2)$ of T_{π_6} because the vertices at level 1 in the trees T_{π_6} and T_{π_7} have different third coordinates. Indeed, the third coordinate of $(\pi_6, 1, D)$ is D, whereas the third coordinate of $(\pi_7, 1, C)$ is C. Thus $[\pi_6, 2, L_2] \neq [\pi_7, 2, L_2]$. The arcs $[(\pi_2, 2, \beta_1)]$, $[(\pi_3, 2, \beta_1)]$, $[(\pi_4, 2, \beta_1)]$, and $[(\pi_3, 2, \beta_1)]$ are all equivalent. However, the arcs $[(\pi_7, 3, Id)]$ and $[(\pi_6, 3, Id)]$ are not equivalent because the paths π_7 and π_6 have different second arcs.

(General) We claim that the object $T_t(\mathcal{N})$ whose vertices are the collection of equivalence classes of vertices of $\mathrm{For}_t(\mathcal{N})$, and whose arcs are the set of equivalence classes of arcs of $\mathrm{For}_t(\mathcal{N})$, is a digraph. First note that the equivalence relation on the vertices of the forest $\mathrm{For}_t(\mathcal{N})$ preserves level. Thus we can extend the concept of level to the vertices of $T_t(\mathcal{N})$ by setting the level of $[\pi_j, j, v_j]$ equal to j. Suppose that $[[\pi, j, \pi_j]]$ is an arc of $T_t(\mathcal{N})$ where π has length τ. If $\rho = \rho_\sigma, \ldots, \rho_1$, if $\sigma \leq \tau$, if $[\rho, k, b_k] = [\pi, j, \pi_j]$, and if $k = j \leq \sigma$, then $\rho_\ell = \pi_\ell$ for all $\ell \leq j$. Thus the vertex $[\pi, j, b(\pi_j)]$ is equivalent to the vertex $[\rho, j, b(\rho_j)]$. That is, the arc $[[\pi, j, \pi_j]]$ has a well-defined initial vertex, namely $[\pi, j, b(\pi_j)]$. If $j = k > \sigma$, then b_j is an empty arc at $b(\rho_\sigma)$. Then π must be a path of length σ that is identical to ρ. Thus in case π has a length less than t, the arc $[[\pi, j, a_j]]$ also has a well-defined initial vertex. Similarly, each arc in $T_t(\mathcal{N})$ has a well-defined final vertex. It follows that $T_t(\mathcal{N})$ is a digraph. Note that each arc in $T_t(\mathcal{N})$ has a final vertex that is at a level one smaller than the level of its initial vertex.

(General) We show that $T_t(\mathcal{N})$ is a tree. We have assumed that N has at least one arc, so $\mathcal{P}_t(\mathcal{N})$ has at least one element. Therefore $T_t(\mathcal{N})$ has a vertex $[\pi, 0, R]$ for some path π. It is also clear that each vertex of $T_t(\mathcal{N})$ is connected by a path to the vertex $[\pi, 0, R]$. Therefore, the digraph $T_t(\mathcal{N})$ is connected. If π is a path and if j is an integer that is at most equal to the length of π, then the vertex $[\pi, j, b(\pi_j)]$ is the initial vertex of an arc whose final vertex is $[\pi, j-1, b(\pi_{j-1})]$. If (ρ, j, ρ_j) is a vertex equivalent to $[\pi, j, b(\pi_j)]$, then for all $\ell \leq j$ the arcs π_ℓ and ρ_ℓ must be the same. This shows that arcs of $T_t(\mathcal{N})$ that have the initial vertex of $[\pi, j, b(\pi_j)]$ are equivalent. If j is greater than the length of π, then there is only one arc whose initial vertex is $[\pi, j, \pi_j]$. Thus each vertex in $T_t(\mathcal{N})$ is the initial vertex of at most one arc.

(General) We can now show that $T_t(\mathcal{N})$ has no cycles. Suppose that $c = (c_r, \ldots, c_1)$ is a cycle consisting of edges c_j (see the beginning of Chapter 2). Each c_j is the undirected edge associated with some arc of $T_t(\mathcal{N})$. Among the vertices of the edges of c, there is a vertex of highest level. Suppose that vertex is $\nu = [\pi, h, v_h]$. The cycle c connects the vertex ν to itself. The edge c_r is associated with an arc a_1 of $T_t(\mathcal{N})$, and the final vertex of the arc a_1 must be at a level $h - 1$ because the initial vertex of a_1 is at the highest level of the vertices that are connected by edges of c. Furthermore, the edge c_r must be associated with an arc a_r that also has its final vertex at level $h - 1$. Thus the edges associated with the arcs a_1 and a_r must be the same edge because each vertex in $T_t(\mathcal{N})$ is the initial vertex of at most one arc. However, a cycle can contain no repeated edges. Therefore $T_t(\mathcal{N})$ has no cycles.

(General) Now that we have constructed the tree $T_t(\mathcal{N})$, we construct a map ϕ from $T_t(\mathcal{N})$ to the graph N. If $\nu = [\pi, j, v_j]$ is a vertex of $T_t(\mathcal{N})$, then set $v_\phi(\nu) = v_j$. If $\alpha = [[\pi, j, \pi_j]]$ is an arc of $T_t(\mathcal{N})$ and $j \leq \text{length}(\pi)$, then set $a_\phi(\alpha) = \pi_j$. If length $(\pi) = \tau < j$, set $a_\phi(\alpha) = \langle b(\pi_\tau)\rangle$, where $\langle b(\pi_\tau)\rangle$ is the empty arc at the vertex $b(\pi_\tau)$.

(General) Suppose that v_ϕ carries a vertex at a level less than t to a vertex ν of N that is not an input vertex of N. We claim that the map a_ϕ is one to one and onto from the arcs that terminate at ν to the arcs in N that terminate at $v_\phi(\nu)$. To see this, suppose that $\pi = \pi_\tau, \ldots, \pi_1$ is a path in N and suppose that $[\pi, j, v_j]$ is a vertex in $T_t(\mathcal{N})$. Let $a_1, \ldots, a_s$ denote the arcs in N that terminate at $v_\phi(\nu)$. If $j = \tau$, then $v_\phi(\nu)$ is an input vertex of N and there is nothing to prove. Otherwise, $v_j = b(\pi_j)$ and each of the arcs $[[\pi, j+1, \pi_{j+1}]]$ terminates at $[\pi, j, b(\pi_j)]$. For each arc a_k, build a path $\rho_k = b_\sigma, \ldots, b_1 a_k \pi_j, \ldots, \pi_1$ that either has length t or that has its initial vertex at an input vertex of N. Suppose that a is an arc of $T_t(\mathcal{N})$ that terminates at $[\pi, j, b(\pi_j)]$. Then $[[\rho_k, j+1, a_k]]$ is an arc of $T_t(\mathcal{N})$ that terminates at $[\pi, j, b(\pi_j)]$. Suppose ρ is a path in N of length at least $j+1$ such that the arc $[[\rho, j+1, \rho_{j+1}]]$ terminates at $[\pi, j, b(\pi_j)]$. The arc ρ_{j+1} of the path ρ must be one of the arcs $a_1, \ldots, a_s$. The vertex $[\rho, j, b(\rho_j)] = [\pi, j, b(\pi_j)]$ because the arc $[[\rho, j+1, \rho_{j+1}]]$ terminates at $[\pi, j, b(\pi_j)]$. Therefore, for each $\ell \le j$, it follows that $\rho_\ell = \pi_\ell$. Thus the arc $[(\rho, j+1, \rho_{j+1})]$ in $T(\rho)$ is equivalent to the arc $[(\pi, j+1, \pi_{j+1})] \in T(\pi)$.

(General) The final piece of the construction of $T_t(\mathcal{N})$ is to assign an order function to the tree. Note that the map a_ϕ carries paths in $T_t(\mathcal{N})$ to paths in N. Each element of $\mathcal{P}_t(\mathcal{N})$ is the image of a path of length t in the tree $T_t(\mathcal{N})$. If $\nu = [\pi, j, b(\pi_j)]$ and if $j < \text{length}(\pi)$, then the map a_ϕ is a one-to-one function on the arcs of $T_t(\mathcal{N})$ that terminate at ν. If the value of the order function at $v_\phi(\nu)$ is $a_1, \ldots, a_s$, then the sequence $a_\phi^{-1}(a_1), \ldots, a_\phi^{-1}(a_s)$ is the value of the order function at the vertex ν. Vertices at level t are leaves of $T_t(\mathcal{N})$. At each of those leaves the value of the order function is the empty sequence. This completes the proof of Lemma A.0.3.

Next we use the tree $T_t(\mathcal{N})$ of Lemma A.0.3 to construction the network $\mathcal{T}_t(\mathcal{N})$. The networks $\mathcal{T}_t(\mathcal{N})$ and $\mathcal{N}$ compute the same function in time t.

Lemma A.0.4. *Assume that Y is a nonempty set. Suppose that F is a function from an s-fold product $Y \times \cdots \times Y$ to Y. Suppose that the $\mathcal{F}$ network $\mathcal{N}$ computes the function F in time t. There is an $\mathcal{F}'$ network $\mathcal{T}_t(\mathcal{N})$ that is represented by an ordered tree $T_t(\mathcal{N})$ of height t that computes F in time t. Furthermore, $\mathcal{F}'$ is the union of $\mathcal{F}$, the composition of functions of $\mathcal{F}$ with projections, projections, and a collection of constants.*

Proof of Lemma A.0.4. To construct the $\mathcal{F}'$ network $\mathcal{T}_t(\mathcal{N})$, suppose that N denotes the ordered digraph that represents $\mathcal{N}$. We use the notation introduced in Lemma A.0.3. Assume that the network $\mathcal{N}$ computes the function F in time t from the initial state σ_0. Lemma A.0.4 states that there is an ordered tree $T_t(\mathcal{N})$ and a map of ordered digraphs ϕ from $T_t(\mathcal{N})$ to N. The map ϕ carries each path of length t in $T_t(\mathcal{N})$ to a path in N that either has length t or has its initial vertex at an input vertex of N.

We continue the definition of an $\mathcal{F}'$ network $\mathcal{T}_t(\mathcal{N})$ with graph $T_t(\mathcal{N})$ by describing an assignment of functions to the vertices of $T_t(\mathcal{N})$. Suppose that $\nu = [\pi, j, v]$ is a vertex of $T_t(\mathcal{N})$. There are three possibilities for the vertex $v_\phi(\nu)$ that depend on the characteristics of the path π. It is possible that:

(i) the path π has length τ, that $j \ge \tau$, and the initial vertex of π is an input line of N;
(ii) the path π has length t, that $j = t$, and the initial vertex of π is not an input line for N;
(iii) the path π has length τ and $j < \tau$.

In case (i) if $j = t$, then we assign a leaf to ν. If in case (i) the integer $j < t$, then we assign to ν the identity function on the set Y.

In case (ii) the initial vertex of π is a vertex of N with a function is $\mathcal{F}$ assigned to that vertex by the network $\mathcal{N}$. At the initial state σ_0 of $\mathcal{N}$, the function at the initial vertex of π is in a state s. We assign to ν the function that is constantly equal to s.

In case (iii), the vertex $v_\phi(\nu)$ has a function in $\mathcal{F}$ assigned to it in $\mathcal{N}$. We assign that function to ν.

Next we need to describe a connection function $C(\mathcal{T}_t)$ for the network $T_t(\mathcal{N})$. Assume that the order function of N is Γ_N. The leaves of $T_t(\mathcal{N})$ are not in the domain of $C(\mathcal{T}_t)$. If $\nu = [\pi, j, v]$ is a vertex of $T_t(\mathcal{N})$ such that length $(\pi) = \tau < j < t$ and if the initial vertex of π is an input vertex for N, then the function assigned to ν is the identity function and the (one) variable of that function is connected to the identity function one level higher than j. That is, $C(\mathcal{T}_t)$ has at the one variable of the function at vertex ν the vertex at level $[\pi, j+1, b(\pi_\tau)]$ along the path in $T_t(\mathcal{N})$ determined by π. If ν falls into case (iii) and if the assignment of the function at ν is a function $f \in \mathcal{F}$, then $\Gamma_N(\nu)$ is a sequence of arcs $a_1, \ldots, a_s$, where s is the number of variables of f. Furthermore, a_ϕ is one to one and onto from the arcs that terminate at ν to the arcs of N that terminate at $v_\phi(\nu)$. The function $C(\mathcal{T}_t)$ assigns to the jth variable of f the initial vertex of the arc $a_\phi^{-1}(a_j)$. This completes the construction of the network $T_t(\mathcal{N})$.

Next we determine an initial state σ_0' for $T_t(\mathcal{N})$. We need only describe the initial state of functions at the vertices of $T_t(\mathcal{N})$ that are not leaves because the leaves of $T_t(\mathcal{N})$ are either input vertices or they are not mapped by v_ϕ to input vertices of N. A vertex that is not mapped by v_ϕ to an input vertex of N has a constant assigned to it. The initial state of a constant is that constant. The initial state of the identity function along a path that is connected to a leaf, but is not a leaf, is an element y_0 chosen arbitrarily in Y.

We can now show that if the network $T_t(\mathcal{N})$ begins in the state σ_0', and if the network $\mathcal{N}$ starts in the state σ_0, then the function computed by $T_t(\mathcal{N})$ in time t is the same as the function computed by $\mathcal{N}$ in time t. Recall that the network $T_t(\mathcal{N})$ is constructed for a given a fixed time t in which the computation takes place. We consider computations carried out by $\mathcal{N}$ and $T_t(\mathcal{N})$ in time $t' \leq t$. The proof uses the second principal of induction[7] on the time t'. We use the following statement as the inductive hypothesis.

$\mathcal{H}(t', \nu)$: for each vertex ν of $T_t(\mathcal{N})$ whose level is greater than or equal to $t - t'$, and for each function $H(x_1, \ldots, x_s)$ computed in time t' starting at state σ_0' whose the vertex ν is its terminal vertex, the network $T_t(\mathcal{N})$ computes $H(x_1, \ldots, x_s)$ at the terminal vertex $v_\phi(\nu)$ in time t' from the initial state σ_0.

[7] The terminology "second principal of induction" is used by Jacobson (1951a; p. 9). The second principal of induction assumes that a proposition $P(s)$ is true for all $s < k$ and uses that assumption to prove that $P(k+1)$ is true.

The inductive hypothesis $\mathcal{H}(0, \nu)$ is certainly satisfied because in the initial state σ_0' each vertex ν at level t of $\mathcal{T}_t(\mathcal{N})$ has the same state as the vertex $v_\phi(\nu)$ has in σ_0.

Suppose that μ is a vertex of $\mathcal{T}_t(\mathcal{N})$ at level $t - t' - 1$ and suppose that the inductive hypothesis is satisfied for all times $t'' \leq t'$ and all vertices in $\mathcal{T}_t(\mathcal{N})$ at levels greater than or equal to $t - t'$. Set $m = v_\phi(\mu)$. If m is an input vertex of N, then the vertex $\mu = [\pi, t' + 1, m]$, where π is a path in N. The initial vertex of the path π is at m and thus the vertex μ has an identity function as its assigned function. That function receives the value of the input line of m at time $t' + 1$. Thus the vertices m and μ have the same state at time $t' + 1$.

Suppose that $0 < t' < t$ and suppose at time $t' + 1$ the network $\mathcal{T}_t(\mathcal{N})$ computes the function $H(x_1, \ldots, x_s)$ at the terminal vertex $\mu = [\pi, t - t' - 1, v_{t-t'-1}]$. Suppose that π is a path whose length is *less than or equal* to $t - t' - 1$. Each such vertex in $\mathcal{T}_t(\mathcal{N})$ is the final vertex of exactly one arc. At time $t - t'$, the initial vertex of each arc that terminates at μ either is in the state of the function at vertex $v_\phi(\mu)$ at time $t = 0$, or the vertex μ is connected by a sequence of identity functions to a leaf. We have already dealt with the first case. Thus suppose that the arc terminating at μ has an initial vertex with the initial state of $v_\phi(\mu)$ assigned to it. If μ is the final vertex of a path whose initial vertex is a leaf, then $v_\phi(\mu)$ must be the final vertex of a path in N that begins at an input vertex of N. The state of μ at time $t' + 1$ is the value, say v_0, at that leaf. Because the time $t' \leq t$, the input vertex connected to $v_\phi(\mu)$ is constantly in the state v_0. Thus at time $t' + 1$ the vertex $v_\phi(\mu)$ is in state v_0.

Suppose at time $t' + 1$ the function $H(x_1, \ldots, x_s)$ is computed by $\mathcal{T}_t(\mathcal{N})$ at the terminal vertex $\mu = [\pi, t - t' - 1, v_{t-t'-1}]$. Suppose that π is a path of length *greater than* $t - t' - 1$. Because the length of path π is greater than the height of the vertex μ, the vertex μ is not a leaf, and it is the final vertex of a set of arcs $\alpha_1, \ldots, \alpha_r$ where $r \geq 1$. The vertex $v_\phi(\mu)$ is the final vertex of exactly the same number of arcs as μ. Suppose that for each $j \leq r$, $a_\phi(\alpha_j) = \beta_j$. Each arc α_j has an initial vertex at a vertex $b(\alpha_j)$, which is mapped by v_ϕ to the initial vertex of the arc β_j. The inductive hypothesis implies that at time t' the state of the function at $b(\beta_j)$ is the same as the state of the function at the vertex $v_\phi[b(\beta_j)]$. The function at the vertex μ is the same function as that at the vertex $v_\phi(\mu)$. Thus in the one unit of time from time t' to time $t' + 1$, the function at the vertex μ and the function at the vertex $v_\phi(\mu)$ compute the same value. Thus at time $t' + 1$ the state of the function at the vertex $v_\phi(\mu)$ is the same as the state of the function at the vertex μ. □

Combining Lemma A.0.3 and Lemma A.0.4, we can conclude that there is an $\mathcal{F}'$ network $\mathcal{N}'$ represented by the tree $\mathcal{T}_t(\mathcal{N})$ that in time t computes the same function as that computed by $\mathcal{N}$ in time t. However, the ordered tree $\mathcal{T}_t(\mathcal{N})$ is not necessarily a complete ordered tree. The following theorem shows that we can replace $\mathcal{T}_t(\mathcal{N})$ by a network whose graph is a complete ordered tree.

Theorem A.0.5. *If an $\mathcal{F}$ network with an output line at a vertex v computes a function $F(y_1, \ldots, y_s)$ in time t from an initial state σ_0, then there is an $\mathcal{F}'$ network represented by a complete ordered tree and an initial state σ_0' for the $\mathcal{F}'$ network such that:*

(i) the $\mathcal{F}'$ network computes the function F in time t, and
(ii) the class of functions $\mathcal{F}'$ consists of the class of functions $\mathcal{F}$, the functions of $\mathcal{F}$ composed with projections, projections, and constants.

Proof of Theorem A.0.5. Lemma A.0.4 shows that there is a network $\mathcal{T}_t(\mathcal{N})$ that is represented by an ordered tree and that computes the function F in time t starting in an initial state σ_0''. Each path from leaf to root in the graph that represents $\mathcal{T}_t(\mathcal{N})$ has length t. Suppose that the maximum in-degree of a vertex in $T_t(\mathcal{N})$ is r. We show that there is an $\mathcal{F}'$ network that is represented by the complete r tree $S[r, t]$ that computes the function F in time t starting from an initial state σ_0'. We prove the theorem by an induction on the computing time t. We use the following statement as the inductive hypothesis:

(i) if an $\mathcal{F}$ network $\mathcal{T}$ is represented by a tree T of height t, if the network has branch vertices with an in-degree bounded above by r, and if the network computes a function $H(x_1, \ldots, x_s)$ starting from an initial state σ_0, then
(ii) there is an $\mathcal{F}'$ network represented by the complete ordered r tree $S[r, t]$ that computes $H(x_1, \ldots, x_s)$ in time t, starting from an initial state σ_0'; and
(iii) the class of functions $\mathcal{F}'$ consists of the class of functions $\mathcal{F}$, functions of $\mathcal{F}$ composed with projections, projections, and constants.

If $t = 1$, then the tree T must have height 1 with $s \le r$ leaves connected to the root R of the tree. If $s = r$, there is nothing to prove. If $s < r$, then replace T with the tree $S[r, 1]$ that has r leaves where each leaf is connected by a single arc to the root $(0, 0)$. We now build a new network with a graph that is the tree $S[r, 1]$. Assign the variable x_j to the vertex $(j, 1)$ of $S[r, 1]$ and assign x_1 to the remaining leaves of $S[r, 1]$. Set $Pr_s(y_1, \ldots, y_r) = (y_1, \ldots, y_s)$. Assign the composition $H \circ Pr$ to the root $(0, 0)$ of $S[r, 1]$. Set the initial state σ_0'' of the network with tree $S[r, 1]$ equal to the state of the function H in the state σ_0'. Then the new network computes the same value as $\mathcal{T}$ in time $t = 1$.

Suppose that the $\mathcal{F}$ network $\mathcal{T}$ has a tree T of height $t + 1$ as its graph, and that the in-degree of each branch vertex of T is at most r. Suppose that the root R of T has an in-degree equal to $r' \le r$. Denote by $\alpha_1, \ldots, \alpha_s$ the arcs of T that have a final vertex R. The initial vertex $b(\alpha_j)$ of the arc α_j is the root of a subtree T_j of T that is the graph of a network $\mathcal{T}_j$. The network $\mathcal{T}_j$ computes a function F_j in time t. The inductive hypothesis states that there is an $\mathcal{F}'$ network $\mathcal{S}_j$ whose graph is the tree $S[r, t]$ that computes F_j in time t starting in an initial state σ_j. Denote by $S_{(j,1)}$ the subtree of $S[r, t + 1]$ that has root $(j, 1)$. Because $S_{(j,1)}$ and $\mathcal{S}_j$ are isomorphic complete r trees, we can assume that $S_{(j,1)}$ represents the network $\mathcal{T}_j$. In particular, this implies that each vertex in $S_{(j,1)}$ has a function assigned to it, each vertex has an order assigned to the arcs that end there, and $S_{(j,1)}$ has an initial state determined by the initial state of $\mathcal{T}_j$. If $s = r$, assign the function that is at the root of $\mathcal{T}$ to the root of $S[r, t + 1]$.

If $s < r$, then for each branch vertex v of $S[r, t + 1]$ that is not connected by a path to one of the $b(\alpha_j)$, assign the function Pr_1 to v. Assign the composition of Pr_s and the function that is assigned to the root of T to $(0, 0)$. The tree $S[r, t + 1]$ now represents an $\mathcal{F}'$ network $\mathcal{S}$.

We require an initial state for $\mathcal{S}$. The initial state of each $S_{(j,1)}$ has already been determined. Choose an element y_0 of Y, and assign y_0 as the initial state at each branch vertex that is not in one of the trees $S_{(j,1)}$. Assign the variable x_1 to each leaf of $S[r, t + 1]$ that is not in one of the trees $S_{(j,1)}$.

Because the function assigned to $(0, 0)$ ignores those variables not computed by the networks with graphs $T_{(j,1)}$, and because the networks whose graphs $S_{(j,1)}$ compute in time t the function computed in time t by the network that has a graph whose root is $b(\alpha_j)$, it follows that $\mathcal{S}$ is a network whose graph is a complete r tree that computes $H(x_1, \ldots, x_s)$ in time $t + 1$. □

Appendix B Appendix to Chapter 3: Real-Valued Functions

Chapter 3, Section 3.2 analyzes the computational complexity of some simple bimatrix games by using Leontief's Theorem as the principal tool. Theorem 3.2.1 of that section states that if a function of 2^N variables can be computed in time N, then the network that carries out the computation is essentially unique. Definition 3.2.2 defines "essential uniqueness," but Theorem 3.2.1 is not proved in Section 3.2. Furthermore, in Section 3.2 the computations are restricted to networks that use elements of $\mathcal{D}_0$ as modules. The justification of that restriction is not given there; instead the reader is referred to this appendix.

The first section of this appendix, Uniqueness Results, proves that under reasonable hypotheses, a network that computes a function $F(x)$ in a neighborhood of a point P can be replaced by a network that computes $F(x) - F(P)$ in the neighborhood of the origin of $\Re^N$ without changing the time required for the computation.[1] Furthermore, the modules used in the replacement network can be assumed to have a neighborhood of the origin of some space $\Re^s$ as their domain and to have the value 0 at the origin of $\Re^s$. The integer s depends on the dimension of the domain of the modules used in the network.

The second part of this appendix, Leontief's Theorem, offers a generalized version of the Leontief Theorem. Leontief's Theorem gives necessary conditions and somewhat different sufficient conditions to ensure that a function $F(x_1, \ldots, x_M, y_1, \ldots, y_N) = C[A(x_1, \ldots, x_N), B(y_1, \ldots, y_N)]$. As we have seen, this is a statement about the possibility of computing the function F by a network whose graph is a tree of height 2. The leaves of the tree receive the variables x_i and y_j. There are two vertices at height 1, with the modules A and B assigned to those vertices by the network doing the computation; the root of the tree is assigned the module C. In the statement of Leontief's Theorem, the necessary conditions are rank conditions on the bordered Hessians of F. The generalization of Leontief's Theorem addresses the problem of finding rank

[1] Note that this can require changing the class $\mathcal{F}$, because the class of elementary functions must include translations of variables and addition of constants.

conditions on matrices of derivatives of a function of 2^N variables that must be satisfied for the function to be computed by a network of sufficiently smooth functions represented by the graph $S[2, N]$. In some discussions of economic theory, computations are carried out by using functions that have a conveniently chosen Euclidean space as the domain and have a subset of a Euclidean space as the range. The generalization of Leontief's Theorem given in this appendix covers the case of vector-valued functions.[2] To be able to extend the results to those functions, the second section of this appendix introduces a generalization of bordered Hessians and discusses the invariance of the rank of these new bordered Hessians under changes of coordinates.

B.1. UNIQUENESS RESULTS

Appendix A and the paragraph following Definition 2.1.10 introduce the complete ordered r tree, a fan-in, $S[r, N]$ of height N. An example of the tree $S[2, 3]$ is shown in Figure 2.1.4 in Chapter 2.

Suppose that an $\mathcal{F}$ network $\mathcal{N}$ is represented by the directed tree $S[r, N]$. We allow the class $\mathcal{F}$ to include functions whose domain consists of r tuples of vectors in $\Re^d$, where the vectors are chosen in a sufficiently small neighborhood of some point. The functions are $\Re^d$ valued. The vertices of the tree $S[r, N]$ are points (i, j) of the plane where $0 \leq j \leq N$ and $0 \leq i < r^j$. The point $(0, 0)$ is the root of the tree and a point (i, j) is a vertex at level j. If $j < N$, the point (i, j) is the terminal point of r arcs whose initial vertices are the points $(ri + k, j + 1)$, $0 \leq k < r$. The network $\mathcal{N}$ assigns to each vertex of $S[r, N]$ a module, that is, function, in $\mathcal{F}$. Thus $\mathcal{N}$ describes a function with the points $(i, j) \in S[r, N]$ as domain and the set $\mathcal{F}$ as range. In Section 3.1 we introduced the notation $\langle i, j \rangle$ to represent the function assigned to the vertex (i, j) by the network $\mathcal{N}$.

Notation. *We denote the function computed by the subtree whose root is the vertex* (i, j)*, by* $\langle |i, j| \rangle$*. Compare this with the notation (given in Section 3.1.2) of Section 3.1.*

As a cautionary note, if the level L is not N or $N - 1$, then the function $\langle |i, j| \rangle$ is not the module $\langle i, j \rangle$.

Suppose that an r-fold product of open sets chosen from $\Re^d$ has a coordinate system

$$\left\{\left\{x_{(0,0)}, \ldots, x_{(0,d-1)}\right\}, \ldots, \left\{x_{(r-1,0)}, \ldots, x_{(r-1,d-1)}\right\}\right\}.$$

The $x_{(i,j)}$ are coordinates in the ith component of the product $\Re^d \times \cdots \times \Re^d$.

[2] As we noted in Chapter 2, vector-valued functions can be used to represent algorithms that use conditional branching.

Definition B.1.1. The d tuple of coordinate functions

$$\underline{x}_i = \{x_{(i,0)}, \ldots, x_{(i,d-1)}\}$$

is a *d variable*. An *independent tuple* of *d variables*,

$$(\underline{x}_1, \ldots, \underline{x}_n),$$

is an n tuple, where each entry in the tuple is itself a d variable $\underline{x}_j = \{x_{(j,0)}, \ldots, x_{(j,d-1)}\}$ such that the full set of variables $[x_{(0,0)}, \ldots, x_{(n,d-1)}]$ is an independent set of real variables. That is, the tuple of variables $\{x_{(0,0)}, \ldots, x_{(n,d-1)}\}$ forms a coordinate system in a neighborhood of a point in $\Re^{nd}$. A function G of r d variables $\{\underline{x}_1, \ldots, \underline{x}_r\}$ is *d vector valued*, if

$$G(\underline{x}_0, \ldots, \underline{x}_{r-1}) = [G_0(\underline{x}_0, \ldots, \underline{x}_{r-1}), \ldots, G_{d-1}(\underline{x}_0, \ldots, \underline{x}_{r-1})],$$

where each $\underline{x}_i$ is a d variable and each $G_i(\underline{x}_0, \ldots, \underline{x}_{r-1})$ is a real-valued function.

A coordinate system in a neighborhood of a point in a space $\Re^N$ is a choice of N sufficiently smooth functions that have a nonsingular Jacobian with respect to a standard coordinate system. It is usual to say that a function is *nonsingular in a variable* at a point if the partial derivative of the function with respect to that variable is nonzero at the point. This is a motivation for the following definition.

Definition B.1.2. A function

$$G(\underline{x}_0, \ldots, \underline{x}_{r-1}) = [G_0(\underline{x}_0, \ldots, \underline{x}_{r-1}), \ldots, G_{d-1}(\underline{x}_0, \ldots, \underline{x}_{r-1})]$$

of r d variables $\underline{x}_0, \ldots, \underline{x}_{r-1}$, which is defined on the r-fold product $\Re^d \times \cdots \times \Re^d$, with values in $\Re^d$ is *nonsingular* in $\underline{x}_i$ at a point P if the Jacobian of the map G,

$$\left[\frac{\partial G_k}{\partial x_{(i,j)}}\right]_{0 \le j \le d-1}^{0 \le k \le d-1},$$

has rank d at P.

(If the functions $G_0, \ldots, G_{d-1}$ have Taylor series at the origin, then nonsingularity at the origin requires that if all the variables are set equal to zero except for one d tuple, say, the tuple $\underline{x}_i$, then the resulting function from $\Re^d$ to $\Re^d$ has a nonsingular Jacobian. That is, the matrix that is the differential (or Jacobian) of the map has a determinant that is not zero. If all the variables in the linear terms of the Taylor series expansions of the functions G_j are zero except for the variables in $\underline{x}_i$, what remains are d-linearly independent linear expressions in the variables of $\underline{x}_i$.)

One new piece of notation is required for Definition B.1.3, which follows.

Notation. *Suppose a space has d variables* $\{\underline{x}_1, \ldots, \underline{x}_M\}$ *as coordinates and suppose that P is a point in that space. If a network* $\mathcal{N}$ *computes a value by using the values of the coordinates* $\{\underline{x}_1, \ldots, \underline{x}_M\}$ *at the point P as inputs, then each of the functions* $\langle |i, j| \rangle$ *computes a value that depends on the coordinates of P. We denote by* $\langle |i, j| \rangle(P)$ *that value computed by the function* $\langle |i, j| \rangle$.

In Chapter 2 the concept of a function computed by a network represented by a tree $S[r, N]$ is treated in detail (see Definitions 2.1.6 and 2.1.4). We restate that concept in the next definition, because the notation used here is different from that used in Chapter 2.

Definition B.1.3. Suppose that $\mathcal{F}$ is a set of C^s functions that are d-vector-valued functions of r, d variables. A d-vector-valued function G of r^N d variables $\{\underline{x}_0, \ldots, \underline{x}_M\}$ can be *computed in a neighborhood of a point P* by an $\mathcal{F}$ network $\mathcal{N}$ represented by $S[r, N]$ if there are functions $\langle i, j \rangle$ indexed by the vertices (i, j) of $S[r, N]$ (each in some appropriate domain) such that:

(i) $\langle i, N \rangle$ is one of the d variables $\underline{x}_k$;
(ii) for each $0 \leq i < r^N$, $\langle i, j \rangle[X_0, \ldots, X_{(r-1)}]$ is a d-vector-valued function of class C^s in a neighborhood of the point $\langle |ri, j+1| \rangle(P), \ldots, \langle |ri + r - 1, j+1| \rangle(P)$;
(iii) $G(\underline{x}_0, \ldots, \underline{x}_{r^N-1}) = \langle |0, 0| \rangle(\underline{x}_0, \ldots, \underline{x}_{r^N-1})$ in some neighborhood of P.

In Chapter 3, Section 3.2, $\mathcal{D}$ networks are replaced by $\mathcal{D}_0$ networks.[3] Computations are assumed to be local; that is, the functions used in the network are all defined on a neighborhood of some given point. Requiring the function to be computed to take the value zero at the given point of interest is not restrictive because in the original class of functions $\mathcal{D}$, the addition of a constant to the function being computed does not change the computation time. When the class $\mathcal{F}$ contains translations of the original coordinate functions, for example if $\mathcal{F} = \mathcal{D}$, then we can replace the original coordinate functions by translated functions and assume that the function is to be computed in a neighborhood of the origin of $\Re^N$.

Lemma B.1.1 states that if the class of functions $\mathcal{D}$ is used to construct networks, and if the function to be computed vanishes at the origin, then the restriction to computations with functions that are zero at the origin is not restrictive. If a function can be computed by a network that uses functions in

[3] Recall that $\mathcal{D}$ is the collection of real valued, twice continuously differentiable, nonsingular functions and $\mathcal{D}_0$ is the subset of functions in $\mathcal{D}$ that take the value zero at the origin.

$\mathcal{D}$, then the function can also be computed by a network of the same length that uses functions that vanish at the origin.

In the case of a $\mathcal{D}$ network with graph $S[r, N]$, we construct a procedure that replaces each module of a network by a new module that has zero as its value at the origin. When one function is so altered, then there is a change in each function that follows it in the graph $S[r, N]$. The construction requires following the changes through the graph of the computation. A moment's reflection by the reader is probably all that is required to see that this is possible, but we included a proof that such a procedure exists.

Definition B.1.4. Denote by $\mathcal{D}^s(r, d)$ the class of functions of r variables, each variable a d variable, that are continuous of class s. Denote by $\mathcal{D}^s(r, d)_0$ the collection of functions in $\mathcal{D}^s(r, d)$ that take the value 0 (the zero vector) at $\underline{0}$ (the origin). Thus $\mathcal{D} = \mathcal{D}^2(2, 1)$.

Because the proof requires the discussion of two different networks, each with diagram $S[r, N]$, we need a slightly more complex notation for the function assigned to a vertex of $S[r, N]$ by a network $\mathcal{N}$. We rarely need to resort to this notation.

Notation. *If $\mathcal{N}$ is a network with graph $S[r, N]$, then denote by $\langle i, j\rangle_{\mathcal{N}}$ the function $\mathcal{N}_{(i,j)}$ (cf. Definition 2.1.1) assigned by $\mathcal{N}$ to the vertex (i, j) and denote by $\langle |i, j|\rangle_{\mathcal{N}}$ the function computed by the tree with the vertex (i, j) as the root.*

Lemma B.1.1. *Suppose $G(\underline{x}_1, \ldots, \underline{x}_M)$ is a C^s function of M d variables $\underline{x}_1, \ldots, \underline{x}_M$, with each d variable taking values in an open set of $\Re^d$. Assume G can be computed by a $\mathcal{D}^s(r, d)$ network, $\mathcal{N}$, whose graph is $S[r, N]$ in the neighborhood of the origin $\underline{0}$. Assume that $G(\underline{0}) = \gamma$. There is a $\mathcal{D}^s(r, d)_0$ network, $\mathcal{N}'$, that computes $G - \gamma$ in the neighborhood of $\underline{0}$.*

Proof of Lemma B.1.1. We proceed by induction on the length N. The inductive hypothesis is; for each function $G(\underline{x}_1, \ldots, \underline{x}_M)$ of M d variables that can be computed by a $\mathcal{D}(r, d)$ network $\mathcal{N}$ with graph $S[r, N]$, there is a $\mathcal{D}(r, d)_0$ network $\mathcal{N}'$ that is an r fan-in of length N that can compute the function $G(\underline{x}_1, \ldots, \underline{x}_M) - G(\underline{0})$. Suppose $N = 1$. The function G is a function of at most r of the d variables $\{\underline{x}_1, \ldots, \underline{x}_M\}$. Set $\langle 0, 0\rangle = G - G(\underline{0}) = G - \gamma$. Suppose that the inductive hypothesis is satisfied for networks with graph $S[r, N-1]$ and assume G is a function of d variables $\underline{\underline{x}} = (\underline{x}_1, \ldots, \underline{x}_M)$ that can be computed by a $\mathcal{D}^s(r, d)$ network $\mathcal{N}$ whose graph is $S[r, N]$. Then

$$G(\underline{\underline{x}}) = \langle 0, 0\rangle_{\mathcal{N}}[\langle |0, 1|\rangle_{\mathcal{N}}(\underline{\underline{x}}), \ldots, \langle |r-1, 1|\rangle_{\mathcal{N}}(\underline{\underline{x}})].$$

For each i, $\langle i, 1\rangle_{\mathcal{N}}$ is a function in $\mathcal{D}^s(r, d)$. Each of the functions $\langle |i, 1|\rangle_{\mathcal{N}}$ can be computed by a $\mathcal{D}^s(r, d)$ network that is an r fan-in of length $N - 1$. Denote

$\langle |i, 1| \rangle_{\mathcal{N}}(\underline{0})$ by $\gamma_{(i,1)}$. The inductive hypothesis states that for each $0 \le i < r$, there is a $\mathcal{D}^s(r, d)_0$ network, $\mathcal{N}_i$, that is an r fan-in and that computes the function

$$\langle |i, 1| \rangle_{\mathcal{N}} - \gamma_{(i,1)} = g^{(i)}.$$

We build a function $\mathcal{N}'_{(i,j)}$ with the vertices of $S[r, N]$ as its domain that has its values in the class $\mathcal{D}^s(r, d)_0$. The first step of the construction consists of reassigning functions to the vertices of $S[r, N]$. The functions $\langle i, j \rangle_{\mathcal{N}'}$ are assigned in order to produce a network whose graph is $S[r, N]$ in order that the subtree with the vertex $(i, 1)$ as the root is the network $\mathcal{N}_i$. Then we make an appropriate assignment to the root of $S[r, N]$. Thus, if $N \ge j > 0$ and $0 \le i < r^N$, write $i = tr^{j-1} + k$, where $0 \le k < r^{j-1}$. Set $\langle i, j \rangle_{\mathcal{N}'} = \langle k, j-1 \rangle_{\mathcal{N}_t}$. Set

$$\langle 0, 0 \rangle_{\mathcal{N}'}(X_0, \dots, X_{r-1}) = \langle 0, 0 \rangle_{\mathcal{N}}\big[X_0 + \gamma_{(0,1)}, \dots, X_{r-1} + \gamma_{(r-1,1)}\big] - \gamma.$$

The function $\langle 0, 0 \rangle_{\mathcal{N}}(X_0, \dots, X_{r-1})$ is in $\mathcal{D}^s(r, d)$, and it is defined on a neighborhood of the point $[\gamma_{(0,1)}, \dots, \gamma_{(r-1,1)}]$. Furthermore,

$$\langle 0, 0 \rangle_{\mathcal{N}}\big[\gamma_{(0,1)}, \dots, \gamma_{(0,r-1)}\big] = \gamma.$$

Thus, for $(X_0, \dots, X_{r-1})$ that is sufficiently close to $(0, \dots, 0)$, the function $\langle 0, 0 \rangle_{\mathcal{N}'}(X_0, \dots, X_{r-1})$ is in $\mathcal{D}^s(r, d)_0$. Finally, using the notation of Definition B.1.3, we have

$$\begin{aligned} \langle 0, 0 \rangle_{\mathcal{N}'}(\langle |0, 1| \rangle_{\mathcal{N}'}, \dots, \langle |r-1, 1| \rangle_{\mathcal{N}'}) &= \langle 0, 0 \rangle\big[\langle |0, 0| \rangle_{\mathcal{N}_1} \\ &\quad + \gamma_{(0,1)}, \dots, \langle |0, 0| \rangle_{\mathcal{N}_{r-1}} + \gamma_{(r-1,1)}\big] \\ &= \langle 0, 0 \rangle_{\mathcal{N}}[\langle 0, 1 \rangle_{\mathcal{N}}, \dots, \langle r-1, 1 \rangle_{\mathcal{N}}] \\ &= G(\underline{\underline{x}}). \end{aligned}$$

□

What conditions must a d-vector–valued function of N variables satisfy to ensure that it is possible to compute the function in time N by using a network of modules that are C^s functions of r d variables? We show that there is a set of simple conditions that is not only necessary and sufficient to guarantee that a sufficiently smooth function can be computed by a $\mathcal{D}_0$ network in time N, but the conditions also imply that the network that computes the function is essentially unique. "Essentially unique" means that the modules that can be assigned to a vertex in the network are equivalent with respect to an elementary equivalence relation. The equivalence relation, called simple equivalence, is a variant of a standard definition for the equivalence of mappings (see Golubitsky and Guillemin, 1973). Simple equivalence differs from the usual definition of equivalence of functions only in that the diffeomorphism on the domain $\mathfrak{R}^d \times \cdots \times \mathfrak{R}^d$ is required to preserve the product structure on the domain.

Definition B.1.5. Suppose that r and d are positive integers and suppose that F_1 and F_2 are functions in $\mathcal{D}^s(r, d)_0$ that are defined on a neighborhood of the origin in $\Re^d \times \cdots \times \Re^d$ (an r-fold product). Assume that for each i, $0 \leq i \leq r$, U_i is an open neighborhood of the origin in $\Re^d$. Denote by $\underline{x}_i$ a coordinate system in U_i. The functions F_1 and F_2 are *simply equivalent* at the origin if for each i, $0 \leq i \leq r$, there is a C^s diffeomorphism (Golubitsky and Guillemin, 1973) g_i from U_i to a neighborhood of the origin in $\Re^d$ such that

$$F_2(\underline{x}_0, \ldots, \underline{x}_{r-1}) = g_r\{F_1[g_0(\underline{x}_1), \ldots, g_{r-1}(\underline{x}_{r-1})]\}$$

in

$$U_0 \times \cdots \times U_{r-1}.$$

We next discuss essential uniqueness.

Theorem B.1.2. *Suppose that* $G[\underline{x}_0, \ldots, \underline{x}_{(r^N-1)}]$ *is a* C^s *function of* r^N d *variables* $\underline{x}_j = [x_{(j,0)}, \ldots, x_{(j,d-1)}]$. *Assume that*

(i) *for each* k *such that* $k < r^{N-1}$, *the function* G *is nonsingular in each of the variables* $\underline{x}_{kr}, \underline{x}_{kr+1}, \ldots, \underline{x}_{kr+r-1}$;
(ii) G *can be computed by a network* $\mathcal{N}$ *that is an* r *fan-in of* $\mathcal{D}^s(r, d)_0$ *functions; and*
(iii) *the assignment of* d *variables to the leaves of* $S[r, N]$ *is fixed and such that* $\underline{x}_j$ *is assigned to the leaf at* (i, N).

Then for each vertex (i, j) *of* $S[r, N]$, *the function* $\mathcal{N}_{(j,k)}$ *given in Definition 2.1.1 or, in the notation of Definition B.1, the function* $\langle j, k\rangle_{\mathcal{N}}$, *is unique to within simple equivalence.*

The proof of uniqueness is tedious; however, a simple example makes clear most of the argument.

B.1.1. An Example

Suppose the function

$$F(x, y, z, w) = x + y + z + w + y^2 + z^2 + w^2$$

of four real variables x, y, z, and w is computed in time 2 (because there are 2^2 variables). This is certainly possible because

$$F(x, y, z, w) = (x + y + y^2) + (z + w + z^2 + w^2).$$

The function F is nonsingular in each of the variables in the sense of Definition B.1.2. That is, F has a nonzero partial derivative with respect to each of the variables. The value of each of the variables x, y, z, and w is required to compute the function. Each computation of the function F in two units of time can be represented by the tree $S[2, 2]$. Figure 2.1.4 represents the tree $S[2, 3]$. The tree $S[2, 2]$ is a subtree of the tree in Figure 2.1.4 whose vertices and arcs are those that are strictly below level 3. The leaves of $S[2, 2]$ are at the vertices $(0, 2)$, $(1, 2)$, $(2, 2)$, and $(3, 2)$. The root of $S[2, 2]$ is $(0, 0) = \underline{0}$. The four variables x, y, z, and w are assigned to the vertices $(0, 2)$, $(1, 2)$, $(2, 2)$, and $(3, 2)$, respectively. A network $\mathcal{A}$ that computes F in time 2 is determined once an assignment of real-valued functions of two real variables is made for each of the vertices $(0, 1)$, $(1, 1)$ and the vertex $(0, 0)$. We use the previously established notation (where we drop the subscript $\mathcal{A}$) for the assignment. Thus $\langle 0, 1\rangle$, $\langle 1, 1\rangle$, and $\langle 0, 0\rangle$ are assigned to $(0, 1)$, $(1, 1)$, and $(0, 0)$, respectively. Each of the functions $\langle i, j\rangle$ has the value 0 at the origin. The network $\mathcal{A}$ computes the composition $\langle 0, 0\rangle[\langle 0, 1\rangle(x, y), \langle 1, 1\rangle(z, w)]$.

Now set $y = z = 0$ in F and in the functions of the network. Then,

$$F(x, y, \underline{0}) = \langle 0, 0\rangle[\langle 0, 1\rangle(x, y), \langle 1, 1\rangle(\underline{0})] = x + y + y^2.$$

However, $\langle 1, 1\rangle(\underline{0}) = 0$. Therefore $F(x, y, \underline{0}) = \langle 0, 0\rangle[\langle 0, 1\rangle(x, y), \underline{0}]$. The function $\langle 0, 0\rangle(U, 0)$ is a function of the one variable U. The substitution of $\langle 0, 1\rangle(x, y)$ for U in $\langle 0, 0\rangle(U, 0)$ must yield the function $F(x, y, \underline{0}) = x + y + y^2$. Therefore, to compute F the only assignment to be made to the vertex $(0, 1)$ is a module simply equivalent to the function $x + y + y^2$. That is, the assignment to $(0, 1)$ is $F(x, y, \underline{0}) = x + y + y^2$ composed with $\langle 0, 0\rangle(U, 0)$. Note that the function $\langle 0, 0\rangle$ must be nonsingular in the variable U because the function $F(x, y, z, w)$ is nonsingular in the variable x. Similarly, the function $\langle 1, 1\rangle$ is simply equivalent to the function

$$F(\underline{0}, z, w) = z + w + z^2 + w^2.$$

Now

$$F(x, 0, z, 0) = x + z + z^2 = \langle 0, 0\rangle[\langle(0, 1)\rangle(x, 0), \langle 1, 1\rangle(z, 0)].$$

Each of the functions $\langle 0, 1\rangle(x, 0)$ and $\langle 1, 1\rangle(z, 0)$ is a nonsingular function of one variable because the function $F(x, y, z, w)$ is nonsingular in each of the variables x and z. Therefore, the function $\langle 0, 0\rangle$ differs from the function $F(x, 0, z, 0)$ only by the possible replacement of the variable x by a nonsingular function of one variable in x and the replacement of the variable z by a nonsingular function of one variable in z. The only assignment that can compute $F(x, y, z, w)$ is one in which $\langle 0, 0\rangle$ is simply equivalent to $F(x, 0, z, 0) = z + w + z^2 + w^2$. A function simply equivalent to

$$F(x, y, \underline{0}) = x + y + y^2$$

is assigned to $(0, 1)$ and a function simply equivalent to

$$F(\underline{0}, z, w) = x + z + z^2$$

is assigned to $(1, 1)$.

We add a cautionary remark. The assignment of $F(x, y, 0, 0)$ to the vertex $(0, 1)$, the function $F(x, 0, z, 0)$ to $(0, 0)$, and $F(0, 0, z, w)$ to $(1, 1)$ does not generally compute $F(x, y, z, w)$. In our example,

$$\langle 0,0\rangle[\langle 0,1\rangle(x,y),\langle 1,1\rangle(z,w)] = x+y+z+w+y^2+(z+w)^2 + 2(z+w)(z^2+w^2)+(z^2+w^2)^2,$$

which is definitely not $F(x, y, z, w)$.

Proof of Theorem B.1.2. The proof is by induction on the integer N. We use the following statement as the inductive hypothesis: If a function of r^N d variables $G(\underline{x}_0, \ldots, \underline{x}_{r^N-1})$ can be computed by a $\mathcal{D}^s(r, D)_0$ network $\mathcal{N}$ represented by the graph $S[r, N]$, then the functions $\mathcal{N}_{(i,j)}$ are unique to within simple equivalence.

Suppose first that $N = 1$. Then the function $G(\underline{x}_0, \ldots, \underline{x}_{r^N-1})$ can be computed in exactly one way by an r fan-in of class C^s and length 1 because we have assumed that the order of the d variables at the leaves of the network is fixed, and the root of the graph $S[r, 1]$ must have the function G assigned to it.

Now suppose that the inductive hypothesis is satisfied for networks with graph $S[r, N-1]$ and suppose that the function G of r^N variables can be computed by two r fan-ins $\mathcal{A}$ and $\mathcal{B}$, where each network has the graph $S[r, N]$. Denote by $T^{(j)}$ the subtree of $S[r, N]$ that consists of the vertices connected to the vertex $(j, 1)$. The tree $T^{(j)}$ has length $N-1$, and it is easy to see that $T^{(j)}$ is an r fan-in of length $N-1$. The vertices in $S[r, N]$ that are at level $N-1$ in $T^{(j)}$ are the points $(jr^{N-1} + a_{r^{N-2}}r^{N-2} + \cdots + a_0, N)$. Denote by $\mathcal{A}^{(j)}$ the restriction of the network $\mathcal{A}$ to the tree $T^{(j)}$. Similarly, denote by $\mathcal{B}^{(j)}$ the restriction of $\mathcal{B}$ to the vertices of $T^{(j)}$.

Fix m such that $0 \le m < r$. Denote by $\underline{\underline{y}}^{(m)} = [y_0^{(m)}, \ldots, y_{r^N-1}^{(m)}]$ the input to the networks $\mathcal{A}$ and $\mathcal{B}$ such that:

(i) $\underline{y}_i^{(m)} = \underline{x}_i$ if $i = mr^{N-1} + a_{r^{N-2}}r^{N-2} + \cdots + a_0$, for some choice of the integers $0 \le a_j < r$; and
(ii) $\underline{y}_j^{(m)} = \underline{0}$ (the zero d vector) otherwise.

Thus, $\underline{\underline{y}}^{(m)}$ is an assignment to the leaves of $S[r, N]$ such that each leaf (i, N) that is in the subtree $T^{(m)}$ receives the variable $\underline{x}_i$, whereas each leaf not in the subtree $T^{(m)}$ is assigned the value $\underline{0}$.

Each of the networks $\mathcal{A}$ and $\mathcal{B}$ computes the function $G[\underline{\underline{y}}^{(m)}]$ from the input $\underline{\underline{y}}^{(m)}$. The network $\mathcal{A}$ computes the superposition

$$\langle 0,0\rangle_{\mathcal{A}}\{\langle|0,1|\rangle_{\mathcal{A}}[\underline{\underline{y}}^{(m)}], \ldots, \langle|r-1,1|\rangle_{\mathcal{A}}[\underline{\underline{y}}^{(m)}]\}$$

given the input $\underline{\underline{y}}^{(m)}$. The function $\langle|j,1|\rangle_{\mathcal{A}}[\underline{\underline{y}}^{(m)}]$ is the superposition computed by the network $\mathcal{A}^{(j)}$. If $j \ne m$, then the d variables that are the leaves of the tree $T^{(j)}$ are assigned the value $\underline{0}$. Thus in the computation of $G[\underline{\underline{y}}^{(m)}]$ by $\mathcal{A}$,

$$G[\underline{\underline{y}}^{(m)}] = \langle|0, 0|\rangle_{\mathcal{A}}\{\underline{0}, \ldots, \underline{0}, \langle|m, 1|\rangle_{\mathcal{A}}[\underline{\underline{y}}^{(m)}], \underline{0}, \ldots, \underline{0}\}.$$

Similarly,

$$G[\underline{\underline{y}}^{(m)}] = \langle(0, 0)\rangle_{\mathcal{B}}\{\underline{0}, \ldots, \underline{0}, \langle|m, 1|\rangle_{\mathcal{B}}[\underline{\underline{y}}^{(m)}], \underline{0}, \ldots, \underline{0}\}.$$

Because the function $G(\underline{x}_0, \ldots, \underline{x}_{r^N-1})$ is nonsingular at the origin in the d variable $\underline{x}_{mr^{N-1}}$, it follows that the function $G[\underline{\underline{y}}^{(m)}]$ is nonsingular in the variables of $\underline{\underline{y}}^{(m)}$. The function $h^{(\mathcal{A},m)}(X) = \langle 0, 0\rangle_{\mathcal{A}}(\underline{0}, \ldots, \underline{0}, X, \underline{0}, \ldots, \underline{0})$, where X is used as the mth d variable, is nonsingular in X. Therefore,

$$h^{(\mathcal{A},m)}\{\langle m, 1\rangle_{\mathcal{A}}[\underline{\underline{y}}^{(m)}]\} = G[\underline{\underline{y}}^{(m)}].$$

Define a new network $\mathcal{A}'^{(m)}$ that has $T^{(m)}$ as the graph and is such that

$$\langle i, j\rangle_{\mathcal{A}'^{(m)}} = \langle i, j\rangle_{\mathcal{A}^{(m)}}$$

if $j \neq 1$, and such that

$$\langle m, 1\rangle_{\mathcal{A}'^{(m)}} = h^{(\mathcal{A},m)} \circ \langle m, 1\rangle_{\mathcal{A}^{(m)}}.$$

It follows that the network $\mathcal{A}'^{(m)}$ computes $G[\underline{\underline{y}}^{(m)}]$. Similarly, define $\mathcal{B}'^{(m)}$, with the graph $T^{(m)}$ such that $\langle i, j\rangle_{\mathcal{B}'^{(m)}} = \langle i, j\rangle_{\mathcal{B}}^{(m)}$ if $j \neq 1$, and such that $\langle m, 1\rangle_{\mathcal{B}'^{(m)}} = h^{(\mathcal{B},m)} \circ \langle m, 1\rangle_{\mathcal{B}^{(m)}}$ where

$$h^{(\mathcal{B},m)}(X) = \langle 0, 0\rangle_{\mathcal{B}}(\underline{0}, \ldots, \underline{0}, X, \underline{0}, \ldots, \underline{0}).$$

Then the network $\mathcal{B}'^{(m)}$, with the graph $T^{(m)}$, also computes $G[\underline{\underline{y}}^{(m)}]$. It follows from the inductive hypothesis that the modules of the networks $\mathcal{A}'^{(m)}$ and $\mathcal{B}'^{(m)}$ are simply equivalent.

We complete the proof of the inductive step by showing that the function $\langle 0, 0\rangle_{\mathcal{A}}$ is unique to within simple equivalence. A vertex at level N of $S[r, N]$ is a point with coordinates $(mr^{N-1} + t, N)$, where $0 \leq m < r$ and $0 \leq t < r^{N-1}$. If

$$\underline{w} = [\underline{x}_0, \underline{0}, \ldots, \underline{0}, \underline{x}_{r^{N-1}}, \underline{0}, \ldots, \underline{0}, \underline{x}_{2r^{N-1}}, \underline{0}, \ldots, \underline{0}, \underline{x}_{(r-1)r^{N-1}}, \underline{0}, \ldots, \underline{0}]$$

is the input to the two networks $\mathcal{A}$ and $\mathcal{B}$, then each network will compute a function

$$H[\underline{x}_0, \underline{x}_{r^{N-1}}, \ldots, \underline{x}_{(r-1)r^{N-1}}] = G(\underline{w}).$$

However, when each of the networks $\mathcal{A}$ and $\mathcal{B}$ receives the input $\underline{w}$, then for each $t > 0$ the leaf $(mr^{N-1} + t, N)$ receives the vector $\underline{0}$. Now examine the modules $\mathcal{A}$ assigned to the vertices at level $N - 1$. The vertex at the point

$(mr^{N-2} + t, N-1)$ is the terminal point of r arcs whose initial points are the vertices $(mr^{N-2} + rt + v, N)$, where $0 \le v < r$. In either of the networks $\mathcal{A}$ or $\mathcal{B}$, if $0 < t \le (r-1)$ then for the input $\underline{w}$, each arc ending at $(mr^{N-2} + t, N-1)$ carries the value $\underline{0}$. If $t = 0$, then each arc whose initial point is $(mr^{N-1} + s, N)$ has constant value $\underline{0}$, with the exception of the arc whose initial point is (mr^{N-1}, N). The arc with the initial point at (mr^{N-1}, N) carries the value of the variable $\underline{x}_{mr^{N-1}}$. After one unit of time, the module of the network $\mathcal{A}$ at the vertex $(mr^{N-2}, N-1)$ computes $\langle mr^{N-2}, N-1\rangle_{\mathcal{A}}(\underline{x}_{mr^{N-1}}, \underline{0})$, where $\underline{0}$ denotes the r tuple that has all entries equal to zero. Similarly, in the network $\mathcal{B}$, the module at the vertex $(mr^{N-2}, N-1)$ computes the function $\langle mr^{N-2}, N-1\rangle_{\mathcal{B}}(\underline{x}_m r^{N-1}, \underline{0})$. Furthermore, in both networks $\mathcal{A}$ and $\mathcal{B}$, if $t > 0$, then each module at a vertex with coordinates $(mr^{N-2} + t, N-1)$ receives $\underline{0}$ as an input for each variable. Thus at level $N-1$, for each $t > 0$ the modules at vertices $(mr^{N-2} + t, N-1)$ constantly compute $\underline{0}$. More generally, the module at a vertex $(mr^{N-j}, N-j+1)$ receives the value $\underline{0}$ from each arc whose initial vertex is at the point $(mr^{N-j+1} + t, N-j+2)$, $t \ne 0$. Thus each module at a vertex $(mr^{N-j} + t, N-j+1)$ constantly has value $\underline{0}$ unless $t = 0$. Therefore the value carried by the arc ending at $(mr^{N-j}, N-j+1)$ is the composition of functions of one d variable. More explicitly, for each vertex $(mr^{N-j}, N-j+1)$, set

$$\langle\langle mr^{N-j+1}, N-j+2\rangle\rangle_{\mathcal{A}}(X) = \langle mr^{N-j}, N-j+1\rangle_{\mathcal{A}} \times(\underline{0}, \ldots, \underline{0}, X, \underline{0}, \ldots, \underline{0}),$$

where X is the mth entry. Then the value carried by the arc ending at $(mr^{N-j}, N-j+1)$ is the composition of functions

$$\langle\langle mr^{N-j+1}, N-j+2\rangle\rangle_{\mathcal{A}} \circ \langle\langle mr^{N-j+2}, N-j+3\rangle_{\mathcal{A}} \circ \cdots \circ \times\langle\langle mr^{N-1}, N-j+1\rangle\rangle_{\mathcal{A}}.$$

Set

$$\phi_m^{\mathcal{A}} = \langle\langle m, 1\rangle\rangle_{\mathcal{A}} \circ \langle\langle mr, 2\rangle\rangle_{\mathcal{A}} \circ \cdots \circ \langle\langle mr^{N-2}, N-1\rangle_{\mathcal{A}}.$$

Similarly, set

$$\phi_m^{\mathcal{B}} = \langle\langle m, 1\rangle\rangle_{\mathcal{B}} \circ \langle\langle mr, 2\rangle\rangle_{\mathcal{B}} \circ \cdots \circ \langle\langle mr^{N-2}, N-1\rangle_{\mathcal{B}}.$$

Then the network $\mathcal{A}$ computes

$$\langle 0, 0\rangle_{\mathcal{A}}\{\phi_0^{(A)}(\underline{x}_0), \ldots, \phi_{r-1}^{(A)}[\underline{x}_{(r-1)r^{N-1}}]\}.$$

Similarly, the network $\mathcal{B}$ computes

$$\mathcal{B}_{(0,0)}\{\phi_0^{(B)}(\underline{x}_0), \ldots, \phi_{r-1}^{(B)}[\underline{x}_{(r-1)x^{N-1}}]\}$$

from the input $\underline{w}$. However, each of $\mathcal{A}$ and $\mathcal{B}$ computes $H[\underline{x}_0, \ldots, \underline{x}_{(r-1)r^{N-1}}]$. Therefore,

$$\langle 0, 0\rangle_{\mathcal{A}}\{\phi_0^{(\mathcal{A})}(\underline{x}_0), \ldots, \phi_{r-1}^{(\mathcal{A})}[\underline{x}_{(r-1)r^{N-1}}]\} = \mathcal{B}_{(0,0)}\{\phi_0^{(\mathcal{B})}(\underline{x}_0), \ldots, \phi_{r-1}^{(\mathcal{B})}[\underline{x}_{(r-1)x^{N-1}}]\}.$$

Because simple equivalence is an equivalence relation, $\mathcal{A}_{(0,0)}$ and $\mathcal{B}_{(0,0)}$ are simply equivalent. □

B.2. LEONTIEF'S THEOREM

We have shown in B.1 that if a function of r^N variables, each a d variable, is nonsingular in each of its variables and if it can be computed by a fan-in of length N composed of modules of at most r variables, then the modules of the fan-in are essentially unique. What are the necessary conditions on a function of r^N d variables that it can be computed by a fan-in of length N? Leontief (1947) and Abelson (1980) have provided conditions that are necessary for a real-valued function to be computed by a fan-in of height 2 that uses modules that are real-valued functions of r real variables. Those conditions are discussed in Chapter 3, Section 3.1, and the proof of the result of Leontief is given in that section.

The statements and proofs address the case of a d-vector–valued function where the inputs to the function are assumed to be real variables. This is not a restriction, because an n tuple of d variables is an nd tuple of real variables. When variables are d variables, the architecture of a network that computes a function of those variables is affected, but the Leontief criterion is not changed. Leontief's conditions involve only a function, a choice of an integer r and a choice of splitting the variables of that function into r distinct groups.

The generalization of Leontief's result (stated in Theorem B.2.4 below) to the case of a d-vector–valued function to be computed by a $\mathcal{D}^s(r, d)$ network with graph $S[r, N]$ is the next goal. To achieve that goal, we first define a generalized bordered Hessian.

Suppose that $X = \Re^n$, $Y = \Re^m$, and $W = \Re^p$ are Euclidean spaces of dimensions n, m, and p, respectively. Let

$$\Phi = [\phi_0(\underline{x}, \underline{y}), \ldots, \phi_{p-1}(\underline{x}, \underline{y})]$$

be a differentiable function from a neighborhood of a point $(\underline{a}, \underline{b})$ in $X \times Y$ to W, with each ϕ_i a real-valued function. We denote by $[d_X \Phi]_{\underline{a}}$ the Jacobian of Φ, considered as a function on X at the point $(\underline{a}, \underline{b})$ (see Golubitsky and Guillemin, 1973, p. 2, or Simon, 1986). Typically, one represents the Jacobian by an $m \times n$ matrix; however, we change the matrix representation of the Jacobian from the notation used either in Golubitsky and Guillemin (1973) or in Simon (1986). The change is made to achieve the form desired for the matrix representation of the bordered Hessian.

We choose as the matrix in standard coordinates $\underline{x} = (x_1, \ldots, x_n)$ of the Jacobian, that is, the matrix of $[d_X\Phi]_{(\underline{a},\underline{b})}$, the array

$$D_{\underline{x}}\Phi_{(\underline{a},\underline{b})} = \begin{bmatrix} \left[\frac{\partial\phi^1}{\partial x_1}\right]_{(\underline{a},\underline{b})} & \cdots & \left[\frac{\partial\phi^p}{\partial x_1}\right]_{(\underline{a},\underline{b})} \\ \vdots & & \vdots \\ \left[\frac{\partial\phi^1}{\partial x_n}\right]_{(\underline{a},\underline{b})} & \cdots & \left[\frac{\partial\phi^p}{\partial x_n}\right]_{(\underline{a},\underline{b})} \end{bmatrix}.$$

Thus, the vectors in $\Re^n$ are written as row vectors, and the matrix of $D_X\Phi_{(\underline{a},\underline{b})}$ acts on a row vector by multiplication on the right side of the vector. See Jacobson (1951, p. 36) for a discussion of this notation.

Our choice of notation changes the form of the Chain Rule (see Simon, 1986, p. 68). Suppose $S : X' \to X$, where $X = \Re^n$, while $X' = \Re^{n'}$, has coordinates $\underline{x}'$. If Y and W are as above and if $\Phi : X \times Y \to W$, then, for a point $(\underline{a}', \underline{b}) \in X' \times Y$,

$$[d_{X'}(\Phi \circ S)]_{(\underline{a}',\underline{b})} = [d_X\Phi]_{S(\underline{a}',\underline{b})} \circ [d_{X'}S]_{(\underline{a}',\underline{b})},$$

whereas

$$[D_{\underline{x}'}(\Phi \circ S)]_{(\underline{a}',\underline{b})} = [D_{\underline{x}'}S]_{(\underline{a}',\underline{y})}\,[D_{\underline{x}}\Phi]_{S(\underline{a}')}.$$

Suppose that X and Y are Euclidean spaces and suppose

$$G = (G_0, \ldots, G_{d-1})$$

is a d tuple of real-valued functions G_i, each G_i with domain $X \times Y$. Let Z be an independent real variable (a coordinate on $\Re$). Then $ZG = (ZG_0, \ldots, ZG_{d-1})$ is a function on $\Re \times X \times Y$ with values in the Euclidean space $\Re^d$. For fixed $\underline{a} \in X$, $ZG(Z, \underline{a}, \underline{y})$ is a d-vector–valued function defined on $\Re \times Y$ with Jacobian $[d_{\Re \times Y}ZG]_{(z,\underline{a},\underline{b})}$. The transpose of the Jacobian, $[d_{\Re\times Y}ZG]^t_{(z,\underline{a},\underline{b})}$, is a map from the dual space of $\Re^d$ to the dual space of $\Re \times Y$.[4] Note that the discussion has thus far been independent of coordinates. If we now let $\underline{a}$ vary, then $[d_{\Re\times Y}ZG]^t_{(z,\underline{a},\underline{b})}$ is a function from X to the space of linear maps from the dual space of $\Re^d$ to the dual space of $\Re \times Y$. We can now give a coordinate-free definition of a generalized bordered Hessian.

Definition B.2.1. Assume:

(i) $G = (G_0, \ldots, G_{d-1})$ is an $\Re^d$-valued C^s function ($s \geq 2$), where each G_i is a real-valued function on $X \times Y$;
(ii) Z is a single real variable and $\underline{x}$ denotes a variable point on X; and
(iii) $(\underline{a}, \underline{b}) \in X \times Y$.

[4] For a discussion of dual spaces and maps between dual spaces, see Jacobson (1951b, p. 56).

Then the bordered Hessian of G with respect to X and Y is

$$[bh_{(X,Y)}G]_{(\underline{a},\underline{b})} = [[d_X[d_{\Re\times Y}ZG]_{(z,\underline{x},\underline{b})}]^t]_{(1,\underline{a},\underline{b})},$$

where the superscript t denotes the transpose transformation from the dual space of $\Re^d$ at $ZG(z, \underline{x}, \underline{b})$ to the dual space of $\Re \times Y$ at $(z, \underline{b})$.

Note that $[bh_{(X,Y)}G]_{(\underline{a},\underline{b})}$ is not the same as $[bh_{(Y,X)}G]_{(\underline{a},\underline{b})}$.

B.2.1. An Example

Suppose that $X = \Re^2$ with coordinates $\underline{x} = (x_0, x_1)$ whereas $Y = \Re^2$ has coordinates $\underline{y} = (y_0, y_1)$. Let $G(\underline{x}, \underline{y}) = (x_0\, x_1\, y_0\, y_1,\ x_0\, y_1 + y_0\, x_1)$. The matrix of the Jacobian $[d_Y ZG]$, as a function of $\underline{x}$, is

$$D_{(Z,\underline{y})}ZG = \begin{bmatrix} G_0 & G_1 \\ Z\frac{\partial G_0}{\partial y_0} & Z\frac{\partial G_1}{\partial y_0} \\ Z\frac{\partial G_0}{\partial y_1} & Z\frac{\partial G_1}{\partial y_1} \end{bmatrix} = \begin{bmatrix} x_0\, x_1\, y_0\, y_1 & x_0\, y_1 + y_0\, x_1 \\ Z\,(x_0 x_1 y_1) & Z\, x_1 \\ Z\,(x_0 x_1 y_0) & Z\, x_0 \end{bmatrix}.$$

The transpose of the map $[d_Y ZG]$ has the transpose of the matrix $D_{(Z,\underline{y})}ZG$ as its matrix, with respect to the dual bases (see Jacobson [1951b]) in $\Re \times Y$ and in $\Re^2$. Therefore, the map $[d_Y ZG]^t$ has the matrix

$$\begin{bmatrix} G_0 & Z\frac{\partial G_0}{\partial y_0} & Z\frac{\partial G_0}{\partial y_1} \\ G_1 & Z\frac{\partial G_1}{\partial y_0} & Z\frac{\partial G_1}{\partial y_1} \end{bmatrix}.$$

For our example that transpose is

$$\begin{bmatrix} x_0\, x_1\, y_0\, y_1 & Z\,(x_0\, x_1\, y_1) & Z\,(x_0\, x_1\, y_0) \\ x_0\, y_1 + y_0\, x_1 & Z\, x_1 & Z\, x_0 \end{bmatrix}.$$

The matrix representation of the map $[d_X[d_Y ZG]^t]$ depends on the order in which a basis for the dual space of $\Re \times Y$ is written. We use two different choices; One is to write each entry of the matrix $[D_{(Z,\underline{y})}ZG]^t$ as a single row. A second choice, the one we use most often, preserves the matrix

$$[D_{(Z,\underline{y})}ZG]^t$$

in its rectangular form. When the entries are single rows, the matrix $[D_{(Z,\underline{y})}ZG]^t$ consists of a single column with each entry a row. That is, in our example,

$$[D_{(Z,\underline{y})}ZG]^t = \begin{bmatrix} \text{Row1} \\ \text{Row2} \end{bmatrix},$$

and the row representing $[D_{(Z,\underline{y})}ZG]^t$ is

$$(\text{Row1}, \text{Row2}) = \left(G_0,\ Z\frac{\partial G_0}{\partial y_0},\ Z\frac{\partial G_0}{\partial y_1},\ G_1,\ Z\frac{\partial G_1}{\partial y_0},\ Z\frac{\partial G_1}{\partial y_1}\right).$$

In our example the single row representing $[D_{(Z,\underline{y})}ZG]^t$ is

$$[x_0\, x_1\, y_0\, y_1\, Z\, (x_0 x_1 y_1)\, Z(x_0 x_1 y_0)\, x_0\, y_1 + y_0\, x_1\, Z\, x_1\, Z\, x_0].$$

To find the derivative of a matrix by a variable means to differentiate each entry in the matrix by that variable. In the example, if we represent $[D_{(Z,\underline{y})}ZG]^t$ by a single row, the Jacobian of the map (with respect to the variables $\underline{x}$) has the matrix that is the 2×6 array

$$\begin{bmatrix} \frac{\partial G_0}{\partial x_0} & \frac{\partial^2 ZG_0}{\partial x_0\, \partial y_0} & \frac{\partial^2 ZG_0}{\partial x_0\, \partial y_1} & \frac{\partial G_1}{\partial x_0} \cdots & \frac{\partial^2 ZG_1}{\partial x_0\, \partial y_1} \\ \frac{\partial G_0}{\partial x_1} & \frac{\partial^2 ZG_0}{\partial x_1\, \partial y_0} & \frac{\partial^2 ZG_0}{\partial x_1\, \partial y_1} & \frac{\partial G_1}{\partial x_1} \cdots & \frac{\partial^2 ZG_1}{\partial x_1\, \partial y_1} \end{bmatrix}$$

$$= \begin{bmatrix} x_1\, y_0\, y_1 & Z x_1\, y_1 & Z\, x_1\, y_0 & y_1 & 0 & Z \\ x_0\, y_0\, y_1 & Z\, x_0\, y1 & Z\, x_0\, y_0 & y_0 & Z & 0 \end{bmatrix}.$$

If $[D_{(Z,\underline{y})}ZG]^t$ is presented as a matrix with a single row, then the bordered Hessian at a point $(\underline{a}, \underline{b})$ is

$$\begin{bmatrix} \frac{\partial G_0}{\partial x_0} & \frac{\partial^2 G_0}{\partial x_0\, \partial y_0} & \frac{\partial^2 ZG_0}{\partial x_0\, \partial y_1} & \frac{\partial G_1}{\partial x_0} \cdots & \frac{\partial^2 G_1}{\partial x_0\, \partial y_1} \\ \frac{\partial G_0}{\partial x_1} & \frac{\partial^2 G_0}{\partial x_1\, \partial y_0} & \frac{\partial^2 G_0}{\partial x_1\, \partial y_1} & \frac{\partial G_1}{\partial x_1} \cdots & \frac{\partial^2 G_1}{\partial x_1\, \partial y_1} \end{bmatrix}$$

evaluated at $(\underline{a}, \underline{b})$, because we are also to set $Z = 1$. Thus for the example, with $\underline{a} = (a_0, a_1)$ and $\underline{b} = (b_0, b_1)$, the bordered Hessian at $(\underline{a}, \underline{b})$ is

$$\begin{bmatrix} a_1\, b_0\, b_1 & a_1\, b_1 & a_1\, b_0 & b_1 & 0 & 1 \\ a_0\, b_0\, b_1 & a_0\, b_1 & a_0\, b_0 & b_0 & 1 & 0 \end{bmatrix}.$$

In the second representation, we write the matrix of $[bh_{X\times Y}G]$ as a single column consisting of the two matrices that are the derivatives of $[D_{(Z,\underline{y})}ZG]^t$ with respect to x_0 and x_1. That is, we use the array

$$\begin{bmatrix} \begin{bmatrix} \frac{\partial G_0}{\partial x_0} & \frac{\partial^2 G_0}{\partial x_0\, \partial y_0} & \frac{\partial^2 ZG_0}{\partial x_0\, \partial y_1} \\ \frac{\partial G_1}{\partial x_0} & \frac{\partial^2 G_1}{\partial x_0\, \partial y_0} & \frac{\partial^2 G_1}{\partial x_0\, \partial y_1} \end{bmatrix} \\ \begin{bmatrix} \frac{\partial G_0}{\partial x_1} & \frac{\partial^2 G_0}{\partial x_1\, \partial y_0} & \frac{\partial^2 G_0}{\partial x_1\, \partial y_1} \\ \frac{\partial G_1}{\partial x_1} & \frac{\partial^2 G_1}{\partial x_1\, \partial y_0} & \frac{\partial^2 G_1}{\partial x_1\, \partial y_1} \end{bmatrix} \end{bmatrix}_{(\underline{a},\underline{b})}$$

as the matrix of $[bh_{X\times Y}G]_{(\underline{a},\underline{b})}$.

Thus in the example where the map $[d_{(Z,\underline{y})}ZG]^t$ is represented by the 2×3 matrix $[D_{(Z,\underline{y})}ZG]^t$, the partial derivative of $[D_{(Z,\underline{y})}ZG]^t$ with respect to x_0 is the 2×3 matrix

$$\begin{bmatrix} \frac{\partial G_0}{\partial x_0} & \frac{\partial^2 ZG_0}{\partial x_0\, \partial y_0} & \frac{\partial^2 ZG_0}{\partial x_0\, \partial y_1} \\ \frac{\partial G_1}{\partial x_0} & \frac{\partial^2 ZG_1}{\partial x_0\, \partial y_0} & \frac{\partial^2 ZG_1}{\partial x_0\, \partial y_1} \end{bmatrix}.$$

The bordered Hessian in this representation is the matrix

$$\begin{bmatrix} \begin{bmatrix} a_1 b_0 b_1 & a_1 b_1 & a_1 b_0 \\ b_1 & 0 & 1 \end{bmatrix} \\ \begin{bmatrix} a_0 b_0 b_1 & a_0 b_1 & a_0 b_0 \\ b_0 & 1 & 0 \end{bmatrix} \end{bmatrix}.$$

In summary, we will use the following notation for the matrices of the bordered Hessians.

Notation. *Suppose:*

(i) X and Y are Euclidean spaces of dimensions N and M, respectively;
(ii) X and Y have coordinates $\underline{x}$ and $\underline{y}$, respectively; and
(iii) $G(\underline{x}, \underline{y}) = (G_0, \ldots, G_{d-1})$ is a d-vector-valued function defined on a neighborhood of a point $(\underline{a}, \underline{b}) \in X \times Y$, where the G_i are real-valued functions defined on a neighborhood of the point $(\underline{a}, \underline{b})$.

We denote by $[BH_{(\underline{x},\underline{y})}G]_{(\underline{a},\underline{b})}$ the matrix of $[bh_{(X,Y)}G]_{(\underline{a},\underline{b})}$ represented as a single column of matrices where the column entries are indexed by the elements of $\underline{x}$. The ith entry in the column is the derivative with respect to x_i of the matrix $[D_{(Z,\underline{y})}ZG]^t$ evaluated at $(Z, \underline{x}, \underline{y}) = (1, \underline{a}, \underline{b})$. Thus

$$[BH_{(\underline{x},\underline{y})}G]_{(\underline{a},\underline{b})} = \begin{bmatrix} \begin{bmatrix} \dfrac{\partial G_0}{\partial x_0} & \dfrac{\partial^2 G_0}{\partial x_0\, \partial y_0} & \cdots & \dfrac{\partial^2 G_0}{\partial x_0\, \partial y_{M-1}} \\ \vdots & \vdots & \vdots & \vdots \\ \dfrac{\partial G_{d-1}}{\partial x_0} & \dfrac{\partial^2 G_{d-1}}{\partial x_0\, \partial y_0} & \cdots & \dfrac{\partial^2 G_{d-1}}{\partial x_0\, \partial y_{d-1}} \end{bmatrix}_{(\underline{a},\underline{b})} \\ \vdots \\ \begin{bmatrix} \dfrac{\partial G_0}{\partial x_{N-1}} & \dfrac{\partial^2 G_0}{\partial x_{N-1}\, \partial y_0} & \cdots & \dfrac{\partial^2 G_0}{\partial x_{N-1}\, \partial y_{M-1}} \\ \vdots & \vdots & \vdots & \vdots \\ \dfrac{\partial G_{d-1}}{\partial x_{N-1}} & \dfrac{\partial^2 G_{d-1}}{\partial x_{N-1}\, \partial y_0} & \cdots & \dfrac{\partial^2 G_{d-1}}{\partial x_{N-1}\, \partial y_{d-1}} \end{bmatrix}_{(\underline{a},\underline{b})} \end{bmatrix}.$$

Suppose $S : X' \to X$ is a C^s function from a Euclidean space X' to the Euclidean space X given by functions $\underline{x} = \{\underline{x}_1(\underline{x}'), \ldots, \underline{x}_M(\underline{x}')\}$. The function S has the map $d_{X'}S$; see Figures B.2.1(A) and B.2.1(B). As the Jacobian near $a' \in X'$. Then

$$\begin{aligned} \left[bh_{(X',Y)}G \circ (S \times Id_Y)\right]_{(a',b)} &= d_{X'}[d_{Z\times Y}[ZG \circ Id_{\mathfrak{R}} \times S \times Id_Y]^t] \\ &= d_{X'}[[d_{Z\times Y}ZG]^t \circ S] \\ &= d_X[[d_{Z\times Y}ZG]^t] \circ d_{X'}S \\ &= [bh_{(\underline{X}\times\underline{Y})}G] \circ d_{X'}S. \end{aligned}$$

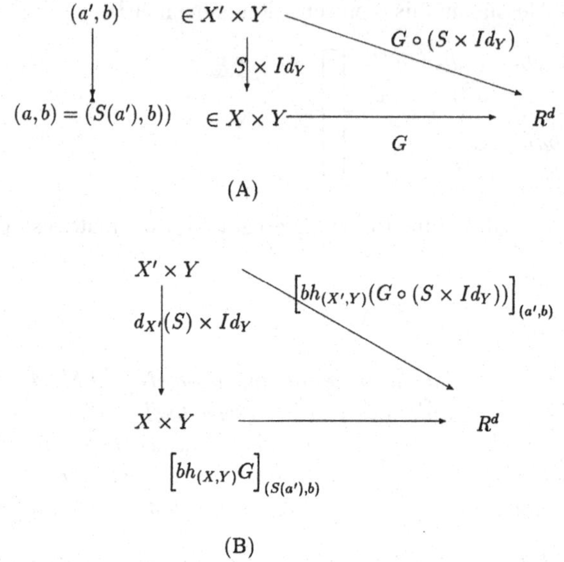

Figure B.2.1.

Thus the rank of $[bh_{(X',Y)}G \circ (S \times Id_Y)]_{(a',b)}$ is bounded by the rank of $[bh_{(X,Y)}G]_{[S(a'),b]}$. It is also easy to check, referring to Figure B.2.2 that the rank of $[bh_{(X,Y')}G \circ (Id_X \times Y)]_{(a,b')}$ is bounded by the rank of $[bh_{(X,Y)}G]_{[a,T(b')]}$. Lemma B.2.1 summarizes the discussion.

Lemma B.2.1. *Suppose that X, X', Y, and Y' are Euclidean spaces and suppose that $S : X' \to X$ and $T : Y' \to Y$ are C^2 functions. Assume that $G : X \times Y \to \Re^d$ is a C^2 d-vector-valued function. For each point $(P', Q') \in X' \times Y'$, the rank of*

$$\left[bh_{(X',Y')}G \circ (S \times T)\right]_{(P',Q')}$$

is bounded by the rank of

$$\left[bh_{(X,Y)}G\right]_{[S(P'),T(Q')]}.$$

The following is tedious to verify, but it is very useful.

Lemma B.2.2. *Suppose that $\underline{x}$ and $\underline{y}$ are sets of real variables that are coordinates for spaces X and Y, respectively. Suppose that $G = (G_0, \ldots, G_{d-1})$ and $F = (F_0, \ldots, F_{d-1})$ are d-vector–valued C^s functions of the variables $\underline{x}$ and $\underline{y}$ that are simply equivalent. For each point $(a, b) \in X \times Y$, the rank of $[bh_{(X,Y)}F]_{(a,b)}$ is equal to the rank of $[bh_{(X,Y)}G]_{(a,b)}$.*

Proof of Lemma B.2.2. It will suffice to show that if U and V are d-dimensional Euclidean spaces, if $(\underline{a}, \underline{b}) \in X \times Y$ and if $K : U \to V$ is a diffeomorphism

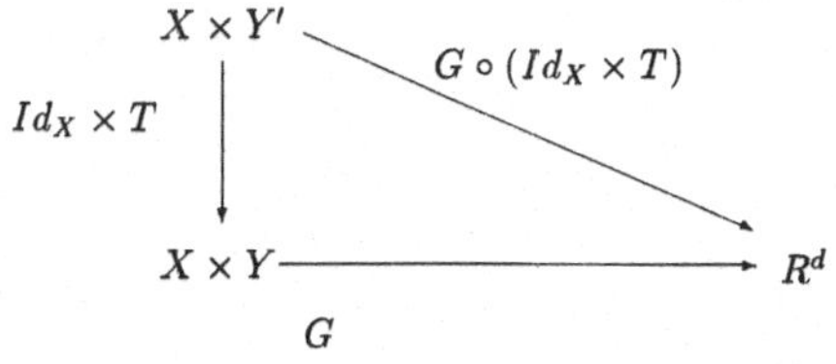

(A)

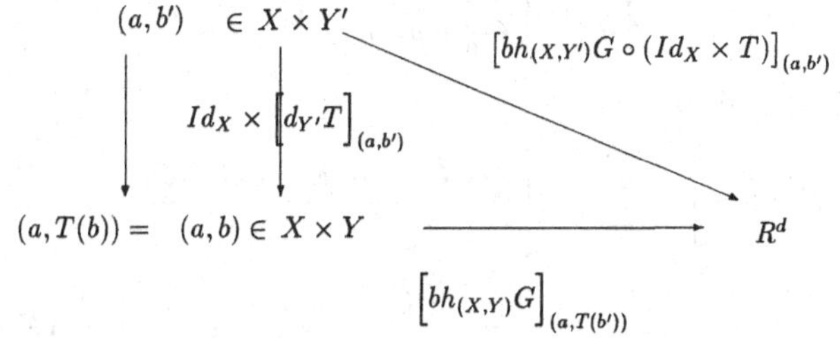

(B)

Figure B.2.2.

from a neighborhood of the point $u = G(\underline{a}, \underline{b})$ in U to V, and $F = K \circ G$, then the rank of $[bh_{(X,Y)}F]_{(a,b)}$ is the same as the rank of $[bh_{(X,Y)}G]_{(a,b)}$. Suppose that U^* and V^* denote the dual spaces of U and V. We assume that X and Y have dimensions N and M and that $\underline{x}$ and $\underline{y}$ are coordinates for the spaces X and Y, respectively. Assume that U has coordinates $\underline{u}$ and that $K = (k_0, \ldots, k_{d-1})$, where each k_i is a real-valued function defined on a neighborhood of $G(\underline{a}, \underline{b})$. We assume that $\mathfrak{R}$ has coordinate Z. The matrix $[BH(\underline{x}, \underline{y})[(K \circ G)]]_{(1,\underline{a},\underline{b})}$ consists of a single column, with the ith entry in the column being a $d \times (M + 1)$ matrix. The entries of that $d \times (M + 1)$ matrix are derivatives with respect to i of the matrix $D_{(Z,\underline{y})}[Z(K \circ G)]^t$ evaluated at the point $(1, \underline{a}, \underline{b})$. The first column of the matrix $D_{(Z,\underline{y})}[Z(K \circ G)]^t$, which we number as the (-1)th column, is $[(K \circ G)_0, \ldots, (K \circ G)_{d-1}]$. The $(j + 1)$st column, which we number as the jth column, has as kth entry $[Z(K \circ G)_k]/\partial y_j$. Thus the kth entry in the (-1)st column is $[(K \circ G)_k]/\partial x_i = \sum_{l=0}^{d-1}(\partial K_k/\partial u_\ell)(\partial G_\ell/\partial x_i)$. The kth entry in the jth column, for $j > -1$, is

$$Z \sum_{\ell=0}^{d-1} \left[\left(\sum_{s=0}^{d-1} \frac{\partial^2 K_j}{\partial u_s \, \partial u_\ell} \frac{\partial G_\ell}{\partial y_j} \frac{\partial G_s}{\partial x_i} \right) + \frac{\partial K_j}{\partial u_\ell} \frac{\partial^2 G_\ell}{\partial x_i \, \partial y_j} \right].$$

Suppose that the first entry in $[BH_{(\underline{x},\underline{y})}G]^t_{(\underline{a},\underline{b})}$, that is, the first $[d \times (M + 1)]$ matrix, is a linear combination of the remaining N entries. Then for some collection of real numbers $(A_1, \ldots, A_N)$ and for each $0 \le \ell \le d - 1$, the following equations are satisfied.

$$\frac{\partial G_k}{\partial x_0} = \sum_{t=1}^{N} A_t \frac{\partial G_k}{\partial x_t},$$

$$\frac{\partial^2 G_\ell}{\partial x_0\, \partial y_j} = \sum_{t=0}^{N} A_t \frac{\partial^2 G_\ell}{\partial x_t\, \partial y_j}.$$

Then,

$$\frac{\partial (K \circ G)_k}{\partial x_0} = \sum_{t=1}^{N} A_t \left[\sum_{\ell=0}^{d-1} \frac{\partial K_\ell}{\partial u_\ell} \frac{\partial G_k}{\partial x_t} \right] = \sum_{t=1}^{N} A_t \left[\frac{\partial (K \circ G)_k}{\partial x_t} \right].$$

If we set $Z = 1$, then

$$\frac{\partial}{\partial x_0}\left[\frac{\partial}{\partial y_j} (K \circ G)_k \right] = \sum_{t=1}^{N} A_t \left[\sum_{\ell=0}^{d-1} \sum_{s=0}^{d-1} \frac{\partial^2 K_j}{\partial u_s\, \partial u_\ell} \frac{\partial G_s}{\partial x_t} \frac{\partial G_\ell}{\partial y_j} + \sum_{\ell=0}^{d-1} \frac{\partial K_j}{\partial u_\ell} \frac{\partial^2 G_\ell}{\partial x_t\, \partial y_j} \right] = \sum_{t=1}^{N} A_t \frac{\partial}{\partial x_t} \left[\frac{\partial}{\partial y_j} (K \circ G)_k \right].$$

Therefore, the rank of $[BH_{(\underline{x},\underline{y})}(F)]_{(\underline{a},\underline{b})}$ is bounded above by the rank of $[BH_{(\underline{x},\underline{y})}(G)]_{(\underline{a},\underline{b})}$. Because K has an inverse, it follows that the bordered Hessians for G and for $K \circ G$ have the same rank at $(\underline{a}, \underline{b})$. □

B.2.2. Example of the General Leontief Theorem in a Low-Dimensional Case

Suppose that $G(X, Y) = [G_0(X, Y), \ldots, G_{d-1}(X, Y)]$ is a function that is $\Re^d$ valued. Leontief's Theorem states necessary conditions that a real-valued function G (that is, the case in which $d = 1$), $G(\underline{x}, \underline{y}) = C[A(\underline{x}), B(\underline{y})]$. As we have seen, the conditions state that the bordered Hessians of G must have ranks bounded by 1. If $d > 1$, if $A(\underline{x})$ and $B(\underline{y})$ are themselves $\Re^d$-valued functions, and if $(\underline{a}, \underline{b}) \in X \times Y$, then G is the composition of a map

$$A \times B \to E \times F = \Re^d \times \Re^d$$

and the map

$$C : E \times F \to \Re^d.$$

We can apply Lemma B.2.1 to conclude that the rank of $[bh_{(X,Y)}G]_{(\underline{a},\underline{b})}$ is bounded by the rank of $[bh_{(E,F)}C]_{(\underline{a},\underline{b})}$. However, the rank of $[bh_{(E,F)}C]_{(\underline{a},\underline{b})}$ is clearly at most d because its matrix consists of a column of matrices, with each entry in the column indexed by a coordinate on E.

Leontief also gives conditions that are sufficient to be able to write

$$G(\underline{x}, \underline{y}) = C[A(\underline{x}), B(\underline{y})].$$

The sufficiency assertions of Leontief's Theorem can be modified to give sufficiency conditions for d-vector–valued functions. The proofs are copies, *mutatis mutandis*, of Leontief's proofs. Slight modifications are required to allow matrix calculations. However, because of the matrices involved, the notation is a bit cumbersome. Therefore, before launching into the statement of the generalized Leontief conditions, we consider an example.

Suppose that $G(\underline{x}, \underline{w}, \underline{y}) = [G_0(\underline{x}, \underline{w}, \underline{y}), G_1(\underline{x}, \underline{w}, \underline{y})]$ is an $\Re^2$-valued function of three sets of variables. We can avoid much of the matrix notation and still see the main thrust of the argument by placing restrictions on the variables $\underline{w}$ and $\underline{y}$. We assume that $\underline{y} = y$ is a single real variable and that $\underline{w} = w$ is also a single real variable. However, we suppose that $\underline{x} = (x_0, x_1)$ is a 2-variable; thus x_0 and x_1 are real variables. Denote by X the $\Re^3$ space of the variables x_0, x_1, and w and denote the space $\Re$ of the variable y by Y. As we have already noted in a similar case, if $G(X, Y) = C[A(X), Y]$ and $A : X \to \Re^2$, then Lemma B.2.1 implies that at the points of $X \times Y$, the rank of $bh_{(X,Y)}G$ is at most 2. The sufficiency conditions of the generalized Leontief Theorem say that if:

(i) $G(X \times Y) = [G_0(X \times Y), G_1(X \times Y)]$,
(ii) $bh_{(X,Y)}G$ has rank at most 2 in a neighborhood of the origin, and
(iii) at the origin the 2×2 matrix

$$\begin{bmatrix} \frac{\partial G_0}{\partial x_0} & \frac{\partial G_0}{\partial x_1} \\ \frac{\partial G_1}{\partial x_0} & \frac{\partial G_1}{\partial x_1} \end{bmatrix} \tag{B.2.1}$$

has a rank of 2,

then there are two functions $C(t_0, t_1, y)$ and $A(\underline{x}, w) = [A_0(\underline{x}, w), A_1(\underline{x}, w)]$ such that $G(\underline{x}, w, y) = C[A(\underline{x}, w), y]$.

To construct C and A, set $A_0(t_0, t_1, w) = G_0(t_0, t_1, w, 0)$ and set $A_1(t_0, t_1, w) = G_1(t_0, t_1, w, 0)$. Because the rank of the matrix (B.2.1) at the origin is 2, we can apply the Implicit Function Theorem (see Simon, 1986, part d, p. 71) to conclude that there is a function

$$H(t_0, t_1, w) = [H_0(t_0, t_1, w), H_1(t_0, t_1, w)] \tag{B.2.2}$$

that is locally a solution of the equations

$$[A_0(x_0, x_1, w), A_1(x_0, x_1, w)] = (t_0, t_1). \tag{B.2.3}$$

Then

$$\{A_0[H_0(t_0, t_1, w), H_1(t_0, t_1, w), w], A_1[H_0(t_0, t_1, w), H_1(t_0, t_1, w), w]\} \\ = (t_0, t_1). \tag{B.2.4}$$

Equation (B.2.4) can be written more compactly as

$$[A_0(H_0, H_1, w), A_1(H_0, H_1, w)] = (t_0, t_1). \tag{B.2.5}$$

A substitution from Equation (B.2.3) into Equation (B.2.5) yields

$$\{H_0[A_0(x_0, x_1, w), A_1(x_0, x_1, w), w], H_1[A_0(x_0, x_1, w), A_1(x_0, x_1, w), w]\} = (x_0, x_1). \tag{B.2.6}$$

Set

$$C^*(x_0, x_1, w, y) = (C_0^*, C_1^*) = \{G_0[H_0(x_0, x_1, w), H_1(x_0, x_1, w), w, y], \times G_1[H_0(x_0, x_1, w), H_1(x_0, x_1, w), w, y]\}.$$

It follows from Equation (B.2.6) that

$$C_i^*(A_0, A_1, w, y) = G_i[H_0(A_0, A_1, w), H_1(A_0, A_1, w), w, y] = G_i(x_0, x_1, w, y).$$

If we set $A(x_0, x_1, y) = A^*(x_0, x_1, 0, y)$, and if we show that the functions C_0^* and C_1^* are independent of the variable w, then that assignment will complete the construction required to verify that the conditions in Section B.2 are sufficient for the example $G(\underline{x}, w, y)$. The matrix of the bordered Hessian $bh_{(X,Y)}G$ is a single column of three matrices M_0, M_1, and M_w. The matrices are

$$M_0 = \begin{bmatrix} \frac{\partial G_0}{\partial x_0} & \frac{\partial^2 G_0}{\partial x_0 \partial y} \\ \frac{\partial G_1}{\partial x_0} & \frac{\partial^2 G_1}{\partial x_0 \partial y} \end{bmatrix},$$

$$M_1 = \begin{bmatrix} \frac{\partial G_0}{\partial x_1} & \frac{\partial^2 G_0}{\partial x_1 \partial y} \\ \frac{\partial G_1}{\partial x_1} & \frac{\partial^2 G_1}{\partial x_1 \partial y} \end{bmatrix},$$

$$M_w = \begin{bmatrix} \frac{\partial G_0}{\partial w} & \frac{\partial^2 G_0}{\partial w \partial y} \\ \frac{\partial G_1}{\partial w} & \frac{\partial^2 G_0}{\partial w \partial y} \end{bmatrix}.$$

The first column of the matrix M_0 and the first column of the matrix M_1 are linearly independent in a neighborhood of the origin, because the matrix (B.2.1) has rank 2.

Because the rank of $BH_{(\underline{x},y)}G$ is at most 2, there are real-valued functions $B(x_0, x_1, w, y)$ and $D(x_0, x_1, w, y)$ such that

$$BM_0 + DM_1 + M_w = 0. \tag{B.2.7}$$

In particular,

$$B\left(\frac{\partial G_0}{\partial x_0}\right) + D\left(\frac{\partial G_0}{\partial x_1}\right) + \left(\frac{\partial G_0}{\partial w}\right) = 0, \tag{B.2.8}$$

$$B\left(\frac{\partial G_1}{\partial x_0}\right) + D\left(\frac{\partial G_1}{\partial x_1}\right) + \left(\frac{\partial G_1}{\partial w}\right) = 0. \tag{B.2.9}$$

The functions B and D are uniquely determined because they are the solution of a system of two linear independent equations. Differentiate each of the equations (B.2.8) and (B.2.9) with respect to y. For $i = 0$ or 1,

$$\left(\frac{\partial B}{\partial y}\right)\left(\frac{\partial G_i}{\partial x_0}\right)+\left(\frac{\partial D}{\partial y}\right)\left(\frac{\partial G_i}{\partial x_1}\right)+B\left(\frac{\partial^2 G_i}{\partial x_0 \partial y}\right)+D\left(\frac{\partial^2 G_i}{\partial x_1 \partial y}\right)$$
$$+\left(\frac{\partial^2 G_i}{\partial w \partial y}\right)=0.$$

It follows from a comparison of the second columns in Equation (B.2.7) that

$$B\left(\frac{\partial^2 G_i}{\partial x_0 \partial y}\right)+D\left(\frac{\partial^2 G_i}{\partial x_1 \partial y}\right)+\frac{\partial^2 G_i}{\partial w \partial y}=0. \tag{B.2.10}$$

Therefore $\partial B/\partial y$ and $\partial D/\partial y$ are the solution of a system of two homogeneous linear equations whose matrix (B.2.1) is nonsingular. Thus the partial derivatives of the functions B and D with respect to y are zero. Therefore the functions B and D are independent of the variable y. Return to Equation (B.2.5) and substitute x_0 for t_0 and x_1 for t_1. Differentiate the resulting equation with respect to w. Then

$$\left(\frac{\partial A_0}{\partial x_0}\right)\left(\frac{\partial H_0}{\partial w}\right)+\left(\frac{\partial A_0}{\partial x_1}\right)\left(\frac{\partial H_1}{\partial w}\right)+\frac{\partial A_0}{\partial w}=0, \tag{B.2.11}$$

$$\left(\frac{\partial A_1}{\partial x_0}\right)\left(\frac{\partial H_0}{\partial w}\right)+\left(\frac{\partial A_1}{\partial x_1}\right)\left(\frac{\partial H_1}{\partial w}\right)+\frac{\partial A_1}{\partial w}=0. \tag{B.2.12}$$

Equations (B.2.11) and (B.2.12) are Equations (B.2.8) and (B.2.9) with $y=0$. Therefore, $B=\partial H_0/\partial w$ and $D=\partial H_1/\partial w$. Substitute these equalities into Equation (B.2.10). The result is the equation

$$\left(\frac{\partial^2 G_0}{\partial x_0 \partial y}\right)\left(\frac{\partial H_0}{\partial w}\right)+\left(\frac{\partial^2 G_0}{\partial x_1 \partial y}\right)\left(\frac{\partial H_1}{\partial w}\right)+\left(\frac{\partial^2 G_0}{\partial w \partial y}\right)=0. \tag{B.2.13}$$

Next compute the partial derivative of $A_0{}^*$ with respect to w. Then,

$$\frac{\partial A_0^*(t_0,t_1,w,y)}{\partial w}=\left(\frac{\partial G_0}{\partial x_0}\right)\left(\frac{\partial H_0}{\partial w}\right)+\left(\frac{\partial G_0}{\partial x_1}\right)\left(\frac{\partial H_1}{\partial w}\right)+\frac{\partial G_0}{\partial w}.$$

Therefore,

$$\frac{\partial^2 A_0^*(t_0,t_1,w,y)}{\partial w \partial y}=\left(\frac{\partial^2 G_0}{\partial x_0 \partial y}\right)\left(\frac{\partial H_0}{\partial w}\right)+\left(\frac{\partial^2 G_0}{\partial x_1 \partial y}\right)\left(\frac{\partial H_1}{\partial w}\right)+\frac{\partial^2 G_0}{\partial w \partial y},$$

because the functions H_0 and H_1 are independent of y. However, Equation (B.2.13) establishes that the function

$$\frac{\partial C_0^*(t_0,t_1,w,y)}{\partial w}$$

is constant in the variable y. It follows from Equation (B.2.4) that

$$\frac{\partial C_0^*}{\partial y}(x_0, x_1, w, 0) = \frac{\partial}{\partial w}[A_0(H_0, H_1, w)] = \frac{\partial x_0}{\partial w} = 0.$$

Therefore, C_0^* is independent of w. Similarly, C_1^* is independent of w.

We now return to discussing the general form of Leontief's Theorem. We will require some new notation.

Notation. *Suppose that $\underline{x}$ and $\underline{y}$ are two independent sets of real variables. Denote by $\underline{x} \cup \underline{y}$ the union of the two sets of variables. For example, if $\underline{x}$ is a single variable x and $\underline{y}$ is the set of variables $\{y_1, y_2\}$, then $\underline{x} \cup \underline{y}$ is the set $\{x, y_1, y_2\}$.*

We split off the proof of the general form of sufficiency as a separate lemma.

Lemma B.2.3. *Suppose that:*

(i) $\mathcal{X}$, $\mathcal{W}$, $\mathcal{Y}$, and $\mathcal{T} = \Re^d$ are Euclidean spaces of dimensions d, p, m, and d, respectively;
(ii) $X \subseteq \mathcal{X}$, $Y \subseteq \mathcal{Y}$, and $W \subseteq \mathcal{W}$ are open neighborhoods of the origin $\underline{0}$ in each of $\mathcal{X}$, $\mathcal{Y}$, and $\mathcal{W}$, respectively;
(iii) $G : X \times W \times Y \to \Re^d$ is a C^2 function;
(iv) the bordered Hessian $bh_{(X \times W, Y)}G$ has a rank of at most d in the neighborhood $X \times W \times Y$ of the point $(\underline{0}, \underline{0}, \underline{0}) \in \mathcal{X} \times \mathcal{W} \times \mathcal{Y}$;
(v) the function $d_X G$ is nonsingular at the point $(\underline{0}, \underline{0}, \underline{0})$ of $X \times W \times Y$.

Then,

(vi) there is a C^2 function A defined in a neighborhood of the point $(\underline{0}, \underline{0})$ in $X \times W$ that takes values in a neighborhood of the origin in T;
(vii) there is a C^2 function C from a neighborhood of the point $(\underline{0}, \underline{0})$ in $T \times Y$ to $\Re^d$; and
(viii) $G = C \circ (A \times Id_Y)$ in some neighborhood of the point $(\underline{0}, \underline{0}, \underline{0}) \in X \times W \times Y$.

Proof of Lemma B.2.3. Suppose that $\mathcal{X}$, $\mathcal{W}$, and $\mathcal{Y}$ have coordinates $\underline{x}$, $\underline{w}$, and $\underline{y}$, respectively. We assume that the point $(\underline{0}, \underline{0}, \underline{0})$ is the origin in the $\underline{x}$, $\underline{w}$, and $\underline{0}$ coordinates. Set $A_j(\underline{x}, \underline{w}) = G_j(\underline{x}, \underline{w}, \underline{0})$, where $\underline{0}$ denotes the substitution $y_j = 0$ for each $y_j \in \underline{y}$. Set $A(\underline{x}, \underline{w}) = [A_0(\underline{x}, \underline{w}), \ldots, A_{d-1}(\underline{x}, \underline{w})]$. Because G is nonsingular in $\underline{x}$ at the origin of the space $X \times W \times Y$, the matrix $D_{\underline{x}}G$ of the Jacobian $d_X G$ is a $(d \times d)$ nonsingular matrix in a neighborhood of the point $(\underline{a}, \underline{b})$ of $X \times W$. The Inverse Function Theorem (see Simon, 1986, part d, p. 71) asserts the existence of a function

$$H(\underline{t}, \underline{w}) = [H_0(\underline{t}, \underline{w}), \ldots, H_{d-1}(\underline{t}, \underline{w})]$$

such that

$$\{A_0[H_0(\underline{t}, \underline{w}), \ldots, H_{d-1}(\underline{t}, \underline{w}), \underline{w}], \ldots, A_{d-1}[H_0(\underline{t}, \underline{w}), \ldots, H_{d-1}(\underline{t}, \underline{w}), \underline{w}]\}$$
$$= (t_0, \ldots, t_{d-1}), \tag{B.2.14}$$

and also such that

$$\{H_0[A_0(\underline{x}, \underline{w}), \ldots, A_{d-1}(\underline{x}, \underline{w}), \underline{w}], \ldots, H_{d-1}[A_0(\underline{x}, \underline{w}), \ldots, A_{d-1}(\underline{x}, \underline{w}), \underline{w}]\}$$
$$= (x_0, \ldots, x_{d-1}), \tag{B.2.15}$$

in a neighborhood of the origin. Equations (B.2.14) and (B.2.15) can be written in a more compact form as

$$A[H(\underline{t}, \underline{w}), \underline{w}] = \underline{t}, \tag{B.2.16}$$
$$H[A(\underline{x}, \underline{w}), \underline{w}] = \underline{x}. \tag{B.2.17}$$

For each $0 \leq j \leq d-1$, set

$$C_j^*(\underline{t}, \underline{w}, \underline{y}) = G_j[H(\underline{t}, \underline{w}), \underline{w}, \underline{y}],$$
$$C^*(\underline{x}, \underline{w}, \underline{y}) = [C_0^*(\underline{x}, \underline{w}, \underline{y}), \ldots, C_{d-1}^*(\underline{x}, \underline{w}, \underline{y})].$$

Then

$$C^*\{H[A(\underline{x}, \underline{w}), \underline{w}], \underline{w}, \underline{y}\} = G(\underline{x}, \underline{w}, \underline{y}).$$

If for each $0 \leq j \leq d-1$ the function $C_j^*(\underline{t}, \underline{w}, \underline{y})$ is independent of each variable in $\underline{w}$, then for $C_j(\underline{t}, \underline{y}) = C_j^*(\underline{t}, \underline{0}, \underline{y})$, and

$$C(\underline{t}, \underline{y}) = [C_0(\underline{t}, \underline{y}), \ldots, C_{d-1}(\underline{t}, \underline{y})],$$

it follows that

$$C[A(\underline{x}, \underline{w}), \underline{y}] = G(\underline{x}, \underline{w}, \underline{y}). \tag{B.2.18}$$

We represent the function $bh_{(X \times W, Y)}G$ as a matrix with rows indexed by the variables of $\underline{x} \cup \underline{w}$. For $x \in \underline{x} \cup \underline{w}$, the row indexed by x is a $d \times (m+1)$ matrix M_x. The first column of the matrix M_x is the transpose of $(\partial G_0/\partial x, \ldots, \partial G_{d-1}/\partial x)$. The matrix whose jth column is the first column of M_{x_j}, $0 \leq j \leq d-1$ is

$$\Gamma = \begin{bmatrix} \frac{\partial G_0}{\partial x_0} & \cdots & \frac{\partial G_0}{\partial x_{d-1}} \\ \vdots & \vdots & \vdots \\ \frac{\partial G_{d-1}}{\partial x_0} & \cdots & \frac{\partial G_{d-1}}{\partial x_{d-1}} \end{bmatrix}.$$

Assumption (v) implies that the matrix Γ is nonsingular. Thus, the matrices $M_{x_0}, \ldots, M_{x_{d-1}}$ are linearly independent. Fix a coordinate $w \in \underline{w}$. Because

$bh_{(X \times W, Y)}G$ has a rank of at most d, it follows from assumption (iv) that there are functions $D_j(\underline{x}, \underline{w}, \underline{y})$, $0 \le j \le d-1$ such that

$$M_w + \sum_{j=0}^{d-1} D_j M_{x_j} = 0. \tag{B.2.19}$$

Therefore, for each $0 \le i \le d-1$,

$$\sum_{j=0}^{d-1} D_j \frac{\partial G_i}{\partial x_j} + \frac{\partial G_i}{\partial w} = 0. \tag{B.2.20}$$

Because the matrix $\Gamma = (\partial G_i / \partial x_j)$ is nonsingular, the D_j are uniquely determined by the $\partial G_i / \partial x_j$ and $\partial G_i / \partial w$. Fix a $y \in \underline{y}$. The partial derivative of Equation (B.2.20) with respect to y yields

$$\sum_{j=0}^{d-1} \left(\frac{\partial D_j}{\partial y}\right)\left(\frac{\partial G_i}{\partial x_j}\right) + \sum_{j=0}^{d-1} D_j \frac{\partial^2 G_i}{\partial x_j \partial y} + \frac{\partial^2 G_i}{\partial y \partial w} = 0. \tag{B.2.21}$$

Each entry of the matrix

$$\sum_{j=0}^{d-1} D_j M_{x_j} + M_w$$

is zero. Therefore, in a neighborhood of the origin,

$$\sum_{j=0}^{d-1} D_j \frac{\partial^2 G_i}{\partial x_j \, \partial y} + \frac{\partial^2 G_i}{\partial y \, \partial w} = 0. \tag{B.2.22}$$

Substitute Equation (B.2.22) into Equation (B.2.21). Then,

$$\sum_{j=0}^{d-1} \left(\frac{\partial G_i}{\partial x_j}\right)\left(\frac{\partial D_j}{\partial y}\right) = 0. \tag{B.2.23}$$

Because Γ is nonsingular, each $\partial D_j / \partial y = 0$. Because y was chosen arbitrarily in $\underline{y}$, it follows that each D_j is independent of each $y \in \underline{y}$. For $w \in \underline{w}$, differentiate Equation (B.2.16) with respect to w. Because $A_j(\underline{x}, \underline{w}) = G_j(\underline{x}, \underline{w}, 0)$,

$$\sum_{j=0}^{d-1} \left(\frac{\partial G_i}{\partial x_j}\right)\left(\frac{\partial H_j}{\partial w}\right) + \frac{\partial G_i}{\partial w} = 0 \tag{B.2.24}$$

when the partial derivatives of the G_i are evaluated at $(H_0, \ldots, H_{d-1}, \underline{w}, 0)$. Equation (B.2.24) is Equation (B.2.20) with all the variables in $\underline{y}$ set to zero. Because the D_j are independent of the variables in $\underline{y}$, it follows that

$$D_j = \partial H_j / \partial w.$$

For $y \in \underline{y}$, differentiate Equation (B.2.24) with respect to y. The result is

$$\sum_{j=0}^{d-1}\left(\frac{\partial^2 G_i}{\partial y\,\partial x_j}\right)\left(\frac{\partial H_j}{\partial w}\right)+\frac{\partial^2 G_i}{\partial y\,\partial w}=0, \tag{B.2.25}$$

because $\partial H_j/\partial w$ is independent of y. Differentiate $C_i^*(\underline{x}, \underline{w}, \underline{y})$ with respect to w. Then

$$\frac{\partial C_i^*}{\partial w}=\sum_{j=0}^{d-1}\left(\frac{\partial G_i}{\partial x_j}\right)\left(\frac{\partial H_j}{\partial w}\right)+\frac{\partial G_i}{\partial w}.$$

For $y \in \underline{y}$,

$$\frac{\partial^2 C_i^*}{\partial y\,\partial w}=\sum_{j=0}^{d-1}\left(\frac{\partial^2 G_i}{\partial w\,\partial x_j}\right)\left(\frac{\partial H_j}{\partial w}\right)+\frac{\partial^2 G_i}{\partial w\,\partial y},$$

because $\partial H_i/\partial w$ is independent of y. It follows from Equation (B.2.25) that $\partial C_i^*/\partial w$ is independent of y. Finally,

$$\frac{\partial C_i^*}{\partial w}(\underline{t}, \underline{w}, \underline{0})=\frac{\partial}{\partial y}G_i[H_0(\underline{t}, \underline{w}), \ldots, H_{d-1}(\underline{t}, \underline{w}), \underline{w}, \underline{0}]=\frac{\partial}{\partial w}(t_i)=0.$$

Therefore,

$$\frac{\partial C_i^*}{\partial w}(\underline{x}, \underline{w}, \underline{y})=0.$$

Thus we have shown that each of the functions $C_j^*(\underline{t}, \underline{w}, \underline{y})$ is independent of each variable in $\underline{w}$. □

The general form of Leontief's theorem is the following.

Theorem B.2.4. *Assume that:*

(i) X and Y are Euclidean spaces of dimensions n and m, respectively;
(ii) G is a C^2 function from a neighborhood of the origin in $X \times Y$ to $\Re^d$;
(iii) there is a C^2 function $A : X \to \Re^d$ from a neighborhood of the origin in X to a neighborhood of the origin in $\Re^d$; and
(iv) there is a C^2 function from a neighborhood of the origin in $\Re^d \times Y$ to $\Re^d$ such that $G = C \circ (A \times Id_Y)$.

Then, near the origin in $X \times Y$, the bordered Hessian $bh_{(X,Y)}G$ has a rank of at most d. Conversely, suppose:

(vi) (i) and (ii) above are true;
(vii) in a neighborhood of the origin in $X \times Y$, the bordered Hessian $bh_{(X,Y)}G$ has a rank of at most d; and
(viii) the map $d_X G$ has a rank of d at the origin of $X \times Y$.

Then, there is a C^2 function A from a neighborhood of the origin in X to a neighborhood of the origin in $\Re^d$ and a C^2 function C from a neighborhood of the origin in $\Re^d \times Y$ to $\Re^d$ such that in a neighborhood of the origin in $X \times Y$,

$$G = C \circ (A \times Id_Y).$$

Proof of Theorem B.2.4. The assertion that if $G = C \circ A \times Id_Y$ then $bh_{(X,Y)}G$ has a rank of at most d follows immediately from Lemma B.2.1. We turn to the sufficiency assertion that when conditions (v), (vi), and (vii) are satisfied, it follows that $G = C \circ (A \times Id_Y)$. We suppose that X has coordinates $\underline{x}$. Because of the assumption that $d_X G$ has rank d in the neighborhood of the origin, we may choose a set of d coordinates, $\underline{x}'$, from among the $\underline{x}$ so that the matrix $D_{\underline{x}'}G$ has rank d near the origin. Denote by $\underline{w}$ the set of coordinates in $\underline{x}$ that are not among the set $\underline{x}'$. Denote by X' the subspace of X that is the set of points where the coordinates $\underline{w}$ are all zero. The space X' has dimension d. Denote by W' the space where all the coordinates of $\underline{x}'$ are zero. Then $X = X' \times W'$. Choose a neighborhood U of the origin in $X \times Y$ so that both $d_X G$ has rank d in U and such that $bh_{(X,Y)}G$ has rank at most d in U. Now refer to Lemma B.2.3. Set $\mathcal{X} = U \cap X'$ and set $\mathcal{W} = W'$. Then conditions (i) through (v) of the lemma are satisfied. The conclusion of Lemma B.2.3 is the required equation $G = C \circ (A \times Id_Y)$. □

The proof of the corollary that follows is a simple induction that we leave to the reader.

Corollary B.2.5. *Suppose that for each $0 \le i \le r-1$, X_i is a Euclidean space of dimension d and that $X = \prod_{i=0}^{r-1} X_i$. Assume:*

(i) G is a d-vector–valued C^2 function in a neighborhood of the origin in X;
(ii) $G(0, \dots, 0) = 0$;
(iii) for each $0 \le i \le r-1$, $d_{X_i}G$ is nonsingular in a neighborhood of the origin in X; and
(iv) for each i, $bh_{(X_i, \prod_{j=0, j\ne i}^{r-1} X_j)}G$ has a rank of at most d in a neighborhood of the origin (in X).

Then there is a C^s d-vector–valued function of d variables $C(\underline{t}) = C(t_0, \dots, t_{r-1})$ and for each $0 \le i \le r-1$ a d-vector–valued function B_i that is a C^s function in a neighborhood of the origin in X_i such that

$$G = C(B_0, \dots, B_{r-1})$$

in a neighborhood of the origin of X.

Notation. *If T is an ordered tree, then we denote by $\mathcal{L}(T)$ the set of leaves of T. If $R \in T$ is a vertex of T that is not a leaf of T, then the collection of all vertices of T that are connected by an arc (directed) to R together with the* *arcs connecting those vertices is a subtree T_R of $S[r, N]$, which we call the full subtree with root R. For a full subtree T with root R, we denote by $\mathcal{L}(T)$ the set of leaves of the full subtree T. If R is a vertex of $S[r, N]$ that is not a leaf, then r arcs have the terminal vertex R. As in Chapter 2, the notation $R(T_0, \dots, T_{r-1})$ denotes the sequence of full subtrees of $S[r, N]$ that have their roots connected to R by an arc. If $i \neq j$, then the set of leaves $\mathcal{L}[T_i(R)]$ is disjoint from the set $\mathcal{L}[T_j(R)]$. If independent d variables are assigned to the distinct leaves of a subtree T of $S[r, N]$, then the collection of real variables that comprises the components of those d variables are coordinates in a Euclidean space. It is convenient to denote that Euclidean space by $X(T)$.*

Corollary B.2.6. *Suppose that N, r, and d are integers greater than zero; that for $0 \leq i \leq r-1$, each X_i denotes a Euclidean space of dimension d; for each i there are (real) coordinate functions $x_{i,j}$, $0 \leq j \leq d-1$, on X_i that take the value 0 at 0; and that $X = \prod_{i=0}^{r^N-1} X_i$. Suppose that G is a d-vector–valued function that is a C^2 function in a neighborhood of the origin of X. Then:*
Necessity.
Assume:

- *(i) for each vertex v of $S[r, N]$ that is not a leaf, there is an assignment of a d-vector-valued function $\langle v \rangle$ of r d variables that is a C^2 function in a neighborhood of the origin of $\prod_{j=0}^{r-1} \mathcal{R}^d$;*
- *(ii) there is an ordering of the d variables of each of the functions $\langle v \rangle$ determined; and*
- *(iii) with the given ordering of variables, if for each $0 \leq i \leq r^N - 1$, $\underline{x}_i = (x_{i,0}, \dots, x_{i,d-1})$ is input to the leaf (N, i), then the network determined by the assignment computes G in time N.*

Then, for each vertex $v \in S[r, N]$ that is not a leaf, there is an open neighborhood of the origin of X such that at points of that neighborhood, for the Euclidean spaces $X_0 = X[T_0(v)], \dots, X_{r-1} = X[T_{r-1}(v)]$ and for each $0 \leq j \leq r-1$,

$$\left[bh_{(X_i, \prod_{j=0,\, j\neq i}^{r-1} X_j)} G\right]$$

has a rank of at most d.
Sufficiency.
Assume :

- *(iv) for each vertex v that is not a leaf of $S[r, N]$ and for the Euclidean spaces $X_0 = X[T_0(v)], \dots, X_{r-1} = X[T_{r-1}(v)]$,*

  $$\left[bh_{(X_i, \prod_{j=0,\, j\neq i}^{r-1} X_j)} G\right]$$

  has a rank of at most d in the neighborhood of the origin in X; and
- *(v) for each v that is not a leaf of $S[r, N]$ and each $0 \leq i \leq r-1$, the map $d_{X_i} G$ is nonsingular in a neighborhood of the origin of X.*

Then, there is a network of d-vector–valued functions of r d variables and an ordered graph $S[r, N]$ such that for each point $\underline{a}$ in some neighborhood of the origin of X, when the coordinates of the components of $\underline{a}$ that are in X_i are input to the network at leaf (i, N), the network computes $G(\underline{a})$ in time N.

Proof of Corollary B.2.6. We first examine the necessary conditions. Assume that G can be computed by a network with graph $S[r, N]$ in time N, and that v is a vertex of $S[r, N]$ that is not a leaf. Fix the variables of X that are not in $X[T(v)]$. Then computing G is reduced to computing a function that is simply equivalent to the function $\langle |v| \rangle$. Lemma B.2.2 shows that $bh_{(X_i, \prod_{j=0, j\neq i}^{r-1} X_j)} G$ has the same rank as the function $bh_{(X_i, \prod_{j=0, j\neq i}^{r-1} X_j)} \langle |v| \rangle$. Lemma B.2.3 shows that latter has a rank of at most d. We turn now to the assertion that (iv) and (v) are sufficient to guarantee the existence of a network that computes G in time N. We proceed by induction on N. The inductive hypothesis asserts that for each $0 \leq i \leq r-1$, there is a network with graph $S[r, N-1]$ that computes B_i in time $N-1$. The assertion for $N=1$ is a consequence of Corollary B.2.5. Assume that the induction hypothesis is true for functions of r^{N-1} variables (with each variable a d variable). We use the notation of (iv) with $v=(0, 0)$ and set $X_0 = X[T_0(0, 0)], \ldots, X_{r-1} = X[T_{r-1}(0, 0)]$. Corollary B.2.5 shows that there is a function A of t d variables, and functions B_i, $0 \leq i \leq r-1$ such that $G\{X[T(0, 0)]\} = A[B_0(X_0), \ldots, B_{r-1}(X_{r-1})]$. Furthermore, each B_i can be computed by a network $\mathcal{B}_i$ with graph $S[r, N-1]$. To see this, note that the function B_i is nonsingular in each of the variables of X_i because G is nonsingular in each of its variables. Furthermore, the function B_i is simply equivalent to the function G with the variables not on X_i hold fixed. It follows that the rank conditions in (iv) are satisfied by B_i because G satisfies the conditions and Lemma B.2.2. shows that the rank conditions on G are inherited by B_i. Now build a network on $S[r, N]$ by building the network $\mathcal{B}_i$ on $T_i(0, 0)$ and assigning the function A to the root $(0, 0)$ of $S[r, N]$. □

Appendix C Appendix to Chapter 5: Application to Games

The Nash solution of the bargaining problem whose frontier is the cubic curve with Equation (5.1.11) is the point on the frontier where $[(1 + A)x - y - a]$ $(y - b)$ takes its maximum value. We use the Lagrange multiplier method to find the maximum. Set the Lagrangian equal to

$$\mathcal{L} = [(1 + A)x - y - a](y - b) + \Lambda\,[y^2 + {}^1\!/_3\, x^3 + (p - {}^1\!/_2)x + q - 1].$$

Then,

$$\Lambda = \frac{(1 + A)(b - y)}{x^2 + (p - {}^1\!/_2)}. \tag{C.0.1}$$

It follows from the condition $\partial\Lambda/\partial y = 0$ that

$$[(1 + A)x - 2y - (a - b)][2x^2 + (2p - 1)] + 4(b - y)(1 + A)y = 0. \tag{C.0.2}$$

Set $a - b = \alpha$. Then

$$(1 + A)x(2x^2 + 2p - 1) - (2y + \alpha)(2x^2 + 2p - 1) + 4b(1 + A)y \\ - 4(1 + A)y^2 = 0. \tag{C.0.3}$$

However, if

$$y^2 = (^{-1}\!/_3)x^3 - (p - {}^1\!/_2)x - q + 1, \tag{C.0.4}$$

then

$$y[-2(2x^2 + 2p - 1) + 4b(1 + A)] = -\Bigg[(1 + A)x(2x^2 + 2p - 1) \\ - \alpha(2x^2 + 2p - 1) + 4(1 + A)\left(\frac{1}{3}\right)x^3 \\ + \left(\frac{2p - 1}{2}\right)x + q - 1\Bigg].$$

Substitute the expression for y into Equation (5.1.11) and clear the denominator. The result is the following equation in x.

$$
\begin{aligned}
&\frac{9}{4}+6A+3A^2-\frac{3\alpha}{2}-\frac{3A\alpha}{2}+\frac{3\alpha^2}{16}-3b-3Ab-3b^2-6Ab^2-3A^2b^2\\
&+3p+3\alpha p+3A\alpha p-\frac{3\alpha^2 p}{4}+6bp+6Abp-3p^2+\frac{3\alpha^2 p^2}{4}\\
&-\frac{21q}{4}-12Aq-6A^2q+\frac{3\alpha q}{2}+\frac{3A\alpha q}{2}+3bq+3Abq+3b^2q\\
&+6Ab^2q+3A^2b^2q-3pq-3\alpha pq-3A\alpha pq-6bpq-6Abpq\\
&+3p^2q+3q^2+6Aq^2+3A^2q^2+\frac{33x}{8}+9Ax+\frac{9A^2x}{2}-\frac{9\alpha x}{8}\\
&-\frac{9A\alpha x}{8}-\frac{3bx}{2}-\frac{3Abx}{2}-\frac{3b^2x}{2}-3Ab^2x-\frac{3A^2b^2x}{2}-\frac{27px}{4}\\
&-18Apx-9A^2px+\frac{9\alpha px}{2}+\frac{9A\alpha px}{2}+6bpx+6Abpx\\
&+3b^2px+6Ab^2px+3A^2b^2px-\frac{9p^2x}{2}-\frac{9\alpha p^2x}{2}-\frac{9A\alpha p^2x}{2}\\
&-6bp^2x-6Abp^2x+3p^3x-\frac{9qx}{2}-9Aqx-\frac{9A^2qx}{2}+9pqx\\
&+18Apqx+9A^2pqx+\frac{75x^2}{16}+\frac{27Ax^2}{8}+\frac{27A^2x^2}{16}+3\alpha x^2\\
&+3A\alpha x^2-\frac{3\alpha^2x^2}{4}+6bx^2+6Abx^2-\frac{51px^2}{4}-\frac{27Apx^2}{2}\\
&-\frac{27A^2px^2}{4}+\frac{3\alpha^2px^2}{2}+\frac{27p^2x^2}{4}+\frac{27Ap^2x^2}{2}+\frac{27A^2p^2x^2}{4}-3qx^2\\
&-3\alpha qx^2-3A\alpha qx^2-6bqx^2-6Abqx^2+6pqx^2-\frac{13x^3}{4}-10Ax^3\\
&-5A^2x^3+\frac{7\alpha x^3}{2}+\frac{7A\alpha x^3}{2}+4bx^3+4Abx^3+b^2x^3+2Ab^2x^3\\
&+A^2b^2x^3-7px^3-7\alpha px^3-7A\alpha px^3-8bpx^3-8Abpx^3\\
&+7p^2x^3+5qx^3+10Aqx^3+5A^2qx^3-\frac{27x^4}{4}-\frac{15Ax^4}{2}-\frac{15A^2x^4}{4}\\
&+\frac{3\alpha^2x^4}{4}+\frac{15px^4}{2}+15Apx^4+\frac{15A^2px^4}{2}+3qx^4-\frac{5x^5}{2}-\frac{5\alpha x^5}{2}\\
&-\frac{5A\alpha x^5}{2}-2bx^5-2Abx^5+5px^5+\frac{25x^6}{12}+\frac{25Ax^6}{6}\\
&+\frac{25A^2x^6}{12}+x^7=0.
\end{aligned}
$$

To find the optima in Example 5.2.1., we computed the partial derivative of P, the payoff function, with respect to y. The result is a quadratic in x with a single solution $S(d, x)$ that is in the interval [0, 1] when $x \in [0, 1]$ and $d \in (0.5, 1.5)$. The solution $S(d, x)$ substituted for y in P. When the resulting function of x and d is optimized, values to be in chosen in [0, 1], the result is the expression $\bar{x}$ given in the second section of Chapter 5. One can then compute the y coordinate $\hat{y}$ for the optimal point. The expression for $\bar{y}$ is the following.[1]

$$\bar{y} = \frac{1}{17424}\Bigg\{-12672 + \sqrt{22}\sqrt{\frac{1}{F5^{1/3}}\frac{1}{\sqrt{F7}}}\text{Sqrt}[(-1965312\ F5^{1/3}$$

$$+ 696960\ d\ F5^{1/3} + 38016\ F1\ F5^{1/3} - 121\ 2^{2/3}\ F2\sqrt{F7}$$

$$+ 2052864\ F5^{1/3}\sqrt{F7} - 15488\ F1\ F5^{1/3}\sqrt{F7} - 3872\ 2^{1/3}\ F5^{2/3}\sqrt{F7}]$$

$$- 2904\sqrt{F7} + 2\sqrt{11}\,\text{Sqrt}\Bigg[\frac{1}{F5^{1/3}\sqrt{F7}}(1965312\ F5^{1/3} - 696960\, d\ F5^{1/3}$$

$$- 38016\ F1\ F5^{1/3} + 121\ 2^{2/3}\ F2\sqrt{F7} + 2356992\ F5^{1/3}\sqrt{F7}$$

$$+ 15488\ F1\ F5^{1/3}\sqrt{F7} + 3872\ 2^{1/3}\ F5^{2/3}\sqrt{F7}$$

$$- 1224\sqrt{22}\ F5^{1/3}\ \text{Sqrt}\Bigg[\frac{1}{F5^{1/3}\sqrt{F7}}(-1965312\ F5^{1/3} + 696960\ d\ F5^{1/3}$$

$$+ 38016\ F1\ F5^{1/3} - 121\ 2^{2/3}\ F2\sqrt{F7} + 2052864\ F5^{1/3}\sqrt{F7}$$

$$- 15488\ F1\ F5^{1/3}\sqrt{F7} - 3872\ 2^{1/3}\ F5^{2/3}\sqrt{F7})\Bigg]\sqrt{F7} + 3554496\ F5^{1/3}\sqrt{F7}$$

$$+ 264\sqrt{22}\ F5^{1/3}\ \text{Sqrt}\Bigg(\frac{1}{F5^{1/3}\sqrt{7}}\ (-1965312\ F5^{1/3} + 696960\, d\ F5^{1/3}$$

$$+ 38016\ F1\ F5^{1/3} - 121\ 2^{2/3}\ F2\sqrt{F7} + 2052864\ F5^{1/3}\sqrt{F7}$$

$$- 15488\ F1\ F5^{1/3}\sqrt{F7} - 3872\, 2^{1/3}\, F5^{2/3}\sqrt{F7})\Bigg)F7$$

$$- 383328\ F5^{1/3}\ F7^{3/2}\Bigg]\Bigg]\Bigg\}$$

Each of the entries $F1, \ldots, F7$ is an expression in d. The expressions are the following.

$$F1 = (65 - 17d),$$
$$F2 = 380224 + 186688d + 18880d^2,$$

[1] The notation "5qnt" denotes the sq. root function.

$$F3 = 1896943 + 1343958\,d + 301026\,d^2 + 20264\,d^3,$$

$$F4 = 3004265473 + 1936930532\,d + 272031648\,d^2 - 23427688\,d^3 - 2691740\,d^4 + 186288\,d^5 - 1584\,d^6,$$

$$F5 = F3 + 9\sqrt{F4},$$

$$F6 = \frac{324}{121} - \frac{2\ F1}{99} + \frac{F2}{1584\,2^{1/3}\ F5^{1/3}} + \frac{2^{1/3}\ F5^{1/3}}{99},$$

$$F7 = \frac{2^{1/3}\ F5^{1/3}}{99} + F6.$$

Bibliography

H. Abelson. Lower bounds on information transfer in distributed systems. *JACM* **27**, 384–92, 1980.

D. Abreu and A. Rubeinstein. The structure of Nash equilibrium in repeated games with finite automata. *Econometrica* **56,** 1259–88, 1988.

M. A. Arbib. *Theories of Abstract Automata*. Prentice-Hall, Englewood Cliffs, NJ, 1960.

M. A. Arbib and P. M. Spira. Computation times for finite groups, semigroups and automata. In *Proceedings of the IEEE 8th Annual Symposium on Switching and Automata Theory*, pp. 291–95. American Institute of Electrical Engineers, New York, 1967.

V. I. Arnol'd. On functions of three variables. *Am. Trans. Soc. Transl.* (2) **28**, 51–4, 1963.

K. J. Arrow. *The Limits of Organization*. W. W. Norton, New York, 1974.

K. J. Arrow and L. Hurwicz. Decentralization and computation in resource allocation. In R. W. Pfouts, editor, *Essays in Economics and Econometrics*, pp. 34–104. University of North Carolina, Chapel Hill, 1960.

K. J. Arrow and L. Hurwicz. On the stability of the competitive equilibrium I. *Econometrica* **26**, 522–52, 1958.

K. J. Arrow, H. D. Block, and L. Hurwicz. On the stability of the competitive equilibrium II. *Econometrica* **27**, 82–109, 1959.

R. J. Aumann. Survey of repeated games. In *Essays in Game theory and Mathematical Economics in Honor of Oskar Morgenstern*, pp. 11–42. Bibliographisches Institut, Zurich, 1981.

E. Ben-Porath. Repeated games with finite automata. *J. Economic Theory* **59**, 17–32, 1986.

E. Ben-Porath. The complexity of computing best response automata in repeated games with mixed strategies. *Games Econ. Behavior* **2**, 1–12, 1989.

C. Berge. *Graphs and Hypergraphs*. North-Holland, Amsterdam, 1973.

L. Bieberbach. *Uber Nomographie*. Die Naturalwissenschaften 10, Berlin, 1922.

L. Blum, S. Smale, F. Cucker, M. Shub, and S. Smale. *Complexity and Real Computation*. Springer, New York, 1998.

A. Cayley. *Collected Mathematical Papers of A. Cayley*. Cambridge University Press, Cambridge, 1857.

Pengyuan Chen. A lower bound for the dimension of the message space of the decentralized mechanisms realizing a given goal. *J. Math. Econ.* **21**, 249–70, 1992.

H. Chernoff. The use of faces to represent points in k-dimensional space graphically. *J. Am. Statist. Assoc.* **68**, 361–8, 1973.

I. K. Cho and Hao Li. Complexity and neural network in repeated games. Technical Report, University of Chicago, 1993.

I. K. Cho. Perceptrons play repeated prisoner's dilemma. *J. Economic Theory* **67**, 266–84, 1995.

G. Debreu. *Theory of Value*. Wiley, New York, 1959.

E. Dehn. *Algebraic Equations*. Dover, New York, 1960.

D. S. Dummit and R. M. Foote. *Abstract Algebra*. Prentice-Hall, Englewood Cliffs, NJ, 1991.

I. Gilboa and D. Samet. Bounded versus unbounded rationality: the tyranny of the weak. *Games Econ. Behavior* **1**, 213–21, 1989.

I. Gilboa and F. Zemel. Nash and correlated equilibria: some complexity considerations. *Games Econ. Behavior* **1**, 80–93, 1989.

M. Golubitsky and V. Guillemin. *Stable Mappings and Their Singularities; Graduate Texts in Mathematics No. 14*. Springer-Verlag, New York, 1973.

D. Hilbert. Mathematische problems. *Vortrang Intl. Math. Kongr. Nachr. Ges. Wiss.* **X**, 253–97, 1900.

D. Hilbert. Uber die gleichung neunten grades. *Math. Annalen* **97**, 243–50, 1927.

L. Hurwicz. Optimality and informational efficiency in resource allocation processes. In Samuel, Karlin, Kenneth J. Arrow, and Patrick Suppes, editors, *Mathematical Methods in the Social Sciences*. Stanford University Press, Stanford, CA, 1960.

L. Hurwicz, S. Reiter, and D. Saari. Constructing an informationally decentralized process implementing a given performance function. Mimeo Notes, Econometric Society World Congress, Aix-en-Province, 1980.

L. Hurwicz. On informational decentralization and efficiency in resource allocation mechanisms. In S. Reiter, editor, *Studies in Mathematical Economics,* Vol. 25, pp. 238–350. The Mathematical Association of America, Northwestern University, Chicago, 1986.

N. Jacobson. *Lectures in Abstract Algebra I – Basic Concepts*. Van Nostrand, Princeton, NJ, 1951a.

N. Jacobson. *Lectures in Abstract Algebra II – Linear Algebra*. Van Nostrand, Princeton, NJ, 1951b.

J. S. Jordan. The competitive allocation process is informationally efficient uniquely. *J. Econ. Theory* **28**, 1–18, 1982.

J. S. Jordan. The informational requirements of local stability in decentralized allocation mechanisms. In T. Groves, R. Radner, and S. Reiter, editors, *Information, Incentives and Economic Mechanisms*. University of Minnesota Press, Minneapolis, 1987.

M. Kachingwe. Corporate knowledge. Mimeo Notes, Nuffield College, Oxford University, 1997.

E. Kalai. Games, computers and O. R. In *Proceedings of the Seventh Annual ACM-SIAM Symposium on Discrete Algorithms*. publ., loc., 1996.

E. Kalai and W. Stanford. Finite rationality and interpersonal complexity in repeated games. *Econometrica* **56**, 397–410, 1988.

E. Kalai, I. Gilboa, and E. Zemel. The complexity of eliminating dominated strategies. *Math. Operations Res.* **18**, 553–65, 1993.

D. E. Knuth. *The Art of Computer Programming*. Addison-Wesley, Reading, MA, 1973a.

D. E. Knuth. *Fundamental Algorithms: Vol. 1 of The Art of Computer Programming*. Addison-Wesley, Reading, MA, 1973b.

A. N. Kolmogorov. On the representation of continous functions by superposition of contiuous functions of one variable and addition. *Am. Math. Soc. Transl.* (2) **17**, 55–9, 1961b.

A. N. Kolmogorov. On the representation of continuous functions by superpositions of continuous functions of a smaller number of variables. *Am. Math. Soc. Transl.* (2) **17**, 55–9, 1961a.

W. Leontief. A note on the interelation of subsets of independent variables of a continuous function with continuous first derivatives. *Bull AMS*, 343–50, 1947.

B. Levitt and J. March. Chester I. Barnard and the intelligence of learning. In O. Williamson, editor, *Organization Theory*. Oxford University Press, Oxford, 1988.

G. G. Lorentz. *Approximation Theory*. Holt, Rinehart & Winston, New York, 1966.

R. D. Luce and H. Raiffa. *Games and Decisions.* Wiley, New York, 1958.

S. MacLane. *Categories for the Working Mathematician*. Springer-Verlag, New York, 1971.

W. McCulloch and W. Pitts. A logical calculus of the ideas immanent in nervous activity. *Bull. Math. Biophy.* **X**, 115–33, 1943.

G. A. Miller. The magic number seven, plus or minus two: Some limits on our capacity for processing information. *Psych. Rev.* **63**, 108–XXX, 1956.

K. R. Mount and S. Reiter. A model of computing with human agents. Discussion Paper No. 890. The Center for Mathematical Studies in Economics and Managerial Science, Northwestern University, Chicago, 1990.

K. R. Mount and S. Reiter. A modular network model of bounded rationality. In M. Majumdar, editor, *Organizations with Incomplete Information*, pp. 306–40. Cambridge University Press, New York, 1998.

K. R. Mount and S. Reiter. On the existence of a locally stable dynamic process with a statically minimal message space. In T. Groves, R. Radner, and S. Reiter, editors, *Information, Incentives and Economic Mechanisms.* University of Minnesota Press, Minneapolis, 1983.

R. B. Myerson. *Game Theory*. Harvard University Press, Cambridge, MA, 1991.

A. Neyman. Bounded complexity justifies cooperation in the finitely repeated prisoners dilemma. *Econ. Lett.* **19**, 227–9, 1985.

G. Owen. *Game Theory,* 2nd ed. Academic, Orlando, FL, 1982.

C. H. Papadimitriou. On players with a bounded number of states. *Games Econ. Behavior* **4**, 122–31, 1992.

V. Pareto. *Manuel d'economie politiqe (Deuxieme edition)*. Marcel Giard, Paris, 1927.

R. Penrose. *Shadows of the Mind*. Oxford University Press, New York, 1994.

R. Radner. The organization of decentralized information processing. *Econometrica* **61**, 1993.

R. Radner. Bounded rationality, indeterminacy, and the managerial theory of the firm. In Z. Shapira, editor, *Organizational Decision Making*. Cambridge University Press, Cambridge, 1997.

R. Radner. Costly and bounded rationality in individual and team decision-making. *Ind. Corp. Change* **9**, 623–58, 2000.

R. Radner and T. Van Zandt. Information processing in firms and returns to scale. *Ann. d'Econ. Statist.* **25–26**, 256–98, 298, 1992.

H. Raiffa. Arbitration schemes for generalized two-person games. Report m 720-1. Engineering Reasearch Institute, University of Michigan, Ann Arbor, 1951.

H. Raiffa. Arbitration schemes for generalized two-person games. In H. W. Kuhn and A. W. Tucker, editors, *Contributions to the Theory of Games, II*, pp. 361–87. Princeton University Press, Princeton, 1953.

S. Reichelstein. Incentive compatibility and informational requirements. *J. Econ. Theory* **32**, 384–90, 1984.

S. Reichelstein and S. Reiter. Game forms with minimal message spaces. *Econometrica* **56**, 661–92, 1988.

S. Reiter. Coordination and the structure of firms. CMSEMS Discussion Paper 1121. The Center for Mathematical Studies in Economics and Managerial Science, Northwestern University, Chicago, 1995.

S. Reiter. There is no adjusment process with 2-dimensional message space for counter-examples. Mimeo, The Center for Mathematical Studies in Economics and Managerial Science, Northwestern University, Chicago, 1979.

A. Rubinstein. Equilibrium in supergames with the overtaking criterion. *J. Econ. Theory* **21**, 1–9, 1979.

A. Rubenstein. Finite automata play the repeated prisoner's dilemma. *J. Econ. Theory* **39**, 83–96, 1986.

A. Rubenstein. On price recognition and computational complexity in a monopolistic model. *J. Polit. Econ.* **101**, 1993.

A. Rubenstein. *Modeling Bounded Rationality*. MIT Press, Cambridge, MA, 1998.

D. Saari and C. P. Simon. Effective price mechanisms. *Econometrica* **46**, 1097–1125, 1978.

P. A. Samuelson. *Foundations of Economic Analysis*. Harvard University Press, Cambridge, MA, 1947.

H. Scarf. Some examples of global instability of the competitive equilibrium. *Intl. Econ. Rev.* **1**, 1960.

E. Schein. *Organizational Culture and Leadership: A Dynamic View*. Jossey-Bass, San Francisco, CA, 1985.

J. P. Serre. *Lie Algebras and Lie Groups*. Benjamin, New York, 1965.

C. P. Simon. Scalar and vector maximization: calculus techniques with economics applications. In St. Reiter, editor, *Studies in Mathematical Economics*, Vol. 25, Part 2, pp. 62–159. The Mathematical Association of America, Northwestern University, Chicago, 1986.

S. Smale. A convergent process of price adjustment and global Newton methods. *J. Math. Econ.* **3**, 107–120, 1976a.

S. Smale. Exchange processes with price adjustment. *J. Math. Econ.* **3**, 211–226, 1976b.

H. Sonnenschein. An axiomatic characterization of the price mechanism. *Econometrica* **42**, 425–60, 1974.

A. G. Vitushkin. *Complexity of Tabulation Problems*. Pergamon, New York, 1961.

D. V. Widder. *Advanced Calculus*. Prentice-Hall, Englewood Cliffs, NJ, 1963.

T. Van Zandt. Organizations with an endogenous number of information processing agents. In M. Majumdar, editor, *Organizations with Incomplete Information*, pp. 239–305. Cambridge University Press, New York, 1998.

Index